THE BOOK OF
EXPLORATION

RAY HOWGEGO

THE BOOK OF EXPLORATION

RAY HOWGEGO

BLOOMSBURY

New York Berlin London

Contents

Introduction

IN THIS BOOK I HAVE ATTEMPTED to present the reader with an entertaining and visually attractive, but nevertheless authoritative and unpatronizing account of the history of exploration from the earliest times to near enough the present day. My commission – a task only slightly less daunting than those described in its pages – was to present the subject in the shape of around 150 relatively brief, self-contained essays commemorating a significant event or celebrating a sufficiently worthy explorer, while as a whole providing a thorough examination of the progress of geographical discovery across the centuries and throughout the globe. What was even more demanding was the decision to dispense the essays in strictly chronological order – a format that, devoid of regional or sequential continuity, would compel each essay to stand alone, paint its own scene and assume no previous knowledge. This will no doubt come as a great relief to the reader with neither the time nor inclination to start at the beginning and finish at the end, but for an author forced to commence each new page on a clean slate as though nothing followed and little came before, it presented a considerable challenge. Even so, the reader will appreciate that no historical event can properly be taken in isolation, especially if it marks one of many milestones in a continuous process of enlightenment. In anticipation, therefore, that even the most committed browser might spare a few moments to read these words, it seemed like a good idea to make use of this introduction to provide a concise overview of exploratory history, its significant landmarks and logical progression, in the hope of establishing a background against which each of the essays may be placed. Not easily done in a couple of thousand words, but here goes.

Long before the dawn of recorded history our earliest ancestors migrated out of their African homeland to the Middle East and onwards into the wider world, and by no less than 12,000 years ago *Homo sapiens* could be found in almost every habitable corner of the globe. Some settled into a nomadic existence, but others organized themselves into the agricultural communities that would blossom into the world's great civilizations. As time went on, the Old World civilizations became increasingly dependent for their cultural development and material welfare on networks of overland and maritime trade routes, and especially on the pathfinders that would pioneer them. These were surely our earliest explorers, their reach extending forever outwards, first into the immediate environment, then, with the development of ocean-going vessels and an increasing awareness of winds and currents, back into contact with distant relatives whose societies, like theirs, had flourished in detached isolation. The commemorative texts of ancient Egypt recall a few of their names, their expeditions up the Nile and to the mysterious land of Punt, but of the unsung heroes that pioneered trade and cultural exchange elsewhere in the world we know little beyond the routes they must have taken.

The Greek and Roman geographers whose works have thankfully survived intact – Herodotus, Strabo and Pliny among them – foraged the scrolls for glimpses of early exploration, leaving us with terse, mouth-watering snippets of illusory voyages and shadowy but named explorers dating back as far as the seventh century BCE. But the most widespread and concrete advances in geographical knowledge accrued from the campaigns of Alexander and the rise of the Roman Empire, which by around 130 CE would allow the venerable Alexandrian geographer Claudius Ptolemy to reasonably describe the shape of the earth from the shores of the Atlantic to India and beyond, and from sub-Saharan Africa to the desolate frontiers of the hyperborean north. Meanwhile, from the opposite direction came emissaries of the Han dynasty in China, opening the eyes of the Chinese for the first time to a civilized world beyond their imperial borderlands and blazing the lonely trails that would bring Eastern and Western humanity into regular contact for the first time.

The 700-year Dark Age that followed Ptolemy's methodical analysis of the known world was refreshingly interrupted by two newly emergent cultures, geographically remote and quite distinct in their motivations, but both dedicated to expansionism and exploration. From the Middle East the spread of Islam united a vast swathe of territory from Spain to the Orient, across which scholars could wander peacefully and unhindered in search of knowledge and enlightenment. From Scandinavia, settlers poured into Russia, to the Black Sea and the Caspian, across the North Atlantic to Iceland and Greenland, and to the coasts of North America where distant relatives of the human diaspora came face-to-face for the first time in tens of thousands of years. However, the voyages of the Vikings, important to them but elsewhere barely recognized, had little impact on a mainland Christendom that was too much involved in its own petty squabbles to worry unduly about the world beyond. But all was to change when Europe found itself rudely awakened from its slumbering isolationism by the arrival on its borderlands of hordes of fearsome Mongol warriors, who from their homelands somewhere in distant Asia were on a mission to subjugate the whole of the known world. Surprisingly, the Mongol invasions were to have a beneficial effect on European explorers, who, rather than having to brave the Islamic south, for years at war with Christendom over the Holy Land, could now wander across Asia under the selectively Europhilic protection of the Mongol khans.

Those few European travellers who did manage to struggle overland to Asia brought back tales of vibrant cultures, silks, spices and other luxury goods so highly valued in the West, but it was not until the fifteenth century, with the development of sturdy ocean-going vessels, that Europe set forth on the reconnaissance, the great age of exploration, that would subsequently bring it into contact with all the peoples of the globe. A procession of Portuguese voyages down the west coast of Africa, initially intended to tap the lucrative Saharan gold trade, eventually rounded the Cape of Good Hope, opened the sea route to India, Malaya and the Spice Islands, and finally located the curiously peripatetic kingdom of Prester John in Ethiopia. However, those like Columbus, who by wishful miscalculation envisaged a more direct passage to the Orient by striking west across the Atlantic, found their visions eclipsed by a seemingly worthless and frustratingly impervious landmass that thwarted their ambitions from pole to pole. In fact, much of the first half-century of exploratory activity in the Americas focused on ways of getting around this impenetrable barrier, rather than getting to know it. Magellan chanced miraculously upon a slender, tortuous passage around its southern tip; Balboa scrambled over an isthmus that kept eastern and western oceans only a hair's breadth apart; Cartier and others optimistically ascended the St Lawrence in misguided anticipation of emerging into the

Pacific; and the English wasted decades fruitlessly chipping away at the maze of ice-bound culs-de-sac that enshroud the continent's northern coasts.

The unanticipated discovery and mindless destruction of two stately civilizations, the Aztec and gold-rich Inca, lured a steady trickle of unsavoury characters, self-seeking adventurers and ruthless treasure hunters who, confident of riches yet undiscovered, launched headlong into impenetrable forest and waterless desert only to find that, in terms of immediate wealth, the American continent had little else to offer. Instead, the Americas, the north in particular, would become the site of a phenomenon quite new to the nations of Europe: the planting of colonies and the acquisition of overseas empire. Settlers looking for a better life, missionaries seeking a New Jerusalem among heathen peoples, sectarian outcasts and political refugees, fur traders and latter-day conquistadors; all of them became the new explorers, expanding the frontier westward across the landscape of North America and into the depths of the Amazonian jungle. Free-roaming privateers menaced the Spanish colonies, while from the Pacific ports galleons commuted with the Philippines, and visionary Christian zealots crusaded on the remotest of South Sea islands.

The seventeenth century witnessed the birth of another phenomenon: the trading company. Merchants that had bartered their wares for purely personal gain, and ships that had plied the seas in courageous solitude, banded together for the common good with a centralized organization, powerful and monopolistic. The Muscovy Company dispersed its merchants into Russia and Central Asia, and vainly sought an ice-free Northeast Passage to China, while the East India companies of England and the Netherlands vied for the richest pickings in the markets of the Orient, dispossessing the Portuguese and establishing colonial empires that would linger into the twentieth century. The westward exploratory excursions of the Dutch company from its base in Java, and the southerly route by which it directed its ships across the Indian Ocean, inevitably led to the first, accidental landings on the desolate and inhospitable coasts of western and northern Australia, and to the earliest European sighting of New Zealand. At the same time Christian missionaries, who had previously confined their activities to India and the coastal cities, braved the high mountain passes of the Himalayas to rediscover the ancient highways of Central Asia, to establish a long-term presence in China, and to make contact with the Buddhist hegemonies of the Tibetan plateau.

Exploration had rarely seen as its primary objective the delineation of the earth's surface, or the discovery of the infinite multifariousness of its flora and fauna, or the appreciation of its rich cultural and ethnological diversity. These had so far been secondary motivations, incidental to the furtherance of trade, religious proselytization, the quest for gold, and the acquisition of empire. But the scientific revolution that stimulated in the mind of men the demand for accuracy and verification, together with the shifting balance of power that brought Great Britain, France and even Russia to dominance in the field of distant exploration, instigated for the first time an era of expansion dedicated to discovery for its own sake. The old maps, some of which still bore names tracing back to Ptolemy, were cast aside or stripped of detail that was centuries old, revealing gaping white spaces that awaited the measurable and verifiable. Massed, state-sponsored expeditions poured into the uncharted wastes of Siberia and beyond, while the invention of the chronometer, which finally removed the guesswork behind longitude, generated a surge of reappraisal which reshaped the continents and placed remote islands for the first time in their correct positions on the map.

By the first decade of the nineteenth century, with the charting of the entire coastline of Australia, the earth's continents, in just fifty years, had been hammered into a profile almost indistinguishable from modern maps. However, vast expanses in the interior of the continents remained unknown or had been little visited for centuries. North America west of the Mississippi and the Great Lakes was still largely unexplored territory. Africa, beyond the well-trodden paths of Ethiopia and a handful of tentative inland excursions, was almost a total blank. Central Asia, a forbidding hotbed of internal strife and warring khanates, had been ignored for many years, and its complex, mountainous, eastern and southern borderlands remained a mystery. Australia was an empty, seemingly useless and impenetrable void. And South America between its ill-defined meandering rivers and populous settlements was known only to indigenous tribes that had so far mercifully escaped the agonies of European contact. But by the end of the century the rivers of Africa had been navigated, its deserts traversed in every conceivable direction, and the continent partitioned into a colourful tapestry of colonial enclaves. Asia had become the favoured haunt of dusty, sunburnt archaeologists, vagrant plant collectors seeking sweetly perfumed adornments for Victorian gardens, and adventurers clamouring at the gates of Lhasa. North America, with the exception of its more remote and impenetrable northern blackspots, had been surveyed from coast to coast in fine detail. And Australia, where the violent climate and absence of natural and human infrastructure presented explorers with their greatest challenge, now had a telegraph line across its dead heart.

In the Arctic the British poured addictively into the quest for the Northwest Passage that had so eluded them centuries earlier, while others struggled relentlessly towards the North Pole. In the far south the first tentative approaches to Antarctica were made in the early decades of the nineteenth century, only to neglect the continent until the end of the century and the great age of heroic exploration that culminated in the attainment of the South Pole. In fact, by the dawn of the twentieth century, beyond the less alluring shores and inner wastes of Antarctica, very few significantly extensive regions of the earth remained untrodden by explorers. The drifting sands of the eastern Sahara, the waterless dunes of the Arabian Peninsula, the complex darkness of New Guinea, the icy Barrens of Canada, the inter-riverine forests of South America, and a few neglected Siberian islands still beckoned, but these would be conquered over the next forty years, by which time the aeroplane had changed the face of exploration forever.

Exploration became something more localized and focused, concentrating on specific attainments like the conquest of mountain peaks, the pursuit of mineral resources, the discovery of uncontacted tribes, or survival in extreme conditions for no reason other than self-satisfaction or the production of a lucrative documentary film. While many would still call themselves 'explorer', the epithet had been devalued. No longer was it one who discovers the unknown, plotting coordinates with sextant and chronometer, but one who could fill the pages of a bestseller, or captivate a breakfast-show audience, with amusing anecdotes and self-congratulatory reminiscences of tedious excursions by 4WD, armed with GPS and PLB. The spirit of genuine exploration lives on in the depths of the oceans, in the subterranean labyrinths of the caver, and even in the unmanned discovery of space; but sadly, for those whose feet remain firmly on the ground, there are few places left on earth where they can muse and linger, certain in the knowledge that no one has been there before.

The Immortal Voyage

The quest for the rare and exotic in ancient Egypt.

1470 BCE

FOR THE EARLIEST EXPLORERS, at least those whose names we know, and whose aspirations resemble those of their more recent counterparts, we must turn to the records of ancient Egypt. Around 2270 BCE the nobleman Harkhuf, celebrated by some as 'the first known explorer', took four expeditions up the Nile, returning with all manner of fine produce and, to the delight of the boy pharaoh Pepi, a 'dancing pygmy', fresh from 'the land of spirits'. As the power and luxury of Egypt increased, so did its need for exotic materials, especially the incenses frankincense and myrrh, which were widely used in its temples and as embalming agents. For these the Egyptians looked towards the southeast, the sacred region out of which the sun rose, the fabled land of Punt.

The earliest recorded voyage to Punt took place around 2450 BCE in the reign of Sahura. Boatbuilding materials were manhandled across the 250 kilometres (150 miles) of parched and torrid landscape that separates the Nile from the Red Sea, beyond which, at the mercy of prevailing winds, the voyage itself could take more than a year to complete. Around 2000, in the reign of Mentuhotep III, an officer named Hennu employed no less than 3000 men to carry out this monumental task. But for the next 500 years voyages to Punt seem to have ceased, its name surviving in the consciousness of the Egyptians as a remote and almost mythical land once visited by their forefathers. More a concept than a place, never the same to all men, for us to speculate on its precise location could be folly.

Queen Hapshetsut, the first woman ever to rule Egypt with the full title of pharaoh, came to power around 1479 BCE. In the struggle to legitimate her position and to immortalize herself through fine deeds and grandiose monuments, she planned a garden of incense for her newly built mausoleum dedicated to the god Amun-Re. However, to acquire the trees that would adorn her garden she needed to re-establish contact with Punt, and for this purpose assembled an expedition of five cedarwood ships manned by 210 men. The expedition arrived back at Thebes laden with myrrh and frankincense trees, ebony, ivory, cinnamon, monkeys, dogs, and even some native 'Puntians' and their children. Hapshetsut achieved immortality beyond her wildest dreams: each day countless tourists halt to admire the vivid depiction of her expedition, inscribed for eternity in the mortuary temple near the Valley of the Kings.

Right A detail of the relief from Hapshetsut's mortuary temple at Deir el-Bahri, showing an expedition to Punt in the 16th century BCE.

600 BCE

Africa Circumnavigated

A westward voyage, but with the sun on the right.

NECHO II, AN EGYPTIAN KING OF THE 26TH DYNASTY, assumed the throne in 610 BCE and ruled Egypt for fifteen years. Confronted by military incursions on Egypt's northeastern borders he waged war against the Babylonians in Syria until defeat at the hands of Nebuchadnezzar forced his retreat to Egypt. Bent on retaliation he ordered the construction of a canal from the Nile to the Red Sea, by which ocean-going vessels might be launched into the Indian Ocean and strike at Babylonia by the back door. The canal constantly refilled with sand and the project was eventually abandoned after 120,000 Egyptians had perished in its construction. Added to this was the distinct possibility that the Babylonians might appear in the Red Sea and use the canal to their own advantage.

Probably to secure the defence of his Asian-facing boundaries in the southeast, Necho assembled a fleet in the Red Sea with instructions to head southward along the coast of Africa and return to the Mediterranean by the Strait of Gibraltar. Aware of his commanders' intense distaste for oceanic voyages, he placed the fleet in the hands of Phoenician sailors who were not only proven navigators but also sworn enemies of Babylonia. Although perfectly familiar with Africa's north and northwestern coasts, they could have had little idea of the extent of the continent to the south. Sadly, the only account of the journey appears all too briefly as a single paragraph in Herodotus' *The Histories*, but from what little it does provide the voyage becomes perfectly plausible. Sailing in July, the north wind and the northeast monsoon would have carried the ships to the equator by March, then to South Africa by the Agulhas Current. Here the navigators reported sailing westward with the sun on their right, a statement that Herodotus, who had no appreciation of the curvature of the earth, found impossible to comprehend.

To sustain themselves the navigators spent prolonged periods ashore, sowing crops in the autumn, or austral spring, and harvesting them the following year. Timed correctly, the Benguela Current and southeast trades would have swept the fleet up the Namibian coast and back to the equatorial regions. After two years it entered the Mediterranean, and in the third returned to Egypt. The account was later hotly disputed by Ptolemy, whose vision of Africa as the extension of a vast and continuous southern continent held sway for 1500 years. Modern scholars have tended to be cautiously sympathetic.

Right This Phoenician trading ship, carved on a sarcophagus now on display in Lebanon's National Museum, is typical of those in which Necho's navigators might have sailed.

Exploration in the Ancient World

Tracing the fleeting narratives of elusive and shadowy pioneers.

500 BCE

THE MOST WE CAN SAY WITH CERTAINTY ABOUT EXPLORERS of the ancient world is that we know not nearly enough about them. Their stories, often reduced long after the event to solitary mouth-watering sentences or terse paragraphs in the works of Strabo, Pliny and Herodotus, are relatively few, suggesting that the real voyage of discovery was far from an everyday occurence. These forgotten explorers were the Amundsens and Livingstones of their day, and, to be remembered centuries later, must have enjoyed immense prestige in their lifetimes. Herodotus tells us of Colaios of Samos who, in the seventh century BCE, was driven by winds into the Atlantic. From the Roman poet Avienus we learn of Himilco of Carthage, who in the fifth or sixth century BCE sailed into the Atlantic to be becalmed in what some have taken to be the Sargasso Sea. About the same time Hanno, a Carthaginian whose narrative survives, rounded the West African coast into equatorial parts, and passed a place where 'torrents of fire entered the sea' – a clear allusion to an erupting volcano, maybe Mount Cameroun. Another, named Euthymenes, a Greek from Massalia, reached the mouth of the River Senegal, wrongly conjecturing it to be the source of the Nile.

Far to the west, Herodotus tells us that the greater part of Asia was explored by the Persian king Darius I and his emissaries. About 515 BCE, Scylax, a Greek in Persian service, was sent out to explore the course of the Kabul and Indus rivers. Descending the latter to the sea, he reconnoitred the shores of the Indian Ocean, rounded the Arabian Peninsula, and after thirty months returned to Persia by the Red Sea. In 470 Sataspes, a nephew of Darius who had raped the daughter of a Persian nobleman, avoided the normal punishment of impaling by opting for something 'even more severe' – a voyage around Africa. In Egypt Sataspes procured a ship and crew, sailed out through the Strait of Gibraltar and continued on a southerly course for many months. Alighting on a coast inhabited by pygmies clothed in nothing but palm leaves, and unable to make headway against the contrary current, he put about and returned to Egypt the way he had come. Back in Persia, King Xerxes decided that Sataspes had failed to accomplish his mission and, with little sympathy for the suffering already endured, had him impaled all the same.

Right A bas-relief showing Achaemenid king Darius I of Persia seated on his throne, attended by an officer and guards. According to Herodotus, Darius was responsible for exploration through much of Asia in the late fifth and early sixth centuries BCE.

Alexander the Great: Conqueror or Explorer?

Domination of the world first depends on knowing its outer limits.

326 BCE

Although the status of Alexander as a discoverer of new lands can easily be overestimated, the impact of his journey on Greek geography was profound in the extreme. A highly cultured man, well versed in history and geography, when Alexander crossed the Dardanelles in 334 BCE to begin his conquest of Asia, he already had a reasonable idea of what lay beyond. The Persian empire, which had reached its apogee under Darius I, spanned half of the known world, from the Bosphorus to the Indus, and almost every corner must have been familiar to its geographers. However, to the east of the Caspian, and southward to the Arabian Sea, Greek geography became increasingly extravagant in its concepts. Disciplined in the Aristotelian notion of the world as an insular landmass surrounded by an extensive and continuous 'Ocean', with no appreciation of the extent of Asia or the existence of the Arabian Sea, Alexander, as he progressed eastward, would find his mental image of the world challenged from every direction.

Obsessed with the notion that domination of the world could be achieved only by penetrating to the shores of the hypothetical Ocean that encircled it, Alexander became as much a true explorer as a conqueror. First the Caspian was not what Greeks had proclaimed to be an inlet of the Ocean, and the plains of Central Asia seemed to stretch to infinity. Then, in the Indus Valley, Alexander heard with despair of the Ganges, a mighty river that would force the fringes of the known world even further from his grasp. In 326, when his weary generals finally declared that enough was enough, Alexander launched despondently on the Indus, certain that it was the Nile and that its descent would bring him back to Egypt. From its delta, which lay not in the Mediterranean but in the Indian Ocean, Nearchus, one of the generals, returned the fleet to Babylon via the Persian Gulf, establishing the Arabian Sea on the Greek map for the first time. Alexander stumbled back through the forbidding Makran Desert, while Craterus, another general, took a wide sweep through southern Afghanistan. Alexander's empire was dismembered by his successors, but journeys to the east continued spasmodically. Around 300, Megasthenes, an Ionian Greek, visited the Indo-Gangetic plain, made a careful study of its people, and composed the four-book *Indica*, which remained the definitive account of the region for centuries to come.

Right A Roman mosaic from the Casa del Fauno in Pompeii, depicting Alexander's battle against the Persians at Issos in 333 BCE.

The Discovery of Britain

While Alexander sought the limit of the habitable world, another explorer had already arrived there.

325 BCE

THE PORT OF MASSALIA, TODAY'S MARSEILLE, had by the fourth century BCE already established itself as an important commercial centre. Founded by Phocaean Greeks around 600 BCE, and ideally situated close to the convergence of the inland trading corridors, it controlled trade around the northwestern Mediterranean and beyond into the barbarian hinterland. Around 325, a date that can be fixed with reasonable certainty, a native of Massalia named Pytheas embarked on a remarkable voyage of discovery that would result in the first documented account of the coastline of northern Europe, the British Isles and the lands of the far north. Little is known of the man himself other than that he was an independent adventurer of limited means; an educated and perceptive mariner of considerable scientific ability.

Pytheas's precise route can only be conjectured from what fragmentary observations survive in the works of later geographers. Whether he reached the Bay of Biscay by an overland route through the Garonne Valley, or by breaking the Carthaginian blockade of the Strait of Gibraltar, is uncertain, but from the bay he rounded the Armorican peninsula, modern Bretagne, and crossed the Channel to what is now Cornwall. In a direction unknown he then set out to circumnavigate 'the islands of the Pretanni', en route visiting the Orkneys and Shetlands and continuing far to the north, to the land of Thule, variously identified as Iceland or the Norwegian coast. Returning south, he sailed for an uncertain distance along the coast of northern Europe. What difficulties he encountered, or how he communicated with the people he met, one can only imagine.

Frequently venturing ashore, Pytheas accurately calculated latitude from the height of the sun, or from the length of the longest day, which in Thule, some six days' sailing from Britain, came close to twenty-four hours. He described what some have taken to be pancake ice, which forms at the edge of drift ice, and he was the first among the Greeks to draw a connection between the tides and the position of the moon. He observed the manners and customs of the inhabitants, the use of fermented liquors made from corn and honey, and the gradual disappearance of various types of grain as one advanced northward. His geographical treatise, *On the Ocean*, written around 320 but since lost, was held in such esteem that it would continue to be quoted by geographers for the next 900 years.

Right Pytheas describes Britain as a place where ancient customs are preserved.

The Mission of Zhang Qian to the 'Western Countries'

China discovers it is not alone in the world.

138 BCE

BEFORE THE ROMAN EMPIRE HAD EMERGED from its Mediterranean heartlands an even greater empire had taken shape in the East. By 210 BCE the Ch'in had expanded from their homeland beyond the great bend of the Yellow River to establish supremacy over the whole of China. The Han dynasty, notably during the reign of Emperor Han Wudi, pushed the boundaries even further, until the empire and its protectorates stretched from Korea to Kyrgyzstan and south to Vietnam. However, expansion to the west was constantly frustrated by the Xiongnu, a nomadic people that had migrated from the north and formed a powerful empire that threatened China's northern borders, displacing an indigenous people, the Yuezhi, deep into Central Asia. In 138, eighteen-year-old Han Wudi resolved to despatch an embassy to the Yuezhi in the hope of eliciting their support for a two-pronged assault on the Xiongnu. The mission, placed in the hands of the courtier Zhang Qian, left the capital Chang'an, modern Xi'an, with 100 followers and a Xiongnu guide.

Far to the west, Zhang Qian's route took him through the territory of the Xiongnu, who detained him and gave him a wife to keep him happy. But Zhang Qian never relinquished his imperial credentials, and after ten years, when the Xiongnu finally lowered their guard, he escaped to proceed on his mission to the Yuezhi, crossing the mountains and after several weeks reaching the kingdom of Dayuan, the Fergana Valley of Uzbekistan. Provided with guides and interpreters, he continued west into Kangju, where Samarqand now lies, then turned south to seek the Yuezhi kingdom around the Amu Dar'ya. Here he found the Yuezhi quite content with their new-found pastures, and in no mood for another war against the Xiongnu. After a year in the region, Zhang Qian set out empty-handed for home, arriving back in Chang'an after an absence of thirteen years, his Xiongnu wife and guide in tow. His report, which richly portrays the lands visited, as well as others more distant, survives as one of the earliest narratives of a true explorer. Zhang Qian opened the eyes of the Chinese for the first time to a civilized world beyond their borders, and he provided the geographical background and stimulus for trade that would result in the opening of the Silk Road, along which the first exchanges would take place between East and West.

Right The world as perceived by the ancient Chinese. The four innermost squares, radiating at consecutive distances of 500 *li* (250km / 150 miles) from the imperial palace, indicate the regions occupied by the various social classes subservient to the emperor. The fifth and outermost square, Huang Fu, was the rest of the world, the 'barbarian' realm beyond the emperor's control.

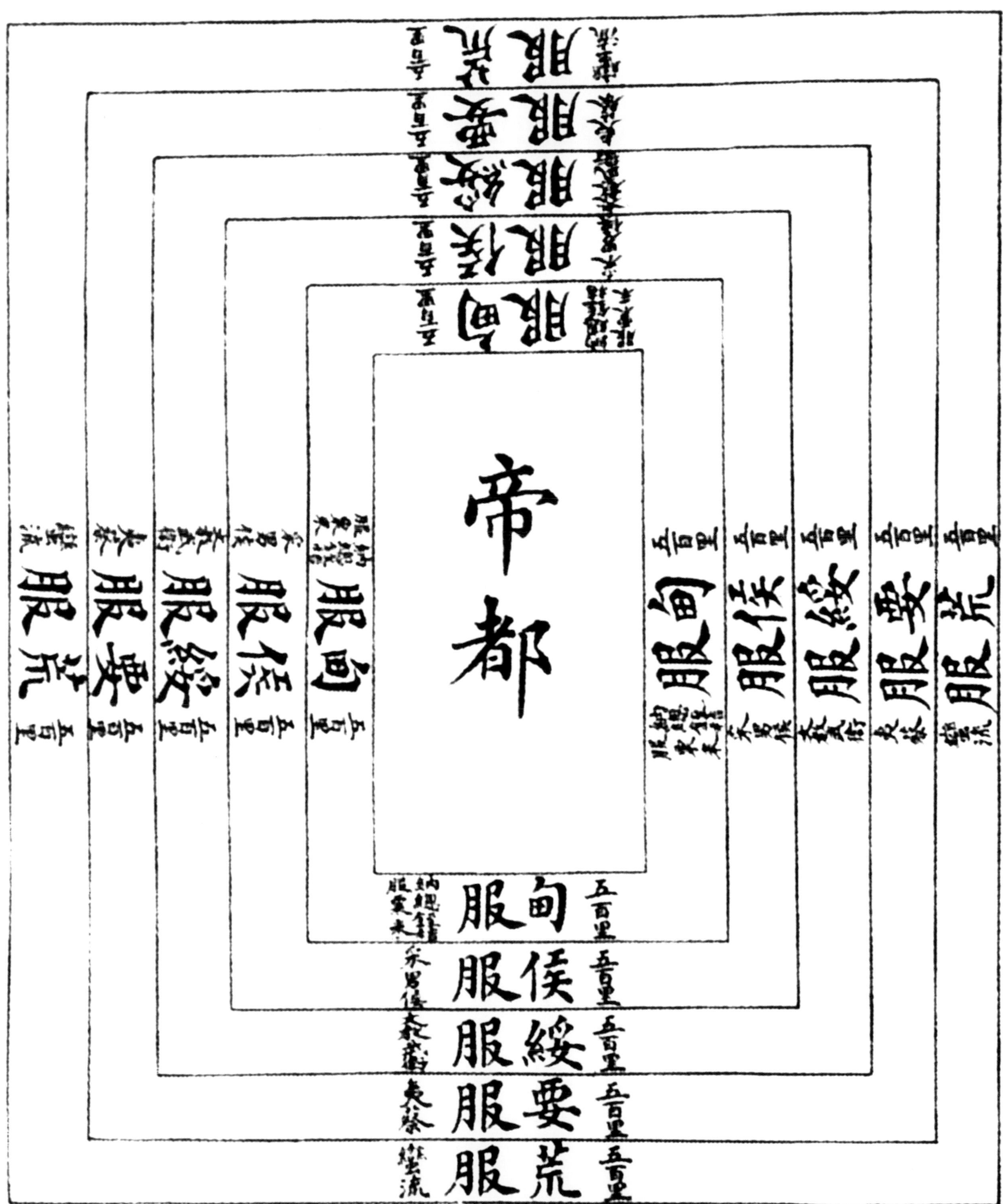
帝都
甸服
五百里
侯服
五百里
綏服
五百里
要服
五百里
荒服
五百里

Exploration under Imperial Rome

Excursions beyond the fringes of empire.

100 CE

BEYOND CHINA AND THE MIDDLE EAST, virtually no significant land journey is recorded prior to the emergence of the Roman Empire. Then, under the Empire, the campaigns of Julius Caesar and his successors in the north brought forth the first reliable accounts of what lay deep in the remote heartlands of France, Britain, Germany and Spain. By 9 BCE Drusus had advanced to the River Elbe, and by 84 CE Agricola had arrived in northern Scotland and despatched a fleet to circumnavigate Britain. Ignorant of Pytheas's voyage four centuries earlier, the fleet subjugated the 'hitherto unknown' Orkney Islands and sighted 'Thule', on this occasion the Shetlands.

To the south of the Mediterranean, in 42 CE Suetonius Paulinus, celebrated for his defeat of the British queen Boudica, crossed the Atlas Mountains and was astonished to see snow-capped peaks. Around 60 CE the infamous emperor Nero sent out two centurions to discover the source of the Nile. Little is known of this important excursion except that after a long journey the men lost the river in an immense marsh choked by reeds and grasses – the notorious Sudd that would become the curse of so many future expeditions. Some twenty years later Septimus Flaccus marched an army southward across the Sahara for three months, reaching a land populated by blacks. Then at a similar date a little-known adventurer, Julius Maternus, struck across the desert for four months to a place where rhinoceroses were found.

Better documented is the disastrously ill-fated campaign of Aelius Gallus, who in 25 CE was sent by Augustus to conclude treaties with, or otherwise subdue, the peoples inhabiting the western parts of the Arabian Peninsula. Disembarking a short distance down the Red Sea coast, he proceeded to march ten thousand men across 1500 kilometres (900 miles) towards Arabia Felix, the fertile coastal district that is now part of Yemen. Sadly, a treacherous Nabataean guide, anxious to rid his homeland of the invaders, steered the advancing army through endless tracts of barren and waterless country, committing countless soldiers to death by hunger and thirst. To add to their misery the troops also suffered a mysterious and terrible illness that could be cured only by administering wine and oil, both of which were in short supply. After six months, his army decimated by death and disease, Aelius Gallus turned back at Marib, in the land of the Sabaeans, and wearily retraced his route back to the coast.

Right A detail from a mosaic pavement at the Sanctuary of Fortuna, to the east of Rome, showing a boat taking soldiers down the Nile.

The Geography of Claudius Ptolemy

Measuring the world by the distance of a day's travel.

130 CE

BY THE END OF THE FIRST CENTURY CE knowledge of the world beyond the Mediterranean had expanded substantially, and the ancient library of Alexandria, restocked after its destruction in 48 BCE, was awash with maps and geographical texts. Around 116 BCE a Greek navigator, Eudoxus of Cyzicus, undertook trading voyages to India, returning with cargoes of perfumes and precious stones and on one occasion discovering on the African coast the wreckage of a vessel he believed had circumnavigated Africa. Anxious to try this out for himself, Eudoxus made two attempts. The first ended in shipwreck on the coast of Morocco, and from the second he never returned.

At a similar date the Greek merchant seaman Hippalos discovered how monsoons could be used to sail directly to India without hugging the coast, while the same period saw the evolution of the Periplus, an early form of coastal pilot, rich in geographical and commercial detail, of which examples survive to the present day. We hear briefly of Diogenes, another Greek merchant, blown southward along the African shore as far as 'the lakes from which the Nile flows', and of Bion of Soli, who ventured to the upper reaches of the Nile and wrote a treatise on Ethiopia, sadly now lost. A Macedonian merchant, Maes Titianus, travelled as far as the 'Stone Tower', a crucial landmark in what is probably now southern Kyrgyzstan, from which he despatched agents into China to trade in silk.

About 100 CE the Greek geographer Marinos of Tyre embarked on the massive task of correlating every scrap of information about the known world and attributing a geographical coordinate to every named place. Unfortunately little or nothing is known of Marinos, and both his map and text are lost, but his work was taken up by another armchair explorer, the mighty Alexandrian scholar Claudius Ptolemy. Ptolemy's *Geography*, written shortly after 130, survives in full as the only book on cartography to have come down to us from the classical period. The maps that accompanied the original have long since been lost, and for the twelve centuries preceeding its discovery by the Byzantine theologian Maximus Planudes, little was known of the book itself. Planudes became the first of many to attempt a reconstruction of the maps, widely used although centuries out-of-date, from Ptolemy's extensive tables of coordinates.

Right One of the many early European world maps reconstructed from the coordinates in Ptolemy's *Geography*; its place names now thirteen centuries out-of-date.

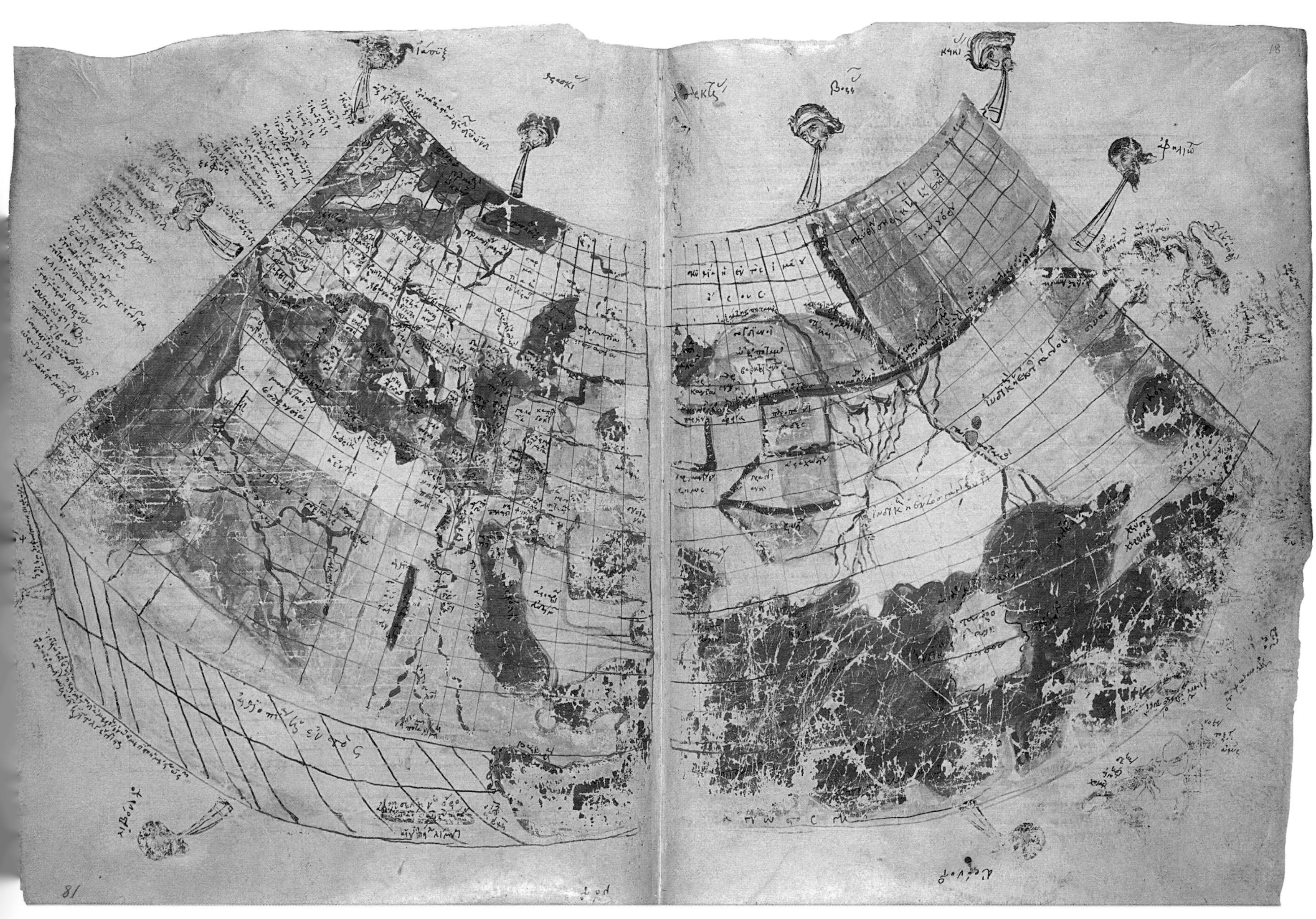

Chinese Pilgrims Seek Enlightenment in India

'Not for riches or fame, but only for the sake of religious truth.'

400–700

Buddhism arrived in China in the first century CE, and by the fifth had come to rival Taoism in popularity. But the fountain-head of the religion, its shrines and sacred texts, lay in far-off India, the way to which was difficult and dangerous. Beyond the Silk Road, underused and largely impassable, lay the fearsome, precipitous tracks of the Karakoram. The Burmese route plunged the traveller into country ravaged by tribal conflict, while the passage by sea would for many incur a tedious detour to the coast. Nevertheless, many Chinese monks would undertake the pilgrimage, impelled by piety and inspired by scholarship to seek the pure texts of the Buddhist scriptures. The monk Yijing, who followed the sea route in 671, records no less than fifty-six such journeys, but for all but a few we have only scant documentation.

Outstanding among those who left detailed narratives of their journeys are Faxian (Fa Hsien), who sought no more than an unmutilated copy of the disciplinary rule-book known as Vinaya Pitaka; and Xuanzang (Hsuan Tsang), whose ambition was to sit at the feet of the masters and collect Sanskrit texts for translation into Chinese. Faxian left Chang'an, modern Xi'an, in 399, and to avoid marauders joined a caravan across the trackless Takla Makan desert, where evil demons summoned sandstorms to disorientate the traveller. Emerging at the flourishing emporium of Khotan, he turned across the snowbound Karakoram, a place 'where dragons spit wind', and descended to Peshawar. After five years he arrived in the plain of the Ganges where, so captivated was he by the monuments and abundance of resources, he remained for six years before making his way home by the Bay of Bengal, Ceylon and Sumatra.

Xuanzang, a man of exceptional intelligence and learning, left Chang'an in 629 and struck out across the Gobi Desert where only heaps of bones and piles of horse-dung guided his way. Following the northern Silk Road, his route to India took him across the Tien Shan and south into Afghanistan where, at Bamiyan, he marvelled at the massive gold-coated statue of Buddha so mindlessly destroyed by the Taleban in 2001. Xuanzang travelled the length and breadth of India, sometimes lingering as long as two years at the major seats of learning. After an absence of sixteen years he returned to China much the way he had come, his twenty-two horses staggering under the weight of 644 sacred texts.

Right The monk Xuanzang on his return from the sixteen-year pilgrimage to India.

Al-rihla fi talab al-'ilm. The Islamic Geographers

The Prophet said: 'Seek knowledge, even as far as China.'

900

THE SPREAD OF ISLAM IN THE CENTURIES FOLLOWING THE ASCENSION of the Prophet Muhammad provided a unification and stability that allowed Arab and Persian scholars to travel uninhibited throughout much of the known world. Geographical knowledge developed through first-hand observation in regions inaccessible to the Greeks and Romans and led to the emergence of a host of prodigious Islamic geographers whose works rivalled those of Ptolemy, Strabo and Pliny. Arab and Persian traders made extensive sea journeys to India, the East Indies, China and Africa, returning with tales both popular and scientific. Ahmad al-Ya'qubi travelled for twenty years between India and North Africa and in 891 completed the *Kitab al-Buldan*, describing all the countries and major cities of the Islamic world. About the same time, Ibn Khurdadhbih delineated the trade routes as far as the Indies, with references to China, Korea and Japan. In 922 Ahmad ibn Fadhlan crossed the Caspian Sea, ascended the Volga, and witnessed a Viking ship burial. Al-Muqaddasi, who wrote around 985, travelled the entire world and produced the first maps in natural colours, similar to those we have today. Around 977 Muhammad ibn Hawqal, who spent thirty years in remote regions, took the caravan route to Darfur and Lake Chad, sailed on the Niger and penetrated as far as the kingdom of Ghana.

Geographical studies in this early period reached their height in the complementary works of Abu'l-Hasan al-Mas'udi and Abu Rayhan al-Biruni. Mas'udi, who has been likened to a Muslim Herodotus, went everywhere between the Caucasus and East Africa, the Mediterranean and India. An intellectual giant of his time, the first to fully appreciate the interplay between geography and history, his monumental *Akhbar az-Zaman* stretched to thirty volumes and encompassed kingdoms well beyond the Islamic world. In 990 Biruni, who has been called the father of both geodesy and anthropology, calculated the latitude of his home town at the tender age of seventeen. He subsequently travelled widely in India, studying the religion and customs of its people. He produced 146 books in every field of natural science and calculated the radius of the earth to within 17 kilometres (10 miles) of its accepted value. In regarding heliocentricity and geocentricity as equally acceptable, philosophical rather than astronomical, Biruni also anticipated the basis of Einstein's relativistic theories. His work would remain unmatched in Christendom for another six centuries.

Right The world according to the Arabic geographer al-Adrisi. Drawn in 1154, it is orientated with north at the bottom of the map.

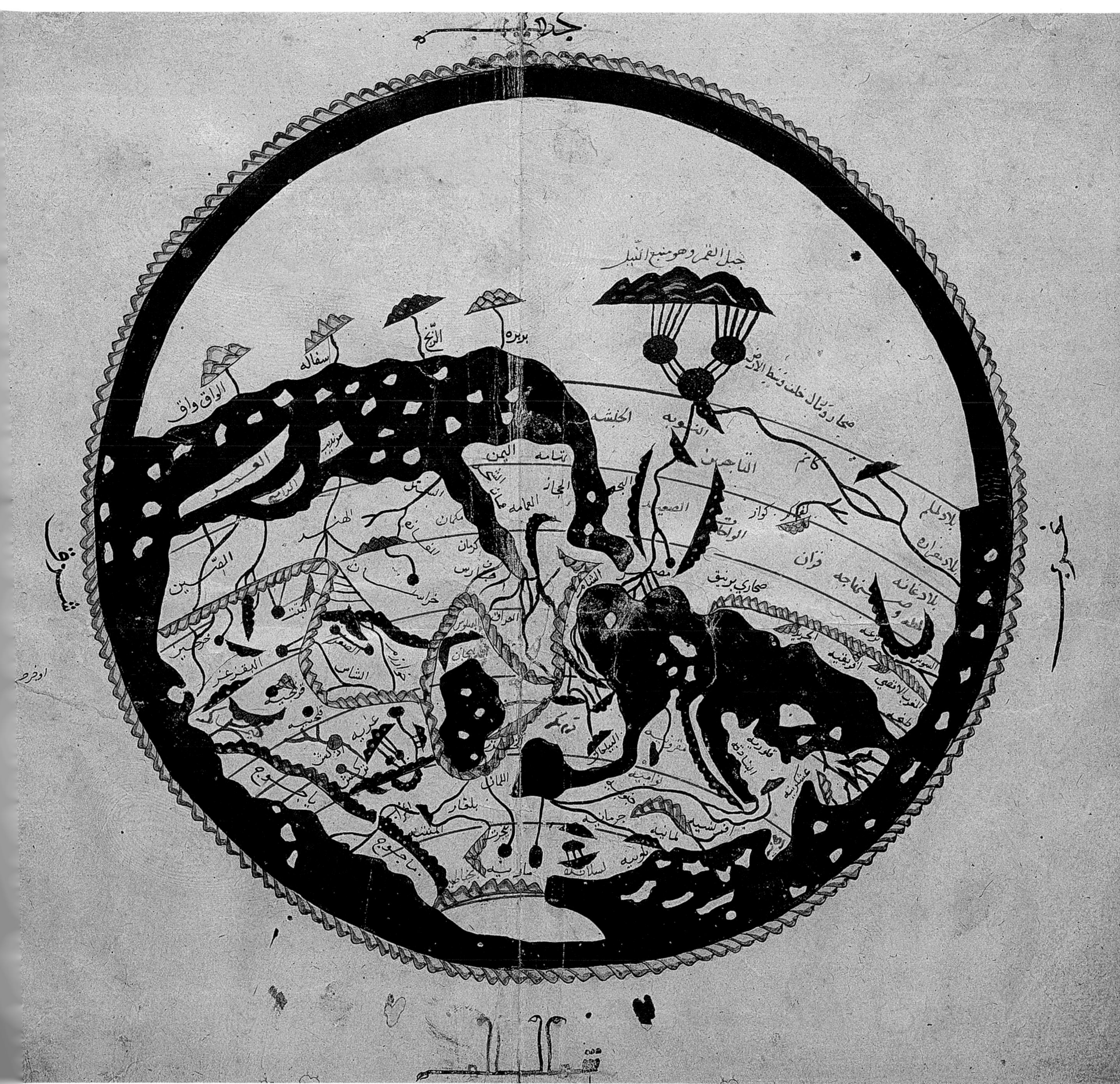

جبل القمر وهو منبع النيل

Eirik the Red and the Discovery of Greenland

Monks and Vikings: island-hopping through the North Atlantic.

982

THE UNLIKELY BUT TRUE PIONEERS OF NORTH ATLANTIC EXPLORATION were humble Irish monks. In rudimentary craft modelled on the traditional currach, with no particular destination in mind, they launched fearlessly onto the open sea, directed by God 'whither He wills'. By the early eighth century they had settled themselves in the Faroes, and around 795 an anonymous group went ashore in Iceland where, at midnight on the summer solstice, they reported: 'The sun hides itself as if behind a little hill.' No doubt others followed in their wake, some, like the almost legendary Saint Brendan, navigating untold distances to the west. It was intelligence gleaned in Ireland and northern Britain that led the Vikings to the Faroes, and around 860 to Iceland, where Norse sagas tell of a community of Irish hermits already ensconced. Then around 930 the Norwegian sailor Gunnbjorn Ulfsson, driven off-course by heavy seas, made the first discovery of 'America' when he glimpsed a small group of islands to the southwest of Iceland. Fifty years later Snaebjorn Galti installed a band of colonists on an adjacent coast, but after a miserable winter his two surviving followers rose up against their leader, murdered him and promptly sailed back to Iceland.

In 982 Eirik Raudi, 'the Red', banished from Norway for manslaughter, then exiled for three years from Iceland for similar misdemeanours, decided that his only option would be to try his luck in Gunnbjorn's mysterious land to the west. When eastern Greenland proved inhospitable he ventured south, rounded Cape Farewell and made his way up the uninhabited west coast, discovering grassy, cultivable slopes rich in wild animals and birds. For three years he lived off the land, explored islands and channels, and marked out the best sites for future settlement. Then, his exile over, he went back to Iceland, armed with irresistable tales of a country he had alluringly christened Greenland. Having recently endured a cruel famine, and suffering a severe shortage of habitable land, the Icelanders needed little encouragement, and when Eirik sailed back to Greenland in 986 he was accompanied by twenty-five ships. Fourteen shiploads of colonists arrived safely to establish the so-called Eastern Settlement, and subsequently the more northerly and smaller Western Settlement. The colonies flourished for 300 years until worsening climate, the erosion of arable land, conflict with the recently arrived Inuit, and remoteness from European trade forced their abandonment and decline.

Right A vellum of the seventeenth-century Danish School, fancifully portraying an heroic Eirik Raudi in full armour.

Thorerus, vel Thoraldus taurinus. Thorer filium habuit Ulf, cujus gnatus fuit Aswaldus, gignens Thorwaldum Erici Rauderi patrem:

Thorwaldus cum filio Erico ob perpetratum homicidium

Effigies Erici Rauderi ad delineationem Einarfi Eiolfsonii adumbrata

e Norvagia in Islandiam aufugit, ubi in promontorio ejusdem insulae caurum versus villam vocatam Drangar ad

vitae

The Norse Discovery of America

Westward to Vinland.

986–1010

WITH SO MANY GREENLAND-BOUND SHIPS plying the stormy North Atlantic in the late tenth century, it would be only a matter of time before one of them chanced upon the mainland coast of North America. In 986 Bjarni Herjolfsson arrived in Iceland to visit his family, only to find that his father had sold up and gone off to Greenland with Eirik Raudi's colonizing expedition. Bjarni determined to follow, but on the third day fell prey to a north wind that swept him to an unknown coast, well forested, hilly, and definitely not his intended destination. But back in Greenland little interest was shown in Bjarni's discovery of Labrador until, fifteen years later, Leif Eiriksson, son of the colony's founder, decided to purchase Bjarni's ship and take a look for himself.

Leif Eiriksson left Greenland some time after the year 1000 with fifteen crew, following Bjarni's course in reverse. His first landfall, Helluland, the mountainous and barren tip of Baffin Island, offered little prospect of settlement, so he continued southward to Markland, the thickly wooded shore of Bjarni's report. Some distance beyond lay Vinland, a distinctly more temperate and balmy locality where he elected to spend the winter. Leif returned to Greenland the following summer, singing Vinland's praises, its grass and grapes, timber and salmon. Maybe vines, if that's what he really meant, did grow there; or was Leif, like his father before him, simply playing the propagandist? Burdened with management of the Greenland colony, he delegated a second expedition to his brother Thorvald Eiriksson, but this ended in disaster when Thorvald fell to a Native American arrow.

No attempt at colonization was undertaken until about 1010 when Thorfinn Karlsefni, an Icelander and Leif's brother-in-law, sailed out with sixty-or-more men, their wives and livestock, to retrace Leif's route and plant a colony in Vinland. The sagas differ in detail, but it appears that the colonists saw out three winters in Vinland, probably the northernmost promontory of Newfoundland, until conflict with previously friendly natives made their position untenable. Archaeological finds confirm beyond doubt the presence of Norsemen in Newfoundland, but the extent to which contact was maintained with North America in later years is uncertain. Fragmentary evidence from the annals suggests that voyages continued until the mid-fourteenth century when the distant colonies fell generally into decline.

Right The controversial Vinland map, now widely regarded as a modern fake, purports to show the Norse discoveries in the New World.

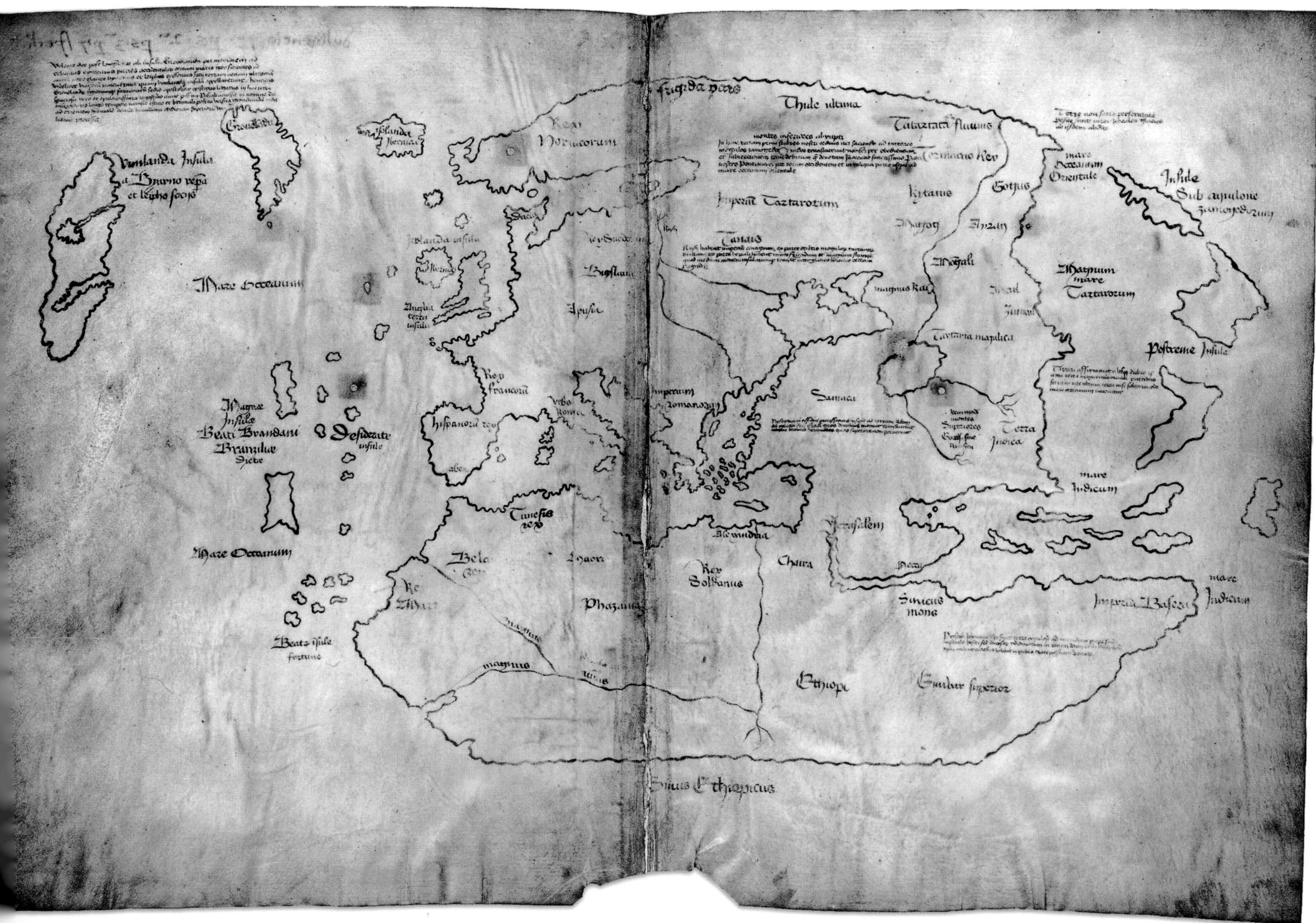
Vinlanda Insula
Mare Occeanum
Thule ultima
Imperium Tartarorum
mare Occeanum Orientale
Insule Sub aquilone
Magnum mare Tartarorum
Postreme Insule
Terra Indica
mare Indicum
Alexandria
Rex Soldanus
Ethiopi
Sinus Ethiopicus

The Journey of Chang Chun to the Camp of Ghengis Khan

The Tao of exploration. Yin and Yang in war-torn Central Asia.

1220

In just two decades the mighty warlord Ghengis Khan had unified the tribes of Central Asia into a collective fighting force and created an empire that stretched from the Tien Shan to the China Sea. In 1219 he stood at the western edge of his dominions, poised to launch an attack on the formidable Khwarezmid empire, which stood between him and the Persian Gulf. But the great khan, now in his late fifties, fearful for his own mortality and concerned that in his ruling 'there may be something wanting', sought passionately the spiritual guidance that only a man of acclaimed wisdom could provide. In tones of uncharacteristic humility he summoned the celebrated seventy-one-year-old Taoist sage Qiu Chuji, better known as Chang Chun, from his residence 3000 kilometres (1800 miles) away on the shore of the Yellow Sea. Anxious to instil in the khan a compassion for the common man, and determined to bring a halt to the indiscriminate killing that had become the hallmark of the Mongol campaign, Chang Chun readily accepted the invitation.

In 1220, with eighteen disciples, one of whom kept a diary of the expedition, Chang Chun first headed north for 1000 kilometres (600 miles) to winter in a remote Taoist monastery. Turning west into the Gobi, where 'no tree is seen for 10,000 li', and surviving the bitter hailstorms of the 'Hugely Cold Mountains', he negotiated the entire breadth of modern Mongolia and by September 1221 had entered northern Xinjiang. When the heat of the sun became intolerable he travelled at night, smearing his horses with blood to ward off evil spirits. Proceeding west to Tashkent and Samarkand, then south across the Hindu Kush, the Mongol camp was eventually located in May 1222 in northeastern Afghanistan. Chang Chun was able to offer the khan no elixir for immortality, but explained instead that life was nourished by a pure heart and the renunciation of worldly desires, and that it was the love of people that formed the foundation of good government. In April 1223 the sage took leave of the Mongol camp, followed his outward track as far as western Mongolia, then by a direct route across the Gobi arrived back in China by the end of the year. Although the Mongols went on to inflict crushing defeats on the Khwarezmids, it is claimed that countless civilians owed their lives to Chang Chun's enlightened ministrations.

Right The Taoist sage Chang Chun meditating on the mysteries of the natural world.

長春丘

European Missions to the Mongol Khan

Christendom meets its match in the heartland of Central Asia.

1245–55

PRIOR TO THE THIRTEENTH CENTURY WESTERN CHRISTIANS had only the haziest impressions of what lay beyond the principalities of European Russia and the crusading grounds of the Middle East. Vague and fanciful notions permeated their perception of Asia, among them the domain of Prester John, a mighty prince who ruled a Christian kingdom somewhere deep in the interior. Curiously, it was the rise of the Mongol empire that finally brought East and West together, wreaking havoc in eastern Europe but thereafter providing the political stability, the *Pax Mongolica*, that would allow a traveller to pass unhindered from Christendom to China. Taking advantage of this, and with an arrogance and presumption that defies comprehension, the pope decided that the 'Great Khan' of the Mongols could be ideal material for recruitment into the Christian fold. Sadly, what he had not anticipated was that the appearance of an emissary before the khan would automatically be taken as a gesture of submission and allegiance, not only by the emissary but also the potentate he represented.

The first mission to the Mongols started from the papal residence at Lyon in 1245, led by the Franciscan friar Giovanni da Pian del Carpini. However, when he and his Polish companion arrived a year later on the River Volga at the camp of Batu, commander of the Mongol western front, they were told that to accomplish their mission they would need to continue on horseback to the court of the supreme khan, a mere 5000 kilometres (3000 miles) to the east. After 106 days in the saddle, their bodies tightly bandaged to prevent chafing, they finally encountered the khan Guyuk at his camp near the Mongolese capital of Karakorum. Not surprisingly, the khan was in no mood to accept Christianity, and in November 1246 he sent the travellers on their way with an imperious and self-asserting reply for the pope. Seven years later, Louis IX of France despatched Friar William of Rubruck on what the king regarded as a fact-finding and diplomatic mission, but what for the friar turned into a profound spiritual quest. Following a route similar to Carpini's, but in the greater comfort of ox-drawn covered wagons, William entered Karakorum on Palm Sunday 1254 and to his surprise came across craftsmen from all over Eurasia, including a goldsmith from Paris. Rubruck's detailed report, sympathetic and observant, survives in full and in certain respects remained unsurpassed until the nineteenth century.

Right The letter from Khan Guyuk, delivered to the court of Pope Innocent IV by Carpini on his return from the Mongols in 1247.

Marco Polo and the Discovery of China

'I have told only half of what I have seen.'

1271-95

THE MONGOL PEACE THAT ATTRACTED RUBRUCK AND CARPINI to Central Asia also opened the way to other diplomatic travellers, all of them seeking favours from the Great Khan. In 1249-51 Friar Andrew of Longjumeau struck deep into the Asian heartland to pursue an anti-Islamic alliance with Khan Guyuk. And in 1254 Hetoum (or Hayton), king of Cilicia, visited Karakorum on a similar mission, the narrative of which became compulsive reading for more than 300 years. Given the stability of the Mongol empire, it would not be long before enterprising merchants, particularly those of Venice, dominant in foreign trade, would take advantage of the situation to reopen the ancient Silk Roads. In fact by the fourteenth century traffic across Asia had become so commonplace that novice merchants could happily set out armed only with one of the handy 'rough guides' in circulation at the time.

As far as we can tell, overland trade with China was pioneeered by two Italian jewel merchants, the brothers Nicolò and Maffeo Polo. Their journey began in 1260, occupied nine years, three of them in Bukhara, and brought the travellers eventually to the court of Kublai Khan, who requested priests and men of learning to educate his followers in the ways of the West. In the event the Polos were unable to satisfy this demand and returned to Venice, but in 1271 they made their way back to China, taking Nicolò's teenage son Marco Polo. Traversing country never before seen by Europeans – the Iranian deserts, the passes of the Pamirs, the Tibetan plateau and the fringes of the Gobi – it was not until May 1275 that they arrived at the Mongol court. For many years Marco travelled in the service of the khan to all four corners of the empire, finally returning to Venice in 1295 by the sea route around Southeast Asia. His narrative, dictated from a Genoese prison cell and popularly known as *Il Milione*, introduced Western readers for the first time to the wealth and vastness of China, the richness of its culture, its science and manufactures. Although initially regarded as fantastic and unreliable, it achieved such distinction that Columbus used it to plan his westward voyage to the Orient two centuries later. Doubts about the book's authenticity which emerged in the 1990s have, at least in this writer's opinion, largely been laid to rest.

Right A detail from the Catalan Atlas of 1375, with a depiction of Marco Polo's caravan, inverted, at the top of the first plate.

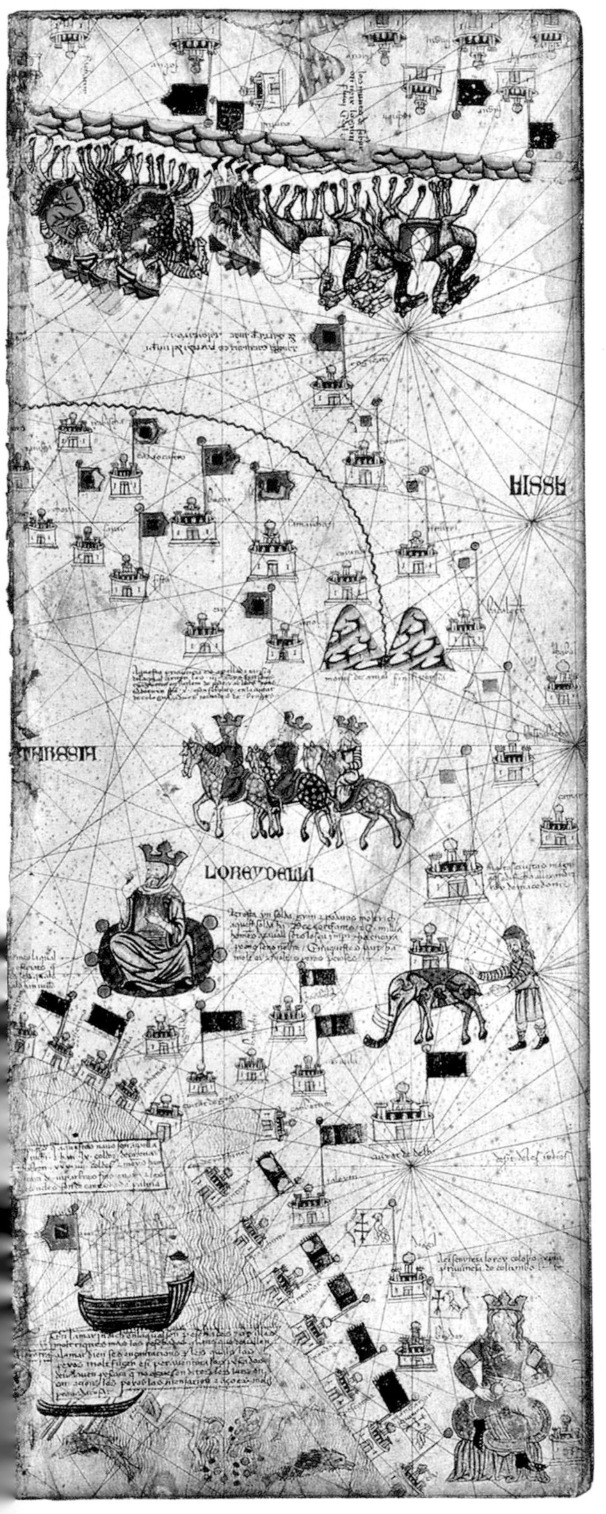
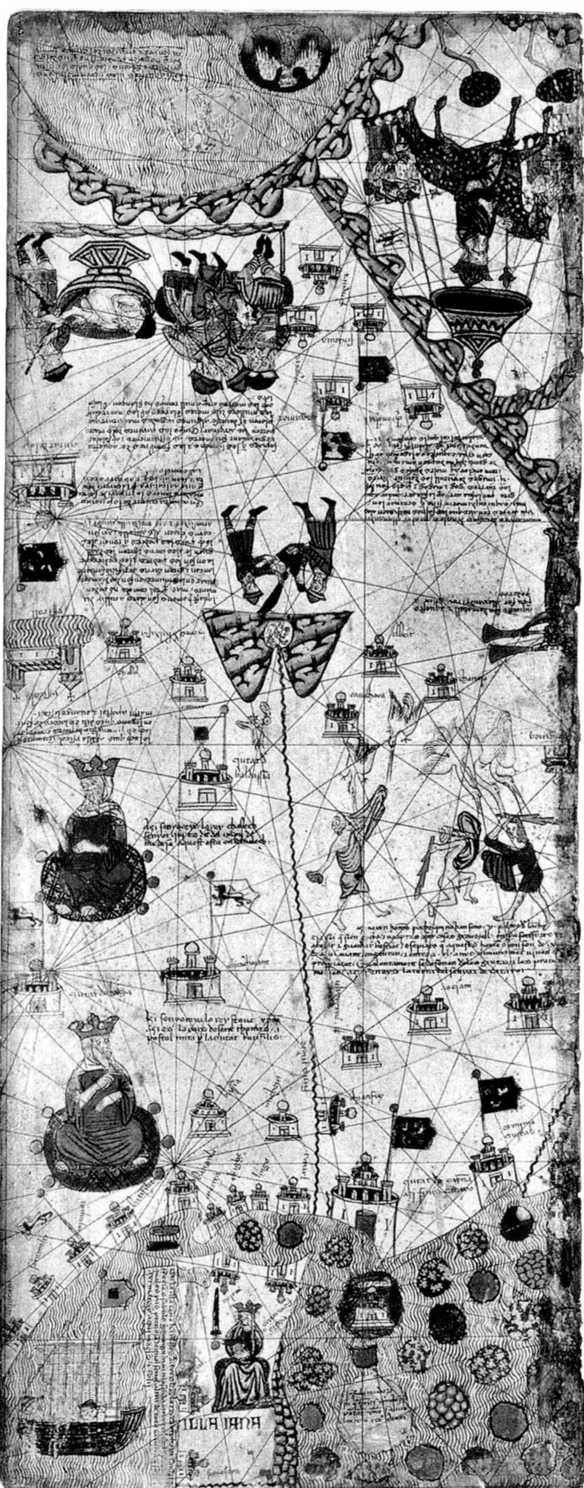
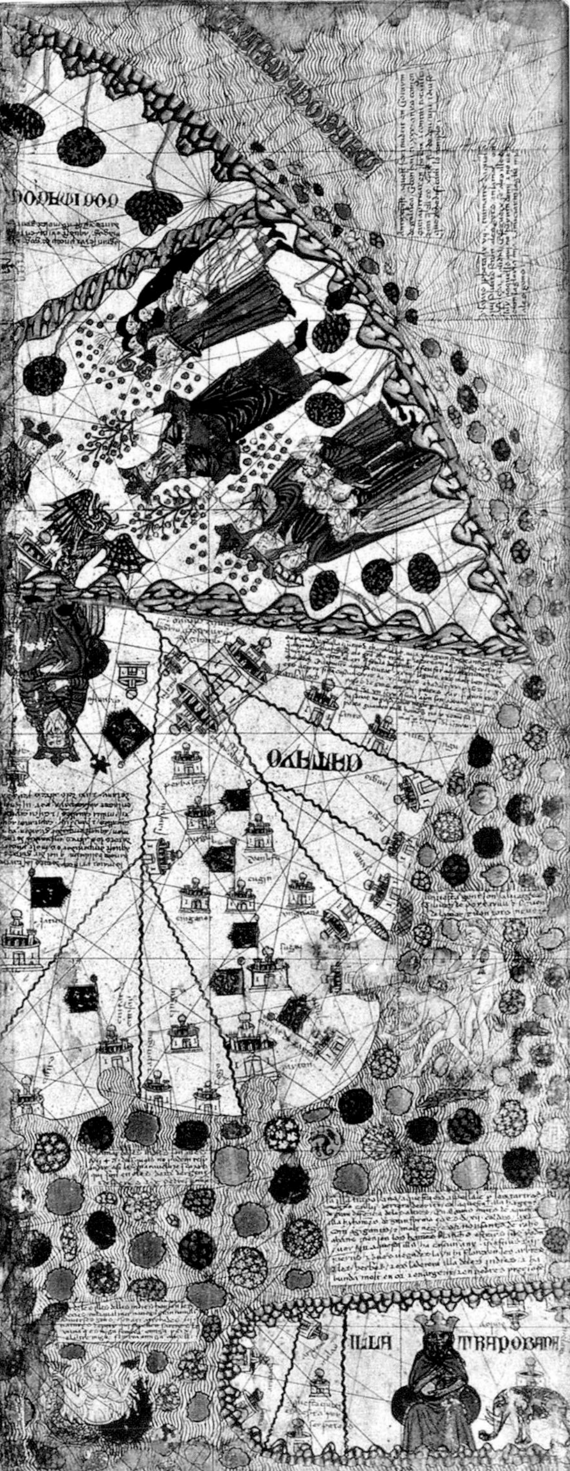

Bar Sauma and Odoric of Pordenone

Christendom seeks allies in the Orient.

1280–1330

WHILE MARCO POLO ENJOYED THE HOSPITALITY OF KUBLAI KHAN IN CHINA, a Chinese Christian, Rabban Bar Sauma, was setting out on a protracted and circuitous ten-year journey to the West. The monk, a cleric of the Nestorian church which had studded the Silk Road with monasteries, headed first for Maragheh, the church's cultural home in northern Iran, which with its observatory and library of 400,000 books was the world's unsurpassed centre of learning. Commissioned to cement a Mongol-Nestorian-Catholic alliance against Egypt, he eventually arrived in Rome in 1287 bearing the welcome news that the khan looked favourably on Christianity and that missionaries might flourish under his patronage. Thus began the remarkable extension of missionary activity that would last until the overthrow of the Mongol dynasty eighty years later. In 1294 the Franciscan missionary Giovanni da Montecorvino was welcomed to Beijing, built a church and subsequently became the city's first archbishop. Others, like Giovanni de Marignolli, were soon to follow, but few complete narratives of their journeys survive or have yet come to light.

Of the Franciscans travelling to China, none left a more detailed account than Odoric of Pordenone, an Italian monk who started his wanderings around 1316. From Iran he sailed to western India, spending a year with the Christian community near modern Chennai, then proceeded by junk to Sumatra, Java and China, arriving about 1322. Three years later, from the khan's capital Cambaluc, modern Beijing, Odoric started home by an overland route through Central Asia, Iran and Asia Minor, arriving back in Padua in 1330. Unfortunately his influential narrative, widely plagiarized by apocryphal travellers like John de Mandeville, is a miscellany of curiosities and anecdotes, entertaining but geographically vague and incoherent. In wide-eyed astonishment he marvelled at the splendour of the khan's palaces; he describes Hangzhou as the 'greatest city in the whole world', and Canton (Guangzhou) as being 'as big as three Venices'. These he actually saw, but as is so common, almost expected in medieval narratives, it is often difficult to distinguish personal observation from material acquired secondhand. Odoric was the first to speak of Tibet and the unusual customs that prevailed there, but whether or not he entered Lhasa has been hotly debated. He died within a year of his return, his tomb at Udine becoming a site of devotion and pilgrimage, a place where many miracles were wrought.

Right This wall painting, showing a procession of Nestorian priests, can still be seen in the Bezeklik Thousand Buddha Caves, where the Silk Road passes to the northeast of the Taklamakan Desert.

Ibn Battuta Recalls Thirty Years' Wanderings

A gift to those who contemplate the wonders of cities and the marvels of travel.

1325-54

FOR HIS ADMIRERS MUHAMMAD IBN BATTUTA is one of the greatest travellers of all time. For nearly thirty years he wandered the Islamic world, an estimated 120,000 kilometres (75,000 miles) through forty-four modern countries, meeting with the wise and the good and committing to memory all that he saw and did. Although more of a traveller than an explorer – it was only on his final journey that he ventured beyond the established commercial routes of *Dar al-Islam* – his narrative survives as one of the most substantial accounts of the fourteenth-century world. A native of Tangier, Ibn Battuta set out in 1325 at the age of twenty-one to make the pilgrimage to the holy shrines of Mecca and Medina, not simply as a duty of faith but also to enhance, by contact with the famous scholars of the East, his suitability for judicial office. However, it was not long before he realized that intellectual fulfilment could not be satisfied by the *hajj* alone, but would require him to continue 'through the entire earth'.

Beyond Mecca, Ibn Battuta took a circuitous route through the classical lands of Islamic culture, then proceeded to the trading posts of the East African coast, South Arabia and the Persian Gulf. In 1332 he turned north to Asia Minor, crossed the Black Sea and examined the western khanates of the Mongol empire. An overland journey through Central Asia and Afghanistan brought him to India, where he remained for nine years before being sent in 1342 as the sultan's envoy to the Mongol emperor of China. This journey took him along the Malabar coast, to the Maldives, Ceylon, Bengal and Assam, then via Sumatra to the great Chinese port of Quanzhou. Returning to Syria and finding the country ravaged by plague, he promptly departed for North Africa and Spain, and in 1351 returned to his home country. Unable to settle until he had seen the last distant outpost of Islam, he set out across the Sahara to the kingdom of Mali, whose previous ruler, Mansa Musa, had passed in splendour through Egypt on a pilgrimage to Mecca. Via Timbuktu, a city that had yet to flourish, and after a second hazardous crossing of the Sahara, Ibn Battuta returned to Morocco in 1354, this time for good. Remarkably, his multi-volume narrative, dictated entirely from memory, languished unnoticed until its rediscovery by scholars 600 years later.

Right The world according to the thirteenth-century geographer Ibn Sa'id, orientated with east at the top.

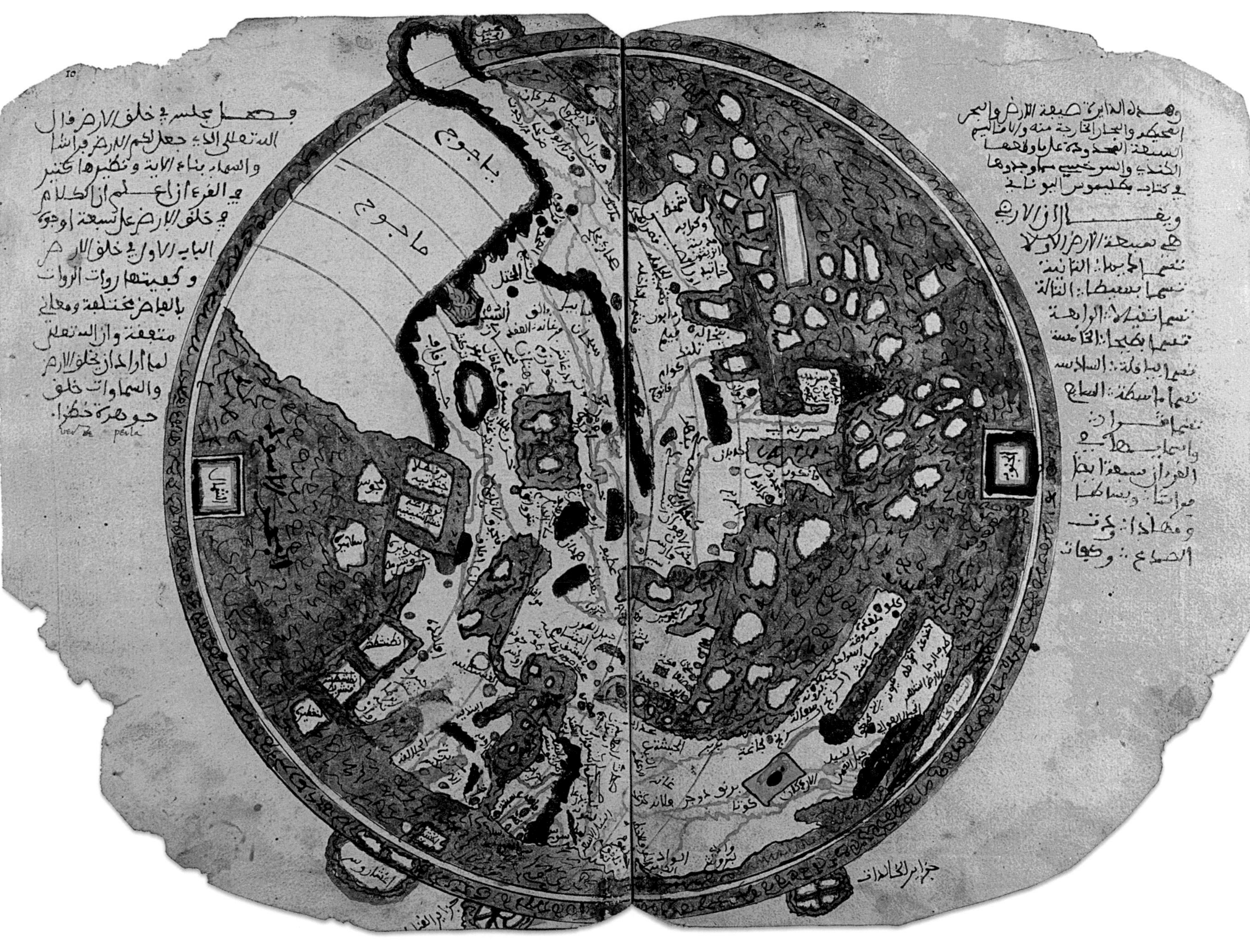
ياجوج
ماجوج

The Seven Voyages of Admiral Zheng He

The rise and fall of China's seaborne empire.

1405-33

THE MONGOL DYNASTY IN CHINA, which had welcomed so many Western missionaries and traders, finally met its downfall in 1368. For the first time in many years a native Chinese dynasty, the Ming, took control of its homeland, restoring an earlier way of life and pursuing an aggressive policy aimed at bringing the most distant borderlands under the aegis of the state. Then, with the succession in 1402 of the third Ming emperor Yongle, the dynasty extended its interests well beyond traditional boundaries, despatching numerous costly, flag-waving missions to every part of Asia and its islands. Hardly exploratory in nature, the routes having been travelled by Chinese merchants for centuries, their object was to reinforce Chinese commercial interests with a massive show of strength, and to bring home exotica which the emperor could claim as the tribute of remote peoples.

By far the grandest and most prestigious of these missions were the seaborne expeditions of Admiral Zheng He, a Muslim eunuch and a favourite at Yongle's court. In seven voyages, over a period of more than twenty years, he would overwhelm the Indian Ocean with vast, awe-inspiring fleets of junks. Zheng He's first expedition comprised sixty-two of them, some of the junks ten times as large as anything seen before, along with 225 support vessels and 27,780 men. For seven years, 1405-11, Zheng's fleets fanned out across the East Indies and reached the Malabar coast of India, while a fourth voyage (1413-15) coasted the Arabian shores and sailed up the Red Sea as far as Jiddah. Foreign envoys frequently accompanied the homeward voyages, and from the fifth voyage (1416-19) Zheng He presented his emperor with a prodigious collection of exotic beasts. A giraffe, which had somehow found its way to Bengal, was deemed so spectacular when it arrived in China that it was revered as an omen of divine provenance. The sixth and seventh voyages (1421 and 1431-33) reconnoitred the coast of Africa, possibly as far as the Mozambique Channel, but despite the wishful thinking of recent commentators there is no firm evidence that Chinese ships ever ventured beyond the Indian Ocean. Yongle died in 1424 and his successor turned his attention towards matters closer to home, slashing the shipbuilding budget and wiping Zheng He's name from the records. Although Chinese merchants would maintain a dynamic trading economy, they had to do so without imperial protection or encouragement.

Right A recently discovered Chinese map of the world, optimistically claimed by some to originate from the time of Zheng He's voyages. However, its conspicuous errors readily identify it as a copy of a European map dating from the early seventeenth century.

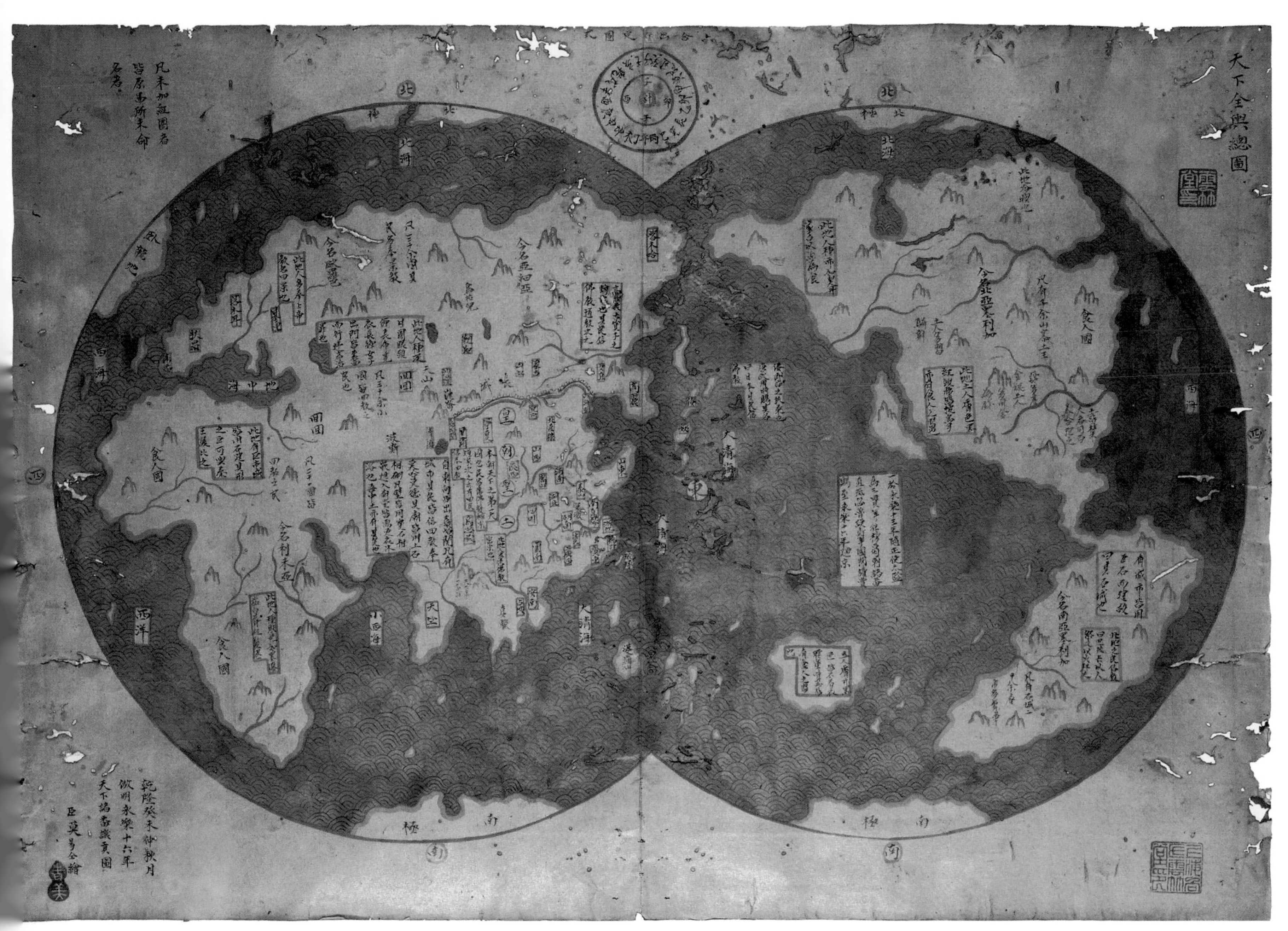
天下全輿總圖
乾隆癸未仲秋月
仿明永樂十六年
天下諸番識貢圖
臣莫易仝繪

The Remarkable Odyssey of Niccolo de' Conti

Travel in disguise.

1414–37

BETWEEN THE MIDDLE OF THE FOURTEENTH CENTURY and the end of the fifteenth remarkably few European travellers succeeded in penetrating much beyond the mercantile emporia of the Levant. In 1404, Ruy Gonzalez de Clavijo, a knight sent out by Henry III of Castile on a diplomatic mission to Tamerlane, managed to reach Samarkand; and in the following years Johann Schiltberger, an obscure German mercenary, found his way by various adventures into Central Asia and the nearer parts of Siberia. However, those that chose to travel entirely in the Islamic world did so only by means of hazardous subterfuge, disguised as Arabs and adopting the outward trappings of Islam, perpetually in fear of exposure. Of these intrepid wanderers the best known and most influential was Niccolo de' Conti, a Venetian trader resident in Damascus around 1414. Fluent in Arabic and familiar with local customs, ideally qualified for travel incognito, Conti decided to take a look for himself at the routes by which spices were arriving in the Persian Gulf. His personal odyssey would occupy him for more than twenty years.

The precise direction and chronology of Conti's travels are conjectural, but his outward route took him across the desert to Baghdad, and from Basra to the major ports of India and Ceylon. He sailed up the Ganges for three months and crossed mountains and plains to the Burmese empire, ascending the Irrawaddy to the capital Ava. Following the normal trade routes, he visited Sumatra, Java and Champa (modern Vietnam) before making his way back via India and the Red Sea to reach Cairo about 1435. Here, during a two-year wait for a passport, Conti reluctantly converted to Islam and lost two of his four children and his Indian wife to the Black Death. Returning to Venice in 1439, and soliciting absolution for renouncing his Christian faith, he sought an audience with Pope Eugenius in Florence. The timing of Conti's arrival proved salutary in the extreme, coinciding as it did with a General Council of eminent scholars, a ready audience which demanded that Conti should dictate his experiences to the pope's secretary Poggio Bracciolini, a humanist scholar of formidable learning. The result, factually precise and devoid of the usual tall stories, was widely circulated in manuscript and exerted considerable influence on geographical thought, particularly with regard to the countries bordering the Bay of Bengal.

Right Fra Mauro's Mappamundi, drawn in 1459 with south at the top. Its depiction of Southeast Asia, and particularly the Spice Islands, relies heavily on Niccolo de' Conti's reports of his travels in that area.

ETHYOPIA
ETHYOPIA OCCID
BENICHILEB
AFRICA
MAVRITANIA
LIBIA
CIRENAICA
ASIA
PARTHIA
TARTARIA
ROSSIA
EVROPA
NORVECIA
SEPTENTRIO
POLVS ARTICVS
TROPICVS
POLVS ANTARTICVS
ORIENS
OCCIDENS

Portuguese Navigators Break into the African Tropics

Voyages into the Torrid Zone.

1435-75

THE WEST COAST OF AFRICA, HAVING NO LONG-RANGE TRADE or established seaports, provided little incentive for exploration throughout the Middle Ages. The great African kingdoms, notably the gold-rich empire of Mali, lay remote from the sea and preferred to conduct their commerce along the vast network of trade routes that for centuries spanned the Sahara. Early coastal voyagers, like the Genoese Vivaldi brothers who in 1291 'sought India by way of the Ocean', or the Majorcan Jayme Ferrer who in 1346 came to grief seeking the elusive 'River of Gold', faced fearsome contrary currents, coasts devoid of food and water, and the constant dread of their ships being burnt up in the heat of the sun. Norman adventurers, fired by a lust for gold, had reached the Canary Islands by 1402, but it was not until 1435 that the Portuguese navigator Gil Eannes finally rounded the notorious Cape Bojador, beyond which lay the impenetrable 'Torrid Zone', or what Arabic geographers had ominously christened the 'Green Sea of Darkness'.

Eannes was just one of a procession of courtly knights and squires who, over a period of some forty years, urged on by Prince Henry of Portugal, relentlessly pressed southward around the bulge of the West African coast. Henry, nicknamed 'the Navigator' despite delegating every voyage to his subordinates, had seen in his destiny the acquisition of an empire in North Africa or the Canaries through which he could tap the Saharan gold trade. When this failed his attention turned towards rivers like the Senegal and Gambia that might provide direct access to the wealth of the interior from the sea. Navigational difficulties that had blighted the earlier galleys were overcome by the development of the ocean-going caravel, rigged for sailing close to the wind. Professional navigators, often Genoese, were employed, and by the time of Henry's death in 1460, the coast as far as Sierra Leone had been charted and the Cape Verde Islands discovered. After a nine-year lull the initiative for further exploration was taken up by Fernão Gomes, a wealthy Lisbon merchant whose captains, within a just year or two, reached Benin on the Niger delta and in 1474 crossed the equator. Gomes's monopoly was rescinded in 1475 when responsibility for further undertakings fell directly to Prince João, heir to the throne and a man wholly committed to the expansion of Portuguese sea power through voyages of exploration.

Right The Catalan-Estense map of 1450–60 portrayed the Mediterranean and northwest Africa with remarkable accuracy, while elsewhere it attempted to insert detail known only with reasonable certainty.

The Extraordinary Voyages of Diogo Cão and Bartolomeu Dias

A cape named Good Hope promises a sea route to the East.

1482-88

WHEN JOÃO II ASSUMED THE THRONE OF PORTUGAL IN 1481 his immediate priority was to capitalize on the African discoveries of the past fifty years. He ordered the construction of a castle at Elmina, west of modern Accra, to control the gold trade and ward off Spanish interlopers, and in 1482 he commissioned Diogo Cão, an experienced sea captain, to prosecute discoveries beyond the furthest known point on the African coast. Cão's instructions were to search for a sea route to India; to mark his progress with the erection of carved stone pillars or *padrões*; and to ascend the major rivers to acquire native intelligence of the kingdom of Prester John, the legendary Christian prince whose domain had somehow shifted from Central Asia to the African interior. Cão discovered the mouth of the Congo, sent emissaries upstream to confer with the local ruler, then proceeded southward some 800 kilometres (500 miles) before turning back on the coast of southern Angola. On a second voyage in 1485-86 he penetrated still further, but slow progress in the face of the Benguela Current frustrated his ambition to round the tip of Africa, halting him at Cape Cross on the desolate coast of Namibia.

It was now evident that such a voyage could not be accomplished by a single ship, so when Bartolomeu Dias set out in August 1487 to sail beyond Cão's furthest point he was provided with three caravels, one a supply vessel. Passing Cape Cross and leaving the supply ship in Lüderitz Bay, Dias neared the mouth of the Orange River, where currents and winds forced him to stand well out to sea, meeting with terrible gales. When a westerly wind failed to return him to the coast, he finally knew for certain that the elusive cape had been rounded, and that by steering north he must reach an eastward-trending shore. In February 1488 his two ships anchored in the tranquility of Mossel Bay, beyond which herdsmen were seen quietly tending their cattle. Determined to continue to India, but outvoted by his crews who feared for what lay ahead, Dias proceeded only as far as the Great Fish River before turning back to the Cape. Whether it was he or his king who named the Cape of Good Hope is uncertain, but in December 1488 Dias sailed safely into Lisbon, having laid the final milestone on the passage to the Indian Ocean.

Right The Henricus Martellus map of 1489 drew on the discoveries of Cão and Dias to show for the first time an open sea route from the Atlantic to the Indian Ocean.

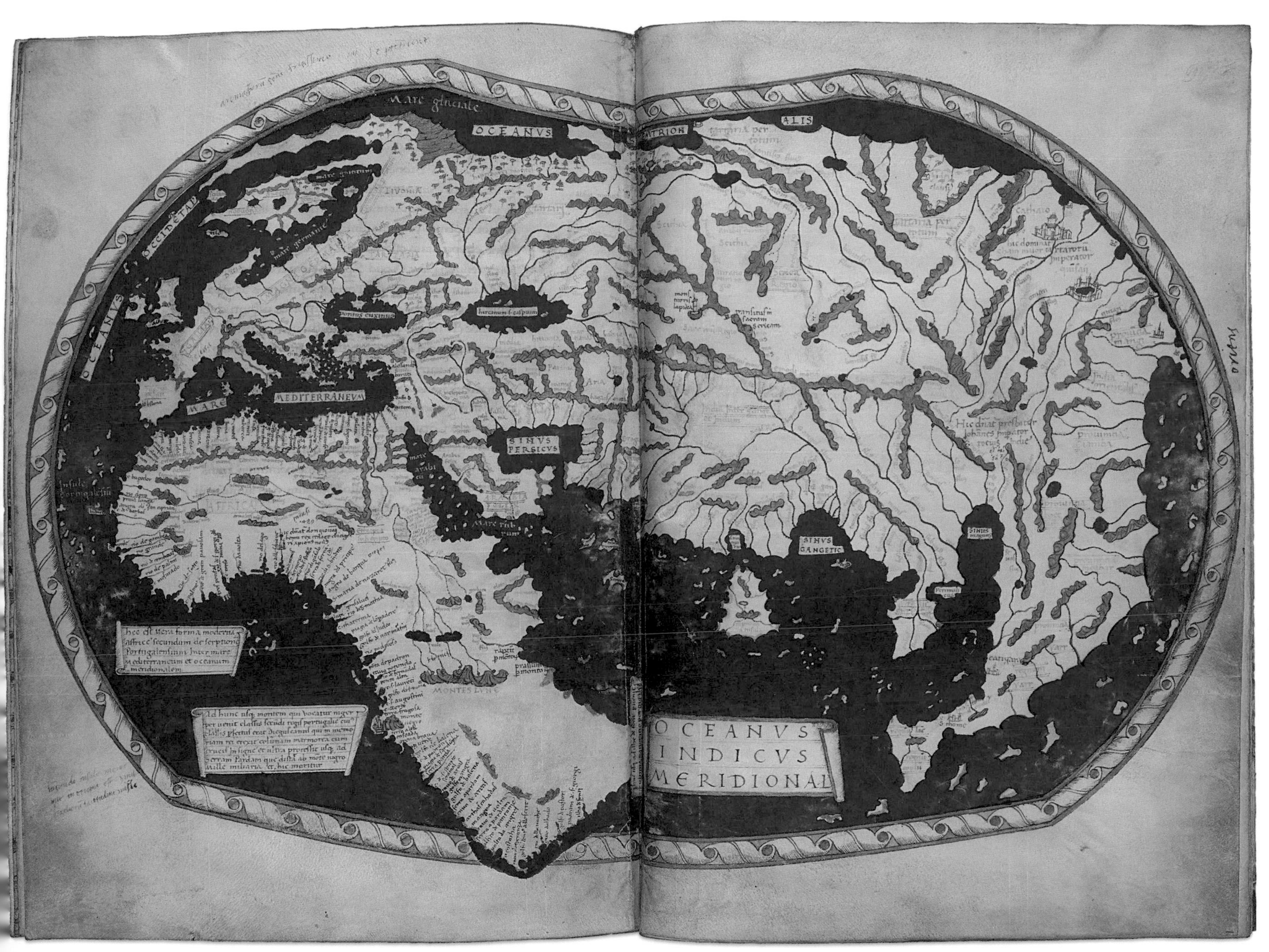

OCEANVS
MARE
MEDITERRANEVM
SINVS PERSICVS
SINVS GANGETIC
OCEANVS INDICVS MERIDIONAL

Pêro da Covilhã Examines the Trade Routes to India

Portuguese spies infiltrate the commerce of the East.

1487-90

The decades surrounding Dias's discovery of the Cape of Good Hope and Da Gama's subsequent voyage to India witnessed a period of fervent exploration and mercantile intelligence gathering, much of it shrouded in the pall of official secrecy that kept new discoveries safe from prying eyes. The stories of so many of its pioneers, names that feature so prominently in books like this, often exist only as fragments or surreptitious 'bootleg' narratives, or have come to us secondhand from others writing long after the event. From Portugal in the 1480s, King João II despatched explorer-ambassadors to discover what they could about India and any Christian kingdoms they might find along the way. An important two-way relationship with Ethiopia, now identified with the realm of Prester John in Africa, had been established with Portugal and Italian mercantile houses, while Arabic documents record the presence of Portuguese ships on the East African coast three years before they were supposed to be there. There is so much about this era of reconnaissance that remains elusive, and so many of its perpetrators forgotten.

Of the surviving reports of agents sent out by King João, the most substantial is that of Pêro da Covilhã, who left Lisbon in 1487 just as Dias was sailing for the Cape. Although Covilhã's story, pieced together from the memories of an old man, contains, like his visit to Mecca and Medina, romantic episodes disputed by modern scholars, it does provide a unique insight into the Portuguese intelligence network. Disguised as Moorish merchants, Covilhã and his companion Afonso de Paiva headed first for Aden where they separated, Paiva travelling to Ethiopia where he died, and Covilhã boarding a dhow for India. After reconnoitring the ports of the Malabar coast, Covilhã surveyed the East African trade route as far as Sofala in Mozambique, then in 1490 returned to Cairo to place an interim report in the hands of Joseph of Lamego, another of João's special agents. Its account of the spice trade and the practicality of reaching India by sea would have been critical to future ventures, but it seems it never reached Portugal. Covilhã departed for Ethiopia where he was amicably confined for the remainder of his life and became a powerful and trusted servant of the emperor. His fate remained unknown until the arrival in 1520 of a Portuguese embassy under Rodrigo de Lima, whose secretary, Francisco Álvares, committed Covilhã's story to print.

Right Rodrigo de Lima's embassy to Ethiopia, 1520, from the narrative of Francisco Álvares.

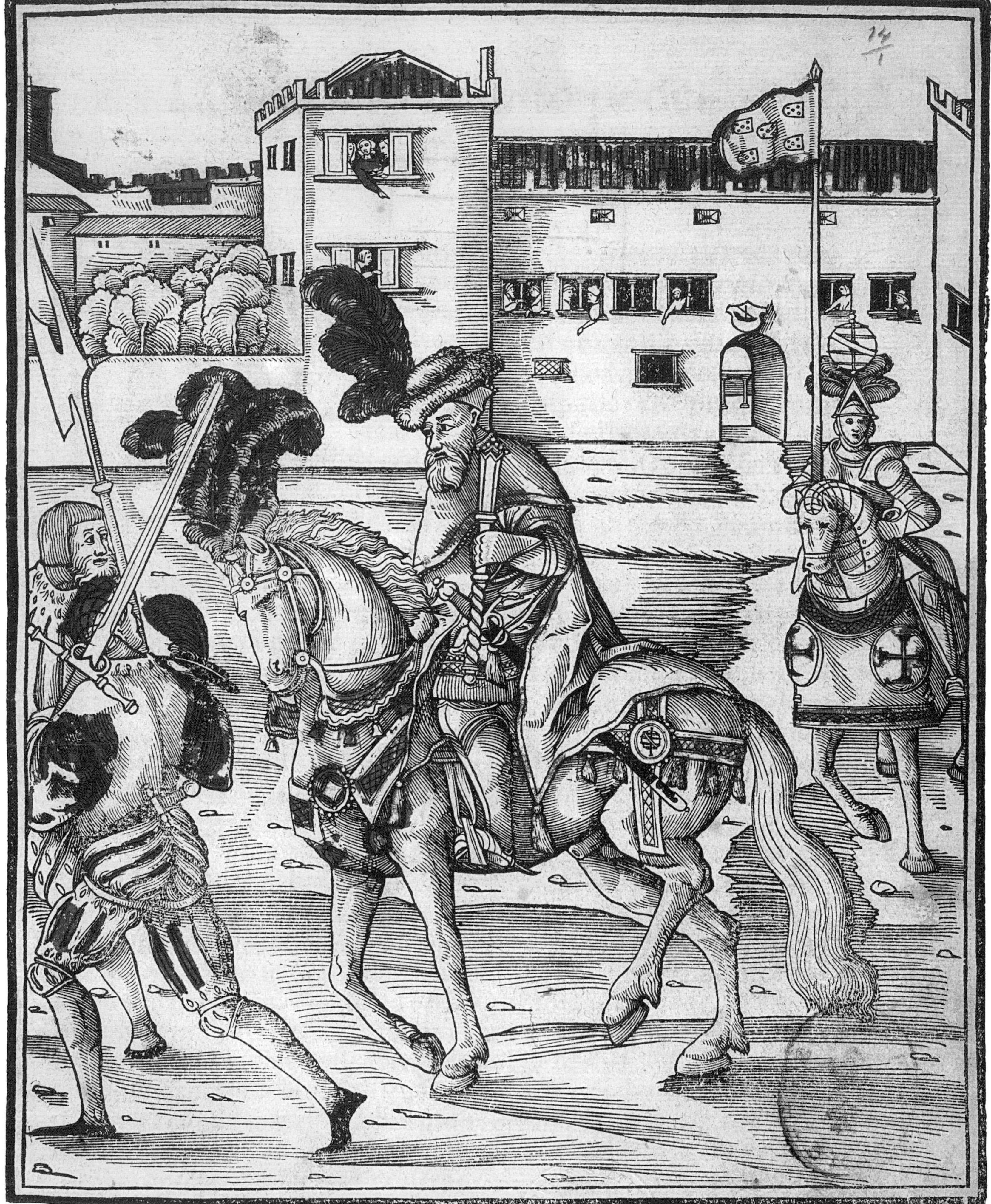

1492

Columbus Establishes a New Horizon in the West

The march of exploration enters a fresh dimension.

For centuries European geographers had witnessed an unfurling of the known world forever eastward, while to the west all they could see was a vast unwelcoming expanse of ocean. The spherical nature of the planet had been appreciated by all but the most simple-minded for more than 1700 years, and its circumference calculated to remarkable accuracy by Greek and Islamic geographers. But for the Atlantic-facing nations the earth might just as well have been a flat disc, from the rim of which the unwary mariner could plunge into boundless space. The rediscovery of the Azores in 1427 had pushed the boundary further west, but scattered beyond were only mythical islands reported by shadowy apocryphal voyagers. When Christopher Columbus, Cristóbal Colón, initially formulated his plans for an eastward voyage he probably had only these in mind, but as the fateful day approached, when he would launch three ships into the unknown, he became increasingly confident that the attainment of Asia, or at least its peripheral islands, was a viable proposition. By miscalculation, selective self-deception, and wildly overestimating the westward trend of the Asian continent, he had reduced the 18,000-kilometre (11,000-mile) voyage to Cathay to a mere 5300 (3300), and to Japan even less. Both were within reach of a well-provisioned vessel, at least with a benevolent wind on the outward passage and, more significantly for the common sailor, on the return.

Whether Columbus was already wise in the ways of the Atlantic is uncertain, but his decision to sail from the Canaries proved favourable in the extreme, the easterlies gently speeding him to the Americas in just five weeks. Land believed to be one of the 1300 offshore islands reported by Marco Polo, but actually somewhere in the Bahamas, was sighted on 12 October 1492, and from here the voyage progressed to Cuba where an embassy trekked absurdly inland to locate the court of the Great Khan. Finding no evidence of organized government, Columbus started back, only to be driven by a chance wind to gold-rich Haiti, home to an advanced indigenous culture that would suffer instant extermination at the hands of Columbus' successors. He would undertake three more voyages to the Caribbean, skirting the coasts of both Central and South America. He would witness the struggle by which cartographers laboured to rationalize his revelations with those of travellers in the true Orient, but he would die seven years before Balboa's discovery of the wide Pacific.

Right This world map, drawn by the pilot and navigator Juan de la Cosa in 1500, attempts to bring together the discoveries made by Columbus and his successors in the New World.

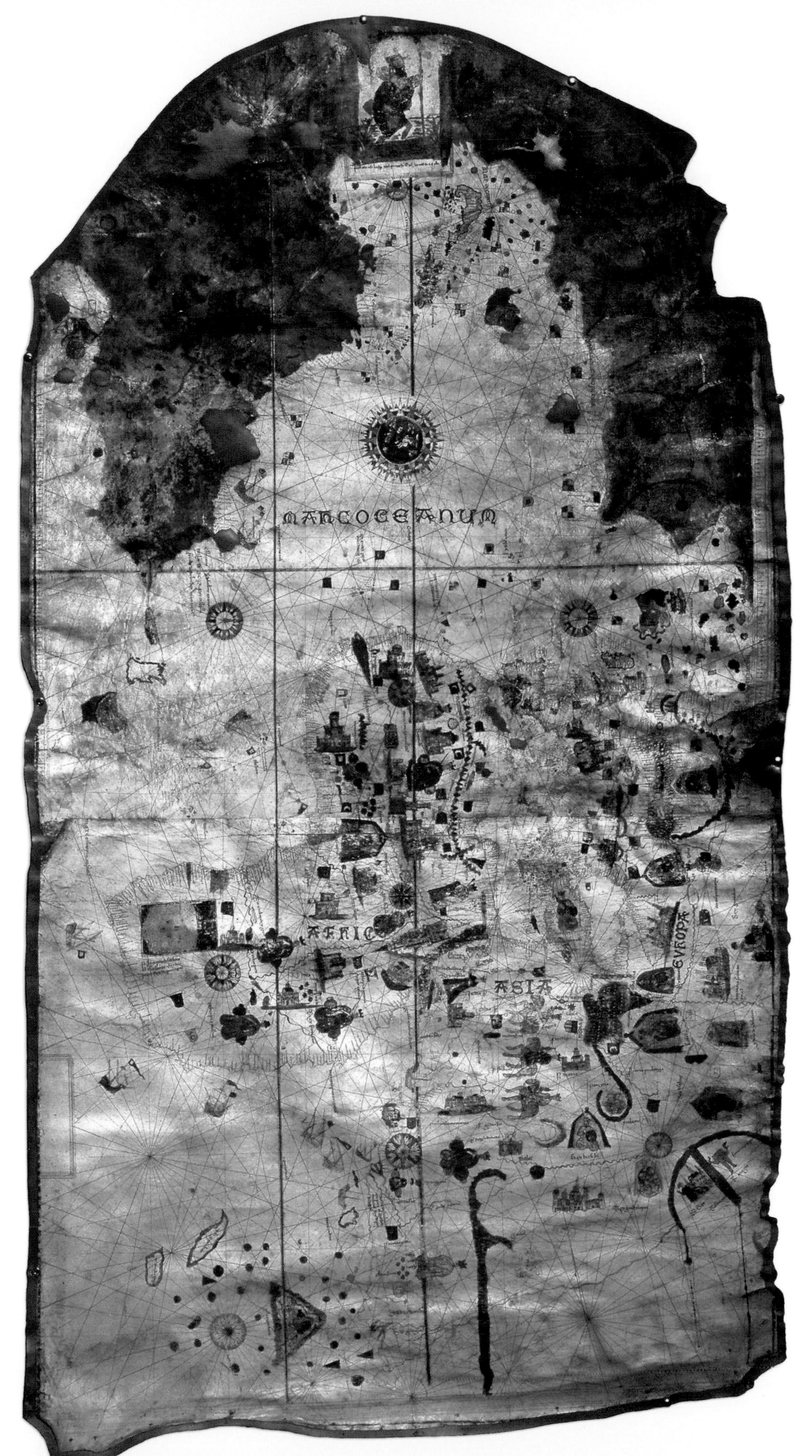
ASIA
EVROPA

1497-98

John Cabot and the Bristol Seamen

England makes its entry on the world stage.

THE TYPE OF VOYAGE THAT SAILS '1800 MILES WEST' and arrives at a country 'rich in grass' where there are 'tall trees' has always been the geographical historian's worst nightmare. But sadly, some of the most crucial pioneering excursions descend into this category, generating a boundless literature of opinion and conjecture which, at the end of the day, serves only to confuse and disorientate the seeker after truth. Of these there are no better examples than the voyages of the Bristol seamen, whose frequent forays into the North Atlantic survive as little more than cryptic, tantalizing fragments and secondhand letters extricated from cobwebbed archives. Although offering somewhat more scope for speculation than most, the same must be said of John Cabot, whose epic voyage, just five years after Columbus, provided the first unequivocal account of a North American landfall since the Vikings. In fact, so little was known of the voyage at the time, and its details so restricted to the privileged few, that the celebrated historian Richard Hakluyt, writing only 100 years after the event, knew even less of it than we do today.

Cabot, a Venetian, arrived in the Bristol shipyards in the 1490s touting a project for a voyage to Asia. By starting in a high latitude he would reach the 'land of the Great Khan', Japan in particular, by a route somewhat shorter than that of Columbus. The idea appealed immensely to King Henry VII, who granted Cabot and his sons dominion under the crown of any lands they might discover. With the small ship *Matthew* and around twenty, mainly Bristolians, aboard, Cabot struck into the Atlantic in May 1497. If Cabot kept a log it has since disappeared, but the handful of secondhand accounts confirm that after little more than a month landfall was made somewhere on the North American coast. For about three weeks Cabot hugged what he thought was Asia but was probably Newfoundland, sending boat parties ashore and finding evidence of human habitation. Returning in early August, his £10 reward lavished on a costume befitting his conquistadorial status, Cabot found no difficulty in enlisting the support of the king and the merchants of London and Bristol for a second and much grander voyage, this time to prosecute former discoveries to the south. Departing in May 1498, his five ships met with a severe Atlantic storm. One returned badly damaged to Ireland, but of the remainder, Cabot's flagship included, nothing more was heard.

Right The letters patent issued in March 1496 by King Henry VII to John Cabot, authorizing his proposed voyage and granting him dominion of any lands he might discover.

8

(8)

De Johanne Cabotto et filiis suis.

Rex omnibus ad quos &c. salutem. Notum sit et manifestum quod dedimus et concessimus ac per presentes damus et concedimus pro nobis et heredibus nostris dilectis nobis Johanni Cabotto civi Venecie ac Lodovico Sebastiano et Sancto filiis dicti Johannis et eorum ac cuiuslibet eorum heredibus et deputatis plenam ac liberam auctoritatem facultatem et potestatem navigandi ad omnes partes regiones et sinus maris orientalis occidentalis et septentrionalis sub banneris vexillis et insigniis nostris cum quinque navibus sive navigiis cuiuscumque portiture et qualitatis existant et cum tot et tantis nautis et hominibus quot et quantis in dictis navibus secum ducere voluerint suis et eorum propriis sumptibus et expensis ad inveniendum discooperiendum et investigandum quascumque insulas patrias regiones sive provincias gentilium et infidelium in quacumque parte mundi positas que Christianis omnibus ante hec tempora fuerunt incognite. Concessimus eciam eisdem et eorum cuilibet eorumque et cuiuslibet eorum heredibus et deputatis ac licenciam dedimus affigendi predictas banneras nostras et insignia in quacumque villa oppido castro insula seu terra firma a se noviter inventis. Et quod prenominati Johannes et filii eiusdem seu heredes et eorum deputati quascumque huiusmodi villas castra oppida et insulas a se inventas que subiugari occupari et possideri possint subiugare occupare et possidere valeant tanquam vasalli nostri et gubernatores locatenentes et deputati eorundem dominium titulum et iurisdiccionem eorundem villarum castrorum oppidorum insularum ac terre firme sic inventorum nobis acquirendo. Ita tamen ut ex omnibus fructibus proficuis emolumentis commoditatibus lucris et obvencionibus ex huiusmodi navigacione provenientibus prefati Johannes et filii ac heredes et eorum deputati teneantur et sint obligati nobis pro omni viagio suo tociens quociens ad portum nostrum Bristollie applicuerint ad quem omnino applicare teneantur et sint astricti deductis omnibus sumptibus et impensis necessariis per eosdem factis quintam partem capitalis lucri sic facti sive in mercibus sive in pecuniis persolvere. Dantes nos et concedentes eisdem suisque heredibus et deputatis ut ab omni solucione custumarum omnium et singulorum bonorum ac mercium quas secum reportarint ab illis locis sic noviter inventis liberi sint et immunes. Et insuper dedimus et concessimus eisdem ac suis heredibus et deputatis quod terre omnes firme insule ville oppida castra et loca quecumque a se inventa quotquot ab eis inveniri contigerit non possint ab aliis quibusvis nostris subditis frequentari seu visitari absque licencia predictorum Johannis et eius filiorum suorumque deputatorum sub pena amissionis tam navium sive navigiorum quam bonorum omnium quorumcumque ad ea loca sic inventa navigare presumencium. Volentes et strictissime mandantes omnibus et singulis nostris subditis tam in terra quam in mari constitutis ut prefato Johanni et eius filiis ac deputatis bonam assistenciam faciant et tam in armandis navibus seu navigiis quam in provisione commeatus et victualium pro sua pecunia emendorum atque aliarum rerum sibi providendarum pro dicta navigacione sumenda suos omnes favores et auxilia impartiantur. In cuius &c. Teste Rege apud Westmonasterium quinto die Marcii.

Per ipsum Regem &c.

De licencia concessa [?]

Rex omnibus ad quos &c. salutem. Cum quedam licet in statuto in parliamento domini H. nuper Regis Anglie Sexti apud Westmonasterium anno regni sui septimo tento edito prohibitum sit ne quis ligeorum nostrorum presumat aliqua regna terras dominia districtus territoria iurisdicciones seu alia loca Regis Dacie [illegible]

The Historic Voyage of Vasco da Gama

The dawn of the Portuguese seaborne empire.

1497–99

ALTHOUGH BARTOLOMEU DIAS HAD DEMONSTRATED the practicality of the Cape route to India, it was by no means a foregone conclusion that Portugal would see its future in this direction. A ten-year lull followed Dias's voyage; King Manuel succeeded his cousin João; and although by the Treaty of Tordesillas the pope had given Portugal the eastern half of the world, court opinion stayed strongly divided over what advantages might be gained in prosecuting discoveries beyond Africa. However, even though the costs and consequences of such enterprises weighed heavily against the arguable benefits, Manuel, inspired by the dubious legacy of Henry the Navigator, would decide in favour of equipping a fleet for India. After much deliberation and political intrigue characteristic of the time, Vasco da Gama was plucked from obscurity to take command.

Four well-equipped vessels and 170 crew departed the Tagus in July 1497, and after a wide sweep of the South Atlantic doubled the Cape of Good Hope in late December, anchoring in Mossel Bay. The next phase of the voyage, the hostile Natal coast that would claim so many sailors' lives, proved the most challenging, storms and the contrary Mozambique Current persistently forcing the ships back on their course. But by April 1498 they had worked their way as far as Malindi, a flourishing port on the Kenyan coast where Da Gama acquired the services of a pilot experienced in the Indian trade. With a benevolent wind the Portuguese reached Calicut in just twenty-three days.

In Western eyes Da Gama's voyage shaped the course of history, but for most Indians it was of little consequence. Da Gama became simply the first of many Portuguese who over the next two centuries would nibble irritatingly at the Indian periphery, while the indigenous empires that actually controlled trade remained largely unaffected. For European geographers Da Gama defined the shape of Africa, but he provided few new discoveries and as an ambassador he was a disaster. He had nothing to offer India and was treated as little more than a poorly equipped trader, derided by the local ruler for the contemptible nature of his gifts. Dejectedly he turned for home in August 1498 but, in choosing the wrong season, lost half his men on the four-month crossing to Malindi. Sometimes with only seven men fit enough to man the two remaining ships, he retraced his nightmarish track back to Lisbon in the summer of 1499.

Right The Cantino world map, dating from 1502 and incorporating information from Vasco da Gama's voyage to India, was one of the first attempts to depict the true shape of the African continent.

Circulus articus:
Tropicus cancer:
Os montes claros em affrica
Serra lioa
Castello damina
Linha equinocialis:
Mare barbaricus:
Circulus capricorni:

Vespucci and the Naming of America

A New World takes shape in the west.

1499-1502

For more than twenty years cartographers wrestled to reconcile Columbus' discoveries with what little they knew about the Asian Orient, while attempts to float the islands of the Caribbean somewhere between Japan and Portugal became increasingly problematic with the discovery of extensive landmasses to the west and south, neither of which seemed to hint very much at Asia. While cartographers like Martin Waldseemuller resolutely moulded the recent discoveries into a completely new continent, wedged somewhat tenuously between Asia and Europe, others conveniently truncated their maps to the east and west in a nebulous void that left everybody guessing. Around the ports of Spain there was no shortage of would-be explorers and maverick empire builders anxious to capitalize on Columbus' discoveries. In 1499 Alonso de Ojeda coasted Venezuela, named by his shipmate Amerigo Vespucci because one of its native villages somehow reminded him of Venice, and in the following year Rodrigo de Bastidas managed to penetrate the Gulf of Uraba before his ship was devoured by Teredo worms.

South America became for a brief moment a moderately sized island, but when in January 1500 Vicente Yáñez Pinzón arrived at Cabo São Roque, its most easterly extremity, intent on sailing around it, he found that the coast trended not westward but towards the south. Turning northwest he chanced upon the delta of the Amazon, which by some curious twist of geography he took to be the mouth of the Ganges. At about the same time Pedro Álvares Cabral landed slightly further down the coast, and in the following January Vespucci reached a broad harbour he called Rio de Janeiro. South America was no longer an offshore island or Asian promontory, but had become a discrete continental landmass, jubilantly christened by Vespucci the 'Mundus Novus' or New World. But Waldseemuller chose to elevate Vespucci to even greater glory, tentatively suggesting in 1507 that the whole of the new southern continent might take the explorer's Christian name. Adopting the Latin form Americus and the requisite feminine ending to comply with Asia, Africa and Europa, it became America. How this name, which was little used at the time, eventually entered common parlance, or how it also came to designate the yet undiscovered North American mainland, is a long story and one of several. But Vespucci, a gifted public relations expert who discovered little and arguably never commanded a voyage of his own, achieved immortality that far exceeded his just dessert.

Right A detail of the Waldseemuller map, which was responsible for disseminating the name 'America' for the new continent, after Amerigo Vespucci.

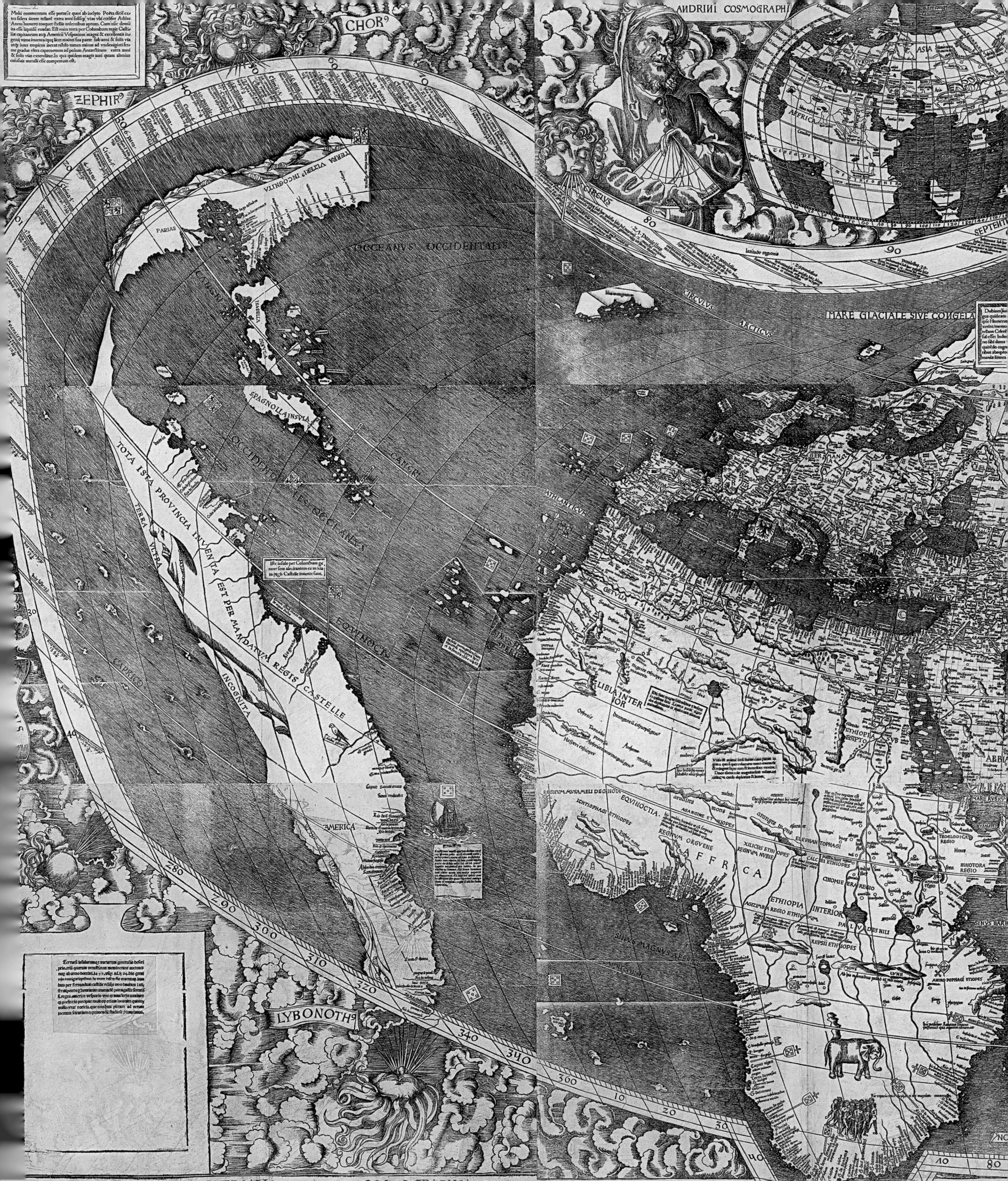

ZEPHIR9
CHOR9
OCCEANVS OCCIDENTALIS
TERRA VLTERI9 INCOGNITA
PARIAS
ISABELLA
SPAGNOLLA INSVLA
TOTA ISTA PROVINCIA INVENTA EST PER MANDATVM REGIS CASTELLE
TERRA VLTRA INCOGNITA
AMERICA
CIRCVLVS ARCTICVS
MARE GLACIALE SIVE CONGELA
LIBIA INTERIOR
AFFRICA
ETHIOPIA INTERIOR
SINVS MAGNVS AFFRICVS
LYBONOTH9
280
290
300
310
320
340

Cabral Decodes the Atlantic and Discovers Brazil

A Portuguese trespasser in the New World.

1500

THE VOYAGE OF PEDRO ÁLVARES CABRAL left two significant legacies. Firstly the pattern by which, over the next four centuries, ships would find their way to the Orient. Secondly the confirmation of the Portuguese as 'legitimate' heirs to a slice of South America that would subsequently become Brazil. Cabral, a gentleman of the patrician class, despatched from Lisbon in March 1500 with thirteen ships to follow in Da Gama's wake to India, had instructions to plant Christianity wherever possible and to foster commercial relationships, both if necessary by force of arms. His predecessors had struggled against contrary winds and currents, which throughout the year frustrated progess towards South Africa; Cabral settled on a more circuitous but ultimately faster track, striking westward from the Cape Verde Islands to take advantage of the northeast trades, then picking up the westerlies that would speed him around the Cape of Good Hope. The concept was sound but the season unfavourable. In the South Atlantic a tempest struck the fleet, sinking four ships and scattering the rest, and only after regrouping off Mozambique did the expedition proceed to India.

Cabral's choice of route did however lead to a particularly propitious event for the Portuguese – a chance landing on the coast of Brazil. Columbus and his successors had already established the existence of a substantial landmass south of the Caribbean, but what was not appreciated was that its coast trended far enough east to bring it within the hemisphere nominated by the Treaty of Tordesillas as Portuguese. This treaty, framed in 1494 by Pope Alexander VI and ratified by the Spanish and Portuguese crowns, had drawn a line from pole to pole, dividing Spanish interests to the west from Portuguese to the east. Placed '370 leagues west of the Cape Verde Islands', it was imagined to pass squarely through the mid-Atlantic, but when Cabral struck the Brazilian mainland in April 1500 he recognized with some delight that he was still well short of the pope's line. The Portuguese claim was staked with the customary erection of a cross and a few prayers, and a ship sent hastily back to Lisbon with the good news. Although the pope's line was subjected to constant diplomatic readjustment (longitude being largely a matter of inspired guesswork) there could be no doubt that Brazil fell firmly within the Portuguese sphere.

Right The ships of Cabral's fleet, from the *Libro de Armadas*.

No Anno de 1500 —
artio Pedralvrz cabral pera a Jndia e 9. de março por Capitão mór de treze vellas, Naos, Navios,
aravellas, das quaes com hũ temporal rijo que lhe deu na travessa do Brazil pera ho cabo de
boa esperança, se perderão quatro, & de todas, estes erão os Capitães
Luis piz
Arribou a portugal.
Guaspar de lemos
de santa cruz trª do Brazil tornou a portugal cō nova do descobrimeto della
Pero diaz
cō a tormenta esgarrou & foy ter a Magadaxó jūto do cabo de guarda fuy, & á tornada se encontrou cō pedralvrz cabral no cabo
Pero de thayde
há tornada se perdeo nos baixos de S. Lazaro & cō a gente salva foy ter a Melinde
Vasq dathayde
perdido com a tormenta
Pedralvrz cabral
Nicolao coelho
Nuno leytão
Simão de miranda
A galarrou na tormẽta cō pedralvrz cabral, & milagrosamente se salvarão
Ayres gomez da silva
perdido com a tormenta,
Simão de pina
perdido cō a tormẽta.
Sancho de thovar
há tornada pera portugal se perdeo cō vento rijo travessão em hũ baixo perto da costa de Mellinde & depoys de toda a gente ser salva lhe poserão fogo
bertolameu diaz
perdido cō a tormenta

Lodovico di Varthema Defines the Course of European Contact with Asia

'The testimony of one eyewitness is worth more than ten thousand hearsays.'

1502-08

Among those solitary travellers who managed to penetrate the darker recesses of the Asian continent before European contact became commonplace, Lodovico di Varthema is exceptional. As an Italian he was exempt from the regime of secrecy that kept Portuguese disclosures under wraps for half a century or so; he could circulate his findings without fear of reprisal or contradiction, and he could be sure of a ready market in a continent starved of reliable tidings from the East. What was equally remarkable was that he travelled not as a merchant, ambassador or would-be colonizer, but as a simple adventurer with a passion for exploration. Sadly, little is known of Varthema beyond what leaks out in his narrative. Formerly a soldier, an educated man with widespread scientific and cultural interests, in 1502 he left his wife and family in his native Bologna and departed for Egypt. Following a tour of the Levant, learning Arabic and pragmatically accepting Islam, he joined a pilgrim caravan at Damascus which brought him to the holy cities of Mecca and Medina, which he was probably the first European to see. Arrested in Aden as a Christian spy, then released, he proceeded to Yemen, Somalia and Iran, then struck overland into Afghanistan in an abortive effort to reach Samarkand.

Returning to the coast at Hormuz, Varthema sailed for India, arriving in 1504, just six years after Da Gama's first visit. However, rather than sticking to the western ports where most of his contemporaries were content to linger, he penetrated far inland, providing a unique description of the mighty Hindu kingdom of Vijayanagar. By his own account he visited Ceylon and followed the sea routes to Burma, Malacca, Sumatra and Java, even as far as Borneo and the Moluccas, the legendary Spice Islands. Returning to India, Varthema spent two years in Portuguese service as a soldier, then in 1508 returned to Europe. His *Itinerario*, first printed in 1510, became an overnight bestseller and saw translation into six languages. Although modern scholars remain suspicious of Varthema's excursions beyond India, invoking questions of chronology and the narrative's relative loss of detail, the fact remains that such a voyage was possible and that Varthema's information, even if secondhand, was essentially accurate. It would become highly influential in determining the direction of Portuguese expansion, and would be used by Magellan in presenting his case for the first circumnavigation.

Right The title page from Lodovico di Varthema's *Itinerario*, which provided European readers with their first comprehensive account of India and Southeast Asia.

Itinerario De Ludouico De Verthema Bolognese ne lo Egypto ne la Suria ne la Arabia Deserta & Felice ne la Persia ne la India: & ne la Ethiopia. La fede el uiuere & costumi de tutte le prefate prouincie. Noua mente impresso.

Balboa Discovers the Pacific Ocean

The lust for gold and the emergence of the conquistador.

1513

OF ALL THE REGIONS ON EARTH THAT ONE MIGHT CHOSE TO FIGHT OVER, the isthmus of Darien, that neck of disease-infested forest and swamp that connects Central with South America, must be one of the least inviting. Even today only the most foolhardy traveller would approach it without fear or trepidation. But for a few brief years, before anything was dreamt of Inca or Aztec, Darien achieved distinction as the most remote outpost of the Spanish empire; a site of bloody conflict, not just with the violently suppressed natives but among the conquerors themselves as they strove to carve petty kingdoms from this unwelcoming backwater. From this arena arose Vasco Núñez de Balboa, the first of the conquistadors whose explorations were fired by personal ambition and the lust for gold. Balboa had first encountered Darien in 1501 as a security guard with Rodrigo de Bastidas's expedition along South America's northern shores. The natives were sometimes friendly, happily trading gold for trinkets and cloth, but most resented the Spanish intrusion. Nevertheless, the lure of gold was irresistible and in 1509 Alonzo de Ojeda arrived to plant the first permanent settlement.

Balboa, who had taken disastrously to farming in Haiti but now saw his fortune in Darien, stowed away on the next supply ship only to find Ojeda's settlement abandoned and in ruins. Out of the ensuing rivalry Balboa emerged dominant, founding a new colony at Santa Maria de la Antigua close to the present-day border of Panama. Gold was plentiful as meagre trinkets and ornaments, but the real source of wealth lay somewhere to the south, along the rivers that emptied into the Caribbean or perhaps even further afield. Balboa's preliminary excursions came to little, but early 1513 brought native intelligence of a great sea, on the far side of which people ate and drank from plates and goblets of gold. In September, with 190 Spanish and 1000 native reinforcements, Balboa plunged into the jungle. Fierce battles, disease and exhaustion rapidly depleted his number, but on 25 September 1513 a party reached the summit of the mountainous divide and looked down on the Gulf of San Miguel, an inlet of a vast ocean never before seen by Europeans. With twenty-six men Balboa marched down to the coast and four days later bathed in the Pacific, claiming possession of the sea and all the lands that bordered it in the name of Spain.

Right An engraving showing Balboa's men standing by while their dogs attacked the natives.

Hernán Cortés and the Conquest of Mexico

The dramatic discovery of cities in the Americas.

1517-21

In the twenty-five years that followed Columbus' arrival in America, Spanish settlers in the Caribbean lived in blissful ignorance of the mighty Aztec and Mayan civilizations that confronted them only a short hop to the west. The conquest of Cuba in 1511 by Diego Velázquez de Cuéllar had found only relatively primitive cultures reminiscent of Hispaniola, while Balboa's crossing of the isthmus of Darien in 1513 had, despite its historic discovery of the Pacific, yielded little other than the hint of a gold-rich civilization lurking somewhere in the distant south. A hapless band of Spanish sailors, shipwrecked from a returning fleet in 1511, had made a life for themselves on the coast of Yucatán but, unable to get word back, their presence stayed unreported for years. However, in 1517 Velázquez despatched a small fleet to the west under the command of Francisco Hernández de Córdoba, its probable mission being the acquisition of slaves to work the fields and mines of Cuba. After a stormy passage Córdoba sighted the first city to be discovered in the Americas, likening its pyramids, naïvely identified as *mezquitas* or 'mosques', to those seen in Egypt and christening it 'El Gran Cairo'. Next year Juan de Grijalva expanded on the discovery, taking four ships around the Yucatán coast to the Tabasco region of southern Mexico.

Hernán Cortés had arrived in Hispaniola in 1503; a restless, mischievous, womanizing eighteen-year-old bored by small-town life in provincial Spain. Over fifteen years, by means often devious, he rose through the civil hierarchy, joining the invasion of Cuba, becoming mayor of its capital Santiago and jostling with governor Velázquez for political ascendancy. Thus, when Cortés and his 400 soldiers debarked illegally on the Mexican coast in 1519, on a mission instigated but on second thoughts revoked by Velázquez, Cortés promptly dismissed the governor's authority and assumed command in the name of King Charles of Spain. Marching inland, his meagre army of 400 incapable by itself of overthrowing the formidable Aztec empire, Cortés and his indigenous mistress manipulated the tribes en route into an overwhelming coalition. In November 1519 the conquering Spaniard was peacefully received into the Aztec capital Tenochtitlan by its unsuspecting emperor Moctezuma II. Cortés had to fight hard to assert his dominance, even against troops sent by Velázquez to displace him, but within two short years Moctezuma was dead, Tenochtitlan lay in ruins, and the Aztec empire had crumbled.

Right The first map of Mexico City, which Cortés built on the ruins of Tenochtitlan, shows a city in transition. The central locations of the Aztec capital are drawn here alongside the new structures planned by Cortés.

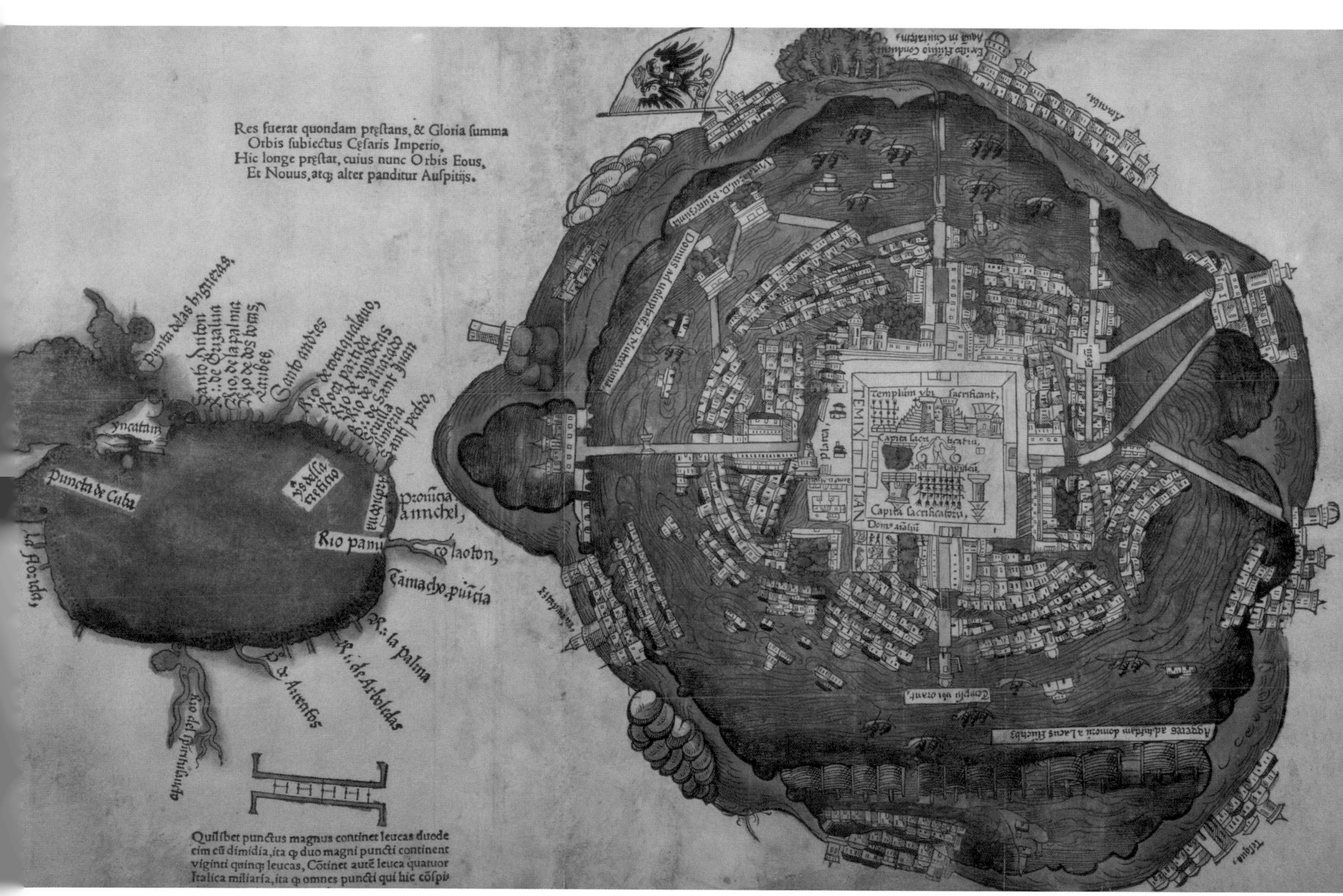
Res fuerat quondam pręstans, & Gloria summa
Orbis subiectus Cęsaris Imperio,
Hic longe pręstat, cuius nunc Orbis Eous,
Et Nouus, atq; alter panditur Auspitijs.
Quilibet punctus magnus continet leucas duode
cim cū dimidia, ita ꝙ duo magni puncti continent
viginti quinq; leucas, Cōtinet autē leuca quatuor
Italica miliaria, ita ꝙ omnes puncti qui hic cōspi

Leo Africanus: Traveller, Apprehended at Sea

A lucky break for European geographers.

1518

ALTHOUGH CLOSELY BOUNDED TO THE NORTH by one of the world's busiest commercial highways, the Sahara Desert received remarkably few first-hand travellers' narratives until the beginning of the nineteenth century. Ibn Battuta's personal account of a trans-Saharan journey taken in 1352-54 was little known in its day, while the more eminent Islamic geographers seemed content to rely on the testimonies of others rather than risk the difficult journey themselves. European travellers, for whom the lure of the legendary riches of Mali would prove an irresistible challenge, were particularly few and far between. An obscure Frenchman, Anselme d'Isalguier, taken into slavery on the Moroccan coast, spent the years 1405-13 in the city of Gao and married a Songhai princess who became the talk of Toulouse. In 1447 the Genoese gold merchant Antonio Malfante ventured inland from the northwest, spent some time at the Tuat oasis and despatched a fairly comprehensive report of his findings. And around 1470 the Florentine merchant Benedetto Dei visited Timbuktu but left us with nothing more than a passing, mouth-watering aside buried inconspicuously in his *Chronicles*. No doubt there were others who, for reasons of commercial rivalry, kept quiet about their adventures or even falsified information to throw others off the scent.

For two centuries virtually the only substantial geography of North Africa accessible to European scholars was that of the traveller known to the western world as Giovanni Leo Africanus, 'Leo the African'. Born Hasan ibn Muhammad al-Wazzan into a wealthy family from Granada, then expelled during the Spanish reconquest, he was educated in Morocco and subsequently travelled extensively on official business to almost every part of North Africa and the Near East. His *Description of Africa*, rich in anecdotal detail and widely read throughout Europe, provides little indication of chronology but does furnish a solid and reliable account of the places visited. After numerous journeys in the north, Leo crossed the Sahara in about 1514 and on a wide sweep visited all the kingdoms of the upper Niger, from Mali to Timbuktu, even as far as Lake Chad. Luckily for Europe, in 1518 he was captured at sea by pirates in the employ of the Knights of St John, handed over to Pope Leo X, and for expediency converted to Christianity. Throughout his ten years in Italy he wrote prolifically and earned a reputation as the leading cross-cultural scholar of his time.

Right A map of Africa, orientated with south at the top, from Leo Africanus' *Descrittione dell 'Africa*, translated from his Arabic notes into Italian in 1526 at the request of the pope.

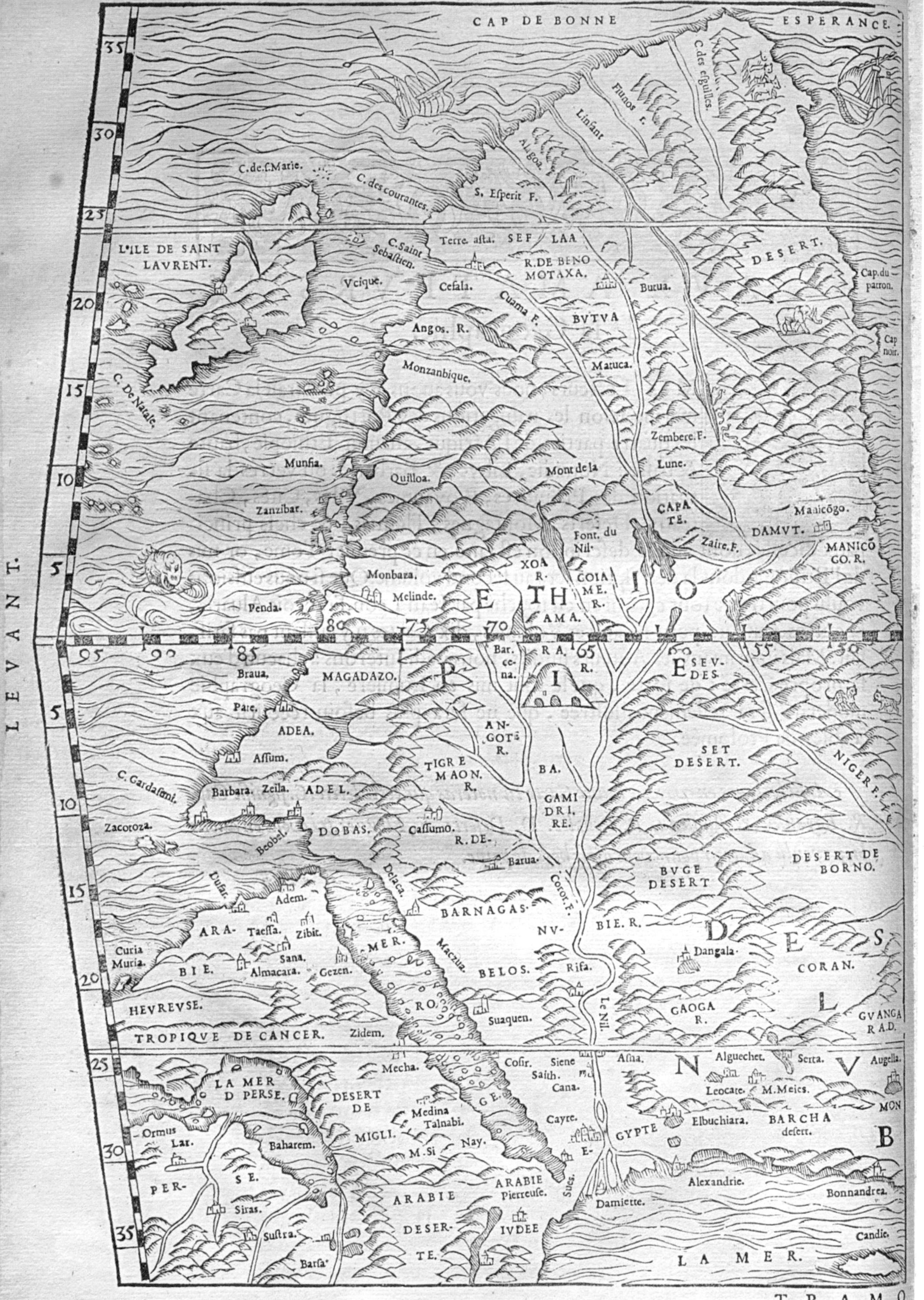

CAP DE BONNE ESPERANCE.

C. des esguilles.
Fiumos r.
Linfant
Alagoa.
C. de S. Marie.
C. des courantes.
S. Esperit F.
L'ILE DE SAINT LAURENT.
C. Saint Sebastien.
Terre. asta.
SEF LAA
R. DE BENO MOTAXA.
DESERT.
Cap. du parron.
Vcique.
Cefala.
Cuama F.
Butua.
BUTUA
Angos. R.
Cap noir.
Monzanbique.
Matuca.
C. De Natale.
Zembere. F.
Munfia.
Quilloa.
Mont de la
Lune.
Zanzibar.
CAPA TE.
Manicōgo.
Font. du Nil.
DAMUT.
Zaire. F.
MANICŌ GO. R.
LEVANT.
XOA R.
COIA ME. R.
Monbaza.
Melinde.
Penda.
E TH I O
AMA.
Bar. ce. na.
RA.
Braua.
MAGADAZO.
P I E
SEV. DES.
Pate.
ADEA.
AN GOTĀ R.
Assum.
TIGRE MAON. R.
BA.
SET DESERT.
NIGER F.
C. Gardafeni.
Barbara.
Zeila.
ADEL.
GAMI DRI. RE.
Zacotoza.
Beobel.
DOBAS.
Cassumo.
R. DE.
Barua.
DESERT DE BORNO.
Dulfar.
Adem.
Delaca.
BUGE DESERT
BARNAGAS.
Cotor. F.
ARA. Taessa.
Zibit.
Sana.
MER
Macrua.
NU.
BIE. R.
D E S
Curia Muria.
BIE.
Almacara.
Gezen.
BELOS.
Rifsa.
Dangala.
CORAN.
HEVREVSE.
RO.
Suaquen.
Le Nil.
GAOGA R.
L
GVANGA RA D.
TROPIQUE DE CANCER.
Zidem.
Mecha.
Cosir.
Siene
Saith.
Cana.
Asna.
N
Alguechet.
Serta.
V
Augella.
LA MER D PERSE.
DESERT DE
Medina Talnabi.
GE.
Leocate.
M. Meies.
MON
Ormus
Lar.
Baharem.
MIGLI.
M. Si
Nay.
Cayre.
E.
GYPTE
Elbuchiara.
BARCHA desert.
B
PER
SE.
ARABIE
ARABIE Pierreuse.
Sues.
Damiette.
Alexandrie.
Bonnandrea.
Siras.
Sustra.
DESER TE.
IUDEE
Candie.
Barsa.
LA MER.

1519–22

Magellan and the First Circumnavigation of the Globe

The ultimate attainment in the history of exploration.

WHATEVER ONE'S CRITERIA FOR EVALUATING the relative heroism, hardship and impact of journeys of discovery, it must be conceded that nothing in the history of exploration can surpass the voyage of Ferdinand Magellan. Born into the minor Portuguese nobility, Magellan (more properly Fernão de Magalhães) had seen service on voyages to India and Malacca before accusations of illicitly trading with the Moors made him *persona non grata* within the Portuguese establishment, abruptly terminating his career prospects and aspirations to imperial distinction. In Malacca he heard that the highly valued spice trade centred on Ternate, a small East Indian island on the edge of the known world, so distant that it took some eighteen months to reach it. But when Magellan suggested that the voyage could be better facilitated by sailing west, Asia being only a short step beyond the Americas, he was shunned by his countrymen but found a ready audience among the bankers of neighbouring Castile. Transferring his allegiance to Spain and declaring his intention to search as far as 75°S to find an opening into the western sea, he sailed from Sanlúcar de Barrameda in September 1519 with five ships and 250 men.

On a voyage fraught with every conceivable hardship – becalmed in the doldrums, winter on the desolate wind-ravaged Patagonian coast, and a tortuous passage in bitter storms through the maze-like channels of the strait that now celebrates the explorer's name – his men mutinied three times, one ship foundered and another went home. But Magellan pressed on into the unknown, his only stroke of luck being that he had entered the Pacific at the moment when the winds were most favourable. By the time Guam was sighted in March 1521 he had been ninety-nine days at sea and his scurvy-riddled crew were reduced to eating ox-hide sail casings, sawdust, and biscuits that stank of rats' urine. When the expedition eventually arrived in the Philippines, Magellan, tempted by imperial adventurism, made the mistake of involving himself in a local conflict, which resulted in his death. Command passed around various members of the crew, one ship having been scuttled while another foundered, until leadership devolved to Sebastian del Cano, captain of the only remaining vessel, the *Vittoria*. This he brought safely back to Sanlúcar in September 1522, the first vessel to circumnavigate the globe, but only after a nightmare voyage across two more oceans and with only eighteen of the crew left alive.

Right A world map by Battista Agnese, 1542, constructed on an unusual oval projection and plotting the route of Magellan's circumnavigation.

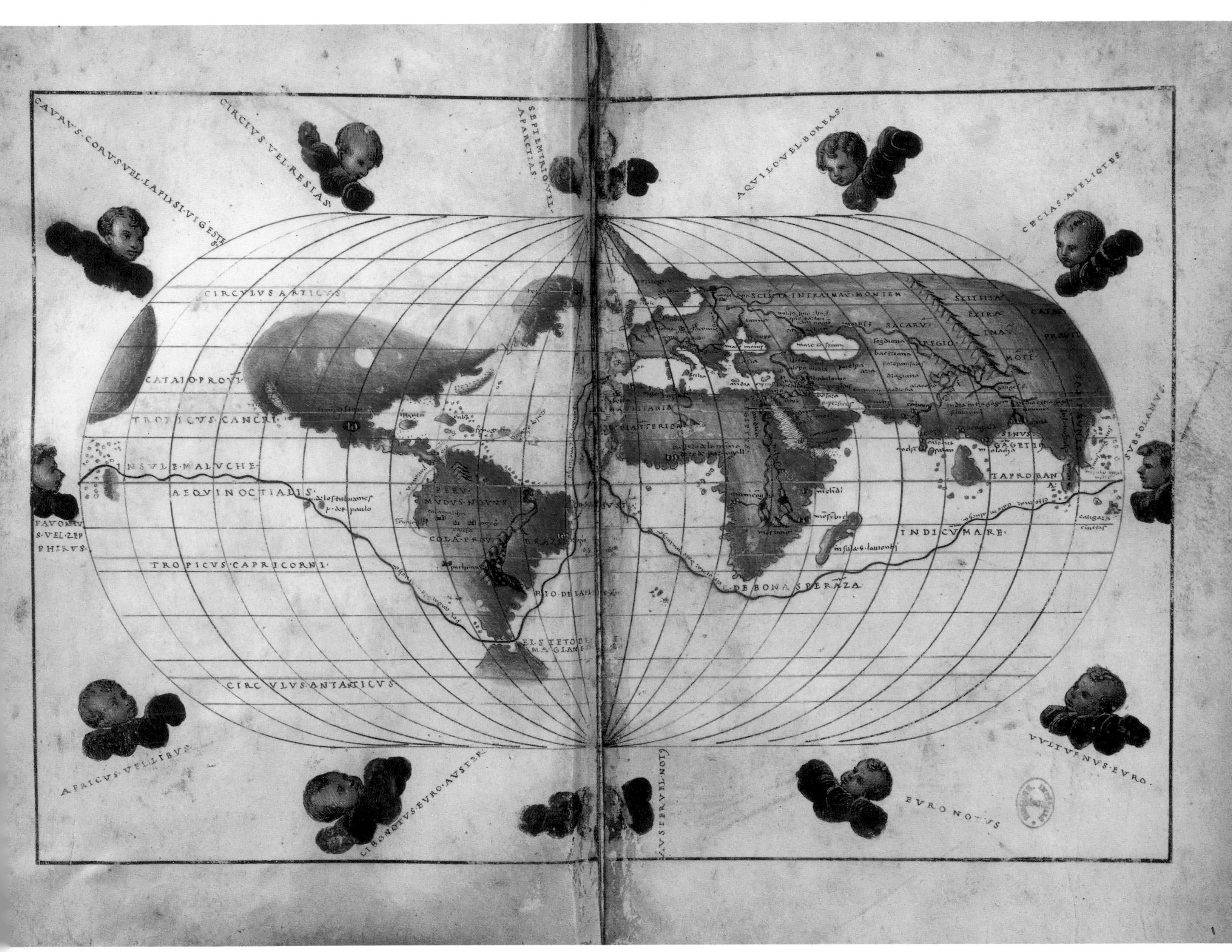
CIRCIUS VEL RESIAS
SEPTEMTRIO VEL APARCTIAS
AQUILO VEL BOREAS
CIRCULUS ARTICUS
TROPICUS CANCRI
AEQUINOCTIALIS
TROPICUS CAPRICORNI
CIRCULUS ANTARTICUS
INDICUM MARE
TAPROBANA
EURO NOTUS

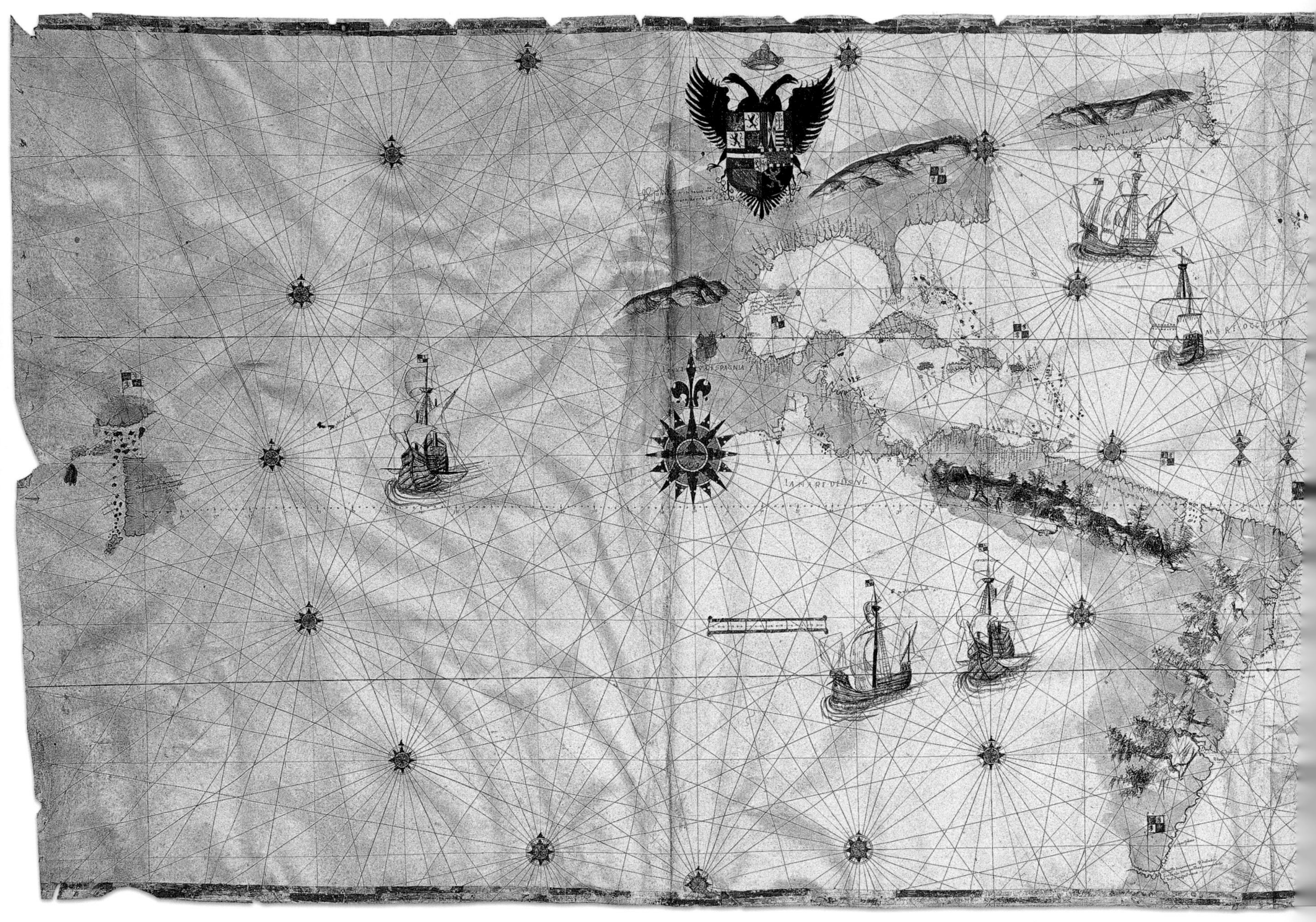

Above This historic and remarkably honest world map by Juan Vespucci, 1526, located only those geographical features known with certainty.

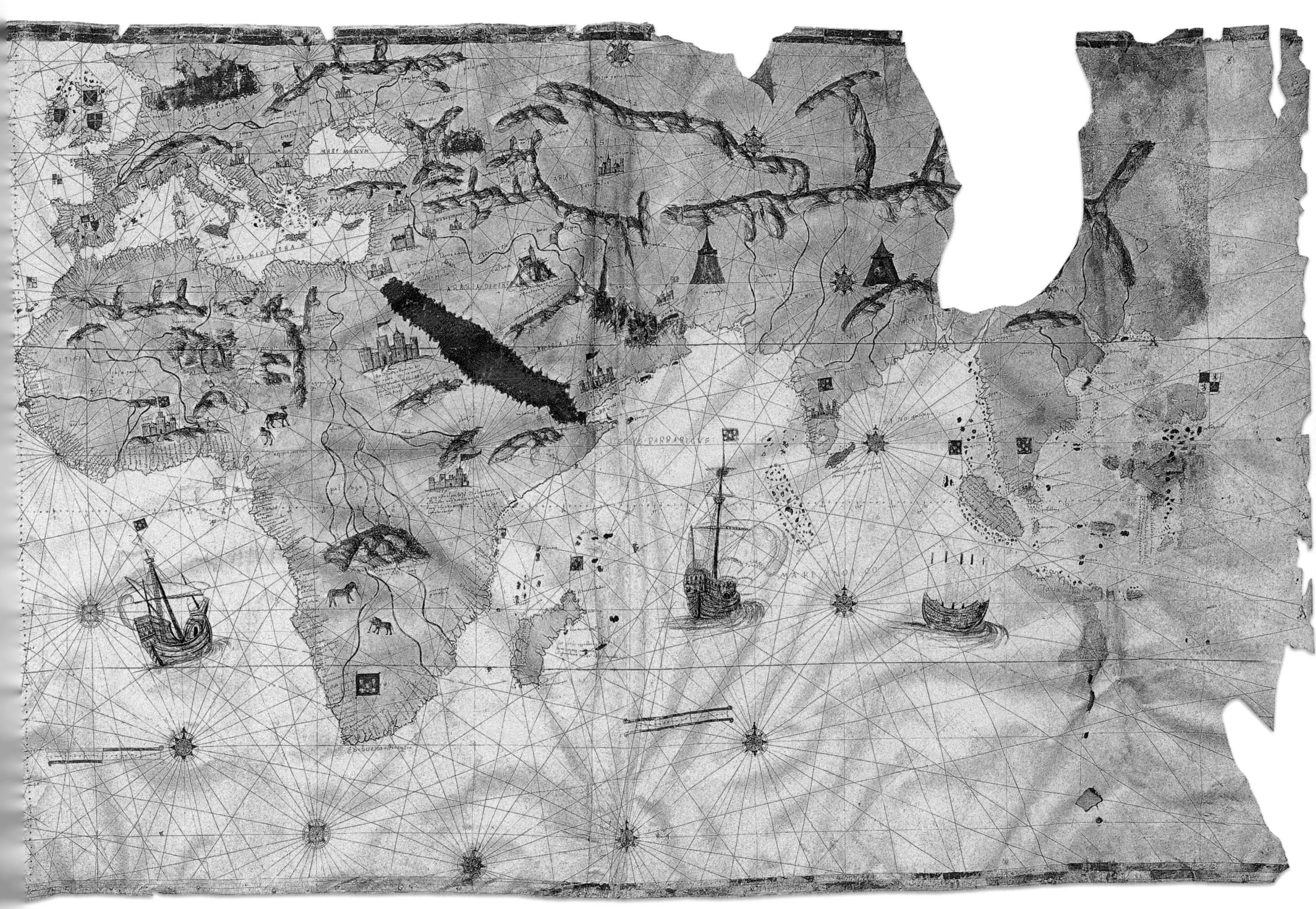

Jesuit Missionaries at the Source of the Blue Nile

Ethiopia promises fresh opportunities for the aspiring explorer.

1520–1635

THE CHRISTIAN KINGDOM OF ETHIOPIA, THREATENED BY TURKS from the Red Sea and surrounded on three sides by petty Muslim warlords, had by the sixteenth century never looked quite so vulnerable. But with the arrival of the Portuguese in the Indian Ocean came the prospect of a strongly armed Christian ally whose intervention might be critical to Ethiopia's survival. A fully fledged Portuguese embassy visited the country in 1520, during which Francisco Álvares became the first to write a detailed explorers' narrative, and in the 1540s a large Portuguese force was instrumental in seeing off a Muslim invasion. The result was that a small but significant missionary presence, latterly Jesuit, lingered in the country well into the following century. Since their arrival in 1577 the Jesuits had recorded some notable 'discoveries', particularly in the region around Lake Tana, the great lake from which the Blue Nile rises, while in the south António Fernandes had made a brave attempt to pioneer an overland route to the Somali coast before falling into the hands of tribal leaders.

In 1613 the Jesuit missionary Pedro Páez received a plot of land for a monastery on the shore of Lake Tana. He subsequently travelled widely through Ethiopia and in 1618 described the springs that he believed were the major source of Tana's waters, and consequently of the Nile itself. In those days Europeans had no concept of a second river, the White Nile that flowed even further southward, and those that passed the confluence of the two Niles somehow always chose to ignore the wider stream. Páez died in 1622 and was succeeded by an even more adventurous traveller, Jerónimo Lobo. The Red Sea now dominated by Turkish shipping, Lobo's first attempt to enter Ethiopia from the Indian Ocean came to grief on the Somali coast, but in 1625 he arrived safely by the somewhat unconventional route through Danakil country. He remained in Ethiopia until the Jesuits were expelled in 1635, travelling widely and following Páez's tracks to the source of the Nile. Lobo's voyage back to Portugal was no less exciting. Shipwrecked on the Natal coast, he and his fellow survivors hastily constructed boats in which they managed to reach Luanda in Angola. To add to Lobo's annoyance, no Portuguese vessel was in port at the time, forcing the frustrated missionary to return via an unscheduled sight-seeing tour of the Caribbean.

Right Ethiopia and the Red Sea, c.1640, from Manuel de Almeida's *Historia de Ethiopia.*

TABOA DAS TERRAS E REINOS DO IMPERIO ABEXIM, OU
ARABIA
M. ROXO
NUBIA BAL LOTS
PRESTE IOAM
Reino de
Rio Tacaze
ETHIOPIA ORIENTAL
RNº FUNHIE
Rº Nilo
R.º MALEG
Fascalo
MAGAZA
TEMBEN
ABARGALE
SALAOA
Bora
DER
DOBAS
GRE
AGA
MER
Bur de Cima
Bur de baixo
AGAUS
REI
BEGAME ME
RNº ANCOTE
HARA
Gedem
RNº DANCALI
RN DO ARÔ
Gongas
gongas NO
GOIAM
RNº BIZAMO
GAFATES
RNº XAOA de cima
MARRABET
OIFATE
XAOA de baixo
RNº GANZ
RNº DAMUT
RNº Guraque
RNº ADEA
REINO OGE
REINO
FATEGAR
Rei NO
BALI
Rº Aoaxe
RNº NAREA
RNº Cambate
ALABA
Galas
Ilhas na Alagoa q Chamao Mar de dam
Esta Alagoa he a Coloe de Ptolo meu Ioam de Barros a Chamma Barcena
R. Zebe
Esta terra Alaba nam Pertence a o Imperio
Patria E Nacimento dos galas
Reino de Adil
CAFRES
OCEANUS ORIENTALIS
Amora
Camaram
Heda
B. da Serra
B. Lebibe
Adem
Baba mandel
Esta rio entra Quatro Jornadas
Cabo Rosbel
Rº dameta
C. dorfuguem
Morocobri
Bandel dan zoada
osbodeis
Oriens
Occidens

1524

Verrazzano Establishes the Continuity of the North American Coast

The fate of the westerly passage to Asia is finally sealed.

LET US PAUSE TO CONSIDER HOW A GEOGRAPHY STUDENT OF THE CLASS OF 1523 might have perceived the world across the Atlantic. Survivors of Magellan's fleet had returned with news that Balboa's 'Sea of the South' was a vast ocean, entry to which was frustrated by the South American continent. In 1513 Juan Ponce de Léon had found the 'island'of Florida, and in 1517 the first Spanish had arrived in Mexico. In 1519 Alonso de Pineda had traced the entire northern shore of the Gulf of Mexico, while in the far north the Cabots and others had alighted on the extremities of Canada. But still an ominous blank remained between Florida and Nova Scotia where the Atlantic might open invitingly into the Pacific and offer the last chance of a direct passage to China. In 1522 the Florentine adventurer Giovanni da Verrazzano, who like the Cabots and Columbus indiscriminately touted his wares to any receptive customer, arrived in France where the silk merchants of Lyon had a vested interest in a short route to the Orient. His object, to seek a strait north of Florida, also aroused the participation of King François I, who was thinking it was about time France joined the clamour of transatlantic migration.

With fifty crew and a caravel named *Dauphine*, Verrazzano started out from around Madeira in January 1524 and after eight weeks struck the coast of North Carolina. After a short exploratory foray to the south, fearing an encounter with Spanish vessels, he turned about and followed the coast northward, visiting New York harbour, christening Long Island 'Louise' after the king's mother and spending fifteen days in Narragansett Bay. Via Nova Scotia he was back on the map, and from Newfoundland a two-month crossing brought him into Dieppe. Although, in establishing the continuity of the eastern seaboard, Verrazzano had failed in his primary mission, hopes of a shortcut to Asia had not entirely been dashed. By a curious error of judgement, or maybe a deliberate deception intended to appease his wealthy patrons, he had identified the Carolina outer banks, that narrow chain of islands that straddles the Pamlico Sound, as an isthmus, behind which lay the broad Pacific. The myth would confound geographers for 100 years, but significantly Verrazzano would never follow it up, instead, on subsequent voyages, aiming much further south. What became of him, whether eaten alive by hostile tribesmen or executed by the Spanish, remains something of a mystery.

Right This world map, 1529–40, by Verrazzano's cartographer brother Gerolamo, gives North America a continuous coastline but shows a vast, non-existent protuberance of the Pacific Ocean into what is now Carolina.

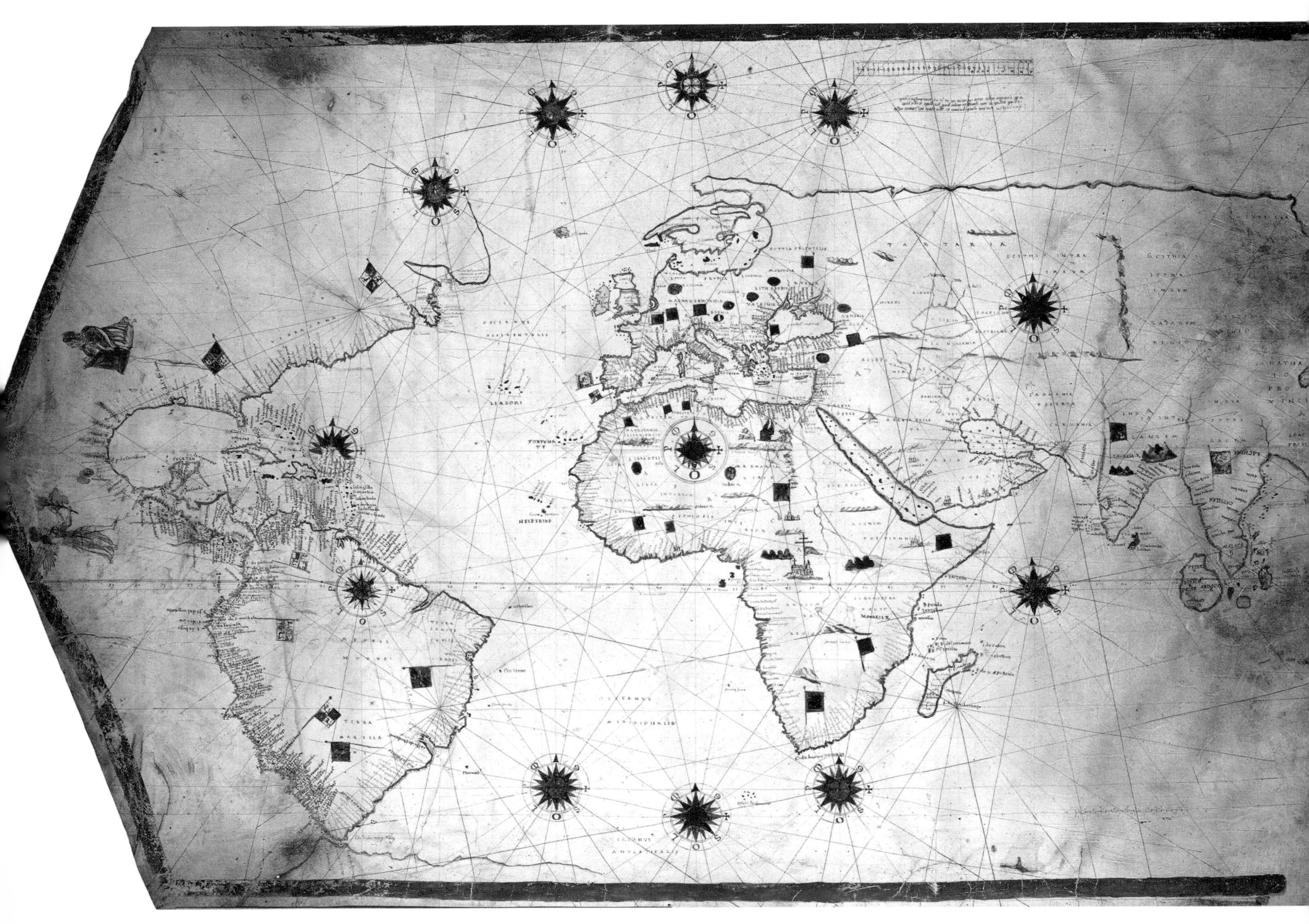

Francisco Pizarro and the Conquest of Peru

The discovery and tragic extinction of the world's last unknown empire.

1526-33

BY THE 1520S EVIDENCE OF A GOLD-RICH CIVILIZATION deep in the heart of South America had begun to filter into Europe. Maritime expeditions down the Atlantic coast had discovered artefacts of precious metal whose source lay deep in the interior, while settlers in Panama learned repeatedly of fabulous cities whose situation lay only a short voyage south. Such rumours were further reinforced by Pascual de Andagoya, one of Panama's co-founders, who in 1522 surveyed along the Colombian coast and subjugated the lands of Birú, a tribal leader whose name, corrupted as Peru, came to represent the entire southern extremity of Spanish colonization. When injury prevented Andagoya from capitalizing on his discoveries the challenge was taken up by one Francisco Pizarro, an illiterate and poorly educated ex-soldier who had accompanied Balboa across the isthmus and had emerged from anonymity and inter-conquistadorial rivalry to become mayor of Panama City.

Pizarro's first venture, a trifling affair undertaken with his henchman Diego de Almagro, turned into a dismal, underfunded and ill-equipped failure, during which Almagro lost an eye to an Indian arrow. His second expedition in 1526-27 fared little better, dumping Pizarro and his long-suffering acolytes in the disease-infested mangrove swamps of southern Colombia. But Pizarro's fanatical determination prevailed. With thirteen brave men he proceeded boldly south and in April 1528 entered the Gulf of Guayaquil to sight his first Inca city at Tumbez. Further landings along the Peruvian coast rapidly confirmed the existence of the advanced civilization he had sought so ardently. Excitedly Pizarro sailed for Spain to acquire royal assent, money and men for a full-scale invasion, a request instantly approved by a queen whose court ladies had already been charmed with lavish gifts of Aztec treasure brought back by Cortés. By 1532 Pizarro was back in Tumbez with a motley crew of would-be conquerors and self-seeking adventurers, determined to emulate the achievements of his Mexican counterpart. Striking inland across the fearful passes of the high Andes with only 185 men he approached the Inca capital of Cajamarca, taking the city against odds of fifteen-to-one and ransoming its monarch Atahualpa for a room stacked with gold. Following the Inca road across the high sierras, Pizarro descended on Cuzco in November 1533, sacking the empire's second city, forcing its leadership into exile and so condemning one of the world's greatest civilizations to extinction.

Right A sixteenth-century engraving depicting Pizarro's siege of Cuzco in 1533.

Sebastian Cabot Seeks the Mountains of Silver

The first hints of the wealth of South America reach Europe.

1527-29

THE EARLIEST PERIOD OF EUROPEAN CONTACT WITH SOUTH AMERICA witnessed some extraordinary feats of exploration. Under-reported at the time and today overshadowed by Pizarro's march on the Inca empire, those involved would put later heroes to shame. In 1516 the Spanish pilot major, Juan Díaz de Solís, seeking a sea route to Asia, discovered the 'Mar Dulce' – the broad estuary of the Rio de la Plata – and sailed up the Uruguay River where he and his comrades were eaten by Indians in full view of the shipboard crew. Another of his sailors, Aleixo Garcia, shipwrecked with others on the Brazilian island of Santa Catalina, struck inland, possibly penetrating as far as the Bolivian Andes in search of a 'White King' who lived in the 'Mountains of Silver'. With silver and copper pilfered from the as-yet undiscovered Inca empire, Garcia headed back. Returning from his staggering 3000-kilometre (1800-mile) adventure he met his death on the banks of the Paraguay, but only after sending some of the booty ahead to his friends on the coast.

In 1527, still a full six years before Pizarro's conquest of Peru, Sebastian Cabot arrived with three vessels in the Mar Dulce. Son of the Bristol seaman John Cabot, but now in Spanish service as Díaz's successor, he had left Spain to discover a passage to Asia shorter than that pioneered by Magellan. Rescuing Garcia's shipmates from their ten-year sojourn on the Brazilian coast, together with their treasure, Cabot continued on his mission to Asia. But the lure of the White King was too great. Cabot abandoned his assignment and headed into the fresh water of what was now christened the Rio de la Plata, or 'River of Silver'. Seeking a navigable route to the 'Mountains of Silver', the unknown Andes, he ventured far up the Paraná River, almost to modern Asunción, until halted by rapids. En route he despatched Francisco César, who after travelling deep into the west allegedly discovered a fabulous city and returned with a rich haul of gold and silver. Whether or not the city existed, it entered South American mythology as the 'Ciudad de los Césares', the City of the Caesars, and would be sought obsessively by explorers for the next 250 years. Although castigated for failing in his specified commission, Cabot returned with the earliest charts of a major South American river system, and the first Inca treasure to be seen in Europe.

Right A remarkably accurate and detailed map of the world by Sebastian Cabot, drawn in 1544 and showing his discoveries in South America.

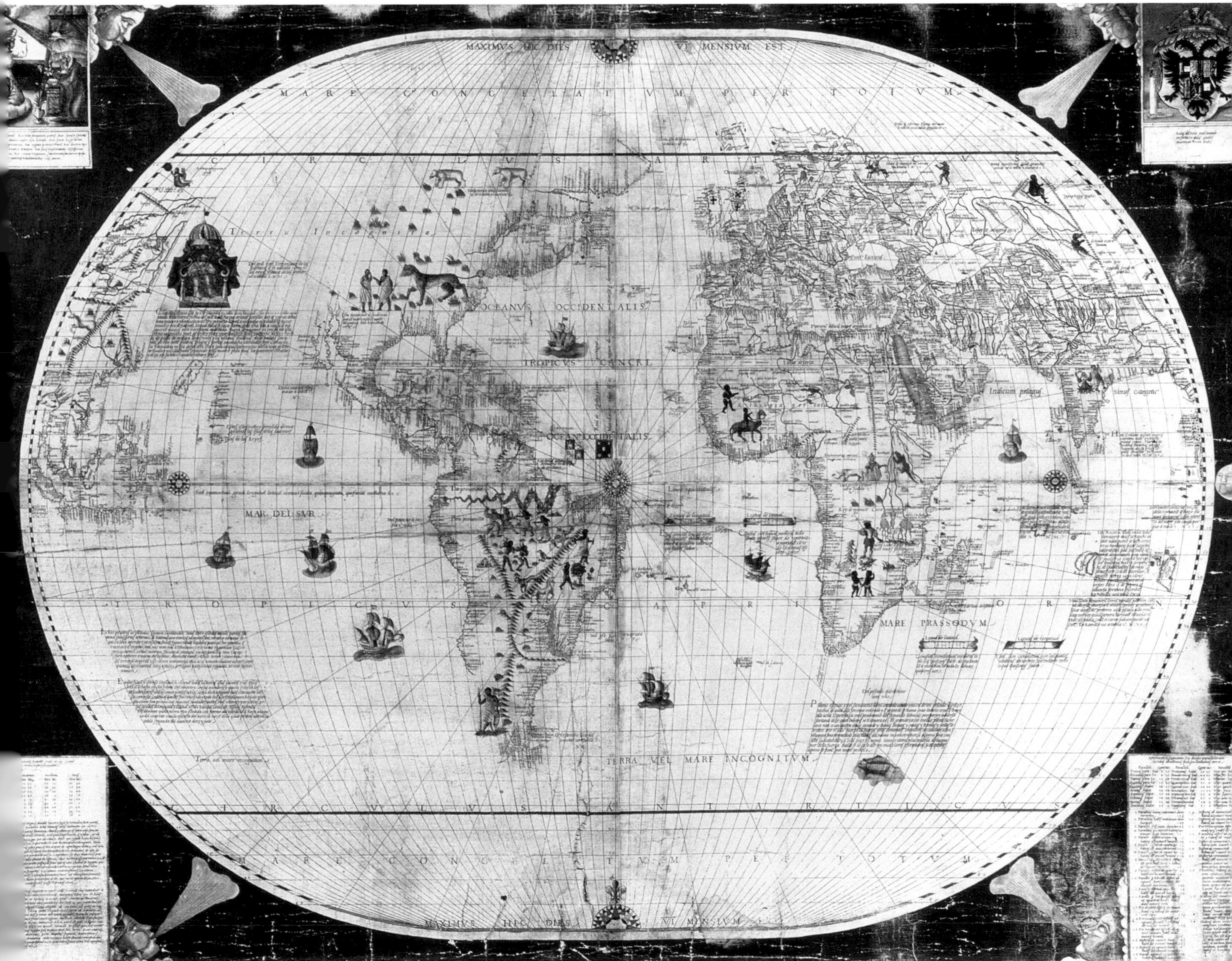
MAXIMVS HIC DIES VT MENSIVM EST
OCEANVS OCCIDENTALIS
TROPICVS CANCRI
MAR DEL SVR
MARE PRASSODVM
TERRA VEL MARE INCOGNITVM

The Narvaéz Invasion of Florida and its Aftermath

The farce that turned to tragedy and enlightenment.

1527–36

IF PÁNFILO DE NARVAÉZ HAD FORESEEN THE CATALOGUE OF DISASTERS that would befall his invasion of Florida he might never have bothered. Funded by investors expecting rich pickings, and with King Charles I of Spain staking his customary five per cent claim on the bounty, Narvaéz left Spain in June 1527 with a force of 600 soldiers, sailors and their wives. His troubles began in Cuba, where 100 deserted in the first month, while the two ships sent to collect horses and supplies from Trinidad sank in a storm, drowning another sixty. The expedition regrouped on Cuba's south coast, but when the fleet got under way in February 1528 it promptly ran aground on a shoal and spent three weeks consuming already dwindling supplies. Liberated by a storm surge, vital reprovisioning at Havana was thwarted by high winds, which drove the fleet deeper into the Gulf until strong currents, frustrating a planned landfall in Mexico, deposited the expedition on the west coast of Florida. Regardless of his plight, Narvaéz ceremoniously laid claim to his worthless domain, losing another two ships in the process, before striking northward into territory where, as always, the locals somehow indicated an abundance of food and gold.

Narvaéz now divided his army into two contingents. As 300 men strove northward, another 100 manned a support fleet to parallel the advancing army by sea. But as Narvaéz and his overland party headed for Apalachee country, ravaged by disease, starvation and Indian attack, the fleet lost contact, eventually giving up the search and heading for home. Marooned with no hope of rescue, the Narvaéz party had little option but to eat their horses (and possibly their dead), melt down their weaponry into raft-building tools, and launch into the Gulf. A hurricane drove the rafts to the coast of Texas, but of the 242 that started out, Narvaéz and 160 others died of thirst and starvation, and two rafts were swallowed by heavy seas. Of the survivors, some went native or were enslaved, while others made a desperate effort to struggle back to Mexico. Of the latter only Álvar Núñez Cabeza de Vaca, the expedition's treasurer, and his party lived to tell the tale and, most significantly, to bring back the first anthropological account of native life. Leaving Texas in 1532 and taking a circuitous route to the west, the survivors turned up four years later near Culiacán, in Mexico's northwestern provinces.

Right The title page of Cabeza de Vaca's influential *Relación*, 1555, which describes his extraordinary adventures in Texas and the southwest and survives as a work of exceptional anthropological and historical significance.

¶ La relacion y comentarios del gouernador Aluar nuñez cabeça de vaca, de lo acaescido en las dos jornadas que hizo a las Indias.

Con priuilegio.

¶ Esta tassada por los señores del consejo en Ochenta y cinco mrs.

German Explorers in Sixteenth-Century South America

A curious anachronism in the history of exploration.

1528–44

In a world where conquistadorial rights had been partitioned between Spain and Portugal, one might be tempted to ask: 'What on earth were German explorers doing in South America in the early decades of the sixteenth century?' But there they were, beating their way across the *llanos* of Venezuela; scaling the Colombian cordillera; seeking elusive riches, the El Dorado that allegedly lay between the Caribbean and Pizarro's empire in the south. Charles I of Spain, who had already witnessed a vast expansion of the Spanish empire, had become a natural candidate for the office of Holy Roman Emperor, but to buy out his rivals required a massive advance from Europe's two major banking companies, the Welsers and the Fuggers. The Welsers, anxious to diversify into misappropriated Indian gold, demanded surety for the loan in the form of rights of exploitation throughout the greater part of northern South America. The agreement was signed in 1528, and within a year the first Welser governor of Venezuela, Ambrosius Alfinger (or Ehinger) was resident at Coro with three shiploads of colonists.

Alfinger quickly embarked on an exploration of his domain, founding Maracaibo and with 170 men advancing inland to the Magdalena, the principal river of Colombia, some 300 kilometres (180 miles) from the coast. Alfinger fell to a poisoned arrow and only thirty-five survivors made it back to Coro. In the meantime Nikolaus Federmann, sent from Germany to succeed Alfinger, struck southwest from Coro in 1530 seeking a land where bearded white men had been reported. His geography was so imperfect that he believed these to be sightings of Sebastian Cabot's expedition to Paraguay. In 1535 Georg Hohermuth advanced 1000 kilometres (600 miles) with 400 men across the Venezuelan *llanos* only to return two years later with nothing to show and three-quarters of his men dead. Then in 1538 Federmann returned to the field, tracing Hohermuth's tracks and ascending the cordillera into the gold-rich Muisca highlands of Colombia, the future site of Bogotá. But Federmann's venture, the only German expedition to achieve anything of distinction, had been trumped. A Spanish contingent under Gonzalo Jiménez de Quesada had already arrived from the north, while a second from the south was just days away. Thereafter the Welsers confined their operations to the *llanos*, culminating in the extraordinary four-year (1541–44) journey of Philip von Hutten to the land of the Omaguas. Their concession was revoked in 1556 and the entire region returned to Spain.

Right A contemporary depiction of the departure of a Welser expedition from Seville in 1534.

The Nightmare of Diego de Almagro's Long March

Madness and barbarism in the Bolivian altiplano.

1535-37

JOURNEYS OF EXPLORATION INEVITABLY ENCOUNTER some measure of misfortune, but for sheer horror, abject hardship and loss of life none can surpass Diego de Almagro's ill-fated excursion to Chile. Almagro had from the beginning been Pizarro's major partner in the Inca conquest, but received in compensation only those territories lying beyond the Peruvian heartlands. Determined to make the best of his meagre concession, and in the hope of staking out a gold-rich personal kingdom southward of Pizarro's domain, Almagro left Cuzco in July 1535, heading along the Inca road towards Lake Titicaca. With him were 570 Spanish cavalry and foot-soldiers, the battle-hardened scum of the earth, and a contingent of 12,000 native porters supplied by the puppet-ruler Manco. Beyond the lake, in the dead of winter, the expedition struck across the barren 3700-metre (12,000-foot) Bolivian altiplano. Food and water became scarce, the soldiers struggled for breath in the rarefied atmosphere, and no clothes were sufficient to protect them from the excruciating cold. One hundred and fifty Spaniards fell by the wayside, while others suffered the agonies of frostbite from which they never recovered. For the native bearers, many hundreds of which perished on the march, death came as a welcome release. Fed on just handfuls of roast maize, the more reluctant were bound in ropes and chains by day and barbarously imprisoned by night.

Eventually the depleted force descended the secluded valley of Salta in northwest Argentina, where it saw out the winter before crossing the high cordillera towards the plains of northern Chile. On the snowbound passes another 1600 natives and 112 horses died, and on reaching Copiapó the remaining natives fled. Almagro duly laid claim to his god-forsaken heritage, but expeditions sent ahead to the borders of the Inca empire found no gold, only sterile lands populated by savage Indians. News of a revolt in Peru, and the opportunity of using the ensuing turmoil to claim Cuzco for himself, caused Almagro to turn back. To avoid the perils of the high sierras he opted for the coastal route, plunging him into the blistering heat of the Atacama Desert where no vegetation relieved the monotonous brown landscape. Recrossing the cordillera, where his troops found their frozen comrades still standing, Almagro reached Cuzco in April 1537, his men blinded by the snow. Defeated in his attempt to win the city, he was imprisoned and beheaded the following year.

Right An engraving of the capture, trial and execution of Diego de Almagro, by order of Francisco Pizarro, after his return from his journey to Chile.

Cartier Opens the St Lawrence Seaway

A river so long that 'no man has been to the end'.

1535–42

By the early sixteenth century the rich fishing grounds off the northeasterly extremities of the American continent were regularly visited by English, French and Iberian navigators. Fishermen, not explorers, by trade, they had little incentive to venture further afield or plunge into the dense forests lining the shores. But a longstanding belief in a golden civilization, lying deep in the interior, shifted its focus in that direction, so that when the king of France commissioned Jacques Cartier, a seaman of St-Malo, to explore the uncharted seas beyond Newfoundland, he had in mind 'islands and countries where there are said to be great quantities of gold'. Failing this there was always the possibility that the waters might open into the broad Pacific and an equally lucrative sea route to China. Cartier's first voyage in 1534, although geographically significant, found the Gulf of St Lawrence comparable in worthlessness to 'the land God gave to Cain', but it did fortuitously introduce him to Donnacona, an Iroquois chief whose people had descended on Gaspé for their annual fishing. Cartier was reassured to hear of a gold-rich land called Saguenay, while also managing to borrow two of the chief's sons for training as interpreters.

Cartier returned with three ships in 1535 to pursue his examination of what would become the St Lawrence River. Ignoring the turnoff to Saguenay, now a land of copper not gold, and passing the village of Stadacona where Quebec now lies, he was warmly welcomed into Hochelaga, an impressively fortified and geometrically planned Iroquois town below the outcrop of Mont Réal. Halted by the rapids further up river, Cartier returned to Stadacona to be greeted by conditions that would plague so many of his successors. The river froze, his ships lay ice-bound until April, scurvy ravaged his crew, and his relationship with the Indians descended into one of mutual distrust. Cartier finally got back to St-Malo in July 1536, then spent the next four years in relative obscurity. A royal commission for a third voyage was granted in 1540, then upgraded the next year to a fully fledged colonizing expedition in which Cartier would play only a secondary role. This poorly documented expedition abandoned its fragile colonies after another winter in the ice, the local diamonds proved to be quartz, and the region's gold was fit only for fools. The St Lawrence was returned momentarily to the Iroquois, and Cartier retired to his estate in France.

Right The Iroquois village of Hochelaga in 1556, as it was depicted by Cartier's contemporary Giovanni Battista Ramusio in his book *Navigazioni e Viaggi*, 1550–59.

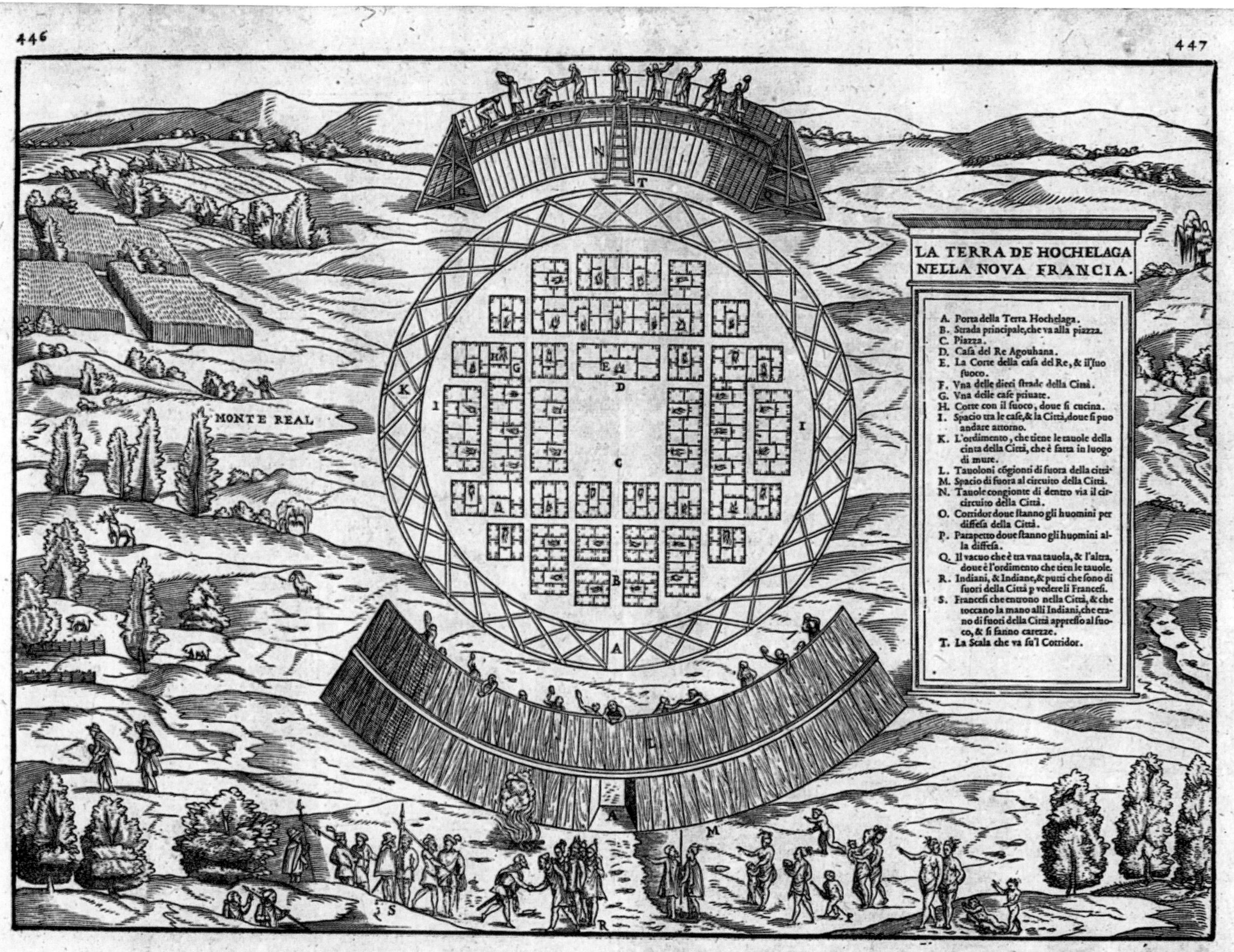
446
447
LA TERRA DE HOCHELAGA NELLA NOVA FRANCIA.
A. Porta della Terra Hochelaga.
B. Strada principale, che va alla piazza.
C. Piazza.
D. Caſa del Re Agouhana.
E. La Corte della caſa del Re, & il ſuo fuoco.
F. Vna delle dieci ſtrade della Città.
G. Vna delle caſe priuate.
H. Corte con il fuoco, doue ſi cucina.
I. Spacio tra le caſe, & la Città, doue ſi puo andare attorno.
K. L'ordimento, che tiene le tauole della cinta della Città, che è fatta in luogo di mure.
L. Tauoloni cógionti di fuora della città.
M. Spacio di fuora al circuito della Città.
N. Tauole congionte di dentro via il circircuito della Città.
O. Corridor doue ſtanno gli huomini per diffeſa della Città.
P. Parapetto doue ſtanno gli huomini alla diffeſa.
Q. Il vacuo che è tra vna tauola, & l'altra, doue è l'ordimento che tien le tauole.
R. Indiani, & Indiane, & putti che ſono di fuori della Città p vedere li Franceſi.
S. Franceſi che entrono nella Città, & che toccano la mano alli Indiani, che erano di fuori della Città appreſſo al fuoco, & ſi fanno carezze.
T. La Scala che va ſu'l Corridor.
MONTE REAL

The Peregrinations of Fernão Mendes Pinto

The first masterpiece of travel literature; the Odyssey of the Orient.

1537-58

The Portuguese so-called 'empire' in Asia, pursued relentessly in the wake of Vasco da Gama's first contact with India, was a curiously nebulous and intangible phenomenon. Contrary to the common perception of empire, it never occupied substantial inland territories. Instead it was essentially seaborne, dominating trade by the forcible occupation of strategic seaports, its landward existence barely apparent beyond a few coastal enclaves. Enterprising viceroys drove navigation eastward in pursuit of the spice trade, Afonso d'Albuquerque occupied Malacca in 1511, and within a few years contact was established with much of the East Indies and Southeast Asia. Portuguese traders and emissaries worked northward up the coast of China, and by around 1542 landed unexpectedly in Japan. Pre-eminent among the many travellers emerging from this restless era was Fernão Mendes Pinto, whose *Peregrinação* captivated audiences across Europe with its tales of pirate raids, desert caravans, court intrigues and narrow escapes, and its colourful descriptions of Asian peoples. Comparable in ambition with Homer's *Odyssey*, and arguably the finest of all works of travel literature, it recalls Pinto's twenty years' wanderings as soldier, merchant, diplomat, prisoner, slave, pirate and missionary.

Born to a poor family of Montemor-o-Velho, Pinto had arrived in India in 1537 and joined a reconnaissance mission to the Red Sea and Ethiopia. Captured by Turks, taken by caravan to Hormuz and ransomed by the Portuguese, he reached Malacca in 1539 and from there ranged far and wide, to Sumatra, Malaya, Siam, Indochina and Japan. In 1549 he introduced a Japanese fugitive to the Jesuit Francisco Xavier who, with Pinto's support, went on to found the first Christian mission in Japan. For the next nine years Pinto sailed on various commissions to Burma and the islands of the East Indies, finally returning to Portugal in 1558. A humane and philanthropic man who strongly denounced the injustices and violence of Portuguese colonialism, he willed his manuscript to a house providing support for former prostitutes, but by the time of its publication in 1614 it had been subjected to considerable diplomatic editing. Later commentators would ruthlessly challenge the veracity of Pinto's narrative, condemning it as anything from a highly coloured romance to an apocryphal display of arrant fiction, but recent scholarship has turned far more sympathetic towards the *Peregrinação*. Its substantial honesty is now admitted, and much of its underlying historical and observational accuracy, at least when extricated from heroic embellishment and subsequent editing, is considered reliable.

Right A detail from the Lopo Homem world map (ca. 1519), which charts the early discoveries of the Portuguese in the East Indies.

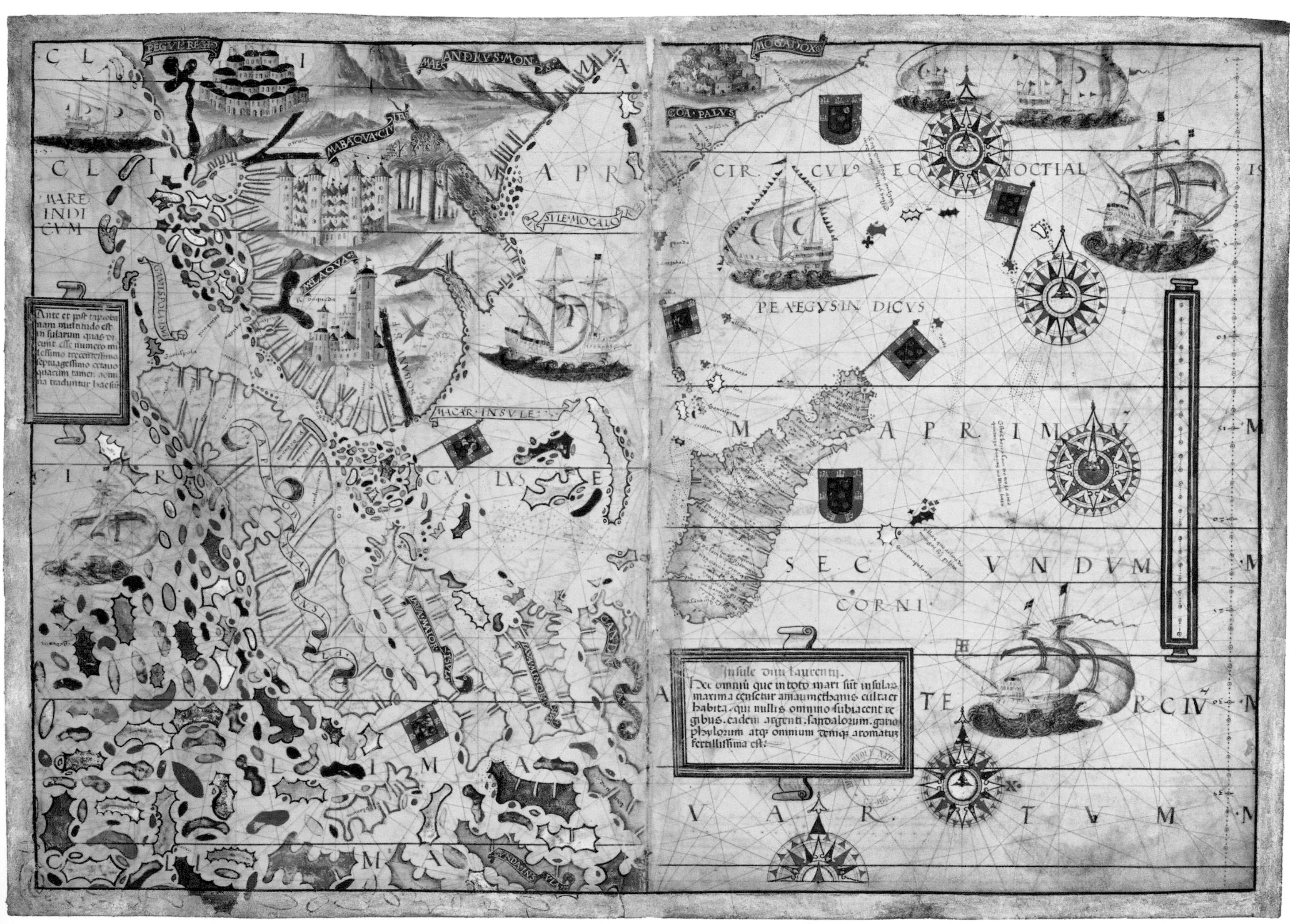

De Soto Seeks a Second Peru in the Southern States

North America is rudely awakened from its slumber.

1539–42

HERNANDO DE SOTO WAS ALREADY ONE OF THE RICHEST MEN ON EARTH. He had helped conquer Central America and had played a major role in Pizarro's campaigns in Peru. Now it was time to settle down in Seville, his stately household bankrolled by a share of the booty, some 500 kilogrammes (1100 pounds) of gold, plundered from the Incas. But the lure of even greater wealth, gleaned from exaggerated accounts of the richness of Florida, soon got the better of him. King Charles I of Spain, who owed him money, had few qualms about making him governor of Cuba and *adelantado* of all that lay in the unexplored depths of the North American hinterland. No expense spared, De Soto disembarked in grand style in Cuba and, leaving his wife in charge of affairs of state, focused on his invasion of Florida, a region which in those days embraced practically the entire southern half of the United States. Determined to avoid the ignoble farce or catastrophic demise of earlier enterprises, he sailed in May 1539 with nine ships, 620 men, tons of heavy armour and equipment, and 500 livestock – the most formidable and meticulously contrived blitzkrieg ever to descend on the unsuspecting native populace.

Landing at Tampa Bay, De Soto, with 400 men and 200 horses, trudged northward to winter in Apalachee country. From here he struck northeast to the savannah, northwest across the Blue Ridge Mountains, then down into present-day Alabama where he suffered heavy losses at the hands of Chief Tuscaloosa. Anxious to escape the embarrassment of returning depleted and empty-handed, he abandoned a proposed rendezvous with his fleet in Mobile Bay and instead turned northwest, forever seeking the gold-rich civilization that furnished metal for the meagre trinkets seen along the way. In May 1541 De Soto spent a month ferrying his troops in rafts across the Mississippi, which he was the first to document as a major artery into the interior. He halted a little beyond where Little Rock stands, and wintered in Arkansas, clashing with fearsome Tula warriors. De Soto met his death, probably from malaria, in May 1542 on the banks of the Mississippi, but his deputy, Luis de Moscoso, continued the quest far to the west until beaten back by tribesmen near the Brazos River. The 300 survivors returned safely in September 1543, descending the Mississippi in rafts and following the coast to Mexico.

Right A watercolour painting from the period showing one of De Soto's men with two Native Americans.

Coronado Seeks the Phantom Cities of North America

An army marches upon an imaginary civilization.

1540-42

JUST A SINGLE GOLD-RICH CITY WOULD NORMALLY BE ENOUGH TO LURE an explorer into the unknown, but the thought of finding seven would seem too good to be true. In fact, legends of 'seven cities' had permeated apocryphal geography since the eighth century, when seven Catholic bishops fled the Muslim invasion of Portugal, crossed the Atlantic and settled on an island called Antilia, where each established a city for himself and his followers. Although transatlantic pioneers would search in vain for the elusive island, the fantasy lingered on, ingrained in the subconscious and corroborated by native accounts of an advanced civilization lurking deep in the North American interior. When in 1539 the itinerant Franciscan friar Marcos de Niza returned from Mexico's northern borderlands singing the praises of the 'seven cities of Cibola', 'rich in gold, turquoises and fleece-bearing cattle', the old legend sprang into life, and within months the viceroy, Antonio de Mendoza, had assembled a force of 1600 Spaniards and natives to lay siege to the place. With command delegated to the local governor, Francisco Vázquez de Coronado, and taking De Niza as a guide, the mighty army headed north from Compostela in February 1540.

Five months later, while subsidiary expeditions scouted the Colorado River, Coronado's main force reached the locality of Cibola, today's western New Mexico. He found only a meagre collection of Zuni pueblos; architecturally stimulating, but hardly the pavements of gold of De Niza's testament. The disgraced friar was packed off to a life of relative obscurity while Coronado's men scoured the countryside for anything that might restore credibility to what was turning into a disastrously futile exercise. But when all seemed lost, fresh hope emerged in the shape of yet another 'golden city'. Named Quivira, it lay far away to the northeast, so from April to July 1541 the invading army, breastplates, helmets and sweat, trudged wearily across vast plains and sandy deserts so featureless that only heaps of cow-dung marked the route. But Quivira, despite its pleasant pastoral setting and tranquil villages of thatched huts, was an even greater disappointment, and the total absence of gold suggested that Coronado had strayed even further from his dream. Dejectedly, the long-suffering army plodded back to New Mexico and camped there until the spring. Reduced to a third of its number largely by conflict with natives, it was back in Mexico by October 1542.

Right This map by Giacomo Gastaldi, dating from around 1553 and incorporating Coronado's discoveries, was the first to show substantial sites of human occupancy in what is now the United States.

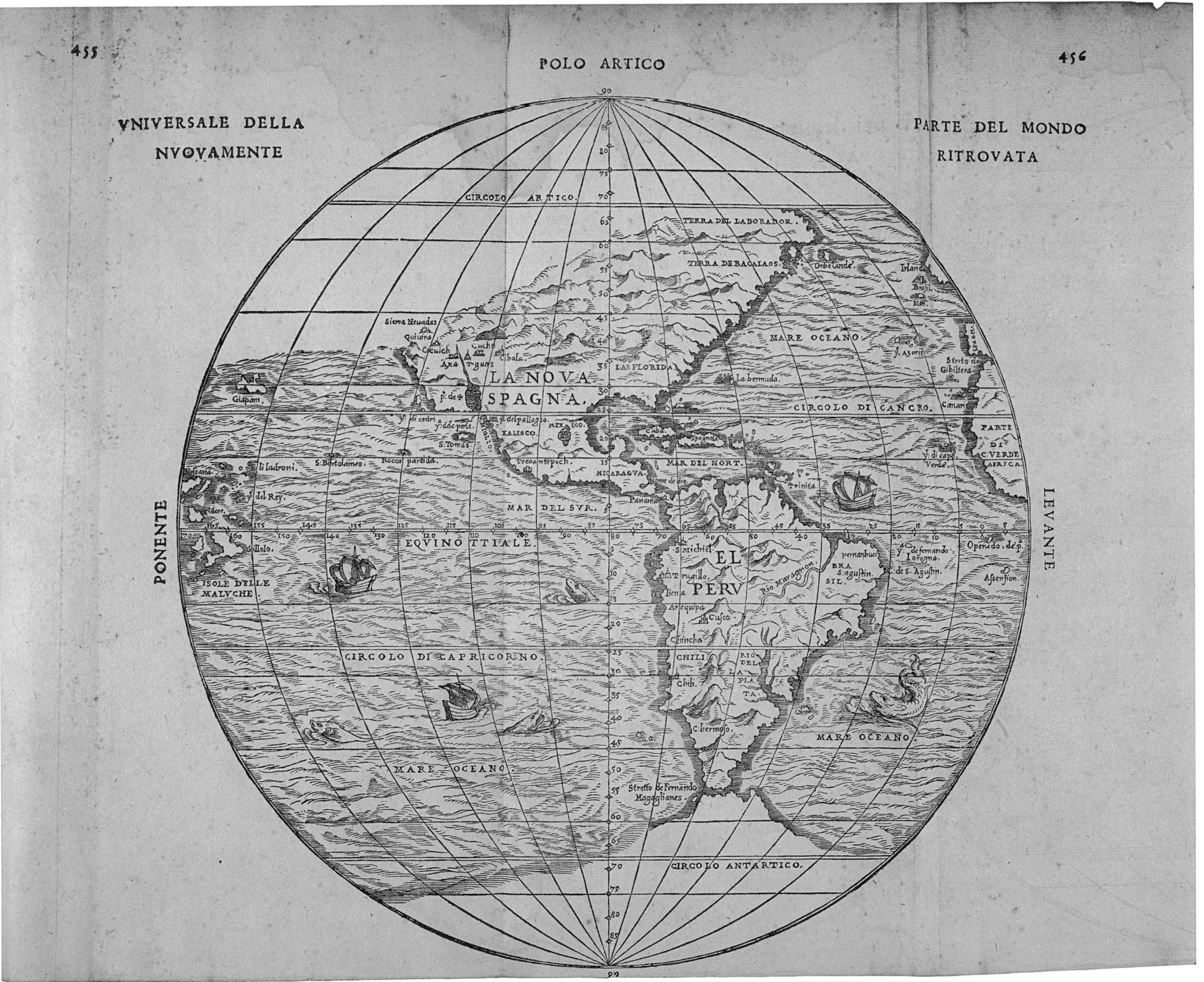
455
456
POLO ARTICO
VNIVERSALE DELLA
NVOVAMENTE
PARTE DEL MONDO
RITROVATA
PONENTE
LEVANTE
CIRCOLO ARTICO
TERRA DEL LABORADOR
TERRA DE BACALAOS
LA NOVA SPAGNA
LA FLORIDA
MARE OCEANO
CIRCOLO DI CANCRO
MAR DEL NORT
MAR DEL SVR
EQVINOTTIALE
EL PERV
CIRCOLO DI CAPRICORNO
MARE OCEANO
MARE OCEANO
CIRCOLO ANTARTICO
ISOLE DELLE MALYCHE
Stretto de Fernando Magaglianes

Francisco de Orellana Descends the River of the Amazons

The first traverse of the South American continent.

1541

Within a few years of Pizarro's conquest of the Andes a bevy of minor conquistadors, intoxicated by rumours of golden cities and mythical kingdoms, descended the bewildering maze of precipitous gorges that flanked the mountains' eastern slopes. Most returned empty-handed from dark impenetrable forests or came to grief at the hands of hostile Native Americans. But gold and silver were not all they sought. Equally precious were the fruits of the forest: spices that might equal those of the Indies, the monopoly of the rival Portuguese. Thus, when Pizarro heard of a 'land of cinnamon' somewhere in the jungles east of Quito he had no hesitation in equipping his brother Gonzalo with an expedition of 300 soldiers and 4000 Indian bearers. The journey began from Quito in February 1541, but on the nightmarish crossing of the cordillera, in snow that turned to weeks of incessant torrential rain, 140 Spanish and countless Indians either deserted or died of exposure. On reaching the Napo, a tributary of the Amazon, a rudimentary vessel was constructed to ferry the weakest downstream, its occupants reduced to eating toads and snakes and the leather of their boots.

In anticipation of an even greater river ahead, Gonzalo despatched fifty men under his second-in-command Francisco de Orellana to investigate. He would never see Orellana again. The swift current of the Napo prevented his return; Gonzalo trudged wearily back to Quito; and Orellana was swept into the main stream of the Amazon, eventually reaching a village of friendly natives. In May, having cobbled together a second and larger vessel, Orellana began his descent of the great river, en route hearing of a race of warrior women who lived deep in the forests and after whom the river would come to be known. Near the junction with the Tapajós the expedition observed its first tides, but the sea was still some 600 kilometres (370 miles) distant and it was not until late August that the party finally broke into the open waters of the Atlantic. The vessels rigged with vines, with blankets for sails, the expedition traced the coast to the safety of the Spanish outpost on the island of Cubagua. Back home, Orellana held the royal court spellbound with tales and exaggerations of his adventures, sufficient to gain assent for an expedition to colonize the river for Spain. His party decimated by disease and Indian hostility, he died of sickness and grief on the river that had immortalized his name.

Right A map of South America by Diogo Homem, 1588, showing Orellana's discoveries on an excessively meandering Amazon.

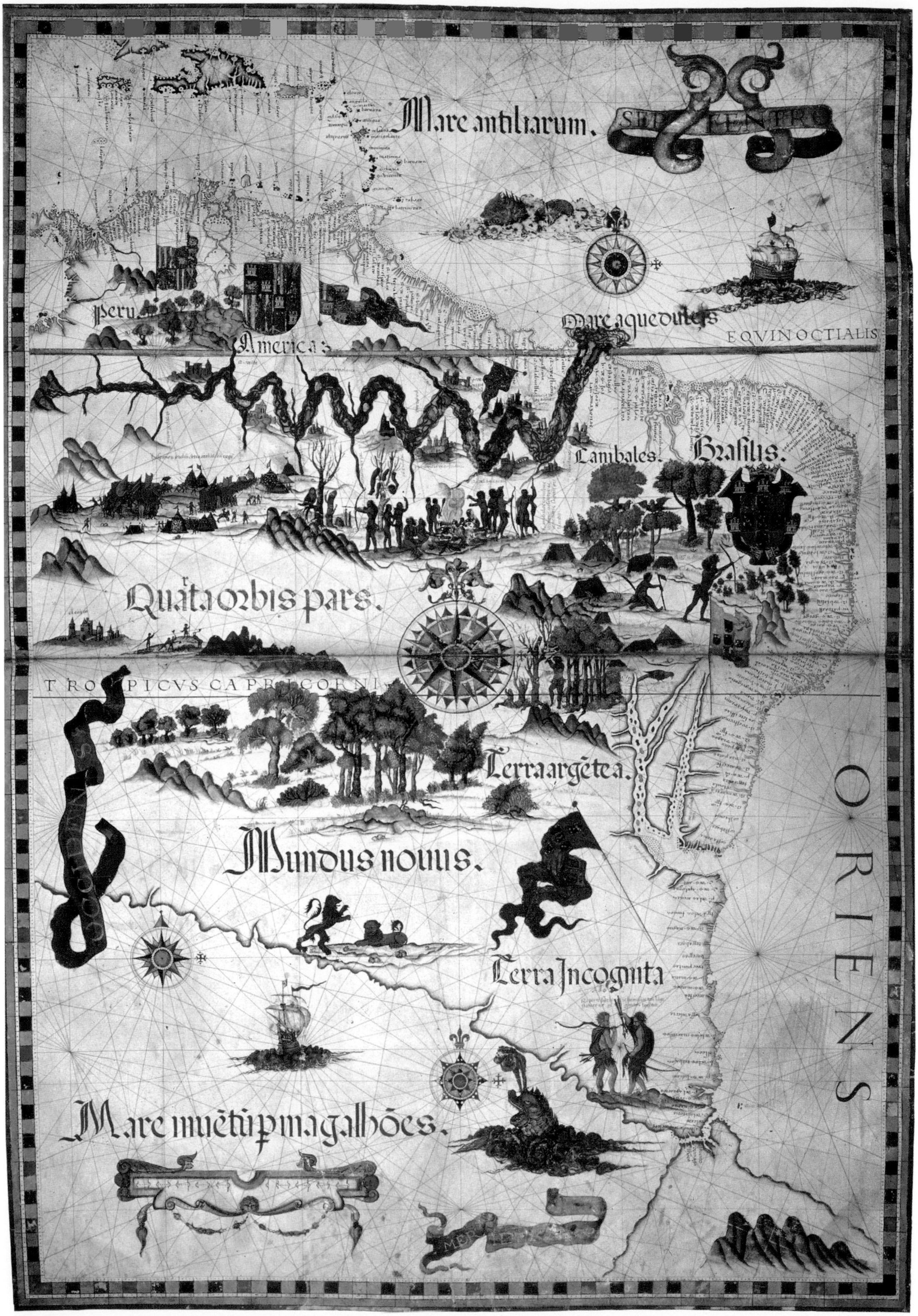

Mare antiliarum.

SEPTENTRIO

Peru

America

Mare aquedulcis

EQVINOCTIALIS

Cambales.

Brasilus.

Quarta orbis pars.

TROPICVS CAPRICORNI

Terra argẽtea.

Mundus nouus.

ORIENS

Terra Incognita

Mare inuẽtu p magalhões.

Francisco Xavier and the Christian Mission in Japan

To go wherever 'His Holiness will command us for the good of souls'.

1541–52

WHILE IBERIAN NAVIGATORS OFTEN TOOK WITH THEM A PRIEST to minister to the sailors and hopefully pick up a few converts along the way, the major Christian orders, seeing it as their apostolic duty to proselytize in 'heathen' lands, despatched independent bands of missionaries who would make important discoveries in their own right. Foremost among such orders was the Society of Jesus which, founded by Ignatius Loyola in 1539–40 at the height of the overseas surge, was exceptional in having missionary activity to 'New Worlds' built into its constitution. The Jesuits lost no time in the matter, and by April 1541 one of their founding fathers, Francisco Xavier, was already on his way to Portuguese India. Wintering in Mozambique, Xavier arrived to spend his first few months ministering to Christians in Goa. After a further two years around the southern tip of India, where he is alleged to have made 30,000 converts, Xavier removed in 1545 to Malacca where, as in Goa, he laboured against immorality and corruption amongst the incumbent Portuguese. The next year he pressed on to the Moluccas, where some 10,000 Christian converts, the result of an earlier Franciscan enterprise, lay scattered amongst the islands.

Returning to Malacca in 1547, Xavier came across a Japanese fugitive named Yajiro who had sought refuge on a Portuguese ship, become a Christian, and whose conversation assured Xavier that Japan might become a lucrative field of missionary endeavour. Collecting a small group of assistants from Goa, Xavier boarded at Malacca a small Chinese pirate junk, which landed him at Kagoshima in Kyushu in August 1549. Cheered by initial successes, Xavier and his party headed for Kyoto, seeking imperial consent to propagate Christianity throughout the entire realm. It was a tedious and wasted journey; they found the emperor mired in political chaos with scant control over his subjects. Leaving his subordinates to further the work of the mission, Xavier returned to Goa, then in 1552 joined a Portuguese embassy to China, his intent being to impress the emperor and hence capitalize on the influence exerted by Chinese culture on Japan. Sadly, the embassy fell apart and Xavier died of fever on the island of Sancian (Shangchuan) while waiting to be smuggled to the mainland. Despite frequent persecutions, the Japanese mission, centred on Nagasaki, flourished until the major expulsions of 1614, then lingered on for several decades more, at its peak claiming around 300,000 converts.

Right An early seventeenth-century screen showing Portuguese traders doing business at a Japanese coastal village.

Anthony Jenkinson on the Trade Routes of Central Asia

The unsung pioneer of English overland exploration.

1555-60

By the early sixteenth century the aspirations of westward-facing European nations, for whom the riches of China were but a direct although somewhat protracted voyage away, had been dealt an unexpected blow by the troublesome discovery of an uninspiring landmass, North America, that stood in the way. For the English, yet to emerge on the world stage but seeking a wider outlet for their woollen goods, the discovery was particularly disheartening and would, by conjecture that the path east must be shorter and easier near the pole, launch them into years of fruitless adventure in high latitudes. In 1553, working on the assumption, with the Greeks, that Asia was encircled by ocean, Richard Chancellor and Hugh Willoughby took three ships in pursuit of a Northeast Passage. Willoughby froze to death in the attempt, but Chancellor fortuitously arrived by sledge in Moscow to enter negotiations with Ivan the Terrible. Trading privileges in hand, Chancellor returned to England and with other interested parties established the Muscovy Company, the world's first joint stock company, for trade with Russia and anywhere further east. For several decades English merchants fanned out across the country, descending the Volga, reaching Persia via the Caspian Sea and returning to inflate the pages of Richard Hakluyt's *Principal Navigations* with vastly understated reports of extraordinary journeys.

While others vainly persisted in their assault on the northern sea route, culminating in the 1580 voyage of Arthur Pet and Charles Jackman to the ice-bound Kara Sea, most company merchants focused their attention on more optimistic overland ventures. In April 1558, Anthony Jenkinson, a merchant widely travelled in the Near East, set out from Moscow with two colleagues to pioneer a land route to China. Descending the Volga through country recently freed from Mongol domination, and joining some local merchants at Astrakhan, he crossed the northern arm of the Caspian and thence proceeded overland to Urgenj (Urganch) in what is now Uzbekistan. By December the party had reached Bokhara, where it stayed four months, entertained by the king and trading its goods. Although haunted by merchants from far afield, the city was a disappointment to Jenkinson. Wars raging to the east obstructed trade with China, and with no further progress in sight the Englishmen dejectedly retraced their route to Moscow. Nevertheless, Jenkinson's report filled a critical blank in the map of Central Asia: a definite no-go region where few Europeans would venture for almost three centuries.

Right A detail from a map by Abraham Ortelius, 1598, showing the results of Jenkinson's reconnaissance of Central Asia.

elapsis.
CAS
SAC
KI
A
GAIA.
TA
R
I.
TVRK
A Mangusla Shayfuram vsq; 20. dierum iter habent, sine vllis sedibus, cum summa aque penuria A Shayfura vsq; Bogar, par itineris interuallum latrocinijs infestum
Kirgessi gens cateruatim degit, id est in hordis. habetq; ritum huiusmodi. cum re diuinam ipsoru sacerdos peragit, sanguinem, lac, & fimu iumentorum accipit, ac terre miscet, inq; vas quoddam infundit, eoq; arborem scandit, atq; concione habita, in populum spargit, atq; hec aspersio pro Deo habetur & colitur. Cum quis diem inter illos obit, loco sepulture arboribus suspendut.
Sur fl.
BO
Amow fl.
SHA
MAR
GHAN.
TASKENT.
Taskent
Ardock fl.
Vrgeme
Shayfure
GH
Kyrmina
AR.
Cante
Cosin
Ougus fl.
Ghudowa
Acsow
KIR
Mare
Boghar vrbs sanctissima
Corasan parua, à Rege Persico adiuuantibus Tartaris 1558. expugnata fuit.
Carakol
Shamarcandia olim totius Tartarie metropolis fuit, at nunc ruinis deformis iacet, vna cum multis antiquitatis vestigijs. Hic conditus est Tamerlanes ille, qui olim Turcaru Imperatore Bayasitē captum aureis catenis vinctum, circumtulit. Incole mahumetani sunt.
Andeghen
Meshent.
Kirshij
GES.
Corasam magna
MHOGOL
SIA.
80 560 640 720 800
Balgh
Cascara, hinc triginta dierum itinere ori

Álvaro de Mendaña Discovers the Isles of Solomon

Imaginary lands in the South Pacific.

1567–95

By the late sixteenth century Spanish ships were becoming an increasingly common sight in the North Pacific, the sailor-monk Andrés de Urdaneta having pioneered the west to east crossing in 1565. But of the South Sea below the equator almost nothing was known. An immense unseen void stretching from the coast of South America to the shipping lanes of the Indian Ocean, it became a convenient resting place for lands of myth and fable: the legendary Incan 'Isles of Gold'; the curiously persistent but strictly hypothetical continent of Terra Australis; the lands of the Amazons; even the wildly misplaced site of King Solomon's mines. So certain were 'men well versed in mathematics' of a 'great unknown southern continent', its lost souls eager for godly enlightenment, its riches ripe for the picking by a future generation of conquistadors, that in 1567 the viceroy of Peru ordered an expedition to locate this imaginary land. Sidelining others who sought prestige from the new discovery, he placed it all in the hands of his nephew, the visionary Galician seaman Álvaro de Mendaña.

Mendaña sailed from Callao in November 1567 with two ships and 150 men, but by mid-January it was obvious that the men of mathematics had been mistaken, and that no elusive continent or fabled islands awaited discovery. Short of drinking water, adrift in an endless sea with little notion of precisely where he was, Mendaña directed the expedition towards New Guinea, another land for which extravagant claims had been made. This too he failed to find, instead stumbling upon an archipelago where in desperation he sought the riches and mineral resources that would have restored face to the luckless enterprise. Although finding none, he alluringly christened the archipelago the 'Isles of Solomon', thereby associating the distant mines of Ophir with the 'Isles of Gold'. The fearful homeward passage, which landed the near derelict ships on the coast of California, did little to deflect Mendaña from his mission, but it would be twenty-five years before he could try again. In 1595 he sailed with four ships and 600 colonists and soldiers, only to lose himself in the vastness of the Pacific and eventually make landfall on the island of Santa Cruz, some way short of his destination. Afflicted by disease and hostile natives, the colonists separated into warring factions. Mendaña died of malaria, but his formidable wife rallied the survivors and with the help of the pilot Pedro Fernández de Quirós led them to the Philippines.

Right A map drawn by Abraham Ortelius in 1589, which incorporates the earliest discoveries by navigators in the Pacific Ocean.

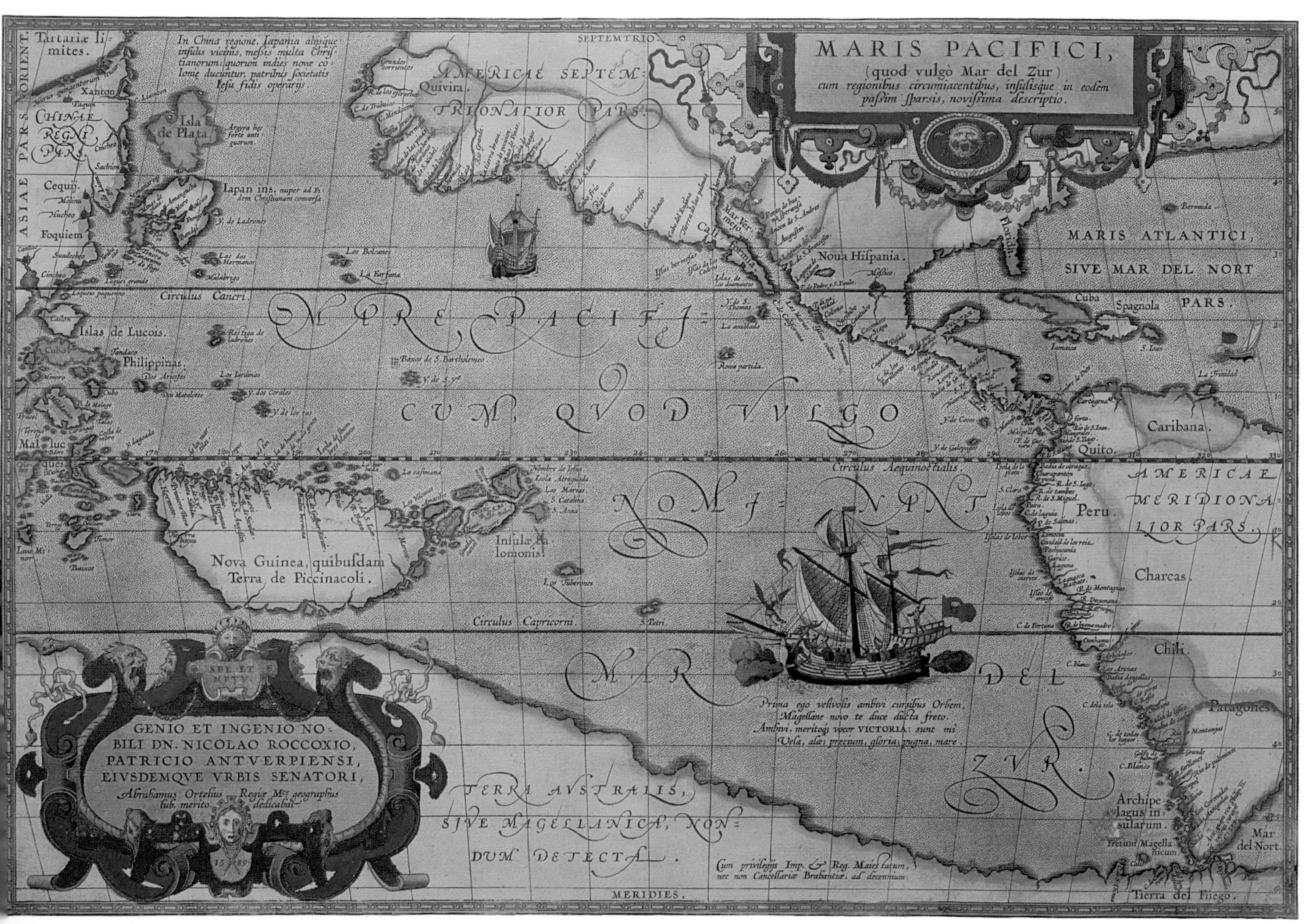
MARIS PACIFICI,
(quod vulgò Mar del Zur)
cum regionibus circumiacentibus, insulisque in eodem passim sparsis, novissima descriptio.
MARE PACIFICUM, QUOD VULGO NOMINANT MAR DEL ZUR.
MARIS ATLANTICI, SIVE MAR DEL NORT PARS.
AMERICAE SEPTEMTRIONALIOR PARS.
AMERICAE MERIDIONALIOR PARS.
TERRA AUSTRALIS, SIVE MAGELLANICA, NONDUM DETECTA.
Nova Guinea, quibusdam Terra de Piccinacoli.
GENIO ET INGENIO NOBILI DN. NICOLAO ROCCOXIO, PATRICIO ANTVERPIENSI, EIUSDEMQUE URBIS SENATORI,
Abrahamus Ortelius Regiæ Mtis geographus lub. merito dedicabat.
Prima ego velivolis ambivi cursibus Orbem, Magellane novo te duce ducta freto. Ambivi, meritoq; vocor VICTORIA: sunt mi Vela, alæ; precium, gloria; pugna, mare.
Circulus Cancri
Circulus Aequinoctialis
Circulus Capricorni
SEPTEMTRIO.
MERIDIES.

Francis Drake Encompasses the Globe

A renegade Englishman intimidates the Iberian world.

1577-80

MAGELLAN'S VENTURE HAD CIRCUMNAVIGATED THE PLANET, but had done so at terrible cost. Of the 250 men that set out, only eighteen struggled to bring the one surviving vessel back to Spain. The crew had faced the most horrific tribulations in the Pacific, and their admiral had died in the Indies. So troublesome was the enterprise that the principal chronicler declared that men would never make such a voyage again. Subsequent attempts to use the Strait of Magellan as a gateway to the Pacific found conditions far worse than Magellan and recommended abandonment of the route. In the event, Portuguese voyages to the East Indies continued to adhere to the well-tried Indian Ocean route, while the Spanish, who had descended on the Philippines in the 1560s, launched their fleets from the Pacific ports of Mexico. The second circumnavigation would not be realized for another sixty years and then not by an Iberian but by a solitary English adventurer.

In 1573 Francis Drake, on his first buccaneering excursion to Central America, its object to relieve the Spanish of gold misappropriated from the Incas, had crossed the isthmus of Panama and prayed aloud that God would spare him to sail just once an English ship upon the glistening waters of the Pacific. With just a handful of men he had terrorized Central America and he could do it again. With a permanent foothold on the isthmus he would achieve naval supremacy on the ocean beyond and make his queen undisputed mistress of the treasures of Mexico and Peru, the loss of which would destroy Spain. Drake left Plymouth in December 1577 with five vessels, but by the time he issued from Magellan's Strait only one vessel, the *Golden Hind*, survived, the others scuttled or returned home. Up and down the South American coast, fearful of a seaborne offensive by a mighty English armada, the unsuspecting Spaniards were placed on red alert while Drake pursued their treasure-laden galleons. From the coast of California, where he contemplated an English colony called New Albion, and having failed to locate the widely conjectured easterly passage into the Atlantic, Drake had no alternative but to strike across the Pacific. Unlike Magellan's, his crossing was relatively uneventful, and after a whistle-stop tour of the Spice Islands he brought the *Golden Hind* back to Plymouth in September 1580, its holds bursting with booty valued at half a million pounds.

Right A Spanish treasure ship is plundered by Drake in the Pacific.

Caca Fogo.
Caca Plata.

Henry Hudson and the Quest for the Northwest Passage

The birth of a typically English obsession.

1577-1610

Elizabethan England, envious of the achievements of Spain and Portugal, was ideally situated and equipped for the launch of a seaborne empire, but despite pretentions to rights of possession in North America it failed to capitalize on the work of its pioneers. Instead it would plough its resources into a desperate search for a northern passage to Asia, sending its misguided mariners into the ice-bound culs-de-sac of the Arctic. Given the rudimentary nature of the ships involved, these voyages were remarkable by any standards, as were their navigators. Some verged on the surreal, like those of Martin Frobisher, who in 1577-78 brought back from Baffin Island hundreds of tons of a supposedly gold-bearing 'black earth', only to find it worthless. In 1587 John Davis ventured up Greenland's west coast to 72°N, declaring 'the sea all open to the west', and in 1616 Robert Bylot reached 78°N and returned with sightings unconfirmed for another 300 years. With him was a genius of navigation, William Baffin, whose extraordinary talent for calculating latitude, even accounting for atmospheric refraction, was 150 years ahead of its time. But the most determined of all Arctic navigators was Henry Hudson.

Hudson's name first comes to light in 1607 when, for the Muscovy Company, he attempted to reach Asia by sailing directly across the North Pole. The understanding was that the Arctic ice occupied only a narrow belt, beyond which the midnight sun kept the ocean warm and clear. His voyage proved otherwise, but it did manage to round the top of Spitsbergen and set a latitude record of 80°N. A second attempt in 1608 landed Hudson on the coast of Novaya Zemlya, and on a third, this time for the Dutch East India Company, he was halted by ice in the Barents Sea. Undeterred, he set course for Labrador and a passage to the northwest, but damage to his ship forced him south, eventually into New York Harbour and 250 kilometres (150 miles) up the Hudson River, which he hoped would take him to the Pacific. For claiming the region for the Dutch he was arrested in London but allowed to redeem himself by taking the next voyage at English behest. This plunged him into the depths of Hudson Bay, where a miserable winter was spent locked in the ice. His men, ravaged by scurvy, starvation and frostbite, mutinied, cast Hudson adrift and eventually limped back across the Atlantic. Poor old Hudson was never seen again.

Right This map of Svalbard by Samuel Purchas, 1625, is largely based on Hudson's first voyage (1607) and incorporates the sightings of English whaling and walrus-hunting expeditions. The main island of Spitsbergen has, by nature of its shape, been misidentified as Greenland.

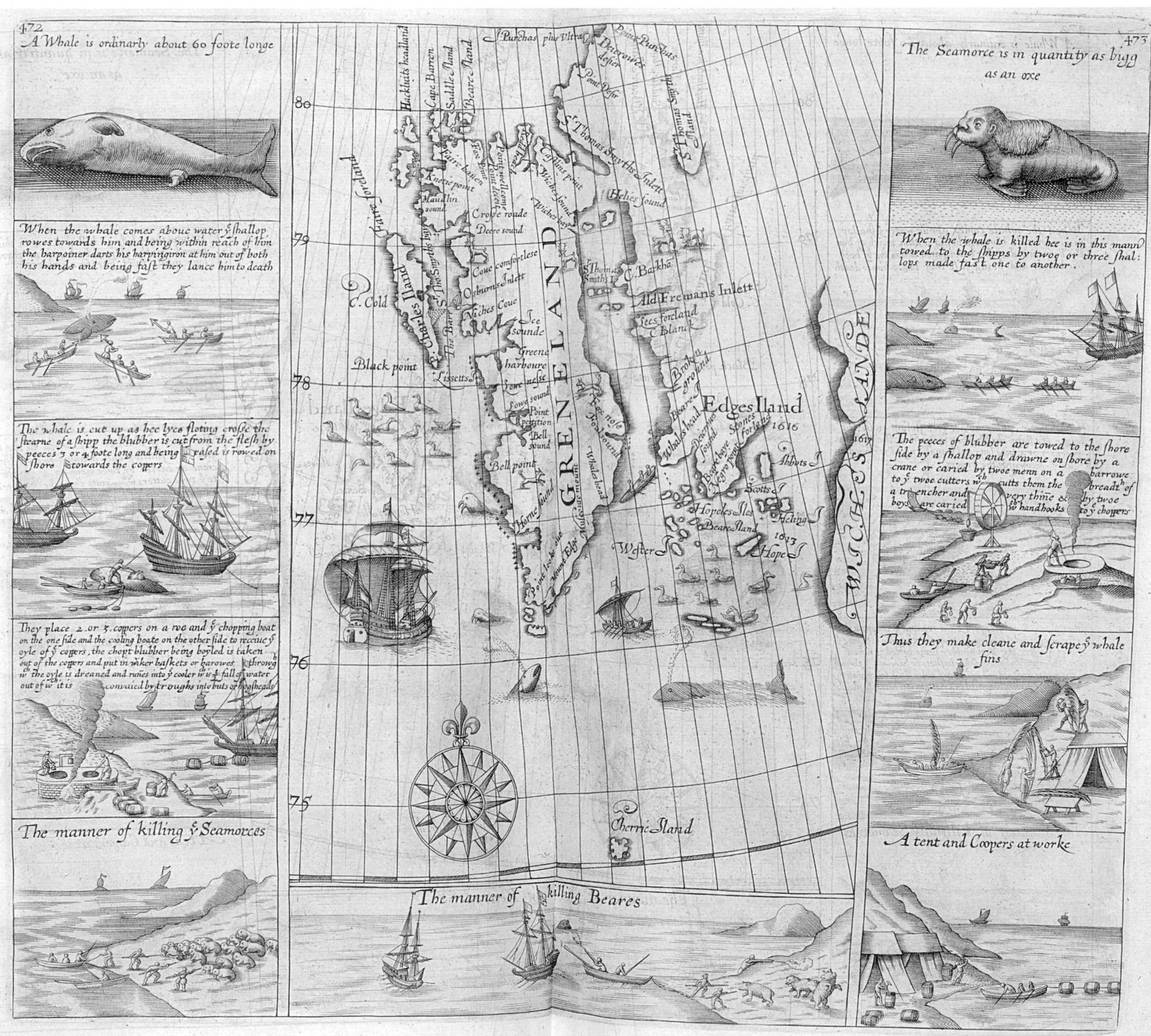
472
A Whale is ordinarly about 60 foote longe
When the whale comes aboue water ÿ shallop rowes towards him and being within reach of him the harpoiner darts his harpingiron at him out of both his hands and being fast they lance him to death
The whale is cut up as hee lyes floting crosse the stearne of a shipp the blubber is cut from the flesh by peeces 3 or 4 foote long and being raised is rowed on shore towards the coppers
The manner of killing ÿ Seamorces
473
The Seamorce is in quantity as bigg as an oxe
When the whale is killed hee is in this mann towed to the shipps by twoe or three shal: lops made fast one to another.
Thus they make cleane and scrape ÿ whale fins
A tent and Coopers at worke
The manner of killing Beares
GRENELAND
Edges Iland
Black point
C. Cold
Cherrie Iland
Hopeles Iles
Beare Iland
Abbots I
Wester I
Hope I
Fairforland
Hacklutts headland
Cape Barren
Saddle Iland
Beare Iland
Purchas plus Vltra
St Thomas Smyths Inlett
Helies sound
Crosse roade
Deere sound
Coue comfortlese
Ice sounde
Greene harbour
Bell point
Horne sound
C. Barkham
Ald. Fremans Inlett
Brok ground
Whales head
1616
1617
1613
75
76
77
78
79
80

1580–1650

The 'Conquistadors' of Siberia

The most prolific slaughter of native wildlife in history.

THE FROZEN WASTES, MARSHES AND FORESTS OF SIBERIA, reaching endlessly with no promise of mineral riches or lost civilizations, offered little incentive to the average European explorer. Despite its vast river systems, navigable by boat in summer and sledge in winter, and forming an almost unbroken chain from the Urals to the Pacific, Siberia had no easily accessible coastline, and its landward approaches lay too remote for the casual visitor. Exploration would necessarily evolve from the interior outwards and would fall to those already on the doorstep, those that could see that riches lay not in gold but in fur.

The pioneers were Cossacks, multi-ethnic free frontiersmen with a crusading zeal reminiscent of the Spanish conquistadors. Allegiant to Mother Russia when it suited them, but more often fired by a passion for personal gain, they would reach the Pacific in a mere sixty years. In 1581–82, backed by the wealthy Stroganov family, the Cossack Yermak crossed the Urals and inflicted a crushing defeat on Kuchum, ruler of Sibir, the last outpost of a fragmented Mongol empire. The way ahead now clear, fur traders surged into regions teeming with wildlife, exacting tribute from the indigenous peoples and fuelling the Russian advance across Asia. From Tobol'sk they spread northward down the Ob, then east to the Yenisey, marking their progress with *ostrogs*, or fortified trading posts. Vasiliy Bugor reached the Lena in 1628, and in 1632 Petr Beketov founded the *ostrog* Yakutsk. Seven years later the first Cossacks reached the Sea of Okhotsk.

In 1643–44 Vasiliy Poyarkov descended on the rich agricultural valley of the Amur, home of the Daur people, distant vassals of the emperor of China. In one of the bloodiest and most gruesome campaigns on record, Poyarkov tricked and tortured his way to the mouth of the river, at one time feeding his men on the corpses of murdered Daur. His successor, Yerofey Khabarov, completed the region's brutal subjugation, opening the Amur to a rabble of adventurers until China reasserted its claim. In the far north, fur traders reached the Lena delta in 1630 and began working their way east along the Arctic coast. Then in 1648 Semyon Dezhnev and Fedot Alekseev rounded the Chukchi Peninsula and entered the Pacific. Dezhnev's report, with its geographically critical recognition of a seaway separating Asia from America, languished anonymously in the Yakutsk archives until its discovery eighty-seven years later.

Right An imaginative eighteenth-century depiction of Yermak, the conqueror of Siberia.

Matteo Ricci Brings the World to China

A pioneer of East-West cultural relations.

1582-1610

CHINA'S STATE-SPONSORED DISCOVERY OF THE OUTSIDE WORLD had come to an abrupt halt with the death of Emperor Yongle in 1424, and although China remained a major trading nation its merchants saw little point in pursuing discoveries in parts of the world that offered nothing China did not have already. In the late fifteenth century Chinese maps filled almost the entire world with the fifteen imperial provinces, everywhere else being relegated to a collection of diminutive islands in a peripheral sea. But, as had happened several times in the past, the outside world would once again be brought to China. For several decades European missionaries, Jesuits and others, had hammered at the door, but none had penetrated beyond Macau and Canton (Guangzhou). However, in 1582 Matteo Ricci, an Italian Jesuit who had spent four years in Goa, arrived in Macau and over the next twenty years would make his way steadily inland, establishing himself first at Zhaoqing, to the west of Canton, then from 1595 at Nanchang, the capital of Jiangxi. Summoned by Emperor Wanli, he entered Beijing in 1601 and remained there the last nine years of his life.

Missionary work in China was an intensely diplomatic affair. Ricci could never overtly announce his intention to preach religion, which would have offended Chinese pride, the country having nothing to learn from foreigners. Instead he appealed to the curiosity of his audience by making the Chinese feel that he had something new and interesting to teach, introducing European novelties such as clocks and sundials, mathematical and astronomical devices, oil paintings and prints, and books magnificently printed and bound. Only when fascination had been aroused by such a process would he gently guide it towards his ulterior goal, subtly placing in a conspicuous position a painting of the Madonna and child. But, in Ricci's opinion, 'the most useful work that was done to dispose China to give credence to the things of our holy Faith' was the map of the world he drew in 1584 at Zhaoqing, which for the first time compelled the Chinese to confront the relatively diminutive extent of their empire compared with the vastness of the 'barbarian' world beyond its borders. For more than a century Jesuit scientists were welcomed into China, introducing astronomical and geodesic skills that, between 1709 and 1718, at the invitation of Emperor Kangxi, culminated in an extraordinarily detailed map of the entire Chinese empire.

Right Matteo Ricci's map of China, 1625.

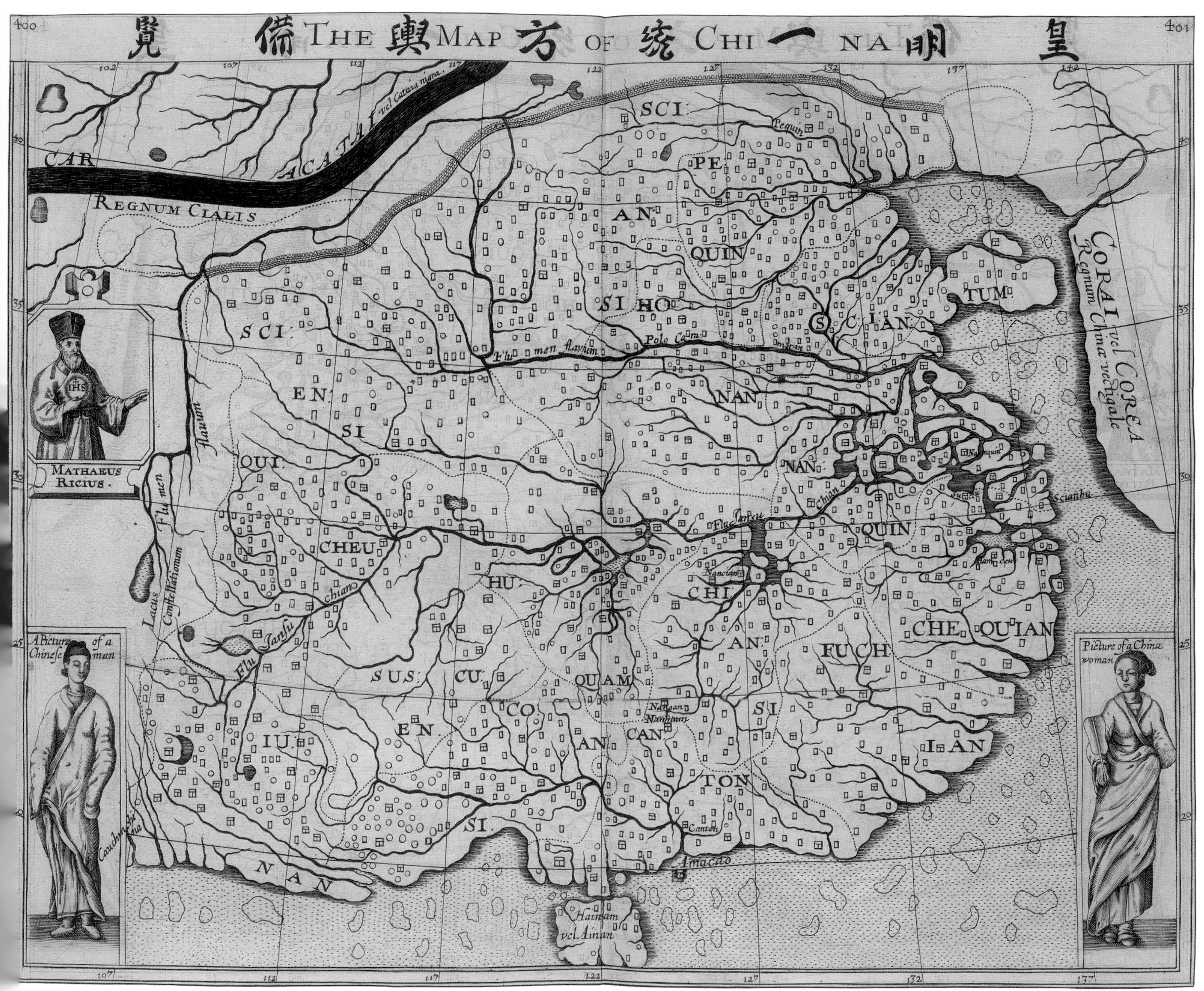
THE MAP OF CHINA
覽 備 輿 方 統 一 明 皇
A Picture of a Chinese man
Picture of a China woman
MATHAEUS RICIUS.
REGNUM CIALIS
CORAI vel COREA Regnum Chinæ vectigale
Flumen flavum
Lacus
Haimam vel Ainan
Amacao
Canton
Pequin

Ralph Fitch and English Reconnaissance in Asia

A neglected pioneer of the British imperialism.

1583–91

Ralph Fitch barely figures in the hierarchy of great explorers, but in Elizabethan England he was a most celebrated and influential merchant traveller. Queen Elizabeth personally furnished him with letters of introduction to the emperors of China and Mogul India; and his ship, the *Tyger*, is named by one of the witches in Shakespeare's *Macbeth*. Although not the first Englishman to see India, an accolade credited to the Wiltshire-born Jesuit Thomas Stephens; nor the first to approach the Indies, Drake and Cavendish having hurried through on their circumnavigations; Fitch was the first to venture beyond the coastal ports and return with detailed reports of the inland peoples and commerce of India, Bengal, Burma, Siam and Malaya. His intelligence was crucial to the early successes of the English East India Company, and it is sometimes said that without Fitch there would have been no British empire in Asia.

In 1581 some London businessmen established the Levant Company, its purpose being to foster direct commercial links with the East and so end the monopoly over the spice trade enjoyed by Spain, Portugal and Venice. Early clandestine explorations proved optimistic, John Newbery having reached Basra by the desert route, then Hormuz by sea, returning to London in 1582. But the next phase would necessarily entail an examination of trade and conditions in India and beyond: a perilous venture, doomed to failure should the Portuguese get wind of it. Under Newbery's leadership, Fitch and three others sailed for Lebanon in February 1583 and reached Basra, where the first of the party elected to stay behind. At Hormuz the travellers were apprehended by the Portuguese, shipped to Goa and released only through the machinations of Thomas Stephens. Fitch, Newbery and William Leedes then proceeded inland to Fatehpur Sikri, Akbar's newly constructed capital, in July 1585. While Leedes settled in the capital, and Newbery started overland for home, never to be heard of again, Fitch departed on his solitary journey eastward. Via Benares, Bengal and Chittagong he arrived at Pegu, the Burmese capital, in December 1586. After a brief excursion to Chiang Mai in modern Thailand he followed the coast southward to become the first Englishman to enter Portuguese-dominated Malacca. Retracing his route through Pegu, Bengal and Ceylon, he sailed from Quilon to Basra, and in Lebanon boarded a ship for England. Fitch returned to London in April 1591, long given up for dead during an absence of eight years.

Right A detail from Joan Blaeu's map of the Mogul empire, 1638, showing the valley of the Indus and the routes to Delhi and Lahore, based on the reports of European ambassadors and merchants.

REGNI
PERSICI
PARS.
CIRCAM
Desertum Lut.
Rachagi
Tebesmisma
Calatia
Camultan
Chibinan
Daragsi
Chimecra
Guadel
I. Sarnaque
Pasir
Macran
Sindu
Bilguri
Gest
Sind
Ziro
Tatta
Tata
Diul
Gjagat
Indus fluvius
Soret
Ninoui
Cacha
Burdiano
Nagar Parker
Nuraquimire
Gundaiaw
Saruna
Luckar
Buckar
Roroo
R. Indus
Multan
Pesinga
Abdun
Coastu
Duruos
Secota
Duckee
Chatzan
R. Lacca
Petto
Lahor
Can Channas
Fetipore
Hoge Moiede
Chiurmul
Sultanpore
Nicondar
Ienba
Pulloceque
GAN
IND
TA
Bando
Ieselmeere
Gislemere
Senavora
Moulto
Chumnao
Toovry
Pucker
Lauara
Bassonpie
Richmal
Mandill
Asmere
Pipera
Iongesgong
Sestrange
Canderupe
R. Padder
Ieloure
Ranas
Mudre
Rudopore
Bilmal
Sariandgo
Bollodo
Carrya
Chitor
MALVA
GUZURATTE,
S. Volo
nunc
CAMBAYA
Resbutos
Reino dos Collys
Armadabad
Mambadabad
Cambaya
Enseada de Cambaya
Iaquete
R. Bahador
Cotiana
Grinal
Mangalor
Choruer
Patan
Nagacerÿ
Nouanagaer
Castellete
Goga
Gundim
Talaia
Dio
Corinar
Sotopapam
I. des Mores
Champanel
Baroche
Surate
Daman
Bassain
Agacim
Bacaim
Tana
Bombaira
I. dos Vacas
DECAN
Dolmbad
Andanagur
Brampore
Chand
Pala
Pale
Narsir
Golcon
MARE
ARABICUM
Nob^mo Spectat^mo viro
D. IOHANNI HUYDEKOPER,
Equiti, Domino in Marsenveen, Neerdyck
etc. Urbis Amsterdamensis Senatori
et Scabino, nec non Concilii Socie-
tatis Indicæ Assessori, Tabulam
hanc D.D. Joh. et Corn. Blaeu.
98
100
102
104
106
108
110

Walter Ralegh's Discovery of Guiana

A gallant knight in search of El Dorado.

1595–1617

EL DORADO, THE GOLD-RICH CITY SOUGHT OBSESSIVELY by generations of adventurers, was never a place at all. First reported in Ecuador in 1535, its name recalled an ancient ceremony practised in the Muisca highlands of Colombia; a coronation by which the heir to the chiefdom would be massaged with gum, coated in gold dust, placed on a raft and floated to the centre of a great lake. To placate the demon of the lake the gilded man, *el dorado*, would consign to the depths a vast cache of gold and emeralds. The custom had vanished shortly before the Spanish arrived, but persistent rumours fired the aspirations of the conquistadors, to whom El Dorado became a kingdom, a Utopian dream that offered its discoverer riches beyond his wildest imaginations. Some sought it in the high Andean cordilleras, the *llanos* of Venezuela, the labyrinthine depths of Amazonia; but to others it was the last resting place of the treasure of the Inca, secreted during a post-colonial diaspora in a land called Guiana, erroneously located a little beyond Peru's eastern borderlands.

It was the last of these suppositions that in 1595 brought the gallant knight, Sir Walter Ralegh, to South America, to where Antonio de Berrío, the celebrated pioneer on the Orinoco, had pinpointed El Dorado on the headwaters of the Río Caroní, deep in the Guiana highlands. Ralegh's El Dorado was the legendary Manoa, overlooking the mighty lake Parima, beyond which lay the domain of the Amazons. The city was a myth, a misunderstanding of Manaos, a gold-trading tribe on the Rio Negro, while Parima was little more than a seasonal flood plain in the Guianan savannahs. After losing himself in the Orinoco delta, Ralegh halted at the mouth of the Caroní before sailing empty-handed for home. But his belief in the richness of Guiana never faltered, and it was this that secured his release from imprisonment in the Tower after serving thirteen years on trumped-up charges of conspiracy against King James. Promising James the 'mountain of gold' he had allegedly seen on the previous voyage, Ralegh embarked in 1617 with some twenty ships. For Ralegh the enterprise turned into a Shakespearean tragedy. His son was killed in an unauthorized attack on a Spanish outpost, and Lawrence Keymis, Ralegh's devoted captain, shot himself in despair for his part in the action. Broken in both health and spirit, Ralegh returned to England to face execution.

Right Ralegh's map of northern South America, orientated with south at the top, showing the lake of Manoa wedged between the Orinoco and the Amazon.

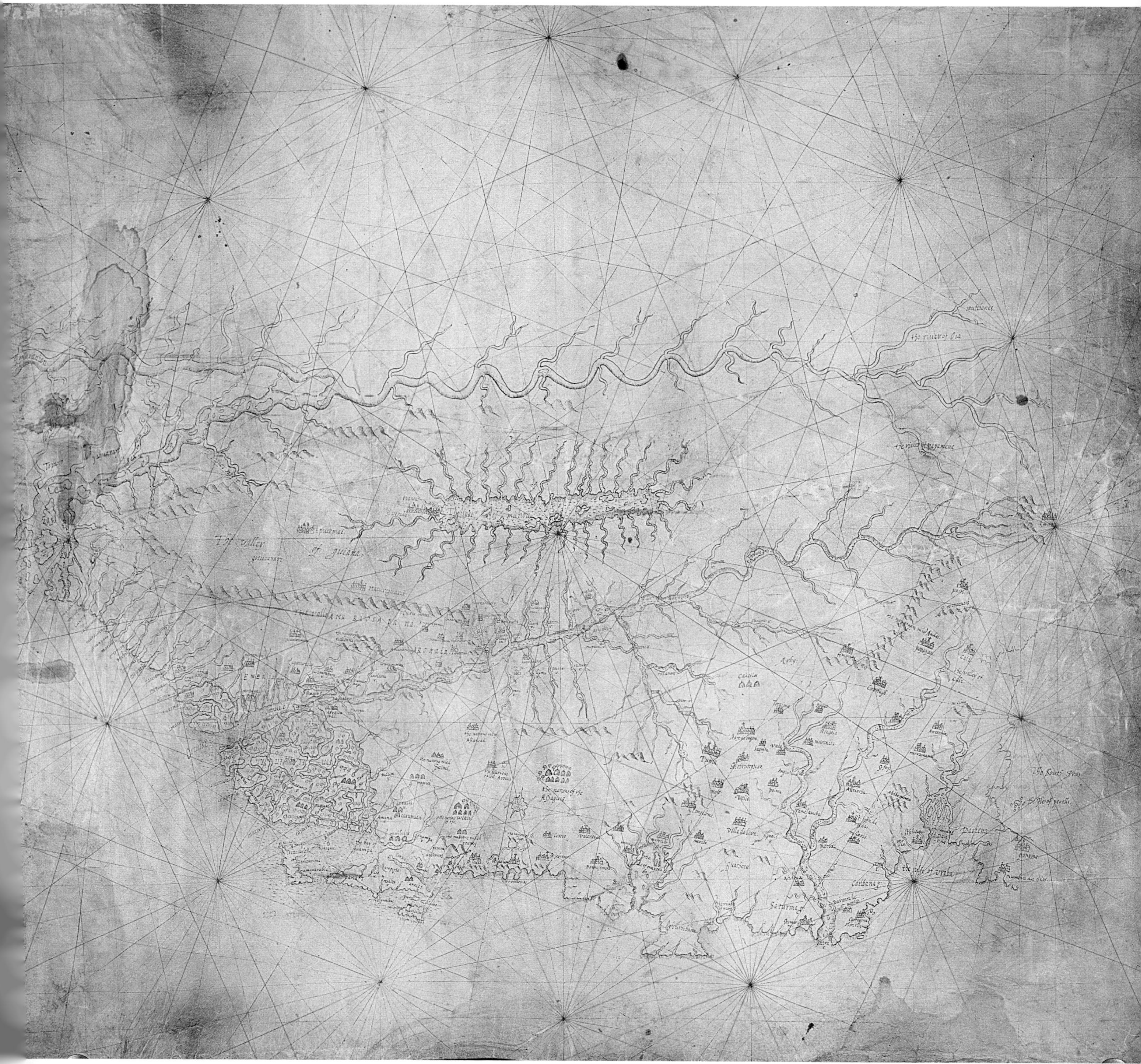

Willem Barents Confronts the Arctic Winter

In pursuit of the Northeast Passage.

1596-97

ALTHOUGH THE QUEST FOR THE NORTH POLE would in later years become an end in itself, sixteenth-century Arctic navigators had little interest in such frivolous and unproductive pursuits, or in displays of heroism that brought no financial reward or profitable return for their investors. Their targets were the riches of the Orient, which in high latitudes were just a stone's throw away through the open waters that, according to the most eminent philosophers, bathed the coast of Asia from Lapland to China. The route beckoned invitingly the principal trading nations of northern Europe, England and the Netherlands, whose maritime aspect was northerly and far removed from the shipping lanes of Spanish and Portuguese rivals. With not the vaguest notion of what really lay ahead, optimistic navigators made sporadic attempts to penetrate this so-called Northeast Passage, only to be halted in the ice-bound Kara Sea. Furthermore, the path was blocked by the sprawling landmass of Novaya Zemlya, beyond which sole access was provided by the narrow strait that separates it from the mainland. However, in 1596 a Dutch expedition piloted by Willem Barents decided on an alternative approach, sailing as far as possible to the north in the hope of rounding Novaya Zemlya beyond its northernmost reach. The voyage would become the first to endure a winter in the extreme Arctic and would furnish our earliest well-documented tale of heroism and survival in the hyperborean wilderness.

At first all went well. The islands of Svalbard were discovered and, by following the edge of the ice eastward, the northern cape of Novaya Zemlya was successfully doubled. But then the ice closed around the ship, cracking its hull and forcing its distressed crew to take refuge on the desolate, treeless shore. From their vessel's shattered timbers they constructed a house furnished with bunks and meagre supplies salvaged from the disintegrating ship. Hot stones warmed their feet, but still their bedding froze into solid boards. Smoke from driftwood fires choked them, and local game, their only sustenance, disappeared in the long polar night. It was not until June that the scurvy-racked survivors escaped their tomb-like incarceration, taking to the ship's boats, which they rowed, sailed or dragged from one open channel to the next. Barents died in the attempt, but thirteen survived the harrowing 2500-kilometre (1,500-mile) trek to the Kola Peninsula where, reunited with their Dutch colleagues, they were restored to normality by draughts of strong Swedish beer.

Right A contemporary engraving showing Barents's ship locked in the ice off Novaya Zemlya; the crew making their way to safety on shore and struggling to salvage what they could from the wreckage.

Bento de Góis Seeks Cathay and Finds China

A Jesuit on the Silk Road.

1602–05

Today the name of Cathay instinctively brings China to mind, but to a sixteenth-century European geographer the words were by no means synonymous. Cathay, derived from Khitai, an ethnic group that had dominated northeastern China in the tenth century, had permeated European literature since the Middle Ages and had been used by Marco Polo to signify China north of the Yangtze. But the first European voyagers landed in the southern ports, Macau and Canton, where the name of Cathay and its capital 'Cambaluc' would have meant little. Matteo Ricci, who resided in Beijing from 1601, believed that Cathay and China, Beijing and Cambaluc, were one, but court customs reported by Polo differed widely from those observed by Ricci. Furthermore, Islamic travellers suggested that Cathay lay directly northeast of India and was peopled with Christians, of which Ricci found none. So to settle the matter, and hopefully to bring the lost Christians of mystic Cathay into the Catholic fold, the Jesuit fathers at Goa decided that an expedition should be mounted. For the task they selected Bento de Góis, a lay brother, born in the Azores, who spoke fluent Persian.

Góis set out from Agra in October 1602 disguised as an Armenian Christian merchant named Abdullah Isai, and at Lahore joined a massive caravan heading north. After eight months in Kabul the caravan proceeded through precipitous, bandit-infested gorges and across the frozen wastes of the Hindu Kush, finally descending in November 1603 to Yarkand (now Shache), the dominant trading centre on the Silk Road. Here Góis conversed with a captured Tibetan 'king', and noted enthusiastically that Tibet appeared to practise a variant of Christianity. In the autumn of 1604 the caravan moved out again, crossing the Taklamakan Desert and following the northern Silk Road through Kuqa and Hami. By the time Góis entered China at Suchow (now Jiuquan) in December 1605, he had concluded that the Cambaluc he sought was in fact Beijing, and that his Islamic informants in Goa, noting superficial resemblances, had confused Christianity with Buddhism. Góis wrote to Ricci in Beijing, but wearied by his ordeal he died in Suchow in April 1607 shortly after the arrival of Ricci's emissary. Góis's all-important diary was returned to Ricci, who wrote to the fathers in India that the journey had proved beyond doubt that Cathay and China were one and the same.

Right An early European engraving depicting the Great Wall of China.

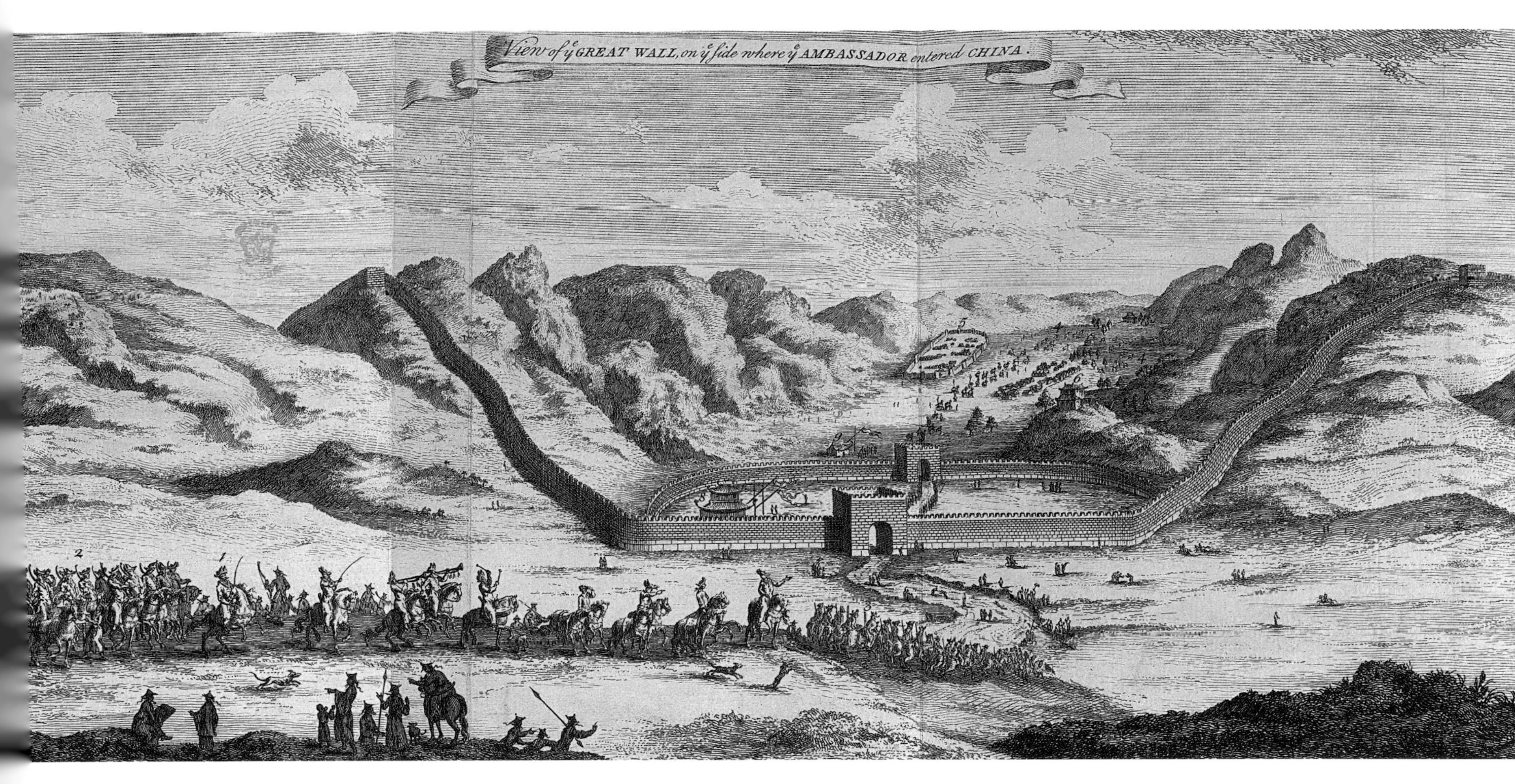
View of ye GREAT WALL, on ye side where ye AMBASSADOR entered CHINA.

Champlain brings France to Canada and Discovers the Great Lakes

The new conquistadors of the North American fur trade.

1603–15

CARTIER'S EXPLORATION OF THE ST LAWRENCE RIVER IN THE 1530S had two objects in mind: gold and the discovery of a passage to Asia. He found neither, and for sixty years the native peoples were left in peace. As time wore on, hopes of finding gold-rich civilizations began to fade, while the growing appreciation of the true size of the North American continent made the discovery of a quick route to China increasingly unlikely. The age of the gallant armour-clad knight was over and in his place came a new breed of conquistador: the fur trader, less sensational but somewhat more realistic about what was on offer. But having nothing of the pre-established infrastructure of Mexico and Peru, and confronted by dense forests and an overwhelming maze of interconnected waterways, the fur traders' conquest would be gradual and altogether more subtle. Cartier had brought the trade to light, and by 1600 a few enterprising Frenchmen had placed ephemeral outposts around the Gulf of St Lawrence, but it was Samuel de Champlain who would spearhead the conquest and establish his nation's presence in what was to become Nouvelle France.

Champlain, a thoughtful and intelligent navigator convinced of the moral and financial advantages of colonialism, had sailed the Caribbean and even advocated the construction of a canal to the Pacific. As royal hydrographer to Henry IV he first came to Canada in 1603, commissioned with charting the waterways and locating the site of a permanent trading factory. Following in Cartier's footsteps, he reached the Lachine Rapids on the St Lawrence and received intelligence of the lakes beyond, then for the next four years he assisted in the search for settlement sites around Nova Scotia, during which he surveyed the New England coast as far as Cape Cod. In 1608 he returned to the St Lawrence, established his centre of operations at what would become the city of Quebec, then the next year charted the Richelieu River in the south and saw the lake that now bears his name. For some time the fate of the colony hung in the balance, plagued by Iroquois attack and decimated by scurvy in the long winters, but Champlain held fast to his conviction and in 1610 returned with the support of Rouen merchants. On repeated visits over the next six years he surveyed the Ottawa River, saw Lake Ontario, and in 1615 crossed the heartland of modern Ontario to Lake Huron.

Right Champlain's manuscript chart of 1607 – the first to accurately delineate the North American coast from New England to Nova Scotia.

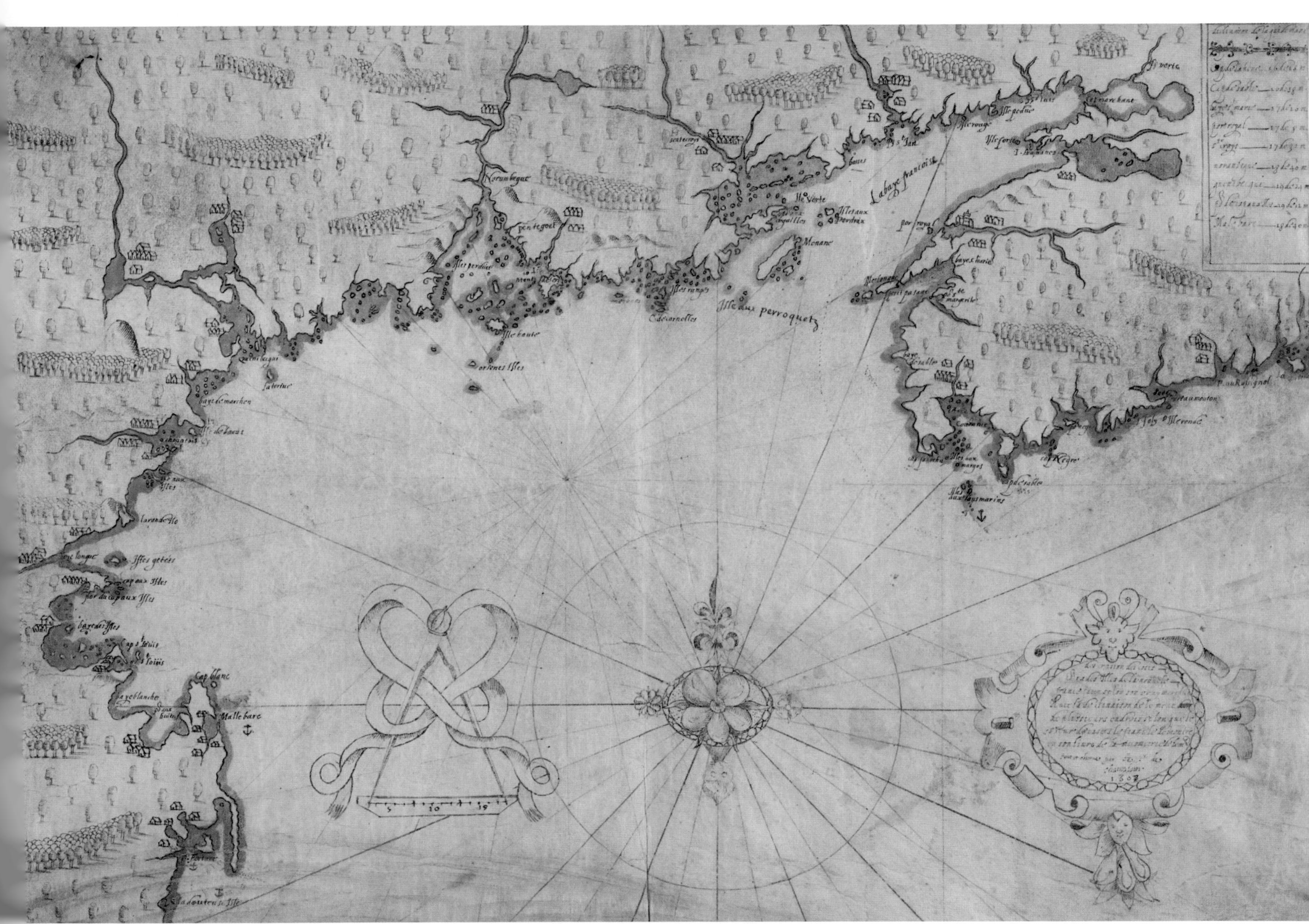
Norumbegue
Menane
Isle haute
Isle aux perroquets
Cap blanc
Malle barc

Pedro de Quirós Seeks the Continent of Lost Souls

A crusader adrift in the Pacific.

1605–06

FOR EXERCISES IN KNIGHT ERRANTRY, those with all the romance of a chivalric fantasy and trappings of a Quixotic burlesque, nothing approaches the voyage of Pedro Fernández de Quirós. This gifted Portuguese pilot knew more of the Pacific than most of his Castilian counterparts, having conducted galleons to the Indies and brought the pitiful survivors of Álvaro de Mendaña's expedition to safety in the Philippines. But his unhappy experiences under Mendaña served only to fire a determination to return to the South Sea, to succeed where Mendaña had failed, and to locate that elusive continent where lost souls cried out for salvation. Finding little favour with the Peruvian authorities, he went directly to Rome, and armed with the patronage of the pope and a fragment of the True Cross, Quirós sailed from Callao in December 1605 with three ships, 300 men and ten friars. His eminently sensible strategy, to ensure nothing was missed, was to zig-zag in a general southwesterly direction, then, if nothing were found, to make for the Santa Cruz Islands. However, his pertinacity in perceiving the expedition as a moral crusade, his prohibition of gambling, swearing and blaspheming aboard ship, brought his long-suffering sailors to the verge of mutiny.

Finding nothing but a handful of diminutive atolls, and with hunger and thirst afflicting his crews, Quirós turned his ships northwest and in May 1606 alighted on a populous island of forests and rolling planes in the archipelago known now as Vanuatu. Satisfied that this was the heavenly Arcady promised to him by the Almighty, the Terra Australis of his heart's desire, he took possession in the name of God and King Philip of Spain, naming it Austrialia del Espiritu Santo, the subtly embedded 'i' recalling Philip's descendancy from the house of Austria. A settlement of New Jerusalem was established beside a river called the Jordan. Every member of the crew, even the most lowly, was created a Knight of the Holy Ghost, a new order of chivalry, and ordered to wear its insignia, a cross of blue silk, on their breasts. But steadily it dawned on the ailing Quirós that his treasured continent was just another Pacific island, and by June all three ships were back at sea. In circumstances that remain forever unclear, Quirós became separated from the fleet and found his way back to Mexico, then to Spain where he spent his last seven years in privation, battling for recognition against a barrage of chastisement.

Right A map of the Pacific by Pedro de Quirós, 1598, wrongly identifying New Guinea as the extremity of an extensive southern continent.

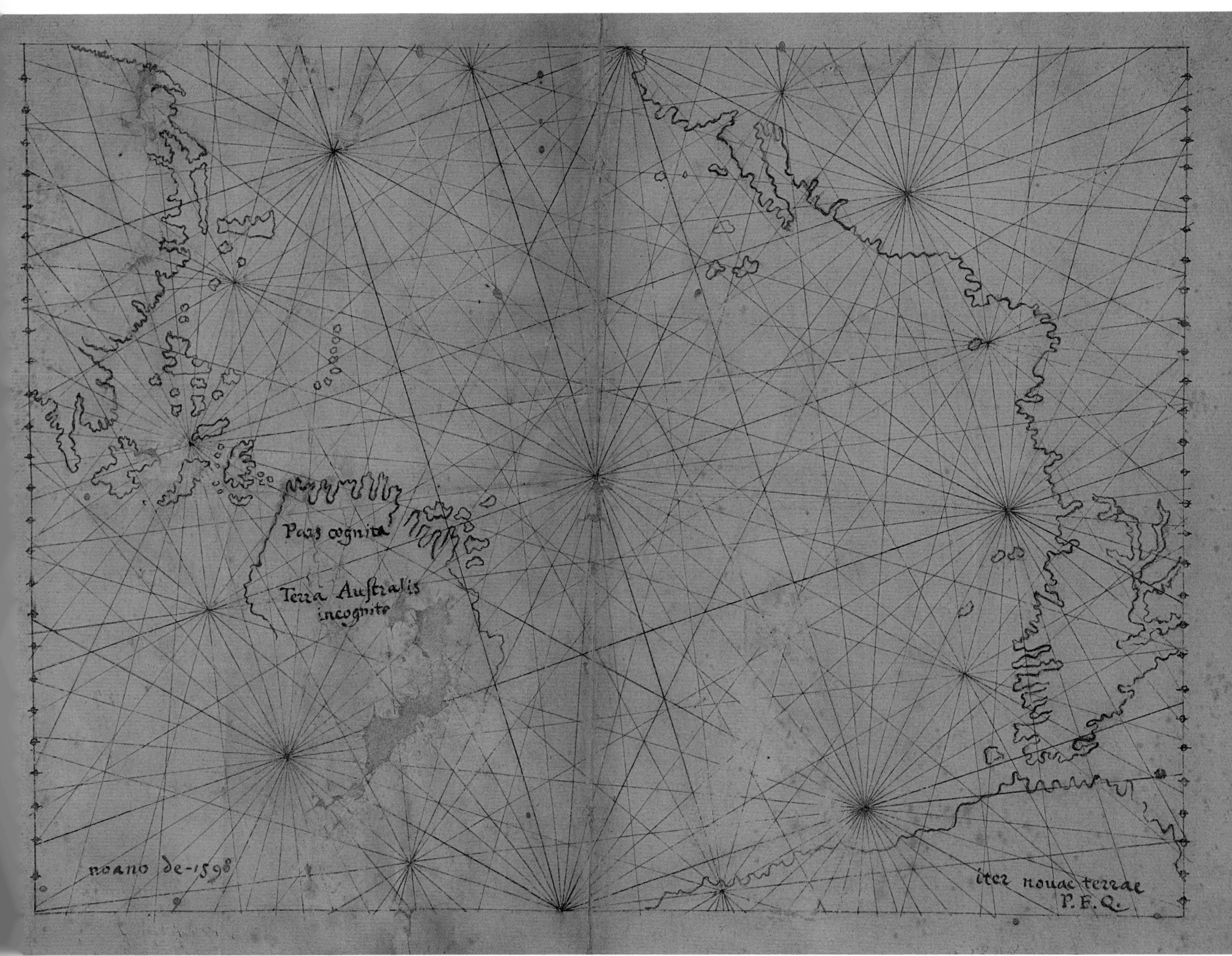
Pars cognita
Terra Australis
incognite
noano de-1598
iter nouae terrae
P. F. Q.

The Unclaimed Discovery of Australia

Ships that pass in the night.

1606

TRY AS WE MAY, AND DESPITE THE IMPASSIONED PLEAS that regularly emanate from advocates of the implausible, uncontroversial documentary evidence of a European discovery of Australia before 1606 is impossible to find. Early cartographic representations of a 'Great South Land', 'Terra Australis', 'Java la Grande', or whatever one might call it, stemmed from a subtle error in Marco Polo's *Travels*, while the extensive northern coastline of a southern continent shown on sixteenth-century French maps was almost certainly an exaggerated misrepresentation of a Portuguese voyage along one of Indonesia's outer islands. While geographers readily assigned New Guinea, discovered in 1526, to the northern extremity of a 'fifth part of the world', Cornelius Wytfliet's statement in 1598 that 'Australis Terra' is 'separated from New Guinea by a narrow strait' was an affirmation debated by his contemporaries and unsupported by hard evidence. And while reports of sailors blown to Australia by storms bear the characteristic hallmarks of accidental landings in New Guinea, those, if any, that really did make it to Australia kept very quiet about it.

By extraordinary coincidence, within seven months of each other, two mariners, Dutch and Spanish, would arrive from opposite directions in the strait that separates New Guinea from Australia. Both were in the enviable position to rightfully claim the discovery of the southern continent, but, as chance would have it, neither did. Willem Janszoon, master of the *Duyfken*, coasted the southern shores of New Guinea and by February 1606 had arrived on the western coast of Queensland's Cape York Peninsula. Copies of his map survive, recording the capes and bays of the Gulf of Carpentaria with extraordinary fidelity, but his log has since disappeared and his map failed to distinguish New Guinea from Australia. In fact the most detailed account of an incident in Janszoon's voyage was preserved into recent times in the oral history of the local Wik people, whose elders could still, three centuries after the event, recall the attempted abduction of an Aborigine woman by one of the Dutch crew. From the other direction came Luis Vaéz de Torres who, inadvertently detached from Pedro de Quiros's expedition to Vanuatu, was heading by a direct route for the East Indies. In September 1606 he successfully navigated the strait that 150 years later would commemorate his name, then continued on his way, blissfully unaware that the tip of a great continent lay only a stone's throw to the south.

Right A chart showing the discovery of Australia in 1606 by Janszoon in the *Duyfken*. The Cape York Peninsula, bottom right, appears as a southerly extension of New Guinea.

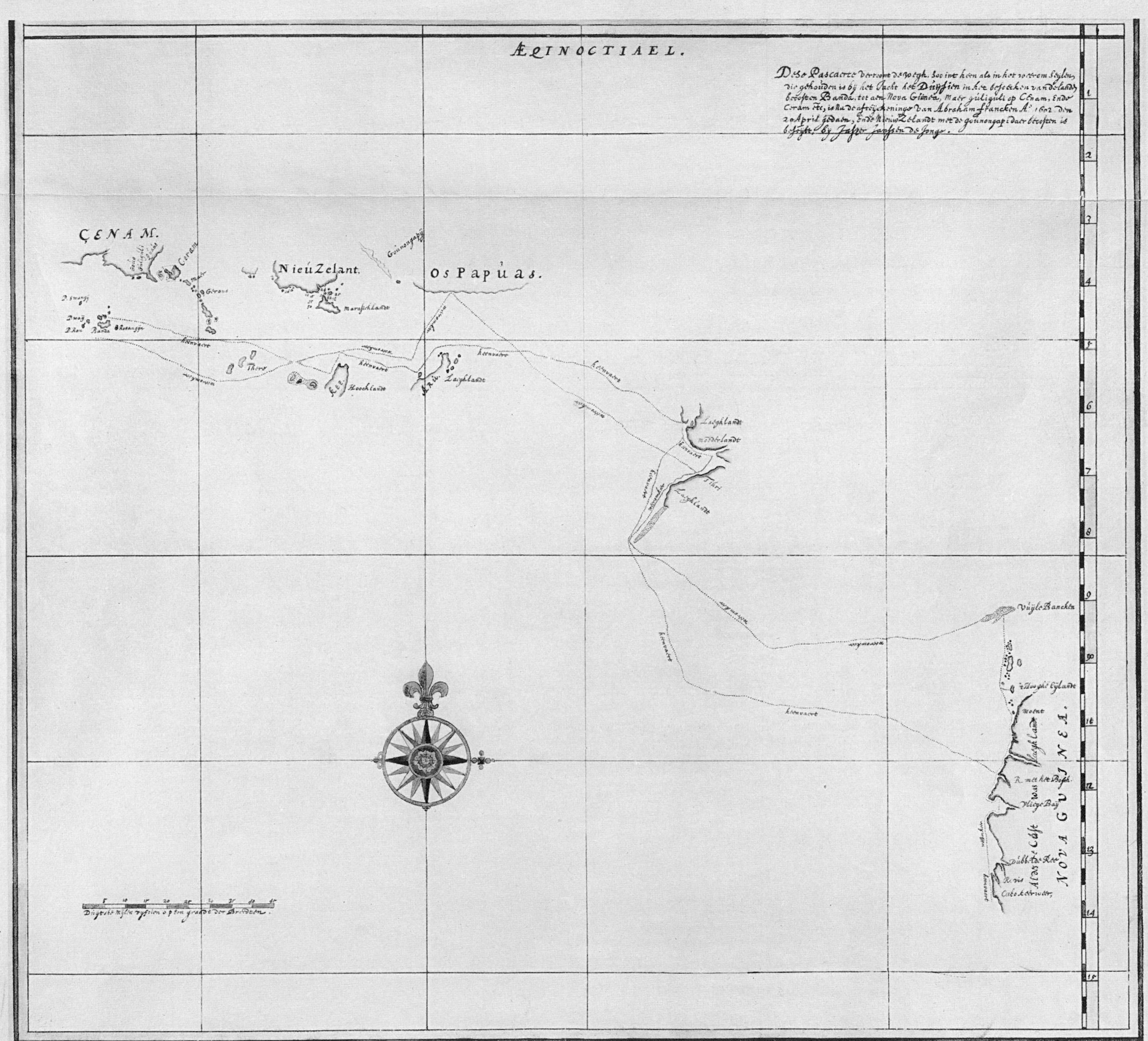

THE DISCOVERY OF AUSTRALIA BY THE YACHT HET DUYFIEN, 1606. — FROM THE SECRET ATLAS OF THE EAST INDIA COMPANY, c. 1670

THE HAGUE – MARTINUS NIJHOFF

Dutch Sailors on the Coast of Western Australia

Shipwreck and survival on a barren shore.

1611–29

By 1602, the year in which the Dutch East India Company was established to regulate Dutch trade with the Orient, as many as seventy Dutch vessels regularly plied the spice route to the Indies. But the arduous voyage around the Cape of Good Hope, north towards India and across the Bay of Bengal, plagued by reefs, contrary currents, monsoons, and by the tropical humidity that spoilt food and water, not only delivered its crew in feeble condition but also encroached on Portuguese and English trading domains. A solution was found in 1611 by Hendrik Brouwer, who had noted that a ship sailing due east from the Cape would be snatched up by the roaring forties, sped rapidly across the Indian Ocean, then taken north to Java by the West Australian Current. It would be only a matter of time before the numerous vessels opting for the Brouwer Route would begin to make landfall on the hitherto unknown Australian coast. Although devoid of food and water, its presence at least provided the welcome assurance that the correct longitude had been reached for the final push northward.

Over the next 100 years around thirty Dutch vessels are known to have visited the Australian mainland, and by the early eighteenth century the continent's western half, from Arnhem Land to the Great Australian Bight, was one of the most accurately charted coastlines in the entire world. While most tarried briefly on the inhospitable shores, others suffered catastrophic shipwreck and the forfeit of rich cargoes, the location of which in recent times would become the sport and obsession of both archaeologists and bounty hunters. Some, like the voyage of François Pelsaert, whose ship *Batavia* ran aground with 340 passengers and crew on a desert island off the Western Australian coast in 1629, generated harrowing stories of disaster and survival. While Pelsaert took a small boat party up the coast and by a remarkable feat of navigation reached Batavia in Java, some of those left behind, scheming mutineers beset by delusions of grandeur, murdered 125 of the survivors, men, women and children, many of them beaten to death, others stabbed with knives or pikes, and some tied hand and foot and thrown into the sea. Pelsaert returned to a scene of bloodcurdling mayhem but quickly brought the principal perpetrators to summary justice, hanging eight on the spot, leaving two to their fate on the mainland and returning the rest to Batavia to face the most appalling punishments.

Right A chart of the Malay archipelago by Hessel Gerritz (corrected to 1631) showing the remarkably accurate delineation of the coast of Western Australia made by Dutch navigators.

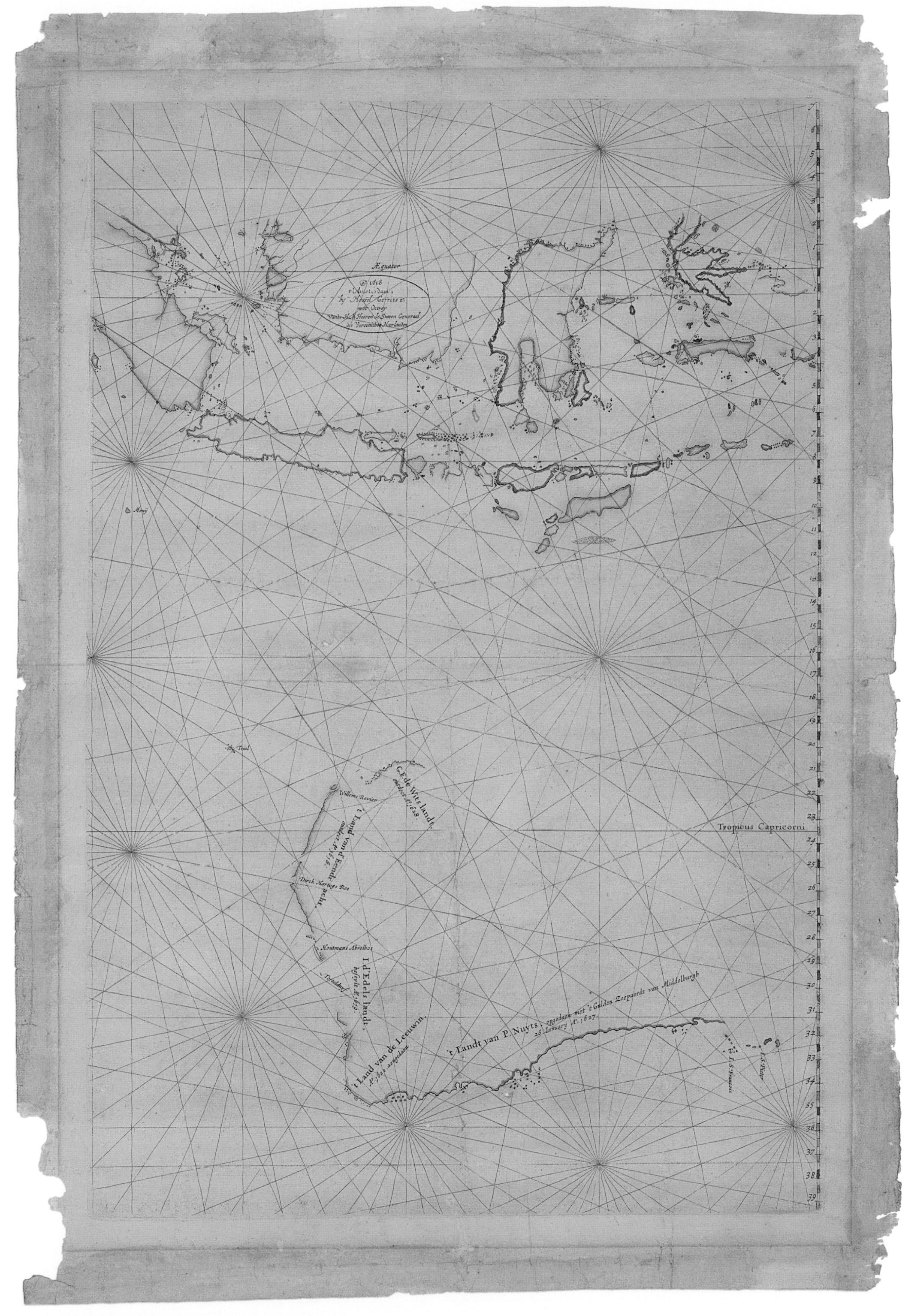
Æquator
1618
t'Amsterdam,
by Hessel Gerritsz.
met Octroy
Vande H. M. Heeren de Staten Generael
der Vereenichde Neerlanden
G.F. de Wits landt.
ontdect A° 1628.
Willems Revier
't Land vand Eendracht.
ontdect A° 1616.
Dirck Hartogs Ree
Houtmans Abrolhos
Tortelduyf
I. d'Edels landt,
beseylt A° 1619.
't Land van de Leeuwin,
A° 1622. aengedaen
't Landt van P. Nuyts, opgedaen met 't Gulden Zeepaerdt van Middelburgh
26 January A° 1627.
I. S. Francois
Tropicus Capricorni

Le Maire and Schouten Round Cape Horn

A new passage into the Pacific.

1615–16

THE PROBLEMS THAT AFFLICTED MAGELLAN'S ENTRY INTO THE PACIFIC meant that no serious voyage of geographical discovery would follow in its wake for nearly 100 years. Francis Drake and his flamboyant mimic Thomas Cavendish, who circumnavigated in 1586–88, were both more concerned with relieving the Spanish of illicitly acquired gold rather than furthering the cause of science, and sped uneventfully from California to the Philippines oblivious to anything of interest. The randomly tortuous voyages of Mendaña and Quirós, reminiscent of the quest for El Dorado, heavily distracted by the dubious assets of a few inconsequential islands, were little more than self-delusive appendices to a conquistadorial past. Not until 1616 did anything like a genuine voyage of discovery, foreshadowing the work of the *grands voyageurs* of the next century, enter the Pacific.

Isaac Le Maire, a principal player in the development of Dutch trade with the East Indies, had tired of the monopoly commanded by the Dutch East India Company, despite having once been its major shareholder. In retaliation he proposed the inauguration of a new route to the Indies; one by which, in sailing west, he would neither trespass on the Company's traditional routes, nor, by locating a new passage into the Pacific, encroach on Spanish terrain. Under Le Maire's son Jacob, the ships *Hoorn* and *Eendracht*, captained by Willem Cornelis Schouten, left the Netherlands in May 1615, calling at Sierra Leone to stock up on 25,000 lemons as protection against scurvy. This measure, along with suitably protracted stopovers on route, ensured that only two fatalities would be recorded, the only major disaster being the accidental loss of the *Hoorn* on the Patagonian coast. Bypassing the Strait of Magellan, the *Eendracht* became the first vessel to round Cape Horn (named after the point of departure) and entered the Pacific. From the Juan Fernández Islands the voyage proceeded due west through many of the ocean's major archipelagos, the Tuamotus, the Society Islands and Tonga, before heading northwest to New Ireland and the coast of New Guinea. Finally, in September 1616, the crew received a warm welcome on the Moluccan island of Ternate. Ironically, however, the Dutch governor at Batavia in Java refused to believe that they had arrived via the Pacific, seizing the *Eendracht* for intruding on Company territory and promptly despatching its commanders back to the Netherlands. Jacob Le Maire died on Mauritius, but Schouten returned to set a new record for a circumnavigation.

Right A contemporary map showing Schouten and Le Maire's route across the Pacific.

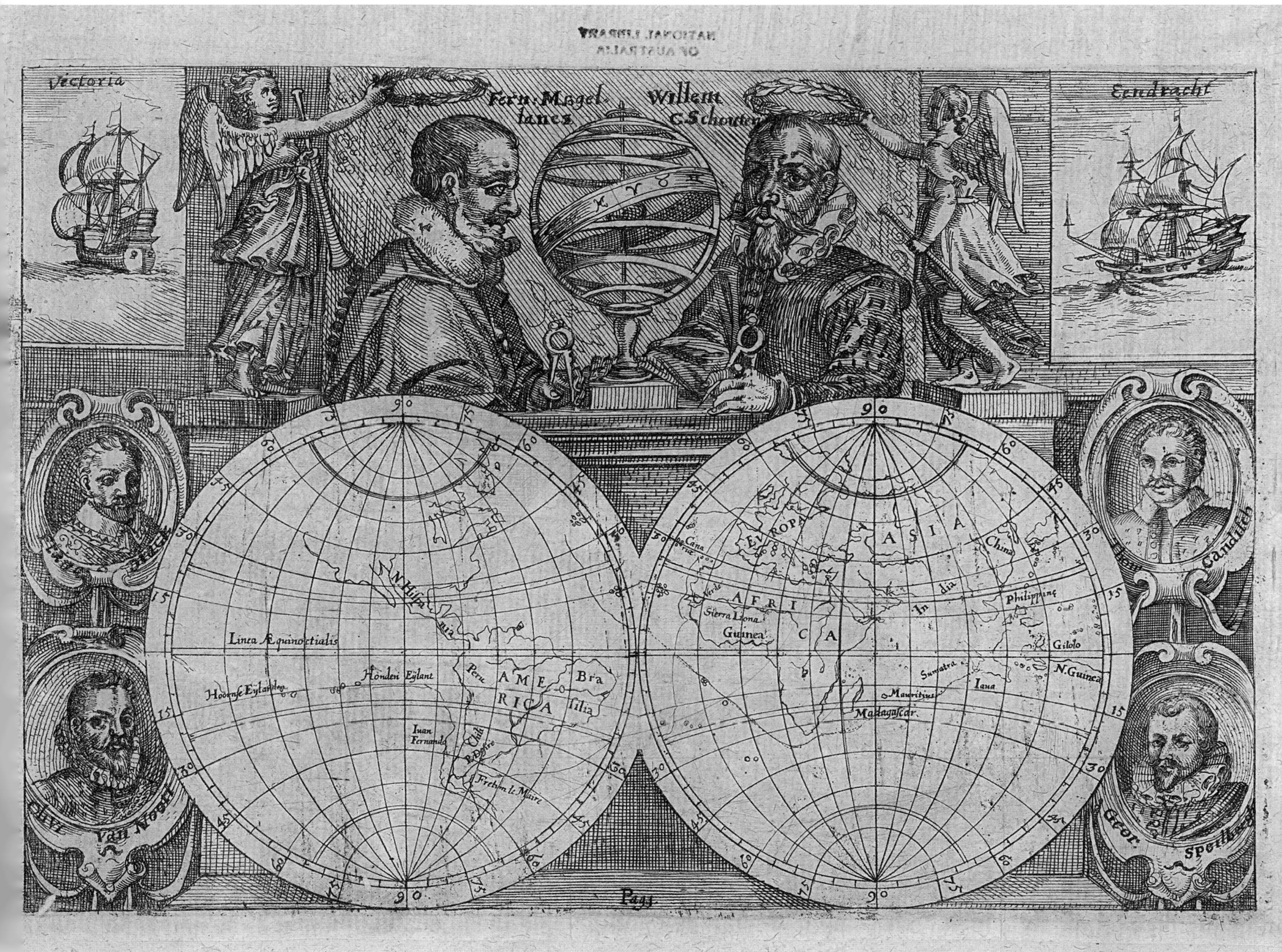
Victoria
Fern. Magel lanes
Willem C.S.Schouten
Eendracht
Linea Æquinoctialis
Hoornse Eylanden
Honden Eylant
N.Hispania
Peru
AMERICA
Brasilia
Iuan Fernandes
Chili
Fretum le Maire
EUROPA
ASIA
China
AFRICA
India
Philippina
Sierra Liona
Guinea
Gilolo
N.Guinea
Sumatra
Iava
Mauritius
Madagascar
Van Noort
Spilberg
Pag

Abel Tasman Ventures into the Southern Ocean

The European discovery of New Zealand.

1642-43

THE DUTCH EAST INDIA COMPANY, more properly the Vereenigde Oost-Indische Compagnie (VOC), was constituted in 1602 to prosecute trade and colonial activity in the East Indies. By 1611 it had established its future centre of operations at Batavia, modern Jakarta, and throughout the first half of the seventeenth century its interests spread across the entire Orient, from Iran to New Guinea and northward to Japan. Exploration became a major feature of its development, particularly during the dynamic ten-year (1636-45) governership of Anthony van Diemen, who displaced the Portuguese from their strongholds in Ceylon and Malacca and sent his sailors far and wide, even to the fabled 'gold' and 'silver' islands of the North Pacific. In fact his vision of a mighty Dutch trading empire saw no bounds, and by the early 1640s Van Diemen was contemplating the little-known lands of the South Pacific, the Islands of Solomon reported by the Spanish, the 'unknown Southland', and even the prospect of a lucrative back-door trade with Chile. It was with these in mind that in 1642 he despatched one of his favourite navigators, Abel Janszoon Tasman, into the uncharted vastness of the southern ocean.

To catch the winds that would propel him along his proposed trajectory, Tasman started from Mauritius, his two ships passing far south of the Dutch discoveries in Western Australia and making landfall on an unknown shore that Tasman dutifully christened Van Diemen's Land – a name it would retain until rechristened for its discoverer in 1856. Two weeks later, the waters so turbulent that only the ship's carpenter could summon sufficient courage to swim ashore and plant the Dutch flag, Tasman pushed eastward in search of the Solomon Islands. After nine days, on 13 December 1642, he chanced upon a coast that seemed to stretch indefinitely from southwest to northeast. Although convinced that he had found the long-sought Southland, he was looking at New Zealand's South Island, and in what Tasman named Murderers' Bay his ships were overwhelmed by fearsome Maori warriors. But Tasman now faced an irreconcilable conflict of duties: to claim newly discovered lands for the Dutch but, at the same time, 'to be patient and long-suffering' with regard to strangers he might encounter. By choosing the later he sacrificed four crewmen and would never set foot on the land he had discovered. Desperately short of water, Tasman charted a course for Batavia.

Right This map of Tasman's voyage gave the first indication of the coasts of Van Diemen's Land (Tasmania) and New Zealand, neither of which were proved to be islands.

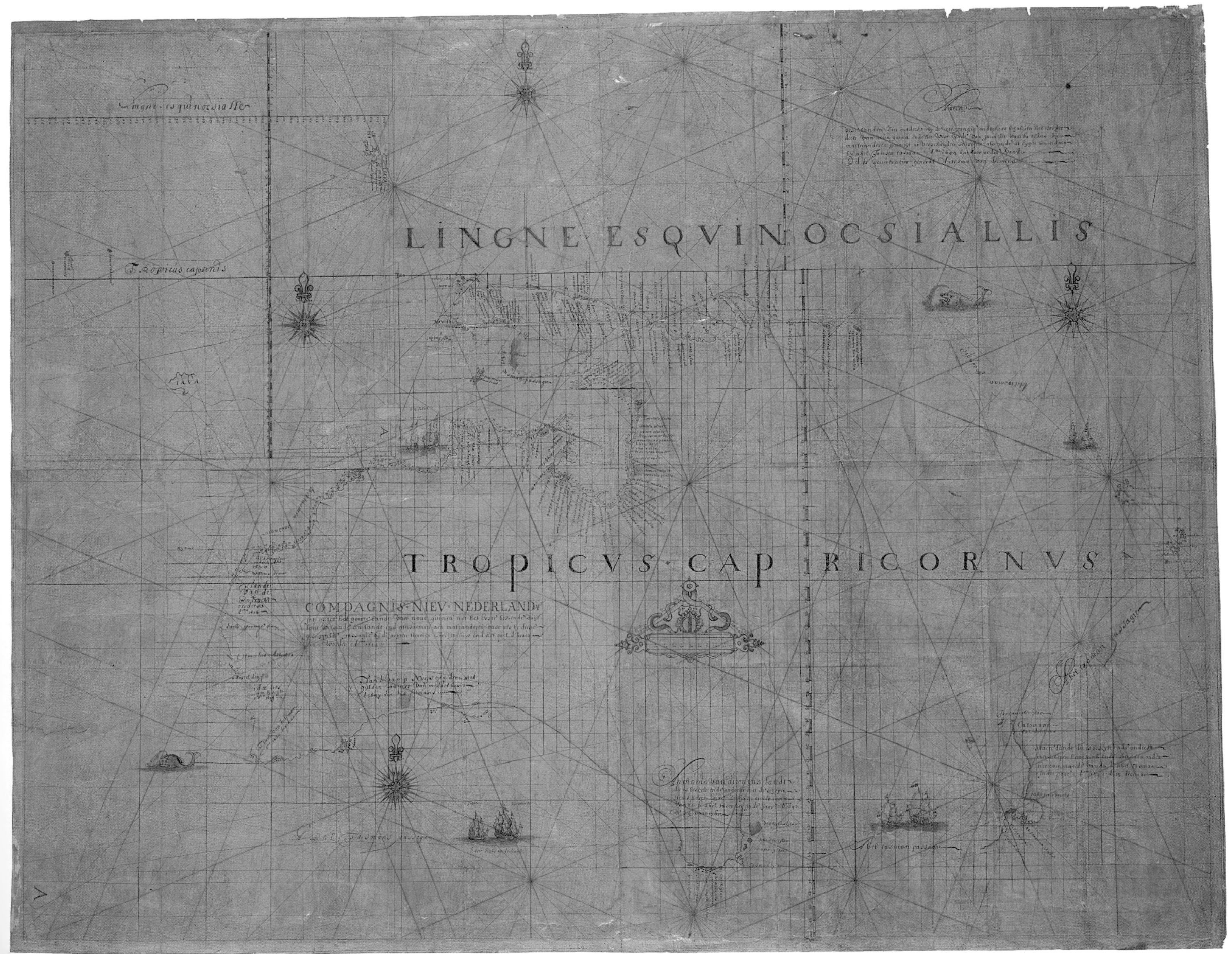
LINGNE ESQVINOCSIALLIS
TROPICVS CAPRICORNVS
COMDAGNIS NIEV NEDERLANDT

Grueber and Dorville Cross the Tibetan Plateau

A journey none dared to repeat.

1661–64

THE JESUIT MISSIONARIES THAT ARRIVED IN CHINA in the seventeenth century suffered mixed fortunes, one moment created high-ranking mandarins in gratitude for their scientific services, and the next finding themselves condemned to death for propagating a foreign religion. Adam Schall von Bell, who had built telescopes for the imperial artillery and had worked for many years on the reform of the Chinese calendar, narrowly escaped execution in 1665 when a violent earthquake terrified the superstitious Chinese into commuting his sentence. However, it was Schall's work on the calendar, condemned in Rome for pandering to local superstition by incorporating lucky and unlucky days, that led quite fortuitously to an extraordinary journey of discovery. When a German assistant, Father Johann Grueber, was despatched to Rome to defend Schall's integrity he found the normal sea route obstructed by a Dutch blockade of Macau. Undeterred, Grueber and his Belgian companion, Albert Dorville, conceived the daring plan of striking overland in a straight line for India, through country that was simply a blank on the map.

Grueber and Dorville left Beijing in April 1661, heading for Xi'an, then west to Xining where they began their ascent into the desolate wastes of the Tibetan plateau. In October, in the kingdom known to the Mongols as Barantola, they became the first Europeans beyond doubt to enter the capital Lhasa. The travellers were welcomed as friends. Grueber drew pictures of the Dalai Lama, an awe-inspiring regent revered as a god, and noted certain outward similarities between Tibetan religion and Christianity, even though 'no Christian was ever in the country before them'. After a month in Lhasa the travellers proceeded southward, crossing the Himalayas by the Lalung Pass and descending to Kathmandu, the capital of Nepal. In March 1662, via Patna and Benares, they reached Agra where Dorville died, 'a victim of the hardships he had suffered'. Taking on a new companion, Father Heinrich Roth, Grueber set out for Rome, descending the Indus to its mouth and striking west across the forbidding Makran Desert. Traversing modern Iran, Iraq and Turkey, they reached Izmir and sailed for Rome, arriving in February 1664. Grueber attempted twice to return to China, first through Russia, then through Central Asia, but he took sick in Constantinople and spent the rest of his life teaching in Europe. His journals, published in Athanasius Kircher's *China Illustrata*, caused a sensation, but few would replicate the journey until modern times.

Right A map of Asia by Joan Blaeu, 1617, compiled from the most reliable sources of the time.

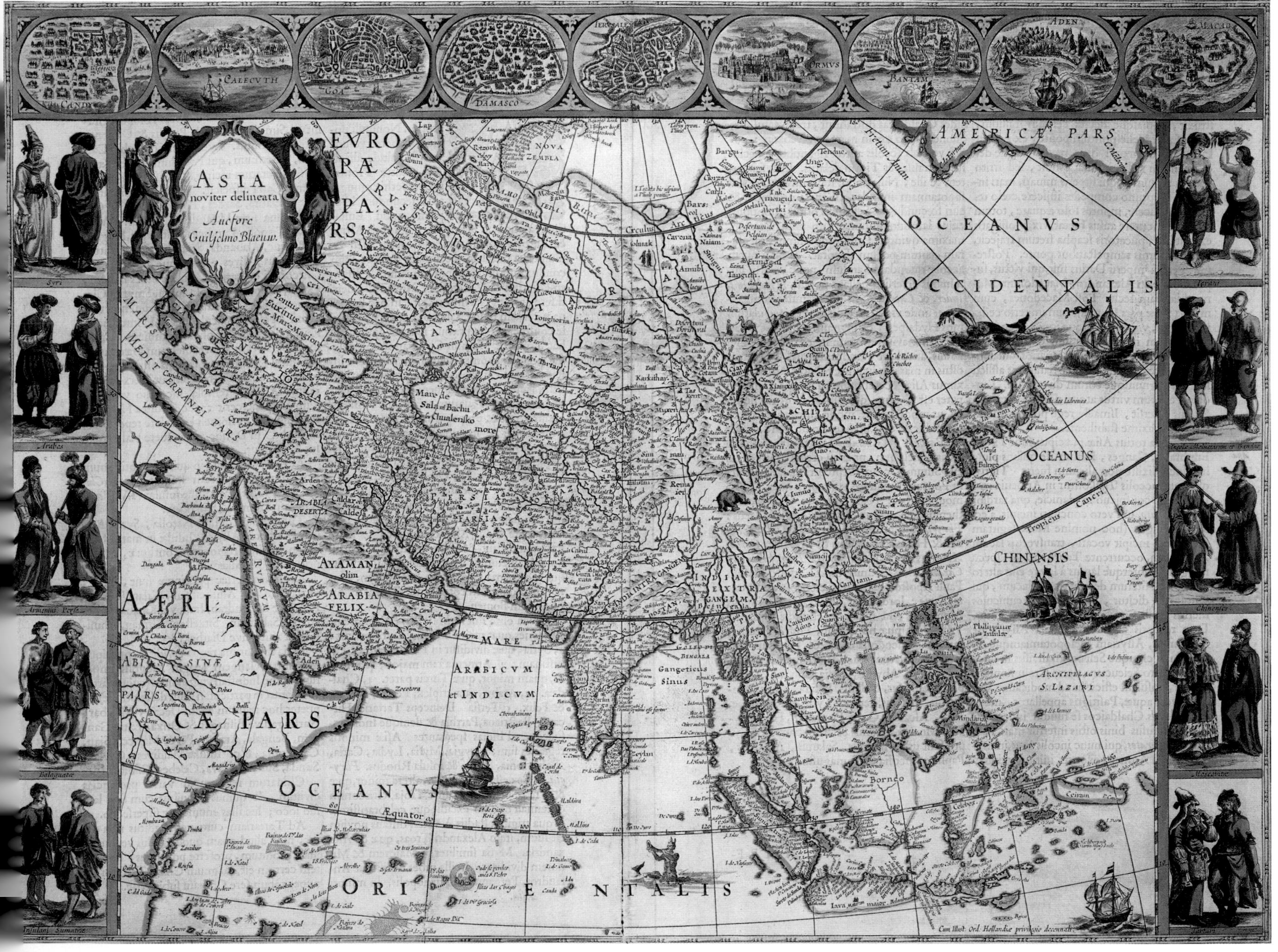
CANDY
CALECVTH
GOA
DAMASCO
ORMVS
BANTAM
ADEN
MACAO
ASIA
noviter delineata
Auctore
Guiljelmo Blaeuw.
EVROPÆ PARS
AMERICÆ PARS
OCEANVS
OCCIDENTALIS
OCEANVS
CHINENSIS
Tropicus Cancri
ARABIA DESERTA
ARABIA FELIX
MARE
ARABICVM
et INDICVM
Gangeticus
Sinus
Borneo
Æquator
OCEANVS
ORIENTALIS
AFRI
CÆ PARS
Syri
Arabes
Chinenses

Jolliet and Marquette Establish the Course of the Mississippi

A question of discovery.

1673

THE DEBATE OVER PRECISELY WHO DISCOVERED THE MISSISSIPPI RIVER will inevitably bring forth an assortment of worthy contenders. Should it be the first to enter its delta, to cross it or to navigate its lower reaches, or should it be the first to recognize the river as a major artery to the interior. As early as 1519 Alonso de Pineda had sailed a few leagues into a great river he devoutly named Espiritu Santo. The castaways of the failed Narvaéz expedition had rounded its delta in 1527, and in 1541 Hernando de Soto, some 500 kilometres (300 miles) from the Gulf, had spent a month ferrying his troops across a mighty river which his survivors would subsequently descend to the coast. But the Mississippi's role as a major thoroughfare into the American heartland was not fully appreciated for another century, and would come from the French colonies far to the north. In 1634 Jean Nicollet, a gifted linguist with Champlain's enterprise, had arrived in Lake Michigan and received native intelligence of a great river that swept into the sea, presumably the Pacific. However, difficulties in travel beyond the security of the French forts prevented further examination, and it was not until 1673 that the government of New France commissioned Louis Jolliet to pioneer an overland route to the river.

Jolliet, an educated man who had renounced his priestly calling to become a fur trader, left Quebec in October 1672. At St Ignace, a mission at the entrance to Lake Michigan, he picked up Father Jacques Marquette, a Jesuit priest under instructions to accompany Jolliet in the hope of doing a little proselytizing along the way. The two companions, one representing the economic and political, the other the spiritual aspirations of New France, departed in May 1673, followed the Fox River from the Jesuit outpost on Green Bay, and reached the limit of known territory after twenty days' navigation. Guided by local tribesmen, they portaged to the Wisconsin River, descended it in canoes and on 15 June finally entered the Mississippi. Jolliet had promised to reach its mouth, hopefully in the Pacific, but the river flowed south not west, entering the domain of hostile tribes and trending uncomfortably towards Spanish territory. Convinced that they were just fifty leagues from the sea they halted short of the Louisiana border and returned via the Illinois River and the Chicago portage.

Right The Marquette map, showing for the first time the upper course of the Mississippi and the approach routes from the 'Lac des Ilinois', now Lake Michigan.

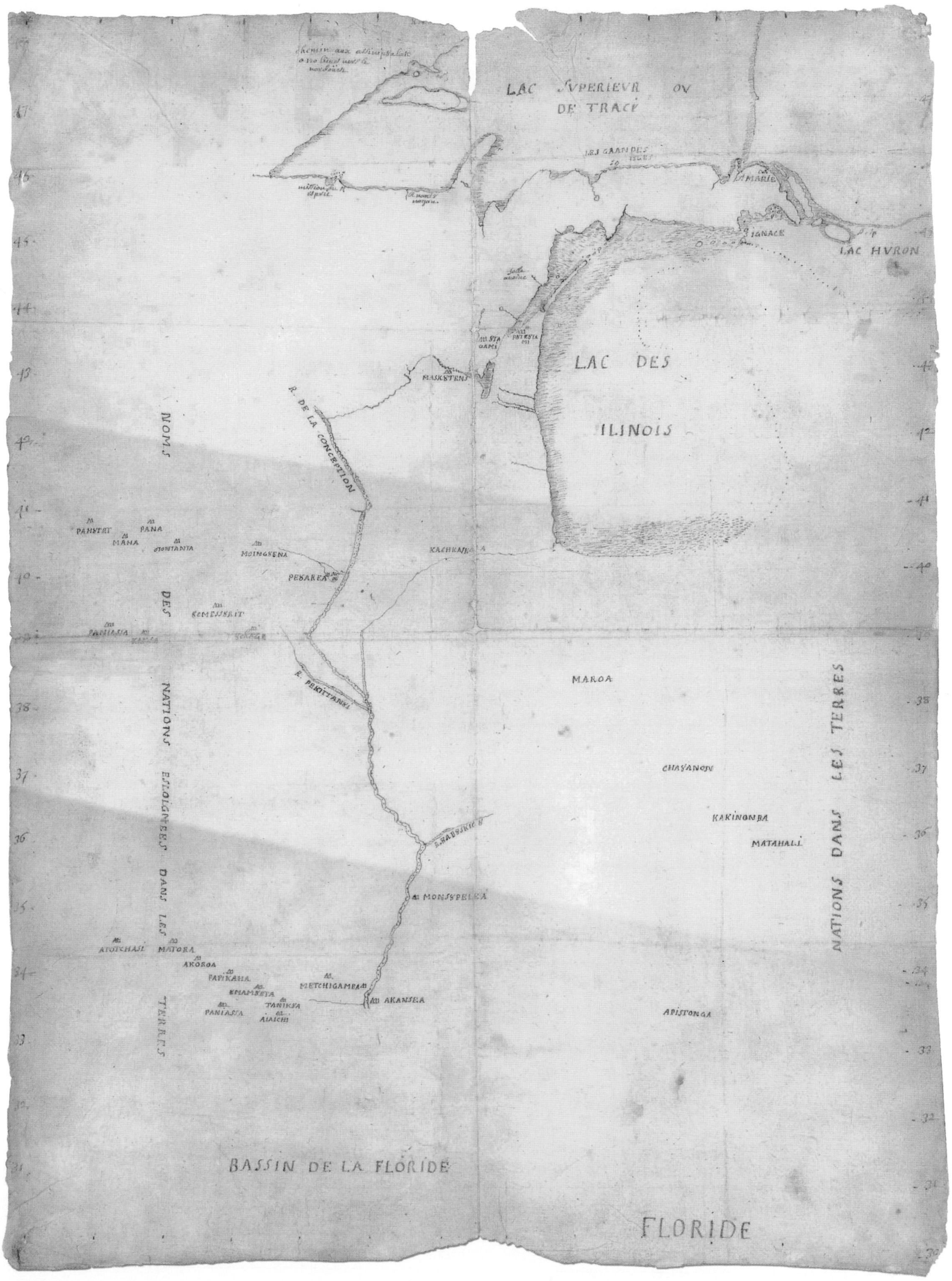

LAC SVPERIEVR OV
DE TRACÉ
LES GRANDES
LAC HVRON
IGNACE
LAC DES
ILINOIS
MASKOVTENS
R. DE LA CONCEPTION
NOMS DES NATIONS ESLOIGNEES DANS LES TERRES
PAHVTET
PANA
MAHA
MOINGVENA
PEOAREA
KACHKASKA
KOMESSERIT
R. PEKITTANVI
MAROA
CHAVANON
KAKINONBA
MATAHALI
NATIONS DANS LES TERRES
MONSOPELEA
ATOTCHASI
MATORA
AKOROA
PAPIKAHA
METCHIGAMEA
AKANSEA
TANIKOA
PANIASSA
APISTONGA
BASSIN DE LA FLORIDE
FLORIDE

La Salle's Vision of Empire on the Mississippi

Exploration for the pursuit of fame.

1679–87

EVEN IN HIS YOUTH RENÉ-ROBERT CAVELIER DE LA SALLE displayed all the qualities of an explorer. Emotional and imaginative, autocratic and fiery, he was ill-suited to the rigid rule of the Society of Jesus, which would spend nine years training him for the priesthood. Denied the opportunity for missionary work which might have satisfied his lust for adventure, and his vows excluding him from a share of the family fortune, he arrived penniless in Canada in 1667, determined to write himself into the record books. However, his attempt in 1669 to discover the Ohio River, 'the way to the Southern Sea, and thereby the route to China', proceeded little beyond Lake Ontario, while his ambition to discover a waterway to the Pacific was to be dashed by Jolliet's unveiling of the Mississippi. But the Mississippi would become the means by which La Salle would indulge his passion to spread the French empire across the North American continent, forestalling any English expansion from Carolina. In 1679, with his faithful lieutenant Henri de Tonty and thirty men, he launched the first ship on the Great Lakes, sailed it into Lake Michigan and built a fort on the Illinois River.

La Salle's first assault on the Mississippi landed him heavily in debt. His ship was lost in a storm, his fort reduced to ruins and his advance party scattered. But in 1682 he regrouped his forces, descended the Illinois and, in February, with twenty-three Frenchmen, launched on the Mississippi. The final descent to the coast was accomplished on 6 April, and three days later La Salle claimed the entire Mississippi basin in the name of Louis IX. La Salle re-ascended the river and returned to France, greeted not as a hero but in a cloud of disapproval. King Louis had his own plans and was not at all sure that he really wanted 'La Louisiane' – effectively the whole of North America from the Appalachians to Mexico. But by falsifying maps to move the river's delta closer to Mexico, La Salle subtly brought the king and his advisers on board, and in August 1684 a massive colonizing expedition sailed for the Gulf. The enterprise turned into a catalogue of misadventures. Overshooting the delta and dumping 320 miserable settlers on the inhospitable Texan coast, it struggled on for two years until La Salle's death at the hands of his own men.

Right This map of North America, 1697, by Louis Hennepin, shows La Salle's discoveries on the Mississippi but places the river too far to the west.

Lieues Communes de France
Lieües d' Allemagne
Lieues d'une Heure de Chemin
BAYE DE HUDSON.
La Bradror
Lac des Poux
Lac des Assenipoils
Port Nelson
NOUVELLE
FRANCE ou CANADA.
Gaspesie
Lac Superieur
Lac des Tibitibis
Lac Piscoutagamy
Lac Timagaming
Lac St Jan
Quebec
Tadousac
Lac Champlain ou Iroquois
Mont Real
Missilimakinac
LAC HURON ou KAREGNONDI
Baye de Puans
Lac des Illinois
Les Illinois
Lac St Joseph
Outoulibis
Fort Pour Empecher Les Assenipoils
Nadouessans
Issati
Tinthonha ou Gens de Prairies
Saut de St Anthoine de Padous
Lac de Pleurs
Kitchiga
Ocitagan
Kikapaus
Fort de Crevecoeur
Fort des Miamis
R. des Illinois
Lac Ontario ou de Frontenac
Grands Villages des Iroquois
LAC D'ERIE OU DU CHAT
LA VIRGINIE
NOUVEAU PAIS BAS
NOUVELLE ANGLETERRE
Boston
Hollandia
MER DE NORT.
Long Eyland
Philadelphia
Apalache
Caroline
C. de Trafalga
FLORIDE.
Tasalaica
Edelano
Vitacucho
Matheo
St. Augustin
Cap d'Canaueral
Cap Carlos
C. d' Agnada
Cap Florida
Bahama
Lucaioneque
Baye de Spirito Sancto
Embouchure de Meschasipi
GOLFE DE MEXIQUE.
NOUVEAU MEXIQUE
Mines de Ste Barbe
PARTIE DE NOUVELLE ESPAGNE.
Rieviere de la Magdelaine
Akansa
Coenis
Quinipissa
Chiquacha
Tamaroa
Massourites
Cap St. Anthoine
Rieviere Ohio
Chiongua R.
Pouhatan
Chesapeak Bay
C. de May
R. de Zud
CARTE
d'un tres grand PAIS
Nouvellement découvert
dans
L'AMERIQUE SEPTENTRIONALE
entre le
NOUVEAU MEXIQUE et la
Mer Glaciale
avec le Cours du Grand Fleuve
MESCHASIPI
Dediée a
GUILLIAUME IIIE
Roy de la Grand Brettagne
Par le R.P.
LOUIS DE HENNEPIN
Mission: Recoll: et Not: Apost:
Chez G. BROEDELET
a Utreght.

William Dampier: the Thinking Man's Buccaneer

A controversial pioneer of scientific exploration.

1683-1711

IT HAS ALWAYS BEEN WITH SOME RELUCTANCE THAT HISTORIANS have admitted William Dampier to the pantheon of great explorers. His association with the most ruthless pirates of the Spanish Main, and the question of whether he really discovered anything previously unknown, have for centuries condemned him to the apocrypha of travel literature. But for those that have reappraised his life, dissected his enigmatic character and assessed his contribution to the growth of geographical knowledge, Dampier emerges as a pioneer of British scientific exploration; a supremely intelligent navigator unequalled in his time; a passionate observer of all he saw around him. Maybe he did sell his soul to the devil to satisfy his thirst for travel, but he was the first to sail three times around the world and the first Englishman to set foot on mainland Australia. He wrote what some regard as the first genuine work of travel literature in the English language, and he compiled a treatise on the winds and currents that remained in use until the twentieth century. His exploits inspired Defoe and Swift, and he bridged the 150-year dark age of British Pacific exploration that preceded the glorious renaissance of the eighteenth century.

Born into a Somerset farming family, Dampier went to sea in 1669 at the age of eighteen. After working as a sugar planter in Jamaica and a logwood cutter in Mexico, he fell in with an unwholesome bevvy of English pirates that ravaged the coastal settlements of Central America. In similar company he embarked in 1683 on a voyage that would take him haphazardly around the world, rounding Cape Horn, crossing from Mexico to the Philippines and in 1688 venturing ashore on Australia's inhospitable northwest coast. Abandoned in the Nicobar Islands, he paddled a native canoe to Sumatra, and from a remote British trading outpost returned via the Cape of Good Hope after an absence of eight years. In 1699, in an almost surreal, Admiralty-sponsored colonizing venture, he took a rotting ship and incompetent, mutinous crew to the site of his earlier Australian landfall, only to spend a month feverously digging for water on a barren and desolate shore. In 1703 his second buccaneering circumnavigation dumped Alexander Selkirk, Defoe's 'Robinson Crusoe', in the Juan Fernández Islands, then in 1708-11 he completed his third circumnavigation as a pilot to the privateer captain Woodes Rogers, in the course of which Selkirk was salvaged from his six-year confinement.

Right The chart and coastal views of Shark's Bay, northwestern Australia, from Dampier's *Voyage to New Holland* (1703).
Following pages Dampier and his companions in their canoe overtaken by a dreadfull [sic] storm.

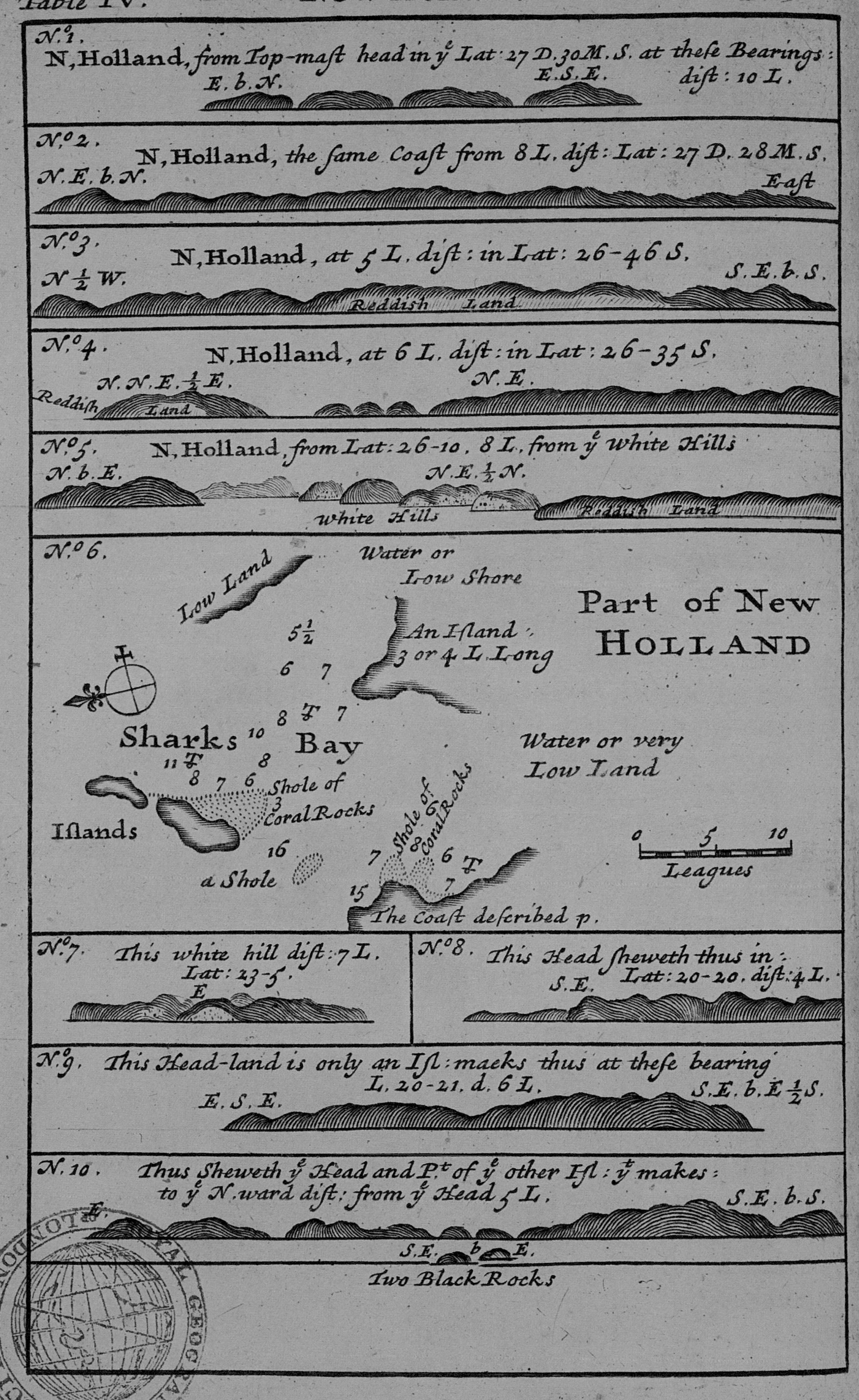
Damp. Voy. Vol. 3. p. 81.
Table IV.
New Holland
N.° 1.
N, Holland, from Top-mast head in yᵉ Lat: 27 D. 30 M. S. at these Bearings:
E. b. N.
E. S. E.
dist: 10 L.
N.° 2.
N, Holland, the same Coast from 8 L. dist: Lat: 27 D. 28 M. S.
N. E. b. N.
East
N.° 3.
N, Holland, at 5 L. dist: in Lat: 26-46 S.
N ½ W.
S. E. b. S.
Reddish Land
N.° 4.
N, Holland, at 6 L. dist: in Lat: 26-35 S.
N. N. E. ½ E.
N. E.
Reddish Land
N.° 5.
N, Holland, from Lat: 26-10. 8 L. from yᵉ White Hills
N. b. E.
N. E. ½ N.
White Hills
Reddish Land
N.° 6.
Low Land
Water or Low Shore
Part of New HOLLAND
An Island 3 or 4 L Long
Sharks Bay
Water or very Low Land
Shole of Coral Rocks
Islands
a Shole
Shole of Coral Rocks
Leagues
The Coast described p.
N.° 7.
This white hill dist: 7 L. Lat: 23-5.
E
N.° 8.
This Head sheweth thus in S. E. Lat: 20-20. dist: 4 L.
N.° 9.
This Head-land is only an Isl: maeks thus at these bearing L. 20-21. d. 6 L.
E. S. E.
S. E. b. E ½ S.
N. 10.
Thus Sheweth yᵉ Head and Pᵗ of yᵉ other Isl: yᵗ makes: to yᵉ N. ward dist: from yᵉ Head 5 L.
E.
S. E. b. S.
S. E. b E.
Two Black Rocks

Dampier & his Companions in the

Canoe, overtaken by a dreadfull Storm.

Fictitious Voyages and Fabulous Worlds

The imaginary and the apocryphal in the literature of exploration.

AS IF TRUTH WERE NOT already stranger than fiction, the literature of exploration abounds with bizarre and extraordinary journeys that never took place; fantastic encounters with mysterious peoples previously uncontacted and never to be seen again; and elusive, beckoning kingdoms that like the island of Fand erupt momentarily from the deep, only to sink without trace into the tranquil void that gave them birth. In fact, narratives of imaginary voyages and invented worlds often proved more appealing and certainly no less convincing than their depressingly authentic counterparts. Nowadays, of course, we are far too well informed, sophisticated and wordly wise to be taken in by such cunning deceits, but in times when fabulous beasts roamed the white spaces of the map, and monsters of the firmament rose menacingly from the seaman's chart, the naïve and unsuspecting public could suffer all too easily at the hands of the dedicated impostor. Among the hoaxers was Daniel Defoe, who could so manipulatively and covertly flood his literature with imaginary voyagers, pirates and idealistic colonists that debate would still rage three centuries later over whether they were real people or simply more of Defoe's little pranks.

It was nothing new; the fictitious voyage already had a long history, and Defoe was merely partaking of a time-honoured tradition. As early as the fourth century BCE, Euhemerus told of his voyage to the mythical island of Panchaea where a golden pillar recorded the chronology of the gods. Around 150 CE Antonius Diogenes narrated in his *Wonders beyond Thule* a conceptualized journey in the hyperborean north which brought the traveller close to the moon. And about the same time, 'having led a humdrum existence with no truth to put on record', the humorist Lucian released his *True Histories*, a hilarious parody which took his mariners to an island packed with the heroes of antiquity, and across the Atlantic to where a giant waterspout lifted them into a fearsome battle between the peoples of the sun and the moon.

The advent of the Middle Ages witnessed the more widespread emergence of the so-called 'apocryphal voyage' – a genre previously characterized by the *Odyssey* and *Argonautica* but ruthlessly dismissed by rational Greek and Roman academia. Plausible enough to have taken place, obscure in pedigree and questionable in authority, its content embellished and sensationalized by copyists and editors, the apocryphal voyage liberally plagiarized incidents from one narrative into another. In fact, like the awesome denizens of the deep and the men with two heads that adorned its pages, the deceit was half-expected, almost demanded by the medieval readership.

Saint Brendan sailed off in a humble curragh to find the 'land promised by the saints', confronting a 'crystal column' (an iceberg) and being lifted on the back of a whale. The Welshman Madoc sought a new life for himself and his followers far across the western sea. Henry Sinclair, laird of the Orkneys, took a fleet to America to secure a resting place for the Holy Grail and other treasures of the Knights Templar. The brothers Nicolò and Antonio Zeno encountered flourishing island kingdoms in the North Atlantic. And the gallant knight John de Mandeville embroidered a mundane excursion to the Holy Land with fabulous pilfered anecdotes of India, Tibet and the Far East. The maps would slowly and somewhat reluctantly relieve themselves of these outlandish discoveries, but the more convincing apocrypha would confuse and confound geographers well into the Age of Enlightenment. The voyages of Lorenzo Maldonado, who in 1588 merrily sailed across the heart of North America to emerge into the Pacific, and Bartolomé de Fonte, who in 1640 did much the same in reverse, rankled the geographical subconscious until late in the eighteenth century.

In 1516 Thomas More's *Utopia*, which placed an ideal imagined world somewhere, literally nowhere, across the Atlantic, inaugurated a genre that employed the discovery of fictitious lands as a vehicle for satire and parody, and for the alleviation of the despair with which idealists and philosophers saw human life evolving around them. Over the next two centuries the genre became so refined and adept in its use of sophisticated props and credible geographical locations that the gap between myth and reality blurred into indistinction. In 1676 Gabriel de Foigny's hero fell from a winged monster into a hermaphroditic, asexual society on the shores of Western Australia; and in 1682 Denis Vairasse, unusually insistent on the veracity of his narrative, drew on recent Dutch discoveries to place his 'land of the Severambes' at much the same spot. The possibility of a vast undiscovered continent deep in the southern seas became welcome succour to a seemingly endless procession of Utopian dreamers. About 1710, somewhere near Kerguelen Island, the shipwrecked mariner Jaques Massé found a 'land of blessing and peace' where men dwelt safe from tyranny and oppression. The English adventurer Morris Williams resided for twenty years in New Athens, a colony founded two millennia earlier by the 100,000 followers of an ancient Greek named Demophilus. Around 1750 François Gabriel Coyer described the island of Frivola, which Lord Anson had chanced upon during his circumnavigation but had forgetfully omitted from his log. Then in

1781 Restif de la Bretonne's hero Victorin made a journey by flying machine to an antipodean land where everything was a mirror-image of French society, even its capital Sirap.

By the late seventeenth century the exponents of the imaginary voyage, motivated perhaps by the prospect of quick financial gain, a fleeting moment of glory or simply a warped form of self-satisfaction, had became so skilled in deliberate deception that their work could quite innocently absorb itself into the burgeoning corpus of authentic travel literature. Some went so far as to place their fabulous creations in perfectly legitimate places, although taking care to choose locations sufficiently exotic and little known for their imposture to pass unheeded. In 1704 the shadowy George Psalmanazar wrote a bestselling and seemingly authoritative account of Formosa, now Taiwan, stunning his audience with lurid descriptions of polygamy, human sacrifice, cannibalism and infanticide. A few years earlier the Frenchman Mathieu Sagean explored west of the Mississippi to find a rich kingdom, its ermine-clothed king, a descendant of Moctezuma, commanding a mighty army from his three-storey palace of solid gold. The inveterate German adventurer Johann Spassvogel wrote copiously of a fortified colony that he and his followers placed surreptitiously on Georgia's Atlantic seaboard. The island of Fonseca, inhabited entirely by women and just a stone's throw from Barbados, saw visits by some of the more fortunate mariners on a number of occasions. And in 1756 Captain David Tompson, by placing his voyage amidst familiar lands, was able to provide a most convincing account of the 'Isle of Reason' where, to the crew's obvious delight, polygamy was the norm.

Needless to say, as the pace of geographical discovery accelerated, our creative travellers found themselves increasingly deprived of the last hiding places for the manifestation of their craft. At first they capitalized on the recent discoveries by Cook and Bougainville in the Pacific, describing with meticulous detail islands that the great navigators had somehow passed by. In the 1780s Guillaume Grivel filled no less than six volumes with a glowing account of *L'Isle Inconnue*, a South-Sea Edenic paradise of babbling brooks and docile fauna. Then in the 1820s an anonymous hero on a Japanese trading voyage spent two years on the islands of Bullanabee and Clinkataboo. But as the market for fictitious Pacific islands neared saturation, so the claims of the imaginary voyager were pressured into even wilder extravagance. Baron Ludvig Holberg's unsuspecting protagonist, Niels Klim, fell down a shaft and entered a subterranean kingdom populated by mobile trees with the heads and feet of humans. And in the late nineteenth century the Cornish mariner Peter Wilkins, shipwrecked at the South Pole, encountered a society of beautiful flying people, one of whom he nursed back to health and subsequently married.

The most remote places on earth having been unveiled, along with the curious folk that inhabited them, there was no option other than to go extraterrestrial. Voyages to the moon, and the societies to be found there, had been popular since the earliest times, particularly amongst those who thought it salutary to place their political satires a little further out of harm's way than a mere island in the South Seas. While most, like Daniel Defoe's *The Consolidator* – 'translated from the lunar language' by a 'true-born English man' – were critiques of life here on earth, others, like John Wilkins's *Discovery of the World in the Moone* (1638) were for their time intelligently reasoned accounts of what a lunar society, if it existed at all, must be like. Stretching the boundaries even further, Chevalier de Béthune gave us a glimpse of life on Mercury as it was in 1750, and Bernard de Fontenelle extended Wilkins's rationale to cover the entire universe. Others, like the philosopher Voltaire, took an opposite standpoint, giving us extraterrestrials descending to earth, only to find this planet a 'great disappointment' compared with their own.

Although the occasional treatise of apocryphal travel literature, conveniently secreted away in darkest Africa or the jungles of Amazonia, would continue to appear sporadically throughout the nineteenth century, the genre as a medium for political or philosophical expression, and particularly as a platform for the elaborately conceived spoof, had few places to go. The tradition was momentarily resurrected by Jules Verne's *Journey to the Centre of the Earth* and Arthur Conan Doyle's *The Lost World*, both of which were set in real places and either of which might in earlier times have passed as perfectly legitimate narratives. But had the days of deliberate deception come to an end? Not at all. The early twentieth-century popular press had few qualms about turning a routinely pedestrian travelogue into an epic of survival and endurance, and as late as 1921 the enterprising adventurer Walter E Traprock – the New York architect George Chappell who never went anywhere very exciting – had little difficulty convincing his more humourless readership of a cruise to the Filbert Islands, 'unmarked on every map from Mercator to Rand McNally', where the fatu-liva bird lays square eggs and the local queen carries a taa-taa as protection against falling nuts. Whether or not a publisher in the current marketplace would ever have the courage to repeat the House of Putnam's noble gesture is difficult to say; but then who would know?

Right An aerial view of the 'Land of Jansenie', 1660, an invention of the Capuchin theologian Ange Lambert Zacharie de Lisieux.

Septentrion
Orient
Midy

Samuel Fritz: Missionary and Cartographer on the Amazon

Spreading the Word of God from a dugout canoe.

1686–1723

THE AMAZON HAD BEEN DESCENDED IN 1542, but it would be a century or more before any firm interest was shown in the river or its natural resources. A scattering of English, Dutch and Irish settlements had sprung up near the delta, and from Ecuador expeditions sought the Omagua, an advanced people that occupied much of the river's upper course. One of these, in 1561 under the bloodthirsty megalomaniac Lope de Aguirre, had actually accomplished a nightmarish descent to the Atlantic. But with the demarcation between Spanish and Portuguese territories so grossly ill-defined, complications arose over which nation had superior rights to the river. Although Portugal and Spain were united under the same king in 1580, their colonial ex-patriots clung strongly to national ties. In fact the Portuguese would exploit the union to their advantage, pushing their conquests far westward and in 1637 despatching Pedro de Teixeira on a flag-flying mission up the Amazon. Teixeira, the first European to fully ascend the river, reached Ecuador in under a year, then retraced his route downstream to become the first to cross South America in both directions.

Precise geographical knowledge of the Amazon and its tributaries remained sketchy until the arrival of the Jesuits in the 1650s. For 130 years they monopolized the ministry to the Indians, enduring formidable hardships to establish missions throughout Amazonia. Particularly forbidding were the countless languages encountered, most of which had no equivalents for abstract concepts like 'belief' or 'spirit', while to expound on the Trinity to the Yancos tribe proved impossible, their word for three being 'poettarrarorincouroac'. However, linguistics was a field in which the intrepid Bohemian missionary Samuel Fritz excelled. He spent the best part of forty years ministering to the Indians from a dugout canoe, and with only rudimentary equipment produced the first detailed map of Amazonia. In the rainy season of 1689 he lay unwell for three months in a Yarimagua village, the waters rising around him, rats and lizards eating his food, while the grunting of alligators kept him from sleep. Seeking medical attention he descended the Amazon to its mouth, only to be imprisoned for eighteen months as a spy. Beloved by the Indians as their saviour from Portuguese slave traders, much of his life was devoted to resettling his flock to the safety of the upper Amazon. He died in 1723, his body horribly mutilated from the bites of insects he had never bothered to brush aside.

Right Samuel Fritz's remarkably accurate map of the Amazon, its tributaries and its peoples. Printed in 1707, it summarizes the results of a century of Jesuit exploration.

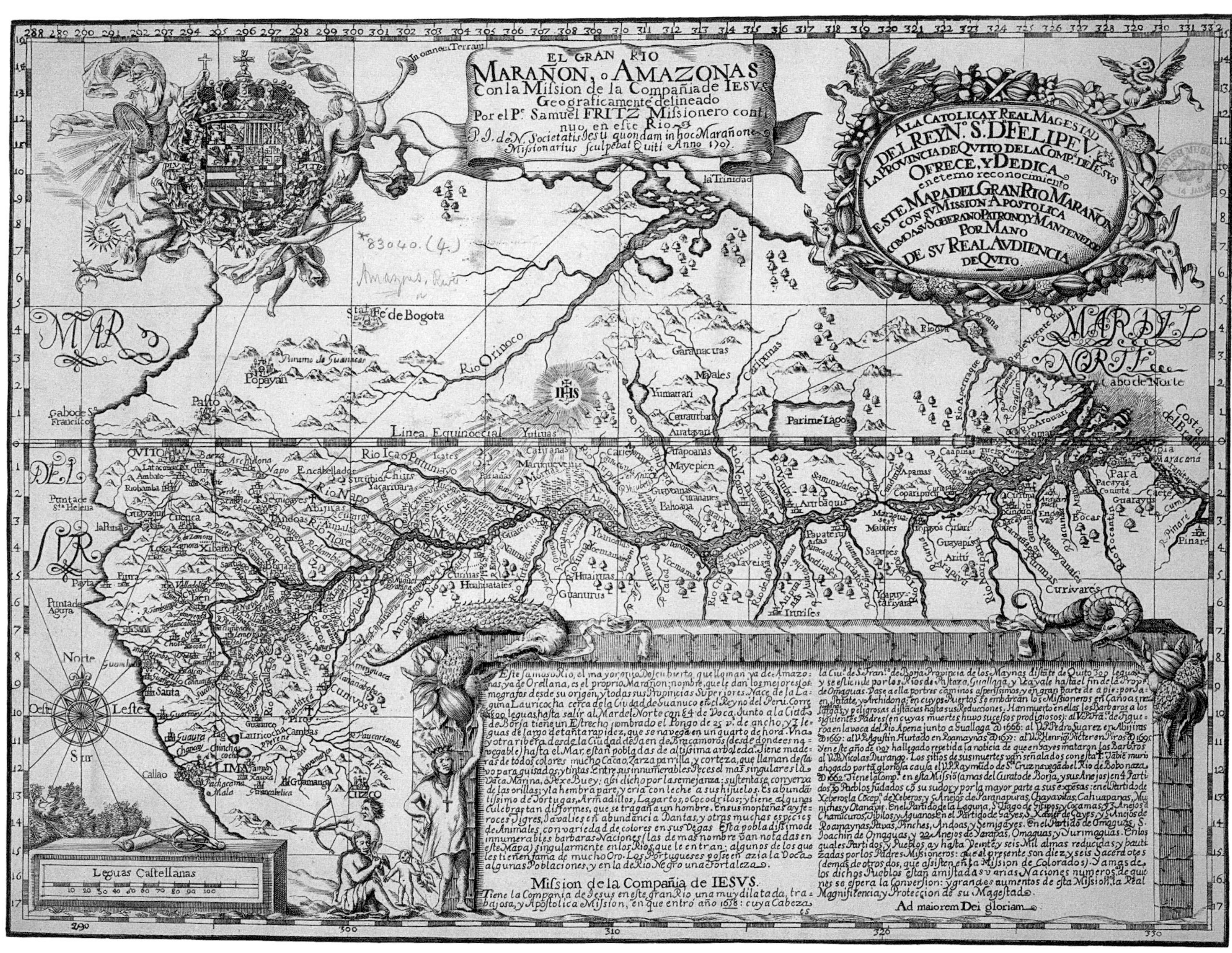
EL GRAN RIO
MARAÑON, o AMAZONAS
Con la Mission de la Compañia de IESVS
Geograficamente delineado
Por el Pe. Samuel FRITZ Missionero continuo en este Rio
P. J. de N. Societatis Jesu quondam in hoc Marañone Missionarius sculpebat Quiti Anno 1707.
A LA CATOLICA Y REAL MAGESTAD
DEL REYN. S. D. FELIPE V.
LA PROVINCIA DE QUITO DE LA COMP. DE IESUS
OFRECE, Y DEDICA
en eterno reconocimiento
ESTE MAPA DEL GRAN RIO MARAÑON
CON SU MISSION APOSTOLICA
COMO A SU SOBERANO PATRON Y MANTENEDOR
POR MANO
DE SU REAL AUDIENCIA
DE QUITO.
MAR DEL SUR
MAR DEL NORTE
Sta Fe de Bogota
Rio Orinoco
Popayan
Pasto
Linea Equinoccial
Parime Lago
Cabo de Norte
Costa del Brasil
QUITO
Rio Napo
LIMA
Callao
Cuzco
Para
Mission de la Compañia de IESVS.
Leguas Castellanas
Norte
Sur
Oeste
Leste
Ad maiorem Dei gloriam

1721-22

Jacob Roggeveen Discovers Easter Island

The world's most remote inhabited outpost.

THE DUTCH WEST INDIA COMPANY never experienced quite the same measure of success as its Eastern counterpart. Founded in 1621 to monopolize trade within the Atlantic rim – a considerably less fertile ground than that enjoyed by its rival – its early fortunes depended heavily on piratical forays into Spanish waters. It did establish colonies on North America's eastern seaboard, one of which became New York, as well as in the Antilles, Surinam, Ghana and Brazil, but within fifty years much had been lost to competing nations. Heavily in debt, the company foundered in 1674 but lingered in a reconstituted form until nationalization in 1791. By comparison with the East India Company it contributed little to geographical discovery, but in 1721 it unexpectedly broke with tradition and acquiesced to the fitting of a fleet of three ships for a voyage into the South Pacific. The destination was the semi-mythical 'Davis Land', sighted thirty-four years earlier by the Englishman Edward Davis and believed to represent the extremity of a vast undiscovered southern continent. The commander was the sixty-two-year-old Jacob Roggeveen, whose father Arent had been a lifelong armchair champion of discovery in the southern seas.

Roggeveen sailed in August 1721 and rounded Cape Horn in the most deplorable weather. Although the sighting of icebergs provided clear evidence for a southern continent, violent winds, snow and hail forced the expedition to turn north to the tranquil haven of the Juan Fernández Islands. From here Roggeveen turned southwest into a navigational black hole where few had ventured before, and on 5 April 1722, Easter Sunday, he came upon a remote island whose population had survived in isolation for hundreds of years. Sadly, Roggeveen's sojourn on the land he christened Paasch Eyland (Easter Island) would be all too brief. He remarks extensively on the dress of the islanders and their manner of cooking without pots, but says regrettably little about the awe-inspiring statues or the traditions that inspired them. Fearful of rising seas, he returned to his ships to leave the islanders in a peace that would endure for another fifty years. A meandering path through the Pacific brought him in December to Java, where he was arrested for infringing on East India Company territory and his ships impounded. As a result, this, the last of the great Dutch voyages would be little known in its time, and its official log would languish anonymously in the archives for more than a hundred years.

Right Roggeveen's three ships at anchor off Easter Island. From Roggeveen's *Tweejaarige reyze rondom de wereld* (1728).

Vitus Bering and the Great Northern Expedition

Russia seeks its limits in the far northeast.

1725-41

THROUGHOUT HIS MANY YEARS AS RULER OF RUSSIA, PETER THE GREAT had striven to draw his country into the modern age, reforming its navy, creating access to the oceans via the Baltic and the Black seas, and establishing Russia as a major world power. Towards the end of his life he looked increasingly to the east, and to the desolate shores of the northern Pacific where there was nothing to bar the Russian advance. But the limit of Russia in the far northeast remained obscure. Did it extend uninterruptedly into America, either via a narrow bridge or a more substantial northerly landmass, or was there a navigable seaway separating the two continents? To solve the mystery, in 1724, the year before his death, Peter summoned Vitus Jonassen Bering, a seasoned Danish navigator serving with the Russian navy. Bering and his assistants started overland from St Petersburg in January 1725, arriving after eighteen months on the Sea of Okhotsk where a vessel was put together to sail the party to Kamchatka. Here a second ship, the *Saint Gabriel*, was constructed, and in July 1728 the expedition finally got underway, following the coast northward beyond Cape Chukotskiy. Poor visibility blighted the mission, concealing the Alaskan coast to the east, so that when Bering halted in 67°18 he was unaware that he had passed through the strait that now bears his name.

Bering returned to St Petersburg in 1730, by which time Peter had died and his niece Anna had assumed the throne. Content to advance her uncle's legacy, and convinced by Bering that Russia's destiny lay in the east, she approved a second and vastly more complex expedition to chart the Siberian coast from the Arctic to China, and to establish the proximity of Japan and America. Although planned to last only two years, Bering's second expedition would blossom into what would become the Great Northern Expedition, detachments from which, over the next ten years, would fan out across almost every part of Siberia. In a nightmare of logistics Bering poured five years into assembling an army of shipwrights and sailors, an array of distinguished scientists and explorers, and to transporting them and their materials to one of the most inaccessible regions on earth. In 1741, wearied by the monumental task he had initiated, he met an inauspicious end, shipwrecked and dying of scurvy on the island, and in the sea named after him.

Right Filip Johan Strahlenberg's monumental map of the Russian empire, incorporating the results of the Great Northern Expedition. **Following pages** A map by Mikhail Tatarinov, 1781, showing the extent of early Russian advances towards Alaska.

MARE GLACIALE
SEPTENTRIO
MARE IAPONICUM
IMPERIUM MOSCOVITICUM
RUSSICA
SIBIRIA
TARTARIA
MONGALIA
SINUS KAMTSCHATKA
PONTUS EUXINUS
MARE CASPIUM
TURKESTAN
PERSIÆ PARS
IMPERIUM MAGNI MOGOLIS PARS
IMPERIUM SINARUM
PEKIN
MARE SINICUM
I. Formosa
Macao
LAOQUO
MERIDIES
OCCIDENS
ORIENS
SPATIOSISSIMUM
IMPERIUM
RUSSIÆ MAGNÆ
recentissimas Observationes
MAPPA GEOGRAPHICA
accuratissime delineatum
opera et sumtibus
TOBIÆ CONRADI LOTTERI
Geogr. et Chalcogr.
AUGUSTÆ VINDEL.
Nota
Scala

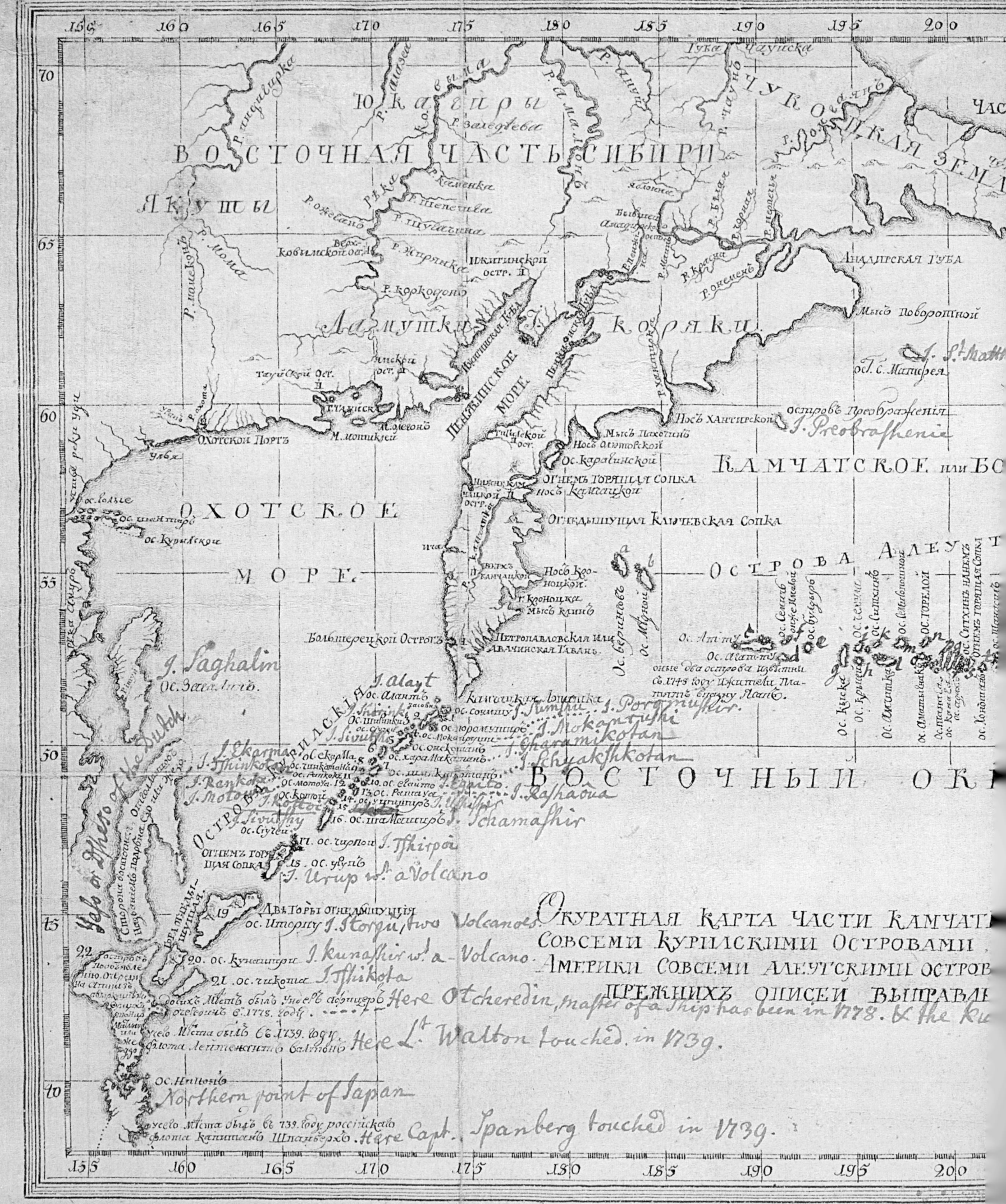

ВОСТОЧНАЯ ЧАСТЬ СИБИРИ
ЯКУТЫ
ЮКАГИРЫ
ЧУКОТСКАЯ ЗЕМЛЯ
ЛАМУТКИ
КОРЯКИ
ОХОТСКОЕ МОРЕ
ПЕНЖИНСКОЕ МОРЕ
КАМЧАТСКОЕ или БО
ОСТРОВА АЛЕУТ
ВОСТОЧНЫЙ ОКЕ
ОСТРОВА КУРИЛСКИЯ
Охотской Портъ
Анадырская губа
Мысъ Поворотной
Огнемъ горящая сопка
Огнедышущая Ключевская сопка
Большерецкой Острогъ
Петропавловская или Авачинская гавань
ос. Беринговъ
ос. Медной
I. Saghalin
I. Alayt
I. Shirinki
I. Sivutsha
I. Ekarma
I. Thinkotan
I. Rankoke
I. Motowa
I. Porgmussir
I. Mokantushi
I. Sharamikotan
I. Schyakshkotan
I. Rashaona
I. Ushisir
I. Schamashir
I. Thirpoi
I. Urup with a Volcano
I. Storgu, two Volcanoes
I. Kunashir with a Volcano
I. Thikota
Isle of Jhesso of the Dutch
I. St. Matth
I. Preobrashenie
Northern point of Japan
Here Otcheredin, master of a Ship has been in 1778. & the R
Here Lt. Walton touched in 1739.
Here Capt. Spanberg touched in 1739.
ОКУРАТНАЯ КАРТА ЧАСТИ КАМЧАТ
СОВСЕМИ КУРИЛСКИМИ ОСТРОВАМИ
АМЕРИКИ СОВСЕМИ АЛЕУТСКИМИ ОСТРОВ
ПРЕЖНИХЪ ОПИСЕЙ ВЫПРАВЛ

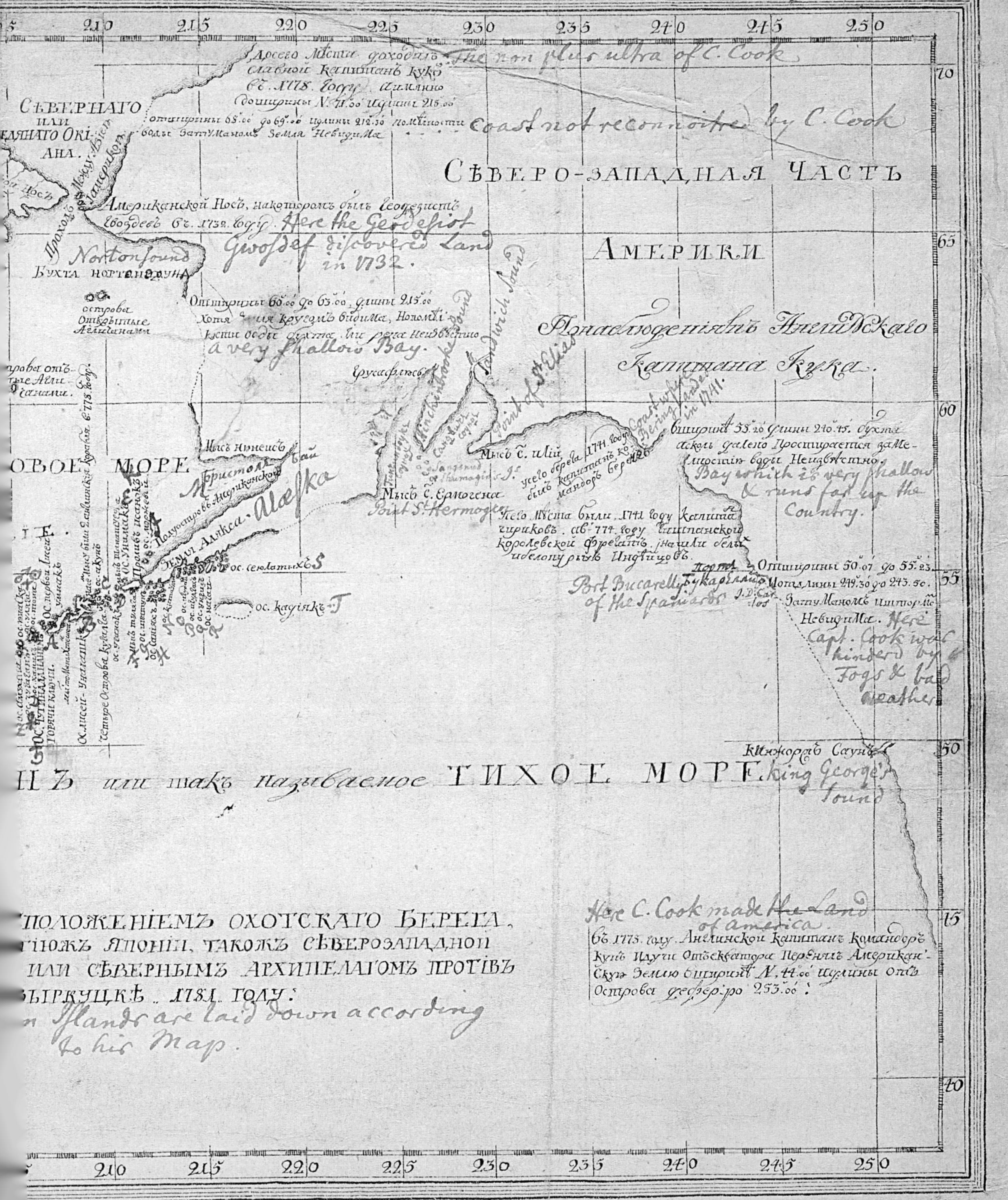

210
215
220
225
230
235
240
245
250
70
65
60
55
50
45
40
The non plus ultra of C. Cook
Coast not reconnoitre by C. Cook
Сѣверо-западная часть
Америки
По наблюденіямъ Аглицкаго
Капитана Кука.
Американской Носъ, накоторомъ былъ Геодезистъ Гвоздевъ въ 1732 году
Here the Geodesist Gwosdef discovered Land in 1732.
Norton Sound
Бухта Нортонсоунд
a very shallow Bay.
Sandwich Sound
Point of St. Elias
Coast where Bering landed in 1741.
Мысъ Ст. Илий
Мысъ Ст. Ермогена
Point St. Hermogen
Alaska
Bay which is very shallow & runs far up the Country.
Port Bucarelli of the Spaniards
Here Capt. Cook was hindered by Fogs & bad weather
Кингжорджъ Саундъ
King George's Sound
Тихое море
Here C. Cook made the Land of America.
Положеніемъ Охотскаго берега,
Иркуцкѣ 1781 году:
n Islands are laid down according to his Map.

La Vérendrye and the Elusive 'River of the West'

A family affair. The opening of the North American prairies.

1731-38

EXPLORERS OF THE MID-EIGHTEENTH CENTURY had barely the slightest concept of the topography of North America's west and northwest. Fur traders Pierre and Paul Mallet had in 1739 reported uncharted mountains at the head of the Platte River, but it was only towards the end of the century that the Rocky Mountains would be recognized as an unbroken chain bisecting the continent. Exploration of the northwest coast was slow to get underway, the Spanish pioneers having charted only the Californian coast, while navigators from the Siberian mainland in the 1740s saw only Alaska. The widely accepted narrative of the apocryphal voyager Bartolomé de Fonte had spawned the myth of a 'Strait of Anian', which directly connected the Atlantic and Pacific, together with a 'Sea of the West' – a vast gulf submerging most of western Canada. The Rockies still unknown, it seemed reasonable to locate the major watershed a little beyond Lake Superior, from where a hypothetical 'River of the West' meandered towards the fabled gulf and hence the Pacific. Native reports seemed to confirm the suspicion, placing a 'great sea' (actually Lake Winnipeg) not too far away to the northwest.

It was the quest for the 'River of the West' that would occupy Pierre Gaultier de Varennes, sieur de La Vérendrye, for twelve years of his life. A Canadian-born ex-soldier, he had spent fifteen years farming in Quebec before joining the fur traders around Lake Nipigon. Assisted by three sons, his explorations began in earnest in 1731, and over the next few years he established a chain of forts between lakes Superior and Winnipeg. In 1738, heavily criticized for concentrating on the profit from furs at the expense of new discoveries, and of delegating too much of the exploratory work to his subordinates and family, he attempted to restore his personal prestige by taking an expedition into Mandan country, present-day North Dakota. There a mighty river, the Missouri, had been reported – surely La Vérendrye's long-sought 'River of the West'. But curiously, after venturing some 2400 kilometres (1500 miles), he halted just a few kilometres short of the river, while a son sent ahead failed to recognize that the river flowed east not west. Now in his fifties and physically exhausted, La Vérendrye placed subsequent expeditions in the hands of his sons who, within a few years, opened vast swathes of territory from South Dakota to Wyoming and northwest to Saskatchewan.

Right A map drawn for La Vérendrye by his native guide Auchagah, showing the extensive network of lakes and portages to the west of Lake Superior.

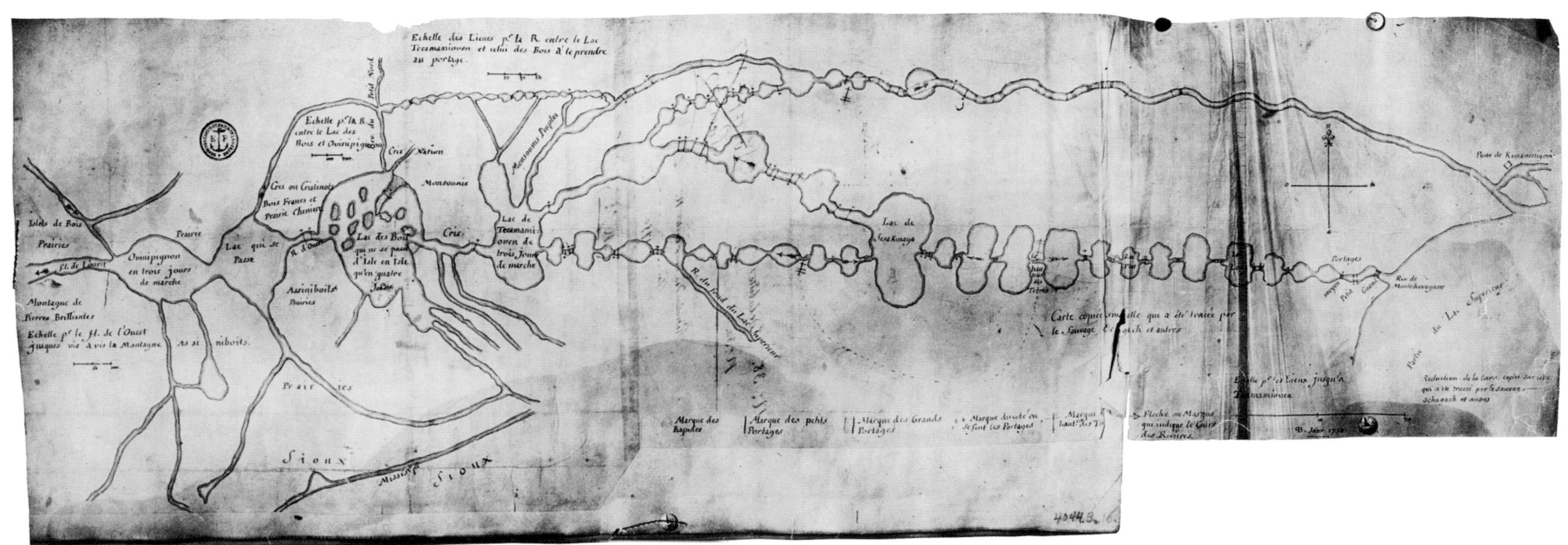
Echelle des Lieues pr la R. entre le Lac Tecamaniouen et celui des Bois à le prendre au portage.
Echelle pr la R. entre le Lac des Bois et Ouinipigon
Cris Nation
Monsounis
Islets de Bois
Prairies
Prairie
Lac qui se Passe
Ouinipignon en trois jours de marche
Fl. de l'Ouest
Montagne de Pierres Brillantes
Echelle pr le Fl. de l'Ouest jusques vis à vis la Montagne
Assiniboils
Prairies
Lac des Bois qui ne se passe d'Isle en Isle qu'en quatre Jours
Cris
Lac de Tecamaniouen de trois Jours de marche
Lac de
Portages
Poste du Lac Superieur
Sioux
Sioux
Marque des Rapides
Marque des petits Portages
Marque des Grands Portages
Fleche ou Marque qui indique le Cours des Rivieres

La Condamine's Expedition to the Equator

South America opens its doors to European scientists and cartographers.

1736-44

THE RAPID ADVANCES IN TECHNOLOGY AND SCIENTIFIC REASONING that accompanied the dawn of the eighteenth century also ushered in a new age of cartography. Approximation gave way to precision measurement, admitting only the verifiable and stripping the maps of blank-filling guesswork, some of it centuries old. Pioneering the new movement was a band of erudite French and Spanish scientists that descended on Ecuador in 1736, its purpose being to establish the shape of the earth. Headed by the aristocrat and mathematician Charles-Marie de La Condamine, they had alighted on the equator to settle a matter of acrimonious debate: was the earth flattened at the poles as proclaimed by Newton, or was it the prolate spheroid advocated by the French. Only by measuring a degree of latitude in the Arctic and at the equator could the battle be decided. While one team busied itself in Lapland, La Condamine and his wayward scholars, plagued by frustration, delay and accusations of being gold seekers in disguise, spent several miserable years in the icy, wind-swept Andean highlands. It was not until 1743 that the last observations were completed, reluctantly confirming the Newtonian position, but by now one of the team had died of fever, another had been stoned to death by a mob, two had gone mad and another two had married.

In eight years the expedition had solved one of earth's greatest mysteries and had accumulated a mass of information on Spanish America, a geographically uncertain region with a longstanding embargo on foreign travellers. La Condamine's curiosity in matters other than mathematics had been so aroused that he decided to return to France, expedition reports in hand, by the difficult route down the Amazon to Belém, then to the French colony in Guiana. He would not only become the Amazon's first foreigner but also its first professional scientist. Apart from the inevitable health problems and the unnerving descent from the Andes, his 5000-kilometre (3000-mile) voyage in a balsa raft was relatively undramatic, allowing him the opportunity to correct existing maps and make detailed observations of tribal customs, flora and fauna, which would for the first time captivate European audiences and prepare the ground for the horde of scientists that would subsequently invade the river. Delayed in Guiana for six months, he finally returned to Paris early in 1745, causing a sensation not so much by his mathematical achievements but by demonstrating the remarkable properties of a previously unheard-of material: rubber.

Right This plan of Quito, surveyed by La Condamine's team, reflects the advances in cartography that characterized this expedition.

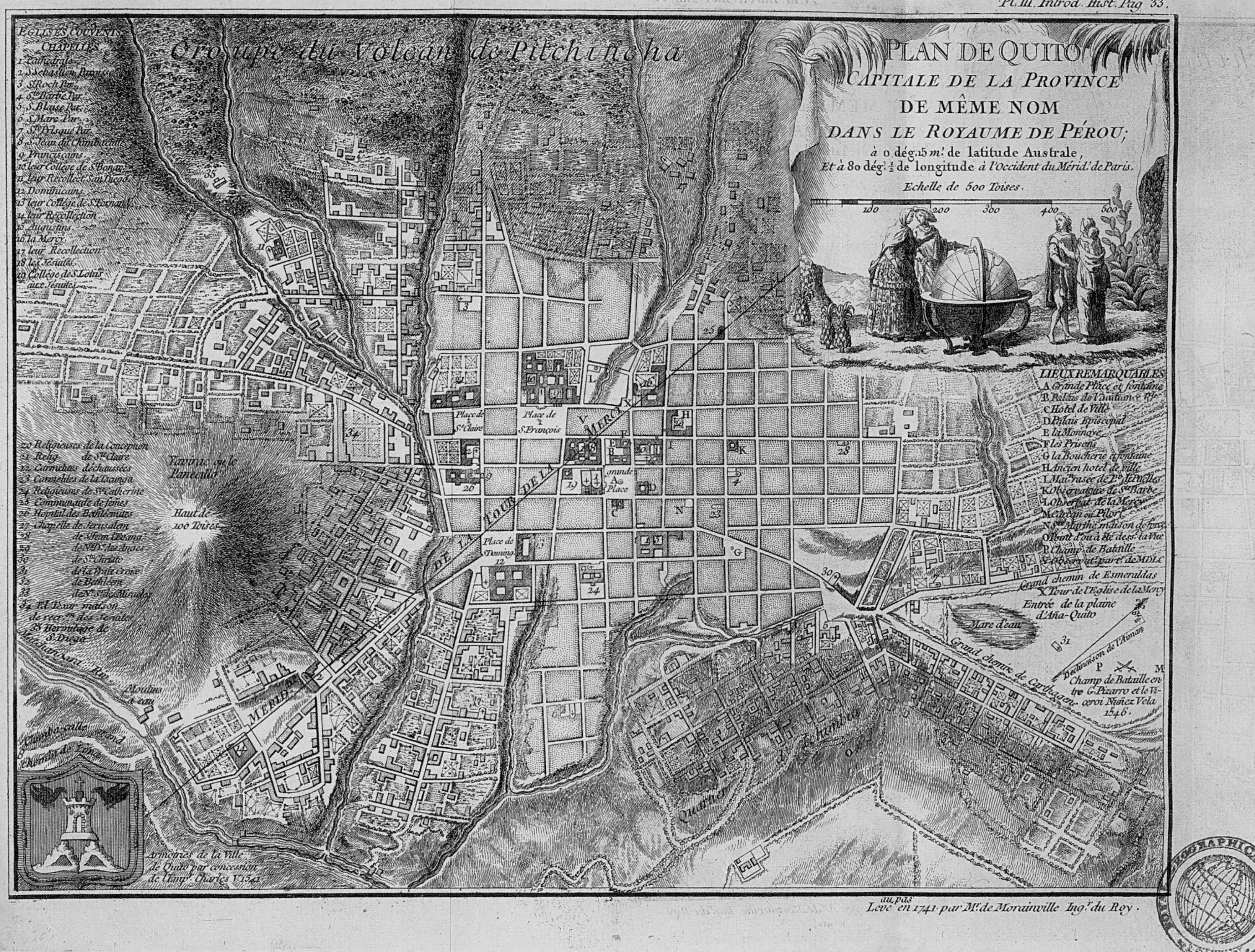
Pl. III. Introd. Hist. Pag. 33.
PLAN DE QUITO
CAPITALE DE LA PROVINCE
DE MÊME NOM
DANS LE ROYAUME DE PÉROU;
Echelle de 500 Toises.
Croupe du Volcan de Pitchincha
LIEUX REMARQUABLES
Grand chemin de Esmeraldas
Grand chemin de Carthagene
Mare d'eau
Champ de Bataille entre G. Pizarro et le Viceroi Nuñez Vela 1546.
Haut de 100 Toises
Place de S. François
Place de S. Claire
Place de S. Domingo
grande Place
Armoiries de la Ville de Quito
Levé en 1741 par Mr. de Morainville Ing. du Roy.

1740-44

The Horrors of George Anson's Voyage Around the World

For the sake of a severed ear.

IN 1731 THE ENGLISH BRIG *REBECCA*, returning peacefully from the West Indies, was boarded by Spanish coastguards who bound its captain, Robert Jenkins, to the mainmast and with a sword sliced off one of his ears. Harassment of English vessels in the Caribbean worsened over the next seven years, and when in 1738 Jenkins related his dramatic story before the Commons, proudly displaying the severed ear, relationships with Spain reached breaking point. Outraged that such a barbaric act should be perpetrated against a humble British citizen, Parliament voted for all-out war against Spain, the third so far that century. By the following year the might of the Royal Navy had assembled off Portsmouth for a massive onslaught on the Spanish empire. Blockading squadrons left for the Bay of Biscay and Gibraltar, and a heavily equipped convoy set out to blitzkreig the Caribbean. A further fleet of six vessels, under the command of Captain George Anson, would depart with instructions to launch a back-door offensive against the poorly defended Pacific ports.

The so-called 'War of Jenkins's Ear' turned into an unmitigated disaster. Men of the incompetently organized Caribbean campaign succumbed in vast numbers to yellow fever; attacks on strategic Spanish ports were successfully repelled; and Anson's voyage would become one of the most tragic stories of the sea.

Anson's rotting and inadequately victualled ships left Portsmouth in September 1740 crammed with 1900 men: 260 of them half-crippled Chelsea pensioners, 200 raw marines and the remainder press-ganged from gin houses and jails. Around Cape Horn they battled for six weeks against tumultuous seas and violent hailstorms that froze the sails and sent them crashing to the decks. Rampant scurvy decimated the crews, two ships went home, one was wrecked in the Chilean archipelago and another was scuttled for shortage of men. By the time the two surviving vessels left the tranquility of the Juan Fernández Islands, little more than 500 crew were left alive. From captured papers Anson learnt that the Caribbean expedition had miscarried, leaving him alone and adrift with no choice other than to abandon a further vessel, transfer the remaining crew to the flagship *Centurion* and strike for the East Indies. After weathering a typhoon in the Marianas, Anson had at least one, redeeming stroke of good luck when he took a Spanish galleon in the Philippines. He anchored off Portsmouth in June 1744, his hold bursting with treasure valued at £400,000.

Right Anson attacks and captures the Spanish galleon *Nuestra Señora de Cabadonga*. A painting by John Clevely.

Byron, Wallis, Carteret and the Scramble for the Pacific

The dawn of a new era of maritime discovery.

1764–69

The conclusion of the Seven Years War, which from 1756 to 1763 had pitted the major European nations against each other, marked a significant turning point in the history of exploration. Described by Winston Churchill as the 'first world war', its repercussions were felt around the globe and would shape the pattern of colonial expansion for decades to come. Great Britain had emerged as the dominant colonial power, the French navy had been crippled, and Spain, which had sided with France, had been enfeebled. But ironically the effects of the war would be most strongly felt in a part of the world left largely untouched by the European diaspora: the remote, beckoning Pacific. For Britain it was an ocean awash with commercial possibility; for France, deprived of its North American territories, it heralded a new imperial frontier; and for Russia, which languished ice-locked across the breadth of Asia, it was the sole gateway to seaborne expansion. Underemployed seafarers, starved of a good war, were diverted into distant exploration, while those that had previously entered the Pacific to plunder Spanish treasure galleons were succeeded by a generation of island hoppers who planted flags on the most inauspicious atolls, rechristening them after captains, crewmen and favoured members of the homeland nobility.

In 1764 Captain John Byron, grandfather of the poet, was rushed to the South Atlantic in the *Dolphin* to claim the Falkland Islands and the mythical 'Pepys Island', either of which might provide a base for Pacific expansion. Following this he was to revive 'New Albion', Francis Drake's whimsical British colony on the Californian coast, and return directly to England via the Northwest Passage. Byron took the Falklands, unaware that the French were there already and had renamed them the Malouines after St-Malo, but then, wearying of the cold, he ignored instructions and departed on a fruitless search for the Solomon Islands. Back in England in 1766, the *Dolphin* was refitted and handed to Captain Samuel Wallis for a voyage to the notoriously elusive southern continent. Initially accompanied by Philip Carteret in the ailing, unseaworthy *Swallow*, Wallis became the first European to enjoy the hospitality of Tahiti (which he named after King George III), then proceeded to claim the Society and Wallis islands. Carteret, despite indescribable hardships, discovered Pitcairn and countless other islands, but his greatest contribution was to finally demolish the myth of a continent hidden in the depths of the South Sea.

Right Wallis's ship, the *Dolphin*, at anchor off Tahiti.

A View of Port Royal Bay at Georges Island
25
Geo. Pinnock

Bougainville Discovers a Paradise in the South Sea

France looks towards the Pacific.

1766-69

In 1766 Louis-Antoine de Bougainville sailed from Nantes with two ships, the *Boudeuse* and *Étoile*, with instructions to circumnavigate the globe. The publicity accorded to the voyage would establish him as a pioneer of French circumnavigation, but he was by no means the first of his countrymen to accomplish this task, nor to range widely through the Pacific. French pirates were there in the late seventeenth century's buccaneering era, and by the 1720s more than 200 French vessels regularly loaded at the ports of Chile and Peru. In 1709 the trader Nicolas de Frondat crossed the Pacific from west to east and continued around the world, and over the next decade at least ten French vessels completed the circumnavigation. Sadly, these privately sponsored voyages attracted little attention at the time and our knowledge of them is fragmentary. By comparison, Bougainville sailed at the command of the king, he took scholars from the Académie des Sciences, and his journal, waxing lyrical about a South Sea paradise where the 'noble savage' lived in a state of blissful innocence, became an influential bestseller in several European languages.

Bougainville, a man of charm and humanity, a mathematician, scientist and diplomat, was a loyal patriot who bitterly mourned the loss of France's North American colonies. With 'the thought of giving to my country in the Southern Hemisphere what she no longer possesses in the northern one', he had established an ephemeral French outpost in the Falkland Islands. But in 1767 his first duty was to hand the colony to the Spanish – a requirement for guaranteeing Spain's continued support in the war with Great Britain. This being done, Bougainville entered the Pacific and like those before him searched in vain for the elusive 'southern continent'. In April 1768 he anchored off Tahiti, which, unaware that the Englishman Samuel Wallis had forestalled him by nine months, he claimed for France, christening the island New Cythera and its local shrub Bougainvillea. It was here that the valet to the expedition's botanist was discovered to be not a boy but a young lady. Named Jeanne Barré, she would become the first woman to encircle the globe. Bougainville's westerly passage halted abruptly at the Great Barrier Reef, diverting him northwest through the Solomon Islands and around the coast of New Guinea. So, once again, by a mere 150 kilometres (90 miles), the vast expanse of Australia's eastern seaboard escaped detection, at least for another two years.

Right Native canoes in the South Pacific. From Bougainville's *Voyage autour du Monde* (1771).

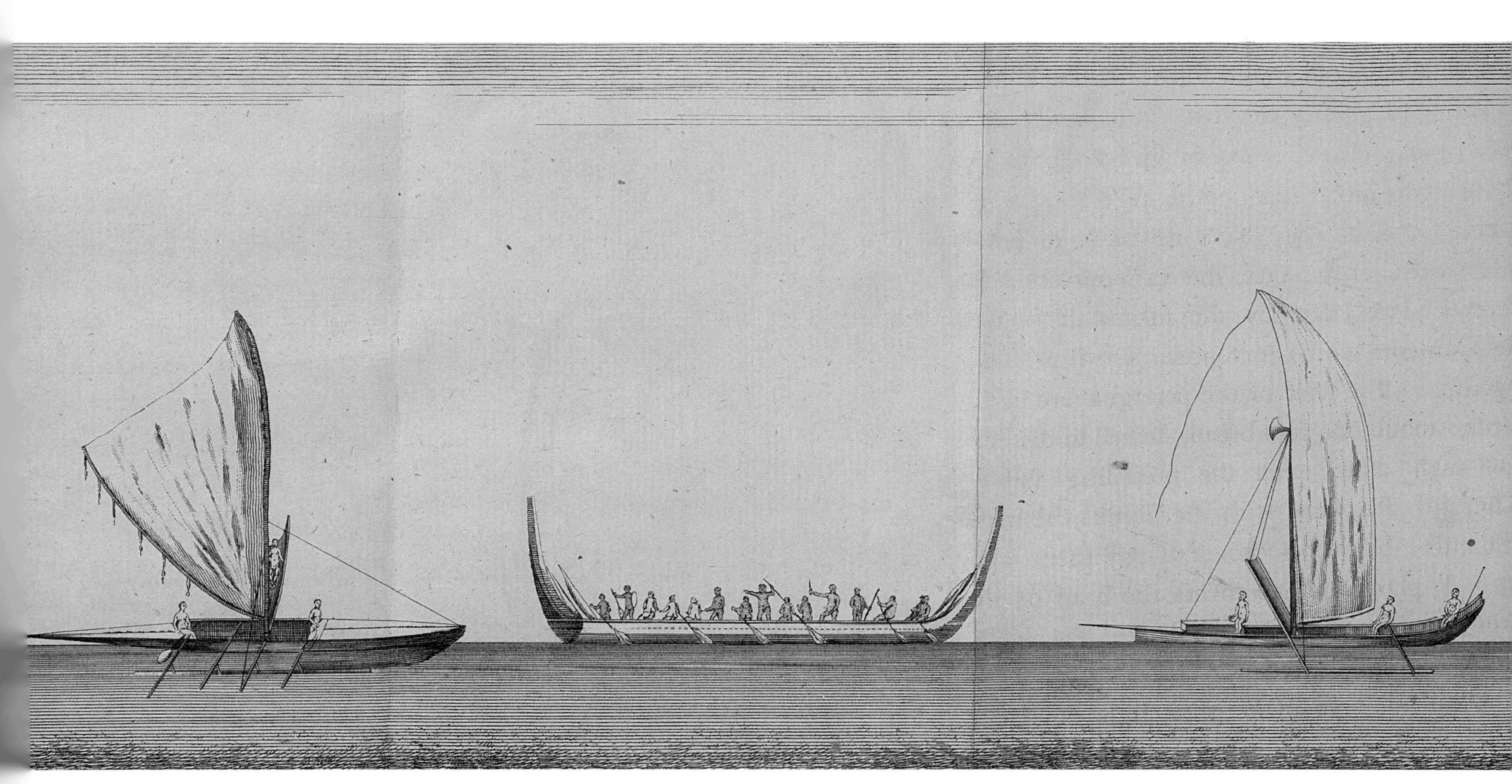

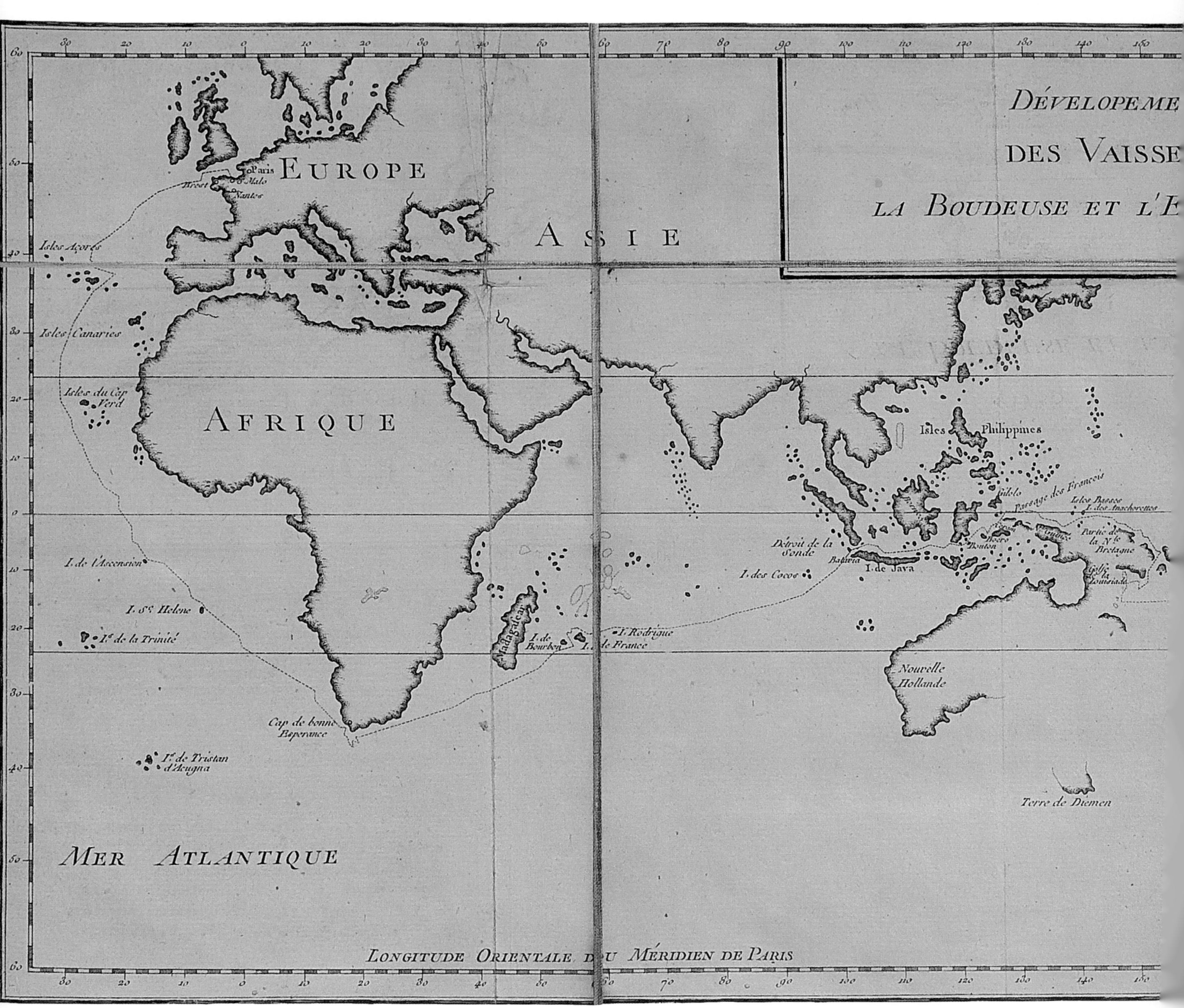

Above The track of Bougainville's ships, *Boudeuse* and *Étoile*, around the world.

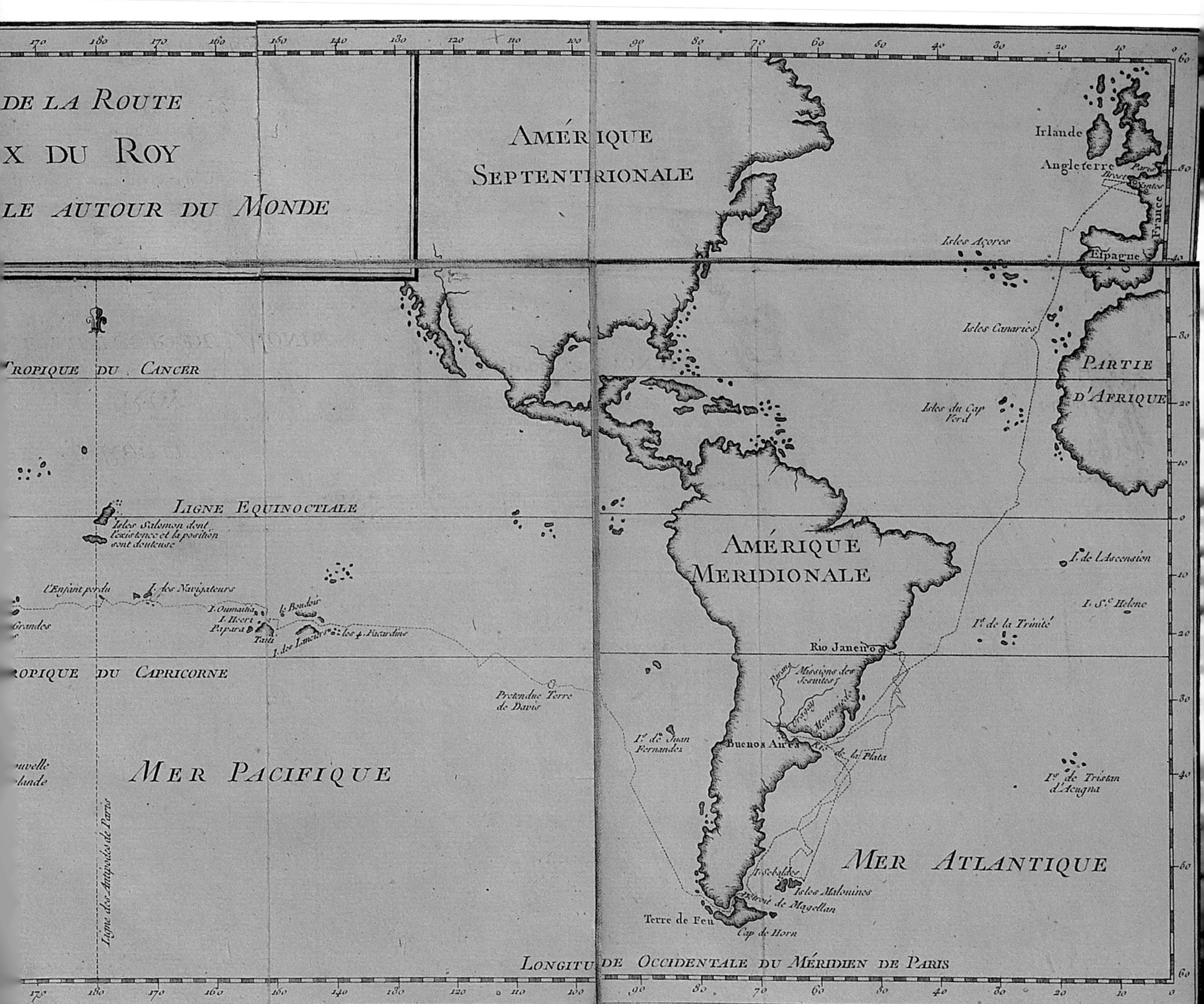
DE LA ROUTE
X DU ROY
LE AUTOUR DU MONDE
AMÉRIQUE SEPTENTRIONALE
Irlande
Angleterre
Paris
Brest
Nantes
France
Isles Açores
Espagne
Isles Canaries
PARTIE D'AFRIQUE
Isles du Cap Verd
TROPIQUE DU CANCER
LIGNE EQUINOCTIALE
Isles Salomon dont l'existence et la position sont douteuse
AMÉRIQUE MERIDIONALE
I. de l'Ascension
L'Enfant perdu
I. des Navigateurs
I. Oumaitia
I. Hoert
Papara
Tati
le Boudoir
I. des Lanciers
les 4 Facardins
I. S.te Helene
Ile de la Trinité
Rio Janeiro
TROPIQUE DU CAPRICORNE
Missions des Jesuites
Pretendue Terre de Davis
Ile de Juan Fernandez
Buenos Aires
la Plata
MER PACIFIQUE
Ile de Tristan d'Acugna
MER ATLANTIQUE
Isles Malouines
Detroit de Magellan
Terre de Feu
Cap de Horn
Ligne des Antipodes de Paris
LONGITUDE OCCIDENTALE DU MÉRIDIEN DE PARIS

Bruce's Travels to Discover the Source of the Nile

A landmark in the evolution of modern travel literature.

1768-73

JAMES BRUCE WAS A GIANT OF A MAN; loud, vain, boastful, brave and self-reliant; a gifted linguist, enthusiastic astronomer and observant amateur polymath. In fact, all that one would expect of the archetypal explorer. But what makes Bruce so unusual, almost unique among his contemporaries, is that he travelled not for missionary, commercial or imperial objectives, but entirely to satisfy a hunger for knowledge and thirst for enlightenment. Even the pursuit of fame, always denied but never far from an explorer's mind, was for Bruce secondary to personal fulfilment. His narrative, the prerequisite of immortality, appeared seventeen years late, and then only to fill the emptiness left by the death of his wife.

Bruce, formerly consul at Algiers, widely travelled in the Near East and fluent in Arabic, left Alexandria in 1768 on a personal odyssey to find the source of the Nile. Leaving the river at Qena, he diverted to the Red Sea and entered Ethiopia by way of Massawa, striking inland to Aksum and Gondar. In November 1770 he rounded the western shore of Lake Tana, visited the Tisisat Falls and ascended the 'Little Abbai', the lake's major feed and hence the primary source of the Nile. After a year in Ethiopia he set out for Sennar, a kingdom ravaged by inter-tribal anarchy where his life was constantly under threat. Descending the Nile to Berber, and taking the notorious caravan route to Aswan, he finally reached Cairo, dressed as a beggar, in January 1773.

Bruce's *Travels to Discover the Source of the Nile* became a milestone in the history of travel literature. Written for the common man rather than established academia, the character of its author, his fears and aspirations, his moments of despair and elation, shine through its pages like a Beethoven symphony. But in the eyes of its detractors, venomous in their ridicule of the towering Scotsman, the book's scholarly imperfections cast doubt upon the veracity of the entire work. Bruce was parodied as a worthy successor to Baron Munchausen, while his denial of his Jesuit predecessors, Pedro Páez and Jeronimo Lobo, did him no favours, nor did his stubbornness in affirming his Nile to be the major stream. However, any attempt Bruce would make to silence his critics faded when he met a premature death, falling headlong down a flight of steps while hurriedly conducting a lady visitor to her carriage.

Right Bruce's map of the Blue Nile accurately plotted its course from source to delta, but showed the White Nile as nothing more than a minor tributary.

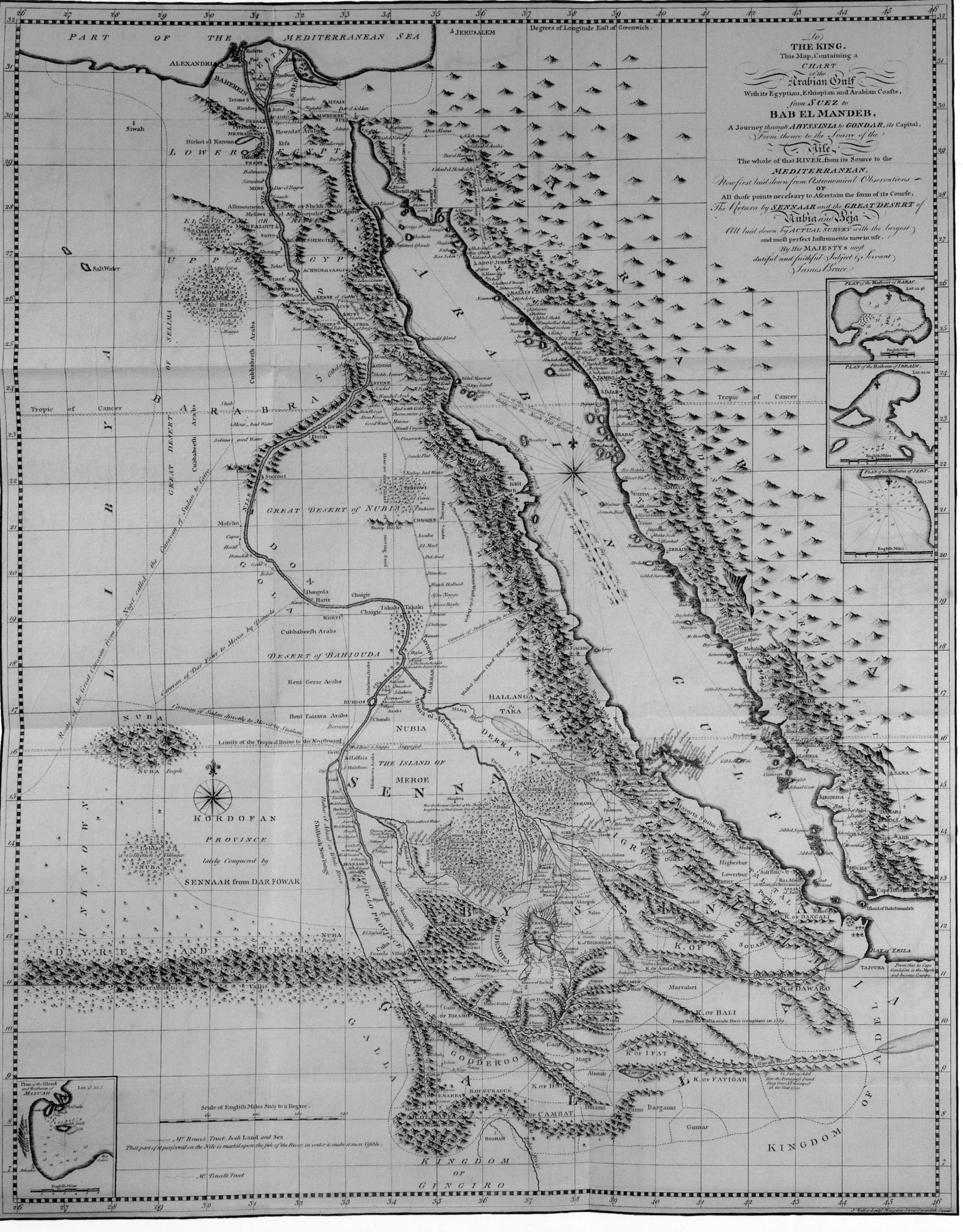
To
THE KING.
This Map, Containing a
CHART
of the
Arabian Gulf
With its Egyptian, Ethiopian and Arabian Coasts,
from SUEZ to
BAB EL MANDEB,
A Journey through ABYSSINIA to GONDAR, its Capital,
From thence to the Source of the
Nile.
The whole of that RIVER, from its Source to the
MEDITERRANEAN.
Now first laid down from Astronomical Observations
OF
All those points necessary to Ascertain the form of its Course,
The Return by SENNAAR and the GREAT DESERT of
Nubia and Beja
All laid down by ACTUAL SURVEY with the largest
and most perfect Instruments now in use.
By His MAJESTYS most
dutiful and faithful Subject & Servant
James Bruce
Degrees of Longitude East of Greenwich.
PART OF THE MEDITERRANEAN SEA
JERUSALEM
ALEXANDRIA
Siwah
LOWER EGYPT
UPPER EGYPT
Salt Water
Tropic of Cancer
GREAT DESERT of NUBIA
DONGOLA
Dongola
DESERT of BAHIOUDA
Beni Gerar Arabs
Beni Faisara Arabs
Cubbabeesh Arabs
NUBA
NUBIA
Limits of the Tropical Rains to the Northward
THE ISLAND OF MEROE
SENNAAR
KORDOFAN PROVINCE lately Conquered by SENNAAR from DAR FOWAR
HALLANGA
TAKA
TIGRE
ABYSSINIA
DYRE AND TEGLA
K. OF DANCALI
BAY OF ZEILA
TAJOURA
K. OF DAWARO
K. OF BALI
K. OF IFAT
K. OF FATIGAR
K. OF CAMBAT
KINGDOM OF GINGIRO
KINGDOM OF ADEL
GALLA
MOCHA
SANA
LOHEIA
Cape Babelmandeb
Tropic of Cancer
PLAN of the Harbour of RABAC
PLAN of the Harbour of IBRAIM
PLAN of the Harbour of SERT
Scale of English Miles Sixty to a Degree
Mr. Bruce's Tract, both Land and Sea
Mr. Poncet's Tract

James Cook Charts the Pacific and Southern Oceans

Unsung in life; heroic in death.

1768-79

IT IS ALWAYS INTERESTING TO CONSIDER THE EXTENT TO WHICH a unique incident or set of circumstances has the ability to catapult an unpretentious explorer to the status of national hero, or to hold a particular voyage of exploration forever in the public eye. If Charles Darwin had not sailed on the *Beagle*, would the ship and its voyage have suffered the same descent into neglect as, say, the *Challenger* or *Rattlesnake*? If Henry Stanley had not made his memorable encounter with Livingstone, would we still recall his more significant explorations on the Congo? And if, on his third voyage, James Cook had not suffered an 'heroic', although inglorious, death at the hands of Hawaiian islanders, would we still regard him as the greatest navigator of all time, devote around 8000 books and articles to him, have a university named after him or erect monuments to his achievements?

Cook's first voyage (1768-71), its primary object being to study the transit of Venus from the island of Tahiti, was just a little too scientific and unsensational to capture the public eye, while Cook himself, a humdrum hydrographer plucked from obscurity, was far less a familiar name than those that sailed with him. As a consequence, the monumental discovery of the eastern seaboard of Australia and the first delineation of the entire New Zealand coast were overlooked by the popular press in favour of the amorous Tahitian exploits of the gentleman botanist Joseph Banks. Cook's magnificent second voyage (1772-75), which charted the entire Southern Ocean and endured extreme conditions to make the closest approach so far to the Antarctic continent, might have survived as a mundanely pedestrian, academic exercise had it not been for the report of an unnamed lieutenant of the *Resolution*, while the sketchy and confused newspaper reports dwelt largely on the arrival in England of a Society islander, or the grisly fate of a boat crew from the *Adventure*, massacred and eaten on the New Zealand coast. In fact it was not until Cook's own account was published in 1777, by which time the captain had departed for his third voyage (1776-79), that the great British public became conscious of a treasure that had somehow evaded valuation. When news of Cook's death reached England in January 1780, obituary writers effused with lamentations for the loss of a national hero but found themselves hard-pressed to unearth even the basic facts of his life.

Right James Cook witnessing human sacrifice on the island of Tahiti.

Samuel Hearne's Journey to the Arctic Shore

'The coast, which I was the first white man ever to see.'

1770–72

THE HUDSON'S BAY COMPANY, which would come to dominate the commerce of the greater part of Canada, was chartered in 1670 after two disgruntled French fur traders had arrived in London to promote exploration in the rich fur country north of Lake Superior. Responsibility for exploration across the bay's entire watershed was embedded in its charter but, despite the eternal French threat to the company's monopoly, its traders seemed reluctant to stray far from coastal depots. In 1715-16 William Stuart made an extensive journey to Chipewyan country, and in 1754 Anthony Henday came almost within sight of the Rockies, but their narratives lacked the geographical precision of trained surveyors. However, the impetus towards exploration was restored in 1767 when two native explorers reported that far to the northwest lay a river, along the banks of which copper could be found in abundance. The metal was desirable because it could be used to ballast the empty supply vessels returning to England and, once arrived, could be sold on to the metalworking and brass industry. In addition, an expedition sent to find it could fly the company's flag in distant parts and hopefully draw uncontacted tribes into its trading posts.

The expedition was given to Samuel Hearne, an ex-navy man, now a company seaman, who had learnt a little about overland navigation from William Wales, one of Cook's future astronomers. Hearne's first attempt to reach the copper river in 1769 was abandoned with the desertion of his guides, while a second, which occupied much of the following year, plunged him into the desolate Barrens around Dubawnt Lake. His guide lost his way, and when a gust of wind damaged Hearne's quadrant there was no alternative but to return to his base at Prince of Wales's Fort. The third expedition departed in December 1770 and headed west into Athabasca country, then north to lakes Aylmer and Contwoyto. Burdened by a 30-kilogramme (60-pound) pack, with canoes suitable only for short river crossings, Hearne trudged across trackless wastes for eight months, patiently following the seasonal movements of buffalo and caribou, his party's only source of food. Then on reaching the Coppermine River in July 1771 he watched in horror as his native assistants took it upon themselves to massacre the local Inuit. Hearne found only worthless lumps of copper, but a few days later he became the first European to see the Arctic from the mainland of North America.

Right Samuel Hearne's chart of his route from Hudson Bay to the Arctic Sea, which he was first to see from the North American mainland.

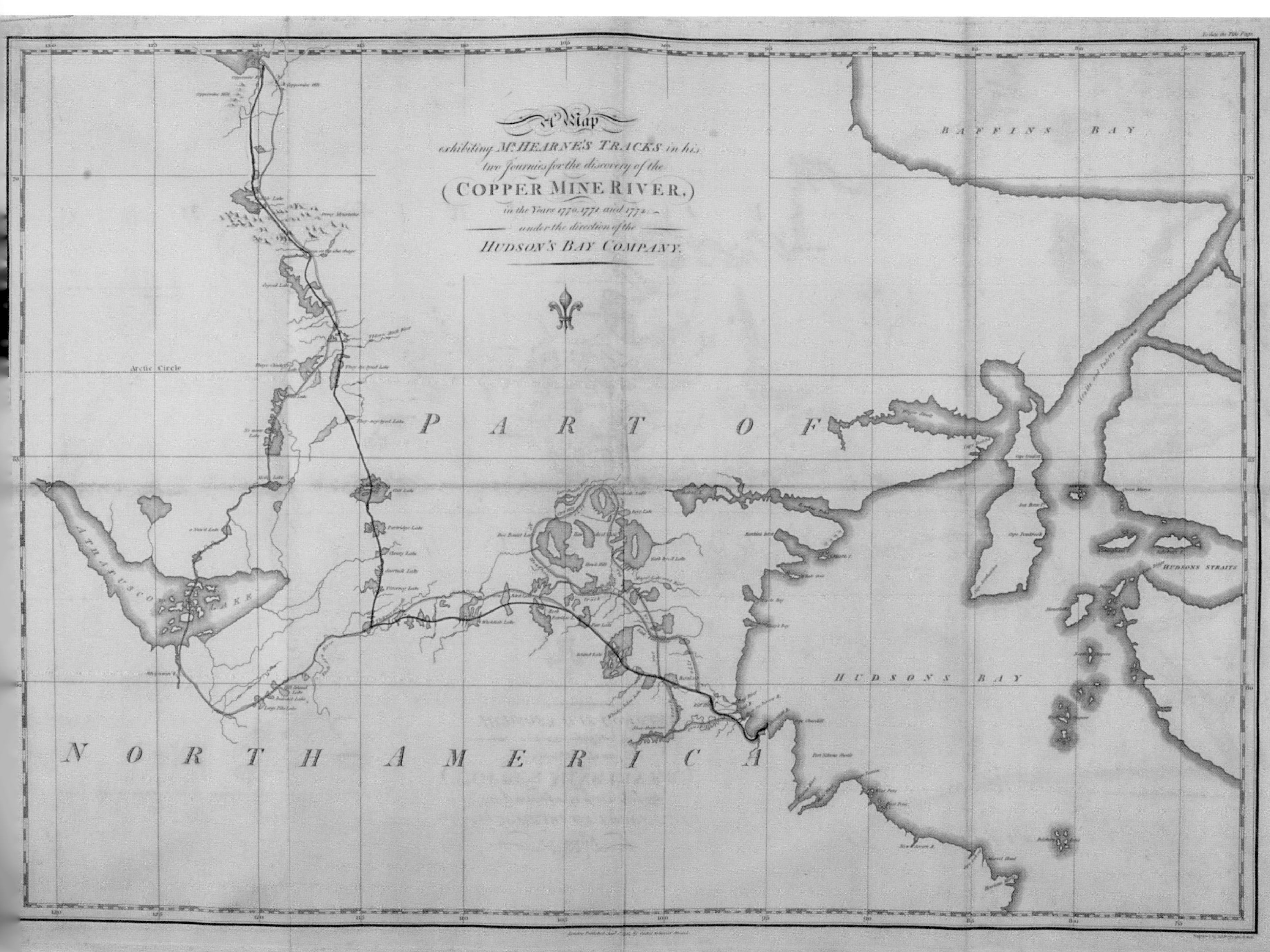
A Map
exhibiting Mr. HEARNE'S TRACKS in his two Journies for the discovery of the
COPPER MINE RIVER,
in the Years 1770, 1771 and 1772.
under the direction of the
HUDSON'S BAY COMPANY.
BAFFINS BAY
PART OF
NORTH AMERICA
HUDSONS BAY
HUDSONS STRAITS
Arctic Circle

The Domínguez-Escalante Expedition to Utah

A Garden of Eden in the heart of the American West.

1776

IT MIGHT COME AS A SURPRISE TO MANY NON-AMERICANS to learn that some of the earliest sites of European settlement in the United States developed not along the eastern seaboard but far to the west, in what is now the state of New Mexico. Juan de Oñate placed a colony on the Rio Grande as early as 1598, and nine years later he established Santa Fe, America's third oldest surviving city. With mixed fortunes, New Mexico hung on as a relatively isolated enclave of white settlement until the early nineteenth century, while in the meantime, the late 1760s, Spanish missionaries started to arrive in California, rapidly establishing more than twenty missions and a number of small towns. However, intercourse between the two colonies, despite their identical latitudes, demanded a circuitous journey into Mexico and outward along the coast, so the search began for a more direct passage to unite the colonies economically and at the same time satisfy the itinerant missionaries. Father Francisco Garcés had in 1775 accomplished a monumental overland trek from California via the Grand Canyon, but his route was difficult and dangerous, and with the creation of the flourishing Monterey missions the focus of attention shifted more to the north.

In July 1776 an expedition of fourteen men left Santa Fe headed by two Franciscan friars, Silvestre Velez de Escalante and Francisco Atanasio Domínguez. With them was Bernado Miera y Pachecho, a retired military engineer who would chart the route and report on the more congenial regions of projected settlement. To outflank the Chiruma, a reputedly cannibalistic tribe, the party headed north into Colorado, then west into the starkly sculpted landscape of southern Utah where a bewildering maze of precipitous canyons dissects the high plateaus. To their relief they eventually emerged into the Utah Valley, a terrestrial paradise of abundant water, pasturage, wildlife and friendly natives. Marking it as a spot ripe for settlement and promising to return within a year, they struck southwest for Monterey, quite unaware of the forbidding country that now lay in their path. In conditions that lunged from blistering heat to driving snow, and with supplies running short, they halted near present-day Cedar City. Turning towards New Mexico and crossing northern Arizona and the River Colorado River, they arrived back in Santa Fe in January 1777. Although forced to abandon their primary objective, their 3000-kilometre (1800-mile) circuit had unveiled a vast swathe of territory never before penetrated by Europeans.

Right The meanderings of the Domínguez-Escalante expedition beyond the Colorado River, with Utah Lake at top left and Sevier Lake below it.

DERROTERO hecho por Antonio Velez y Escalante. Misioneros para mejor conocimiento de las Misiones, pueblos de Indios y Presidios que se hallan en el Camino de Monterey a Santa Fe de Nuebo Mexico. Laus deo Anno Domini 1777
Sierra de Timpanogos
LAGO DE TIMPANOGOS
Ind.s Yamparicas
S. Mateo
Sta Lucia
Sta Catalina
Nombre de Dios
S. Andres
Sierra de S. Buenaventura
S. Cosme
S. Francisco
Sta Rosalia
Nacimiento del Rio Colorado
S. Pedro
S. Anastasio
Sta Rosa
Cienega
S. Bernardo
Rio de San Buenaventura
Serrania de S. Bernardo
Laguna
S. Luis
Sta Isabel
Laguna de Abajo
S. Luis Bajo
Rio de S. Javier
Valle Salado
Ind.s Rapapui
S. Bernardo
Rio Salado
Agua Escondida
LAGO SALADO
Territorio descubierto
Arroyo Tesedon
Sierra de los Guacaros
Ind.s Yutas Tabeguachis
Rio de los Dolores
LLANOS DE N.S.A DE LA LUZ
Sta Brigida
S. Rustico
Rio de las Animas
Indios Timpabachis
RIO NAVAJOA
S. Josep
Guacaros Bajos
Concepcion
Diego
El Rastrillo
Indios Nabajoa
Ugolino
S. Bartolomé
Puerto de Bucareli
RIO JAQUESITA
Sta Gertrudis
Indios Moqui
Indios Cosninas
Orayb
S. Samuel
Rio Colorado
Indios Jumbuicrariri
Pais de Navajoa

David Thompson Defines the Geography of the Canadian West

The resurrection of an unknown hero.

1784-1812

DAVID THOMPSON HAS BEEN DESCRIBED AS THE GREATEST LAND SURVEYOR that ever lived: a title few would deny him. His twenty-eight years in Canada's western provinces took him over 90,000 kilometres (55,000 miles) and filled a blank on the map of around five million square kilometres (two million square miles) – an area ten times that of France. Yet he emerged from the humblest of beginnings and would die in almost total obscurity, buried beside his long-suffering wife in an unmarked Montreal grave. Born in London to an impoverished Welsh migrant family, he received only a rudimentary, charity school education before joining the Hudson's Bay Company as a fourteen-year-old apprentice. Although consigned to clerical duties, his acquaintanceship with Samuel Hearne inspired a passion for exploration, and in 1786 he went inland to help establish an outpost on the South Saskatchewan River. Over the next two years a religious experience committed him to a life of self-imposed abstinence and piety. A fractured leg left him permanently lame and his navigational training blinded him in one eye, probably through staring too long at the sun.

Thompson's extraordinary meanderings through the mountains and valleys of Canada are too overwhelming for just a few words to convey. His chart of a route to Lake Athabasca earned him promotion to surveyor, but a yearning to explore further afield led to his defection in 1797 to the rival North West Company. In the same year he delineated the nearer section of the US-Canada border; he spent several seasons in Alberta with frequent excursions into the Rockies; then in 1798 he surveyed an area from Lake Winnipeg to the headwaters of the Assiniboine and Missouri rivers. In 1806, now a full partner in the NWC, he was sent west to chart the basin of the Columbia River, siting trading posts throughout present-day Montana, Idaho and Washington. In 1811, to counter John Jacob Astor's vision of a United States trading community on the Pacific coast, Thompson flew the British flag over the entire length of the Columbia. He retired to Quebec the next year and in 1814 completed a map of the Canadian west so comprehensively accurate that it remained in use for 100 years. Plagued by financial misfortune, which forcefully returned him to survey work, and for six years blind in both eyes, he died in 1857, leaving his partially completed autobiography and his seventy-seven field notebooks languishing in manuscript until their resurrection in 1916.

Right Thompson's remarkably accurate 1814 map of the Canadian interior, from Hudson Bay to the Rockies and beyond. It was the result of twenty-eight years of travel and observation.

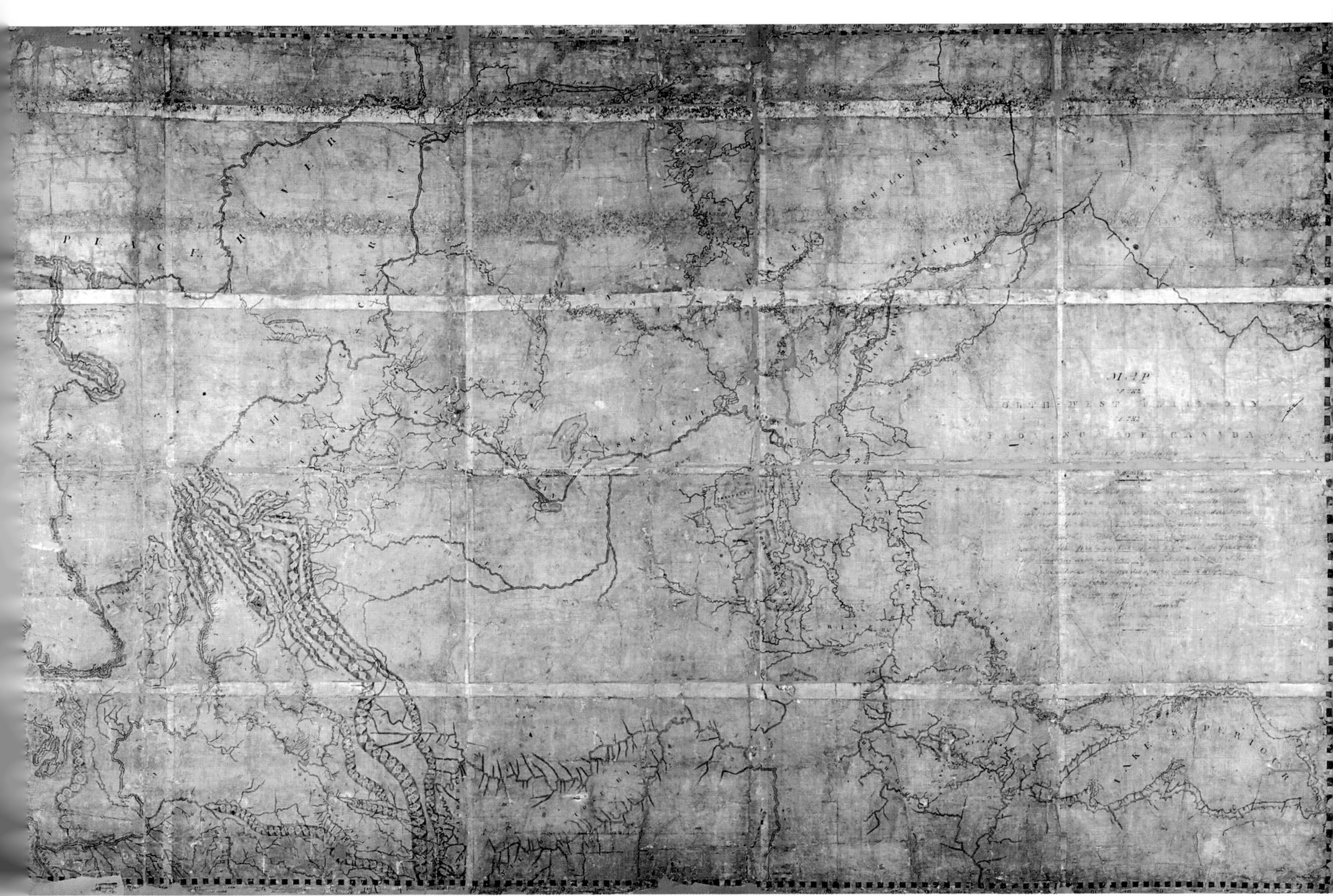
MAP

La Pérouse Fills the Blanks in the Pacific Rim

Cook's French counterpart tackles the work left undone.

1785–88

JAMES COOK HAD CHARTED VAST SWATHES of the Pacific and Southern oceans, but his premature death in Hawaii in 1779 left significant blanks on the map that, had he lived longer, might perhaps have been filled by a fourth or fifth voyage. In the event, nothing of similar magnitude would be undertaken by the British for another twelve years and it would fall to the French, whose navy had reformed since its decimation in the Seven Years War, to take up Cook's mantle. In 1785 Louis XVI, whose keen interest in geography made him an enthusiastic proponent of exploration, proposed a voyage of discovery that would complement Cook's work in regions unvisited, notably the islands deep in the South Atlantic, the northwest coast of America and, most significantly, the Pacific coast of Russia beyond the mouth of the Amur – one of the few expanses of temperate coastline to have consistently escaped definition. Two ships, the *Boussole* and *Astrolabe*, were fitted, and a host of eminent naturalists, astronomers and artists volunteered their services. The expedition was placed under the command of a proven navigator of thirty years experience, Jean-François de Galaup de la Pérouse.

The expedition left Brest in August 1785, rounded Cape Horn in fine weather, headed north to Chile, Easter Island and Hawaii, and between June and September 1786 mapped the coast from Alaska to California. Crossing the Pacific to Macao and the Philippines, it struck north to the uncharted coast of Korea, the island of Sakhalin and the beaded chain of the Kuril Islands. From Kamchatka the reports and charts of the expedition so far were sent back to France, then in September 1787, new instructions in hand, La Pérouse took his ships south to Australia, anchoring in Botany Bay just four days after the first batch of convicts arrived from England. In March 1788, after six weeks recuperation, the expedition weighed anchor and headed northeast for Tonga, never to be seen again. Shipwrecked by a cyclone in the Santa Cruz Islands, those that swam ashore mostly died of fever or were felled by hostile natives. A small group sailed off in a craft moulded from the wreckage, only to disappear into oblivion. Although gripped by revolution, France found time to despatch a search expedition under Joseph-Antoine d'Entrecasteaux, but the site of the tragedy and the fate of La Pérouse would remain a mystery for nearly forty years.

Right A painting showing La Pérouse discussing his intended voyage with King Louis XVI.

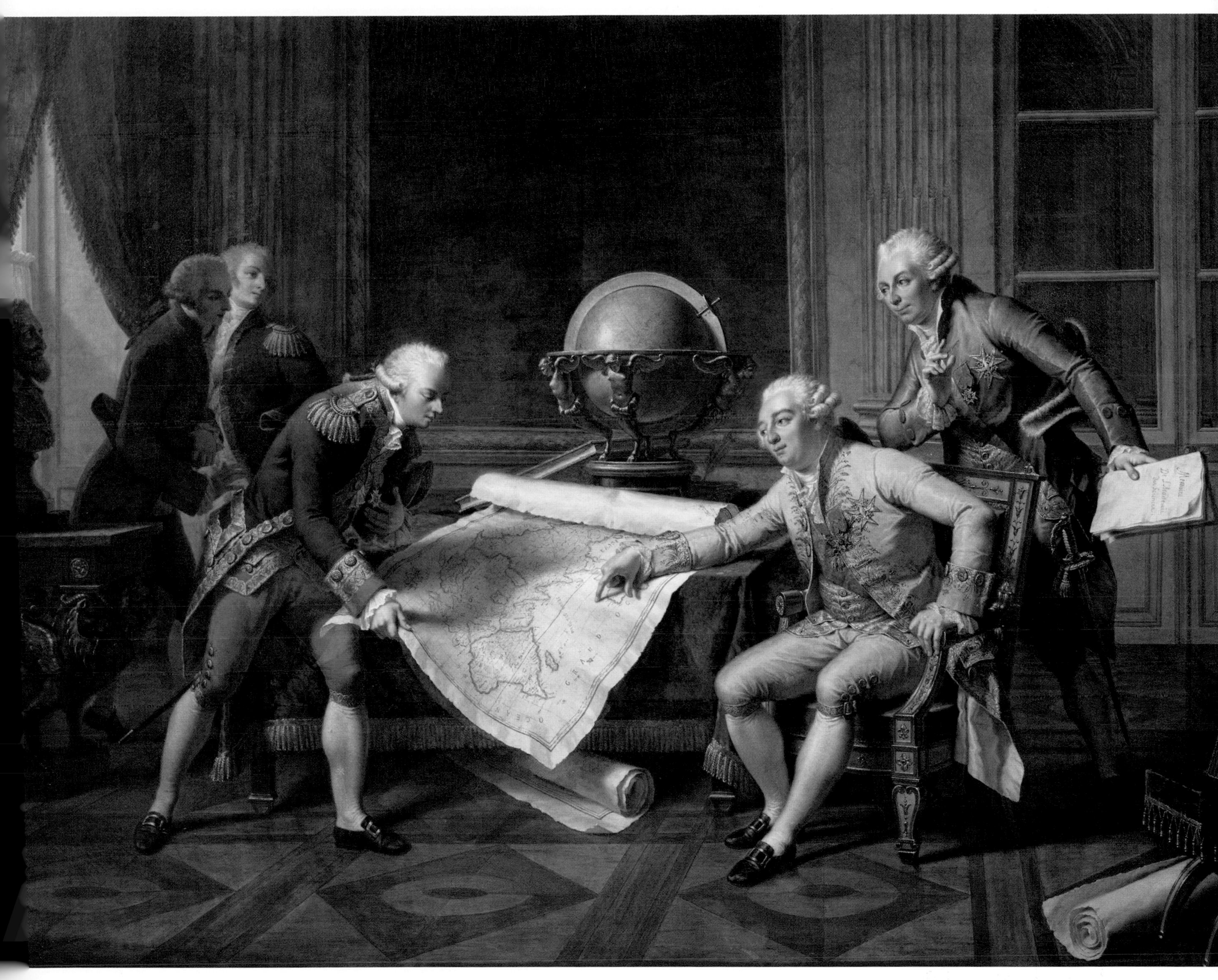

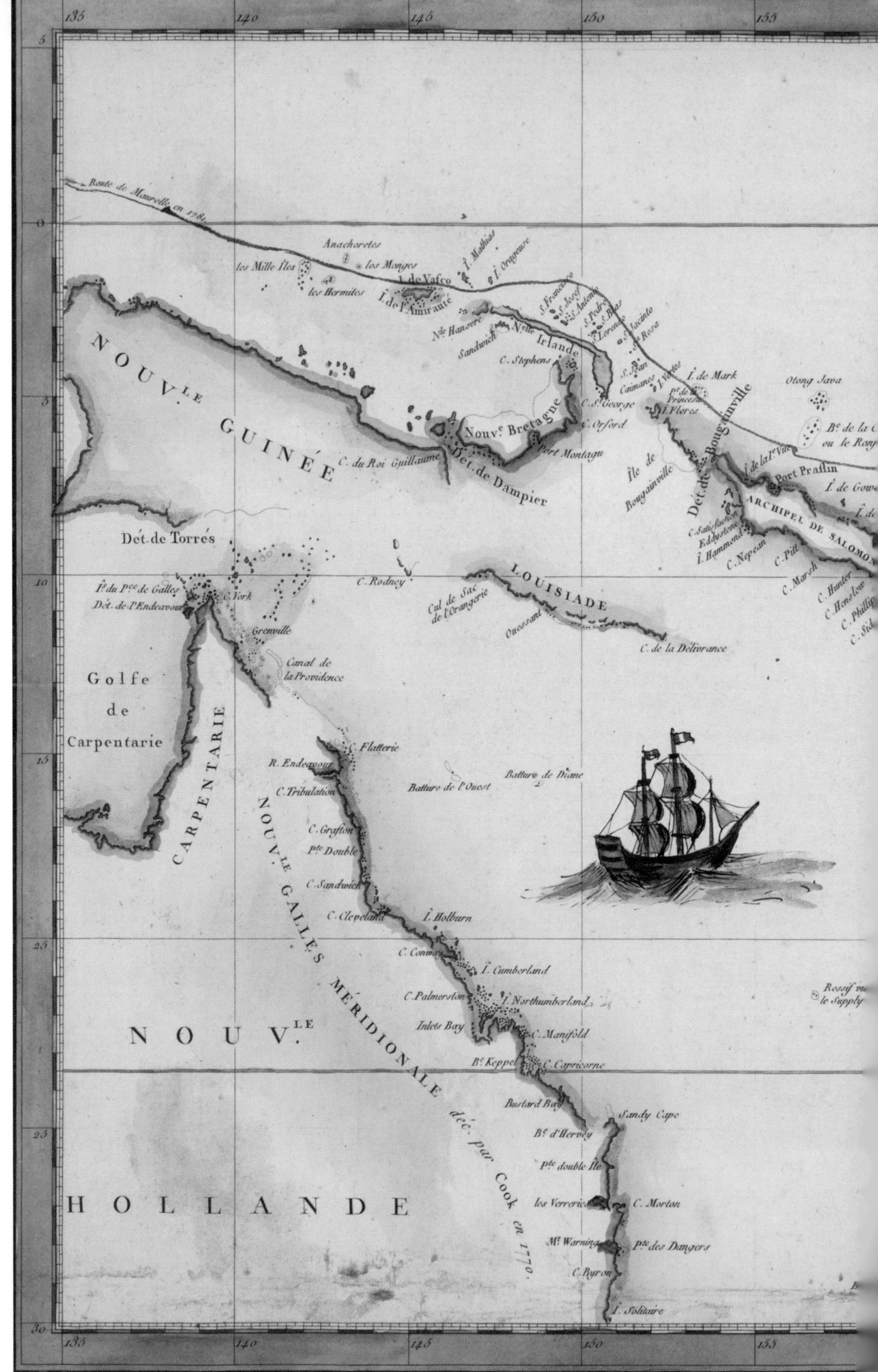

Right A contemporary French map of the islands of Melanesia, 1781, based on the voyage of the lesser-known Spanish navigator Franco Antonio Maurelle. It was during the process of adding detail absent from this map that La Pérouse disappeared without a trace.

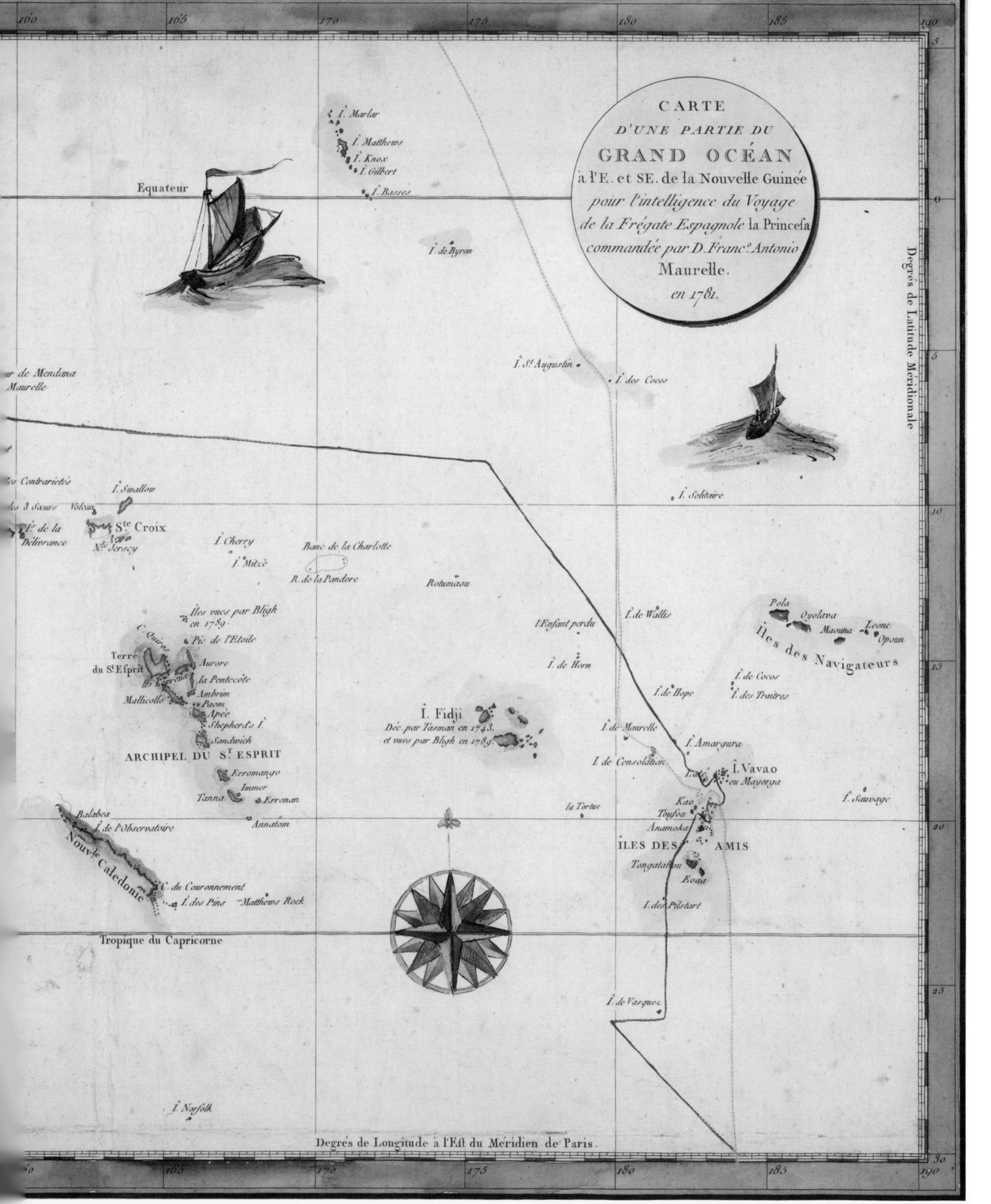

CARTE
D'UNE PARTIE DU
GRAND OCÉAN
à l'E. et SE. de la Nouvelle Guinée
pour l'intelligence du Voyage
de la Frégate Espagnole la Princesa
commandée par D. Franc.o Antonio
Maurelle.
en 1781.
Equateur
Î. Marlar
Î. Matthews
Î. Knox
Î. Gilbert
Î. Basses
Î. de Byron
Î. St. Augustin
Î. des Cocos
Degrés de Latitude Méridionale
Î. Solitaire
Î. Swallow
Volcan
Ste. Croix
Nle. Jersey
Î. Cherry
Î. Mitzè
Banc de la Charlotte
R. de la Pandore
Rotumaou
Îles vues par Bligh en 1789.
Pic de l'Etoile
Terre du St. Esprit
Aurore
la Pentecôte
Mallicollo
Ambrim
Paom
Apée
Shepherd's Î.
Sandwich
ARCHIPEL DU St. ESPRIT
Erromango
Immer
Tanna
Erronan
Annatom
Balabea
Î. de l'Observatoire
Nouvle. Caledonie
C. du Couronnement
Î. des Pins
Matthews Rock
Tropique du Capricorne
Î. Fidji
Déc. par Tasman en 1743.
et vues par Bligh en 1789.
l'Enfant perdu
Î. de Wallis
Î. de Horn
Pola
Oyolava
Maouna
Leone
Opoun
Îles des Navigateurs
Î. de Cocos
Î. des Traitres
Î. de Hope
Î. de Maurelle
Î. Amargura
Î. de Consolation
Î. Vavao
ou Mayorga
Kao
Toufoa
Anamoka
la Tortue
Î. Sauvage
ÎLES DES AMIS
Tongatabou
Eoaa
I. des Pilstart
Î. de Vasquez
Î. Norfolk
Degrés de Longitude à l'Est du Méridien de Paris.
160
165
170
175
180
185
190

Alexander Mackenzie: First Across the North American Continent

The Nor'Westers expand the fur trade deep into the Canadian heartlands.

1789-93

TWO MAJOR EVENTS OF THE 1760S would bring about radical changes in the expansion of the fur trade and the subsequent pattern of North American exploration. The ceding of Canada to Great Britain allowed British fur traders, mostly ex-patriot Scots, to base themselves in Montreal and form into partnerships; while the American Revolution, which would deprive traders of their former stomping grounds south of the Great Lakes, provoked them into widening their horizons into the untapped northwest. Although much of this territory was nominally under the aegis of the Hudson's Bay Company, the HBC had shown little interest in exploring its monopoly. James Finlay built a post in the Saskatchewan Valley around 1767, and in 1778 Peter Pond reached the Athabasca River and discovered rich pickings in the surrounding region. However, it rapidly became apparent that exploitation of the trade could be pursued more effectively by merging the smaller partnerships, always at loggerheads and sometimes in bitter conflict, into larger companies, and in the winter of 1783-84 the North West Company was born.

Alexander Mackenzie, one of the NWC's leading lights and anxious to expand the scope of the company right across the continent, set out in 1789 to discover the course of a great river that Pond had seen flowing out of the Great Slave Lake. Pond, for whom longitude was always a serious weakness, assumed that the river emptied on the coast of Alaska and would hence provide a valuable outlet to the Pacific. But as Mackenzie followed the river that now bears his name he soon recognized that it trended far to the north. After just two weeks descent he had confirmed that its estuary lay in the Arctic Ocean, whereupon he named his discovery the 'River of Disappointment' and turned about without even bothering to view the ocean itself. In 1792 he decided to try again, this time by ascending the Peace River to its source in the Rockies, a little beyond which he hoped to find a stream on the western slope that would lead to the Pacific. Crossing the divide in June 1793, he reached the valley of the hitherto unknown Fraser River, then, forewarned by Indians of the length and hazards of the Fraser, he turned west towards the Dean Channel. On 20 July he arrived on the Pacific some 500 kilometres (300 miles) north of present-day Vancouver, the first man to traverse the entire North American continent.

Right A map from Mackenzie's voyages, 1801, showing his ascent of the Mackenzie River and his route across the Rockies to the Pacific.

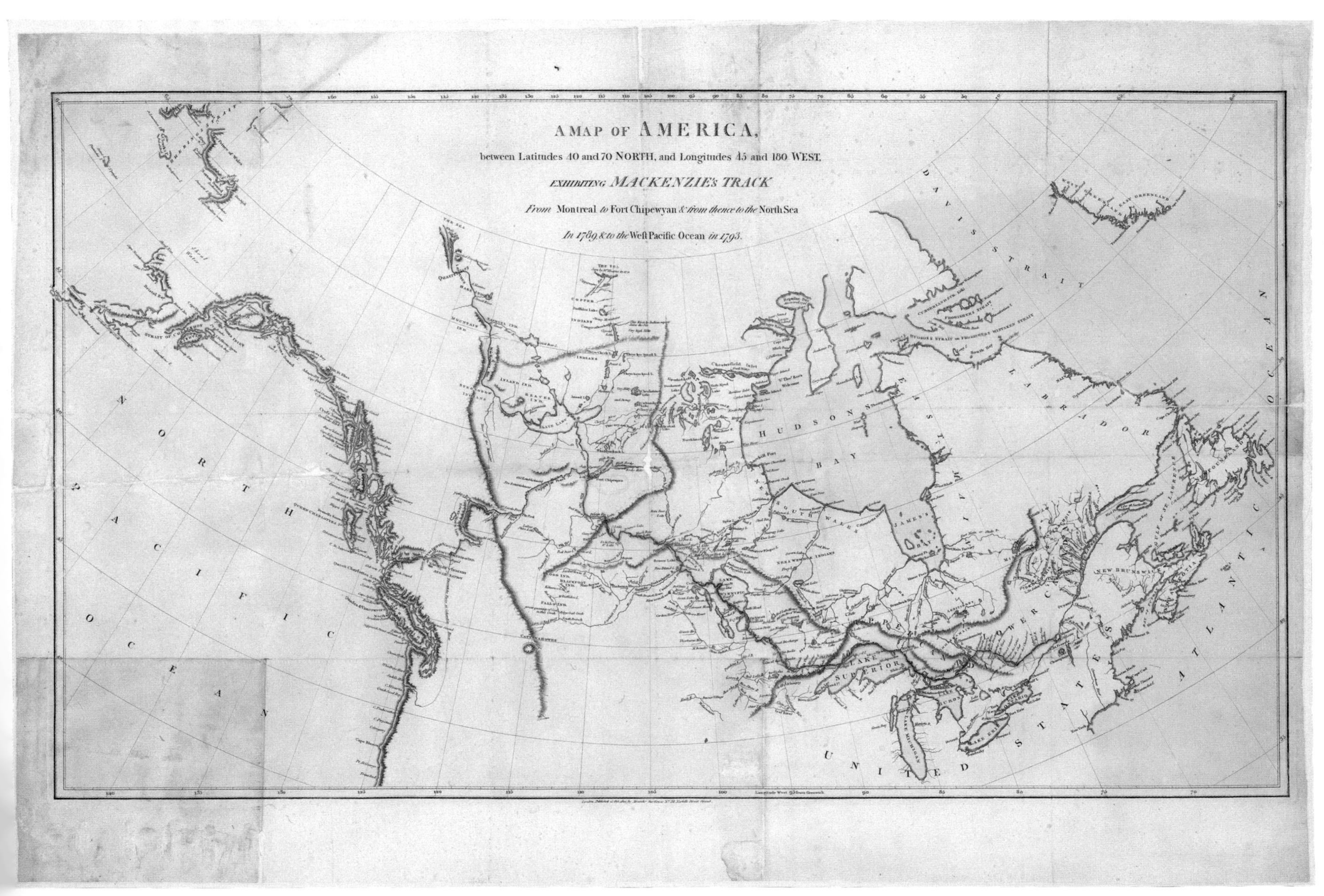
A MAP OF AMERICA,
between Latitudes 40 and 70 NORTH, and Longitudes 45 and 180 WEST.
EXHIBITING MACKENZIE'S TRACK
From Montreal to Fort Chipewyan & from thence to the North Sea
In 1789, & to the West Pacific Ocean in 1793.
HUDSONS BAY
LABRADOR
DAVIS STRAIT
NORTH PACIFIC OCEAN
ATLANTIC OCEAN
UNITED STATES
NEW BRUNSWICK
LAKE SUPERIOR
SOUTH WALES

The Malaspina Expedition: Censored into Obscurity

The triumph of politics over science.

1789-94

BY THE LATTER HALF OF THE EIGHTEENTH CENTURY – the benevolent hegemony of the knowledge-loving despot Carlos III – Spain had devoted more of its financial resources to scientific exploration than any other European country. When the empires of Britain and France had scarcely begun to colour the map, Spain already administered a continuous blanket of territory from California to Cape Horn, a vast natural laboratory of biological, topographical and ethnological science constantly traversed by research missions. But now Spain looked enviously on the great voyages of Cook, La Pérouse and others that were beginning to invade the 'Spanish Lake' – the broad Pacific into which faced the ports and harbours of the far-flung Spanish empire. In 1788 Alessandro Malaspina, an Italian-born officer in the Spanish navy, proposed a voyage of exploration that in its scope would rival anything so far achieved by British and French. Although flaunting its undeniably scientific credentials on the European stage, and hence recruiting the wholehearted support of instrument and chart makers from competing nations, its overriding purpose would be one of imperial inspection – the gathering of information about the geography and economies of an empire that over the years had grown increasingly distant from the homeland, its defences insecure, its commerce and government approaching autonomy.

Malaspina and his fellow-officer José Bustamente, with an august company of naturalists, ethnologists, cartographers and artists, sailed from Cádiz in July 1789 in two purpose-built corvettes, *Descubierta* and *Atrevida*, on a voyage that would last five years. Their route took them around Cape Horn, up the Pacific coast of the Americas, then across the ocean to the Philippines, returning via New Zealand, Australia and South America. Numerous diversions were made to islands nominally off-route, while considerable time was spent at strategic points ashore, and a thorough survey conducted of much of the Pacific coast from Chile to Alaska. The voyage generated 300 journals, 450 albums of astronomical data, 1500 hydrographic reports and 183 charts, and Malaspina started work on a report that would dwarf the narratives of his predecessors. But politics intervened to condemn one of the finest voyages of scientific discovery to more than a century of obscurity. Malaspina's recommendations for greater autonomy for the colonies were treated as heresy by the reactionary ministry that had replaced his friends in government, and publication of the expedition's reports was prohibited. For eight years Malaspina languished in prison until released to spend his last inconspicuous days in his Italian homeland.

Right A watercolour of natives of Tonga, painted in 1793 by Felipe Bauzá y Cañas, a naval officer, artist and cartographer who sailed with Malaspina.

George Vancouver Adds 388 Place Names to the World Map

Accuracy unsurpassed until the twentieth century.

1791-95

WHEN COOK SAILED FROM DEPTFORD IN 1772 at the commencement of his second voyage he took with him in the *Resolution* a young midshipman, 'aged about thirteen and a half', the son of a customs officer in King's Lynn. Little did this 'quiet, inoffensive young man', George Vancouver, realize that one day his name would be commemorated by one of the world's major islands, cities in Washington State and British Columbia, two capes, several bays and a Canadian mountain. For the young seaman, three years in the *Resolution* provided a training that was second to none, and by 1779, having now completed his second voyage with Cook, Vancouver already possessed many of the qualities that would qualify him as a worthy successor to his mentor. So when the Nootka Sound Agreement of 1790 confirmed the rights of Great Britain on America's northwest coast, Vancouver jumped at the opportunity to undertake a far-reaching hydrographic survey of the complex region of islands and inlets that Cook had left on his chart as a single unbroken line. In so doing, he would accomplish one of the century's greatest voyages of discovery, and he would chart the Pacific coast from California to Alaska to an accuracy unequalled until the era of satellite navigation.

Vancouver sailed from Falmouth in April 1791 with the *Discovery* and *Chatham* at the start of one of the longest continuous voyages on record; one that would last nearly five years and cover an estimated 88,000 kilometres (55,000 miles). Of the 180 men that sailed with the expedition, all but five would return safely. Vancouver's outward route around the Cape of Good Hope provided the opportunity of accurately placing some of the remote islands of the Southern Ocean, and of taking formal possession of the southwestern tip of Australia. This done, he proceeded directly to New Zealand and Tahiti, then to Hawaii, which would become his overwintering base for excursions to the northwest coast. In three summer surveying seasons, 1792-94, Vancouver's men navigated more than 16,000 kilometres (10,000 miles) in small boats and delineated over 2700 kilometres (1700 miles) of coastline, during which Vancouver Island was circumnavigated, the Columbia River examined and the bewildering network of British Columbia's coves and channels charted. All this despite Vancouver's failing health and the ferocity of his violent mood swings, probably the effect of a thyroid condition known as myxoedema. Within two-and-a-half years of his return to England Vancouver would be dead, his half-million word journal within 100 pages of completion.

Right One of Vancouver's numerous maps of the coast of northwest America, charted with an accuracy unequalled until modern times.

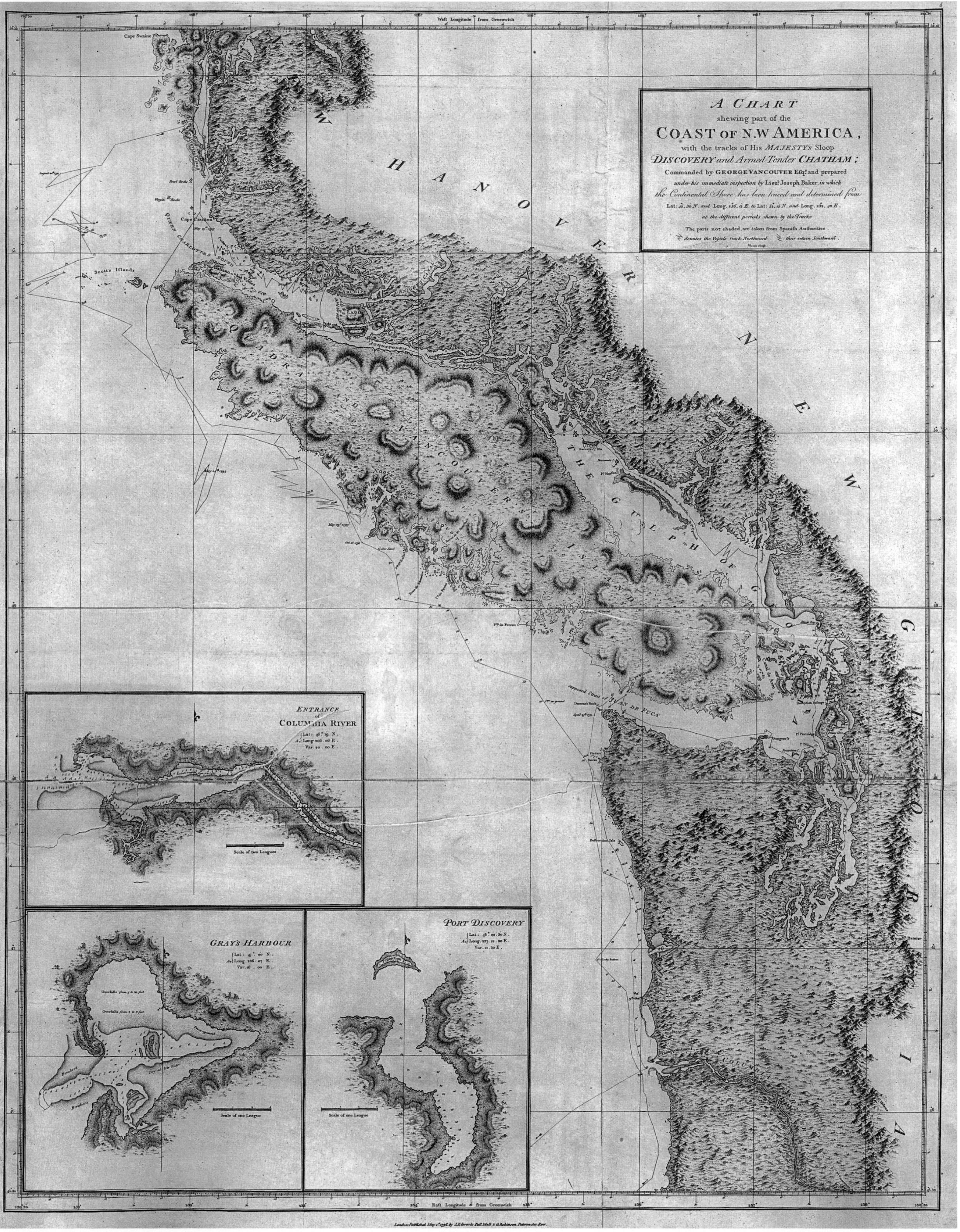

West Longitude from Greenwich
A CHART
shewing part of the
COAST OF N.W AMERICA,
with the tracks of His MAJESTY'S Sloop
DISCOVERY and Armed Tender CHATHAM;
Commanded by GEORGE VANCOUVER Esq.r and prepared
under his immediate inspection by Lieu.t Joseph Baker, in which
the Continental Shore has been traced and determined from
Lat: 45. 30 N. and Long. 236. 12 E. to Lat: 52. 15 N. and Long. 232. 40 E.
at the different periods shewn by the Tracks
The parts not shaded, are taken from Spanish Authorities.
denotes the Vessels track Northward
their return Southward.
NEW HANOVER
NEW GEORGIA
Cape Caution
Scott's Islands
QUADRA AND VANCOUVER'S ISLAND
THE GULPH OF GEORGIA
ENTRANCE of COLUMBIA RIVER
Lat: 46. 19 N.
Long. 236. 06 E.
Var. 20. 00 E.
Scale of two Leagues
GRAY'S HARBOUR
Lat: 47. 00 N.
Long. 236. 07 E.
Var. 18. 00 E.
Scale of one League
PORT DISCOVERY
Lat: 48. 02. 30 N.
Long. 237. 22. 30 E.
Var. 21. 30 E.
Protection
Scale of one League
East Longitude from Greenwich
London: Published May 1st 1798, by J. Edwards Pall Mall & G. Robinson Paternoster Row.

Mungo Park's Discovery of the Niger

'As wide as the Thames at Westminster, and flowing slowly to the eastward.'

1795-1806

The River Niger, its detached meandering course for centuries scribbled haphazardly across maps of North Africa, was one of geography's greatest mysteries. Glimpsed only by a handful of apocryphal European adventurers, but known to geographers and desert travellers since the earliest times, it had no recognizable beginning or end, while even its direction of flow was uncertain. Did it debouch into the Atlantic via the Senegal or Gambia, or did it flow west, as many conjectured, to become a tributary of the Nile or to quietly evaporate from a vast undiscovered desert lake? Were its banks really lined with populous gold-rich cities? For the explorer the approach from every direction was fraught with danger and those that attempted the journey came to grief at the hands of fanatics or, more commonly, died of disease having barely left the coast. But to the African Association, founded in London in 1788, such minor considerations were no excuse for an ignorance of Africa, which it regarded as the 'reproach of the present age'. The problem was in finding anyone brave, foolhardy or desperate enough to take on the challenge.

The Association found the ideal candidate in Mungo Park, a twenty-two-year-old unemployed Scottish doctor, recently returned from Sumatra and eager for another adventure. Park approached his goal by ascending the Gambia, but beyond the calm of the British outposts, which he left in December 1795, he faced every conceivable difficulty. Already he had contracted malaria, but now, to tribesmen who had never before countenanced a white man, he was at best a freak of nature and at worst an infidel spy. Escaping a four-month imprisonment with only a compass and a horse, he reached the Niger at Segou in July 1796, then followed the river for 125 kilometres (75 miles) before turning back destitute, half-naked, racked with fever and fearful of the 'merciless fanatics' along its banks. Long given up for dead, he reached the Gambia a year later, and from there went back to Scotland and penned an overnight bestseller. Bored with life as a Peebles G.P., he was returned to Africa in 1805, determined to trace the Niger to its end. Of the large contingent of soldiers and sailors that started out only Park and three companions survived to descend the river to within 800 kilometres (500 miles) of the delta. They perished in the Bussa rapids while trying to swim for the bank.

Right An engraving of a bridge over the Ba-fing River, Senegal, from a sketch by Mungo Park. Unusually, the explorer himself is pictured in the bottom right corner.

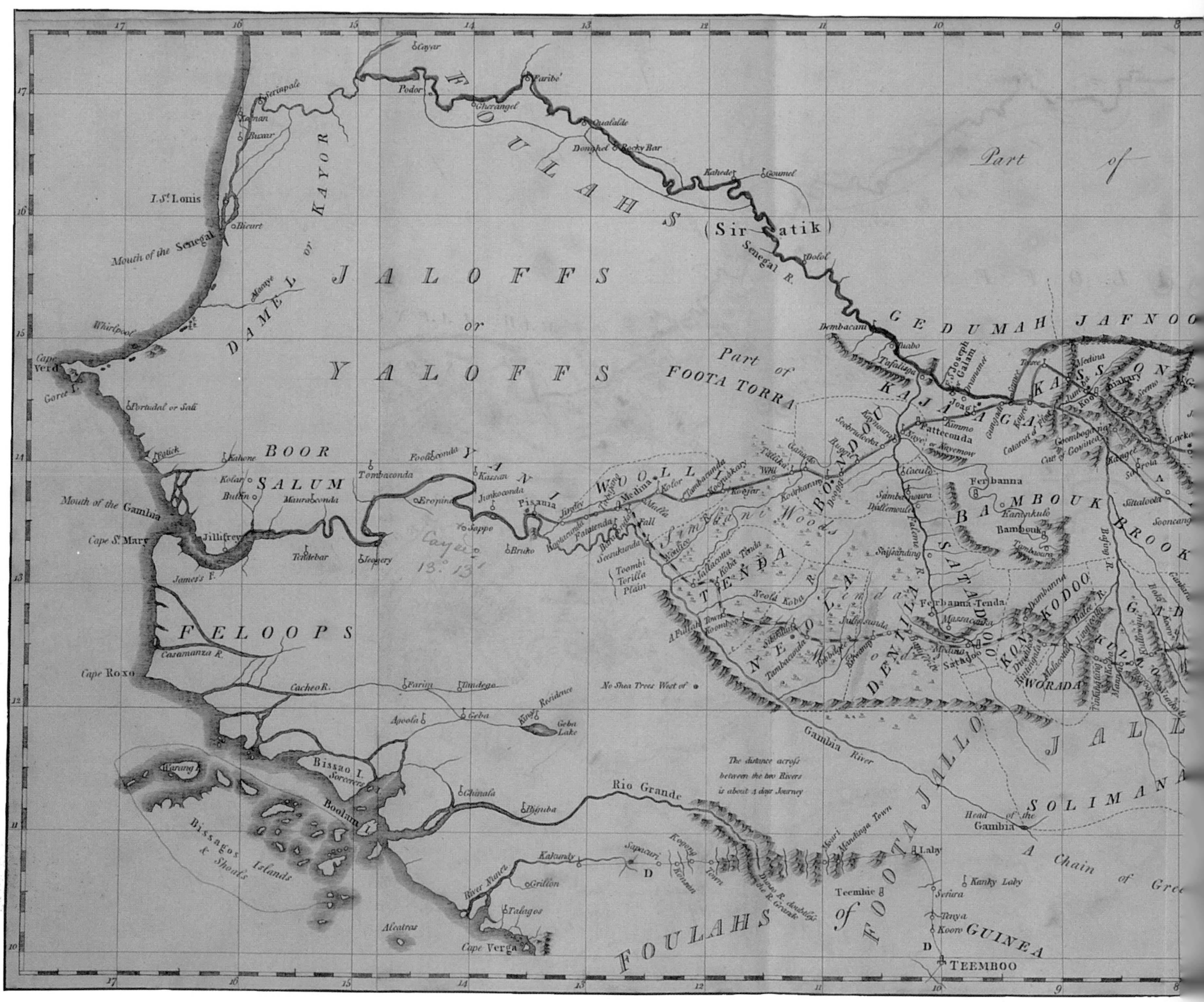

Above The map of Park's first expedition to the Niger, from his *Travels into the Interior of Africa*, 1798.

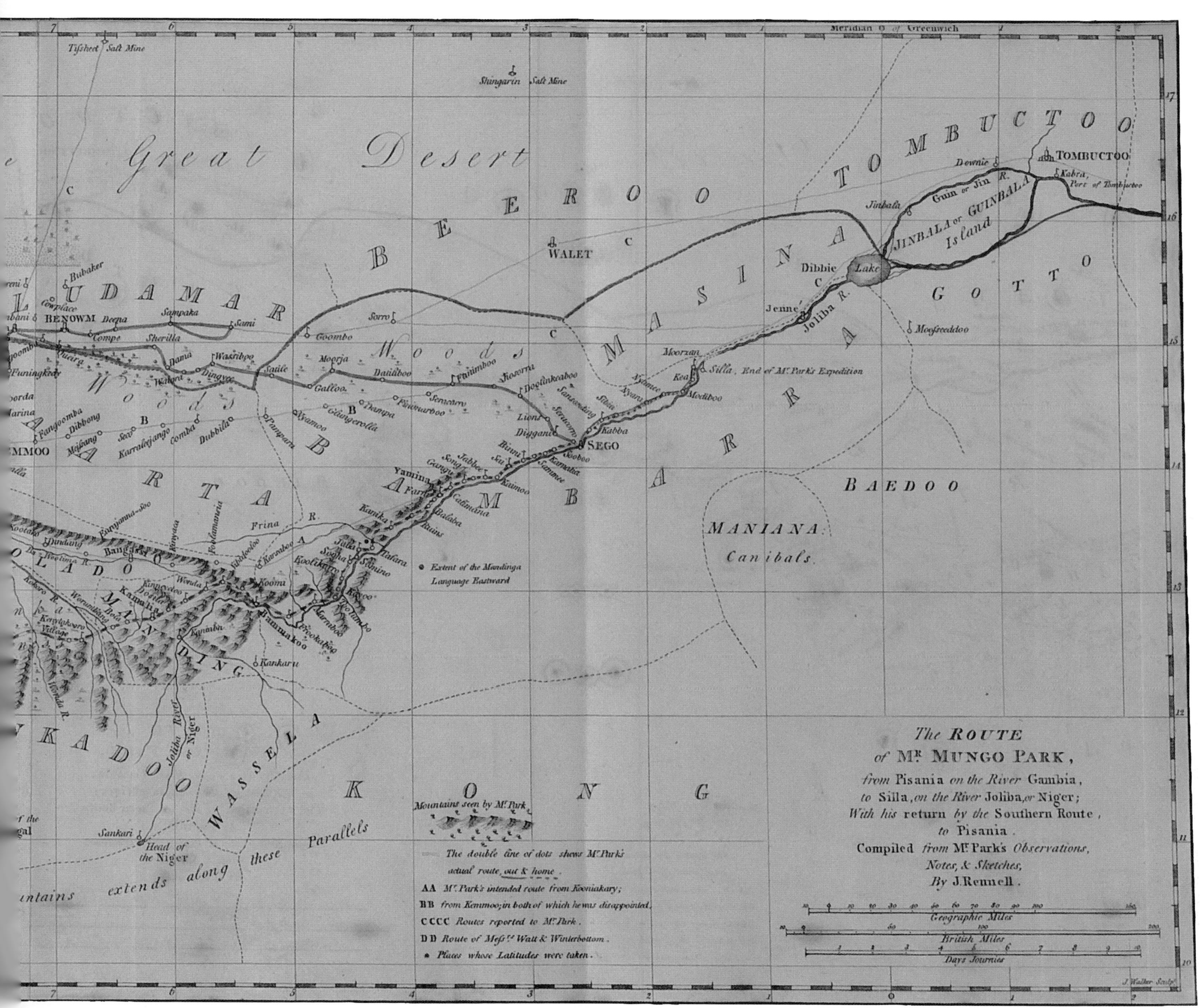

The ROUTE
of Mr. MUNGO PARK,
from Pisania on the River Gambia,
to Silla, on the River Joliba, or Niger;
With his return by the Southern Route,
to Pisania.
Compiled from Mr. Park's Observations,
Notes, & Sketches,
By J. Rennell.
Geographic Miles
British Miles
Days Journies
Mountains seen by Mr. Park
The double line of dots shews Mr. Park's actual route, out & home.
AA Mr. Park's intended route from Kooniakary;
BB from Kemmoo; in both of which he was disappointed.
CCCC Routes reported to Mr. Park.
DD Route of Messrs. Watt & Winterbottom.
Places whose Latitudes were taken.
Great Desert
TOMBUCTOO
BEROO
MASINA
BAMBARRA
GOTTO
BAEDOO
MANIANA Canibals
LUDAMAR
KONG
WASSELA
MANDING
Tisheet Salt Mine
Shingarin Salt Mine
WALET
BENOWM
SEGO
Jenne
Dibbie
Lake
Silla, End of Mr. Park's Expedition
Kabra, Port of Tombuctoo
JINBALA or GUINBALA Island
Joliba R.
Extent of the Mandinga Language Eastward
Sankari
Head of the Niger
Kankaru
Meridian of Greenwich
J. Walker Sculpt.

Friedrich Hornemann's Mission to the Niger

'Born for some enterprise of travel that will do him honour in the eyes of his contemporaries.'

1797-1801

THE AFRICAN ASSOCIATION HAD BEEN FOUNDED in London in 1788 by Joseph Banks and other like-minded gentlemen for the exploration of Africa, its most pressing objective being to resolve the course of the River Niger, the direction of which had been a mystery since ancient times. When the explorations of James Bruce, and of William George Browne who had reached Darfur in 1793, had failed to confirm the most appealing conjecture that the Niger was a tributary of the Nile, the mystery had thickened even further, the Niger apparently emerging from one void in the interior only to disappear into another. The Association decided therefore that, to locate both the beginning and end of the river, a two-pronged attack should be launched, one from the west coast and another from across the desert to the north. Likely candidates for such dangerous missions were hardly in abundance, and although the westerly approach had been eagerly volunteered by the young Scots adventurer Mungo Park, there was a shortage of suitably qualified candidates foolhardy enough to risk the hazardous trek across the Sahara. One, however, would emerge from obscurity to accept the challenge: Friedrich Conrad Hornemann, a young German theology graduate who had spent much of his youth preparing himself for life as an African explorer.

Hornemann arrived in Cairo in 1797 only to find his departure frustrated by financial difficulties and a surge of anti-European fanaticism triggered by Napoleon Bonaparte's invasion of Egypt. In the event the situation turned in his favour. He was befriended and patronized by Bonaparte himself, and in September 1798, disguised as a Muslim trader and accompanied by Joseph Frendenburg, a German convert, he joined a caravan heading for Murzuq in what is now southwestern Libya. Frendenburg died of malaria, but Hornemann lingered in Murzuq for seven months before joining a caravan heading south across the Sahara, bound for Bornu, west of Lake Chad. He sent his final despatch to London in April 1800 but was never heard of again, and it would be nineteen years before two British explorers arrived in Murzuq to unravel the mystery of his disappearance. Hornemann had in fact become the first European of his era to have crossed the Sahara, and on reaching the country around the lower Niger had been greatly loved by the people who regarded him as a healer and a holy man. Sadly, he had died of dysentery in 1801 soon after his arrival.

Right A map of Hornemann's route across the Sahara, drawn by James Rennell in 1802 to accompany the publication of Hornemann's *Journal.*

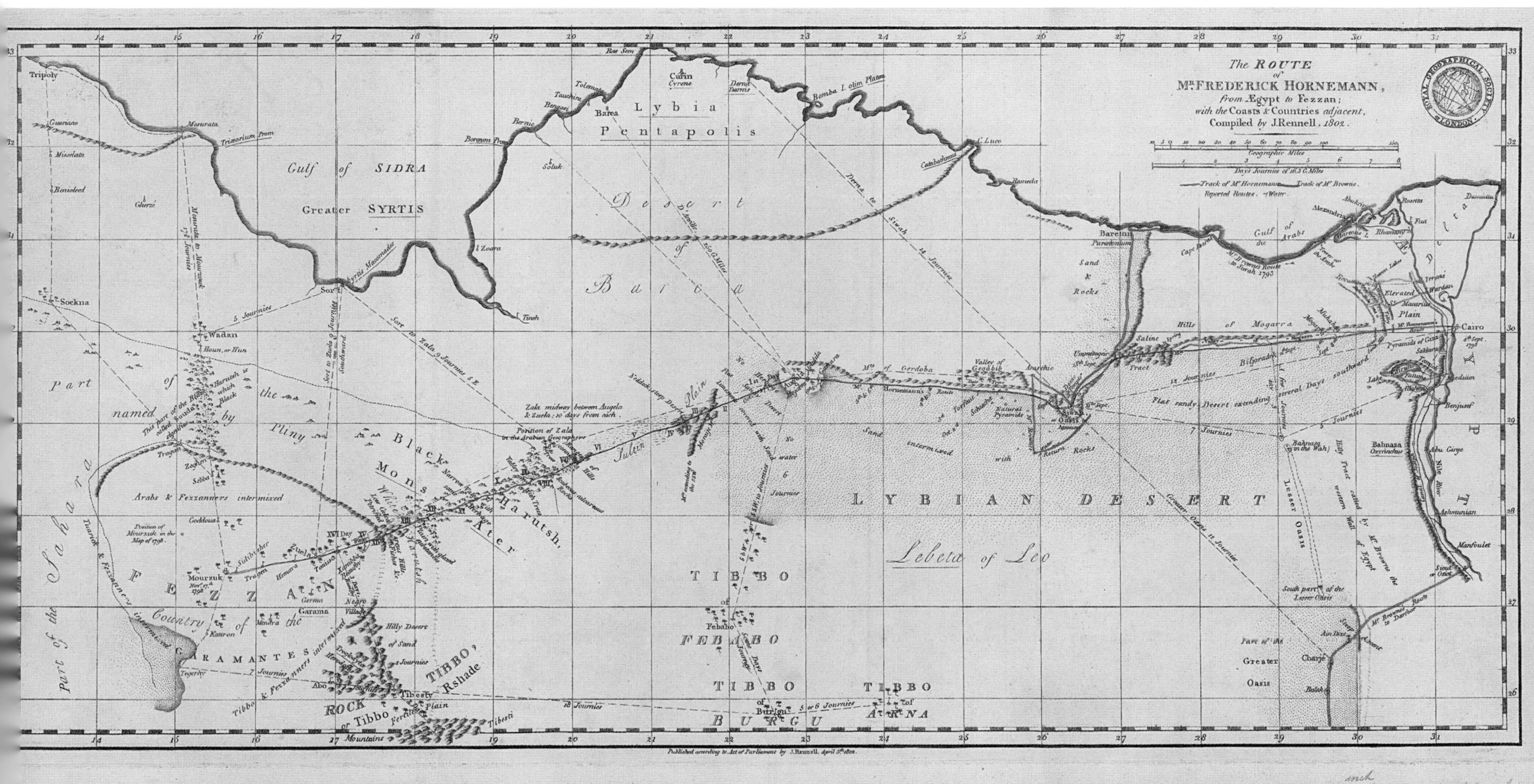
The ROUTE of Mr. FREDERICK HORNEMANN, from Ægypt to Fezzan; with the Coasts & Countries adjacent, Compiled by J.Rennell, 1802.
ROYAL GEOGRAPHICAL SOCIETY LONDON
Geographic Miles
Days Journies of 16,3 G.Miles
Track of Mr. Hornemann
Track of Mr. Browne.
Reported Routes.
Water.
Tripoly
Mesurata
Gulf of SIDRA
Greater SYRTIS
Lybia
Pentapolis
Desert of Barca
Barca
Curin
Cyrene
Derne
Sockna
Wadan
Sort
Part of the Sahara
Mourzuk
FEZZAN
Country of the GARAMANTES
Black Mons Harutsh
Ater
TIBBO
FEDABO
BURGU
Rshade
ROCK Tibbo
LYBIAN DESERT
Lebeta of Leo
Siwah
Alexandria
Rosetta
Abukeir
Gulf of Arabs
Delta
Cairo
Elevated Plain
Hills of Mogarra
Part of the Greater Oasis
Lesser Oasis
EGYPT

1799–1802

Humboldt and Bonpland Bring Organization to the Cosmos

'Nature in all her variety of grandeur and splendour.'

ALEXANDER VON HUMBOLDT HAD FOR TWENTY YEARS CHERISHED THE DREAM of travel in remote and distant lands. Self-taught in languages, schooled in the physical sciences, trained in geology and topology, he was already by his late twenties a man of prodigious intellect and learning. But he knew little of botany, and for years his search for a botanist willing to plunge headlong into the jungles of South America came to nothing. Then in 1798, on the stairs of a Paris hotel, he bumped into Aimé Bonpland, a newly qualified doctor with a passion not only for botany but also for adventure. In Madrid they charmed the court with their expertise, obtaining passage to South America in exchange for intelligence of the continent's mineral resources. Escaping an English blockade, surviving howling gales and a raging shipboard epidemic, the two companions landed at Cumana, Venezuela, in July 1799. They took a trip into the hinterland, moved west to Caracas, then headed south across the savannah to the Orinoco, which they ascended to the Brazilian border.

What the explorers sought was the Casiquiare, the elusive forest-clad watercourse that linked the Rio Negro, a tributary of the Amazonian system, with the northward-flowing Orinoco. The river had long been rumoured, and some had even reported sailing on it, but the idea of a stream that fed two adjacent watersheds, evidently flowing in opposite directions at the same time, was anathema to many geographers. Nevertheless, in May 1800 Humboldt and Bonpland navigated its entire 300-kilometre (180-mile) course, reporting it to be 'as broad as the Rhine' and envisioning it as a great artery of future commerce. Returning to the coast and postponing a visit to Mexico, they headed for Colombia, ascended the Río Magdalena and followed the roof of the Andes to Ecuador and Peru, on route in 1802 climbing 5900 metres (19,300 feet) up Mount Chimborazo and setting a new world altitude record. The impact of the expedition on the scientific world was profound. Humboldt's discoveries and observations filled more than twenty volumes, and Bonpland catalogued more than 3000 new species, instantly doubling the number previously known across the entire globe. Humboldt's formidable learning grew with time, enabling him to perceive the interplay between everything that existed on earth 'from the firmament to the tiniest moss on a rock', and to recognize the subtle interdependence of species, the hierarchy by which the highest of life-forms might be threatened by the extinction of the lowest.

Right A portrait of Alexander von Humboldt at work somewhere in the forests of South America.

Flinders and Baudin Give Shape to Australia

Scientific collaboration between captains at war.

1800–03

AUSTRALIA IN 1800, DESPITE ITS CONSIDERABLE RESIDENT POPULATION, was in European eyes a *terra nullius*, a no-man's-land there for the taking by any nation interested enough to seize possession of its inhospitable shores. Britain, relieved of its American colonies and deprived of an overflow for its swollen prison population, had in 1788 established a miserable enclave of outcast rejects in Sydney Cove. Seemingly impenetrable mountains hampered progress inland, but survey voyages had delineated the coast southward and in 1798 confirmed Van Diemen's Land, Tasmania, to be an island. James Cook had revealed much of the shape of Australia's east coast, and the general aspect of the continent's western half had been established by accidental landfalls of seventeeth-century Dutch navigators, but neither had planted colonial settlements. In the meantime, France, from its position of dominance in the Indian Ocean, was beginning to show a keen interest in the western and southwestern coasts, several of its expeditions having alighted there.

Britain and France had been at war for eight years when two rival Australian coastal expeditions, led respectively by naval captains Matthew Flinders and Nicolas Baudin, requested mutual safe conduct to protect them from seizure by ships of the opposing navies. Sanctioned by enlightened men who understood that mere political squabbles, however deep-rooted, should never encroach on the progess of science, the two expeditions sailed within ten months of each other, Baudin with the *Géographe* and *Naturaliste* in October 1800 and Flinders in the *Investigator* in July 1801. While Flinders had to make do with second-rate supplies and equipment, the best the Admiralty could offer in a time of war, Baudin's expedition, eagerly patronized by Napoleon himself, took the best scientific materials and *savants* that France could muster. Between them, the two expeditions charted almost the entire periphery of the continent, Baudin concentrating on the south and west, and the island of Tasmania, and Flinders on the southeast, the northeast and the Gulf of Carpentaria. By extraordinary coincidence the captains met amiably at the very point where the Murray River enters the sea, but remarkably neither identified the river and so left the crucial question of Australia's inland drainage unsolved for many years. Their destinies linked, both captains would meet their nemesis on the island of Mauritius, Baudin dying there of disease, disgraced and alienated by his officers and scientists, Flinders apprehended as a spy and forced to endure six years in obscurity before repatriation to England.

Right An anonymous portrait miniature of Matthew Flinders, 1801, together with some of his personal possessions.

Above Sydney Harbour as Flinders last saw it in 1800.

Lewis and Clark Seek a Viable Trade Route to the Pacific

A commercial enterprise to which geographical knowledge was secondary.

1803–06

THE VAST SWATHE OF TERRITORY KNOWN AS LOUISIANA, embracing much of the Mississippi and Missouri valleys, had been settled by the French towards the end of the seventeenth century, then offloaded to Spain in 1763, and in 1800 surreptitiously clawed back by Napoleon Bonaparte for the future hub of a Caribbean sugar empire. However, when Bonaparte failed to reclaim Haiti the promise of American empire collapsed and Louisiana, regardless of the Spanish who still thought it was theirs, was sold to the United States for $15 million. For President Thomas Jefferson, a visionary committed to westward expansion, it was a dream come true, but with the Spanish nibbling at the southern fringes, the British in the north, and the French suspiciously eyeing the northwest, time was of the essence in consolidating United States influence over its newly acquired baby. Within weeks Jefferson had appropriated $2500 for an expedition to explore the Missouri, to establish friendly relations with the indigenous nations and to discover a commercial route to the Pacific. Command of the expedition was offered to Captain Meriwether Lewis, who in turn recruited 'Captain' William Clark as his assistant. Linked by prior friendship, their wildly contrasting but complementary temperaments made for an ideal partnership.

The expedition was underway by July 1803, picking up volunteers en route and wintering at the mouth of the Missouri. Progress resumed in May 1804, entering Sioux country and spending the next winter with the Mandans of North Dakota. Here Lewis and Clark acquired the services of Sacajawea, the young Shoshone wife of a French trader who knew the Rockies and spoke a number of languages. In the spring of 1805 the expedition ascended the Missouri and in September, by a circuitous route, crossed the high divide into the watershed of the Columbia. Via the Snake River, a swift descent of the Columbia brought it to the Pacific in the first week of November. The return journey, following three uncomfortable months in a makeshift fort on the west coast, was by comparison arduous and dispiriting. The party was forced to scavenge for food, scrounge from the locals and barter for horses, and despite numerous excursions and divisions of reconnaissance parties, no commercially exploitable route could be found. Finally disbanded at St Louis in October 1806, Lewis and Clark's expedition, despite the landmark acclaim it would subsequently receive, had 'for the purpose of extending the external commerce of the United States' been a heroic failure.

Right Two woodcut engravings by Patrick Gass, who accompanied Lewis and Clark, illustrating his personal account of the expedition.

William Moorcroft, the Wandering Horse-Doctor

A prelude to the 'Great Game' in Central Asia.

1812-25

Born in Lancashire in 1767, William Moorcroft had no intention of becoming an explorer. An outbreak of cattle plague had steered him towards veterinary surgery, an occupation in its early days belittled and derided. He returned from studies in France to establish a lucrative veterinary practice in Oxford Street, London, but then lost everything in a vain attempt to market his patented machine-made horseshoes. Facing destitution, in 1808 Moorcroft eagerly accepted employment with the East India Company as superintendent of its stud farm near Patna, entrusted with improving the cavalry's chargers. In 1811, when adjustments to feed and conditions failed to bring about the required results, he decided to embark on a tour of the Indian horse fairs in the hope of locating better breeding stock. Thus began Moorcroft's career as an explorer. In May 1812, disguised as a Hindu trading pilgrim, with fifty-four porters and livestock, he and his partner, Captain Hyder Jung Hearsey, headed for Tibet, crossing the Himalayas by the Niti Pass and becoming the first Englishmen to set eyes on the sacred Mount Kailas, revered by Hindus and Buddhists as the abode of the gods and the navel of the world. Imprisoned on the journey back, and released only after considerable diplomatic wrangling, Moorcroft faced chastisement for sneaking clandestinely into forbidden territory, and for seven years suffered refusal for any comparable 'wild and romantic excursions'.

What Moorcroft coveted most were the Turkmen horses from the plains of Central Asia, so when permission arrived in 1819 to proceed 'towards the northwestern parts of Asia' he jumped at the opportunity. But by now the Company had an ulterior motive. Fearful of Russian advances, the first murmurings of the 'Great Game' in Central Asia, Moorcroft's excursion could provide crucial intelligence from a mysterious and impenetrable backwater. In the company of a recently arrived nineteen-year-old lawyer named George Trebeck, Moorcroft and his 300-strong party crossed the Sutlej in March 1820. For two years they examined the Buddhist kingdom of Ladakh, then continued to Srinagar, the Khyber Pass and Kabul. Crossing the Hindu Kush and descending to the plains of Turkestan, relentlessly harassed by petty warlords, they entered Bokhara in February 1825, the first Englishmen there since Anthony Jenkinson, 250 years earlier. Unlike Jenkinson, neither Moorcroft nor Trebeck would return, both of them meeting their death, probably poisoned for their possessions, in northern Afghanistan.

Right Moorcroft and Hearsey (left) in native dress, riding yaks on the road to Lake Mansarowar. They encounter two Tibetans, mounted on horseback with a loaded yak.

1815-36

The Riddle of Australia's Inland Waterways

Rivers that flowed away from the sea.

FOR TWENTY-FIVE YEARS THE FORMIDABLE PEAKS and dense impenetrable valleys of the Blue Mountains, barely 50 kilometres (30 miles) inland from where the first party of convicts were landed at Sydney Cove in 1788, presented an intimidating challenge for the explorer and a frustration to a succession of governors desperate for grazing land to feed the colony's burgeoning population. A few tentative steps had been taken to break out of the isolated enclave, some of them by absconders whose notion of precisely where they had been deposited was so imperfect that they regarded the mountains as an easy escape to China, but it was not until 1813 that Gregory Blaxland and two associates penetrated the range sufficiently to distantly descry enough grazing land 'to feed the colony for thirty years'. Others were soon to follow, descending the rivers that rose to the west of the mountains and penetrating ever deeper into the continent's interior. In 1815 George Evans found the Lachlan River, then in 1817-18 John Oxley examined the Lachlan and traced the Macquarie River for some 300 kilometres (180 miles) before clambering heroically back across the Great Dividing Range.

Although Oxley had found in the Liverpool Plains the fertile country demanded by the growing colony, his newly discovered rivers trended inexplicably to the northwest. Flinders's and Baudin's surveys of the Australian coastline had found no significant river emanating from the interior, leading to the conclusion that a great lake must lie deep in the heart of the continent, a beckoning Arcadia where the continent's rivers converged. The mystery of Australia's enigmatic drainage system, its lonely watercourses that, reminiscent of the Nile, meander anomalously through ceaseless tracts of desert and grassland, would engage explorers obsessively for more than fifteen years. In 1829 Charles Sturt followed the Macquarie north and alighted on the banks of 'a noble river', the Darling. The next year, his attention turning southward, he descended the Murrumbidgee to its union with the Murray River, then followed the Murray to its inconspicuous debouchment on the South Australian coast. The final piece in the jigsaw was provided by Thomas Livingstone Mitchell, who in 1835-36 traced the courses of the Lachlan and Darling rivers and confirmed that every major river eventually connected with the Murray. The myth of the great lake was finally dispelled and the secrets of the Murray-Darling basin laid open.

Right Sturt arrives at the confluence of the Murray and Darling rivers and solves one of the greatest mysteries of Australia's inland waterways.

Junction of Darling and Murray R

Captain Sadleir Strikes Across the Arabian Peninsula

Not for fame or glory, but entirely in the cause of duty.

1819

THE LONG HISTORY OF CONFLICT BETWEEN CHRISTENDOM AND ISLAM, coupled with the widespread myth that infidel travellers would inevitably meet a gruesome end at the hands of fanatical desert tribes, meant that for centuries European explorers nibbled only at the fringes of Arabia. Maps of the desert interior, littered with misplaced and unlikely names, some surviving since the Middle Ages, were less reliable than those of the Pacific islands. Remarkably, the first European to penetrate further than 200 kilometres (125 miles) from the coast, a lowly British captain named George Forster Sadleir, would happen to become the first to cross the entire Arabian Peninsula. Unsung in his day, and absent even now from the hierarchy of the great and good, his journey would not be replicated for 100 years. Even more exceptional was that Sadleir blazed his trail across fanatical Arabia in full military uniform, insensitive to local customs or opinion, alone and heedless of danger. All in a day's work, he made no claim to fame, and by the time his report circulated fifty years after the event, Sadleir had expired in obscurity.

In 1819, Captain Sadleir, 47th Regiment of Foot, serving in India, received instructions to proceed to the camp of the Egyptian commander, Ibrahim Pasha, to congratulate the pasha on his successes against the Wahabis and to seek his cooperation in cleansing the Persian Gulf of pirates. He was also to ceremoniously present the pasha, whose camp lay near the Gulf, with a sword of honour. However, on arrival at the Arabian port of Al Qatif, Sadleir found to his dismay that Ibrahim had departed on a pilgrimage to Mecca. Undeterred, he struck fearlessly into the desert, following the pasha's tracks to Al Hufuf where he fell in with a detachment of Egyptian soldiers. After two months hurriedly in pursuit, he reached Ar Rass, the dead centre of Arabia, only to discover that his quarry had escaped again. With no guarantee of safe passage back to the Gulf, Sadleir had little alternative but to press on, finally tracking his prey to Bir Ali, a mere five kilometres (three miles) from Medina. Sword and congratulations duly presented, an escort was provided to conduct the officer to the coast. Sadleir returned quietly to India, apparently oblivious to the significance of his achievement, served out a routine military career, retired to Cork in 1837, then emigrated with his wife to New Zealand.

Right Captain Sadleir's map of his route across Arabia, the first crossing of the peninsula by a European explorer but unheralded at the time.

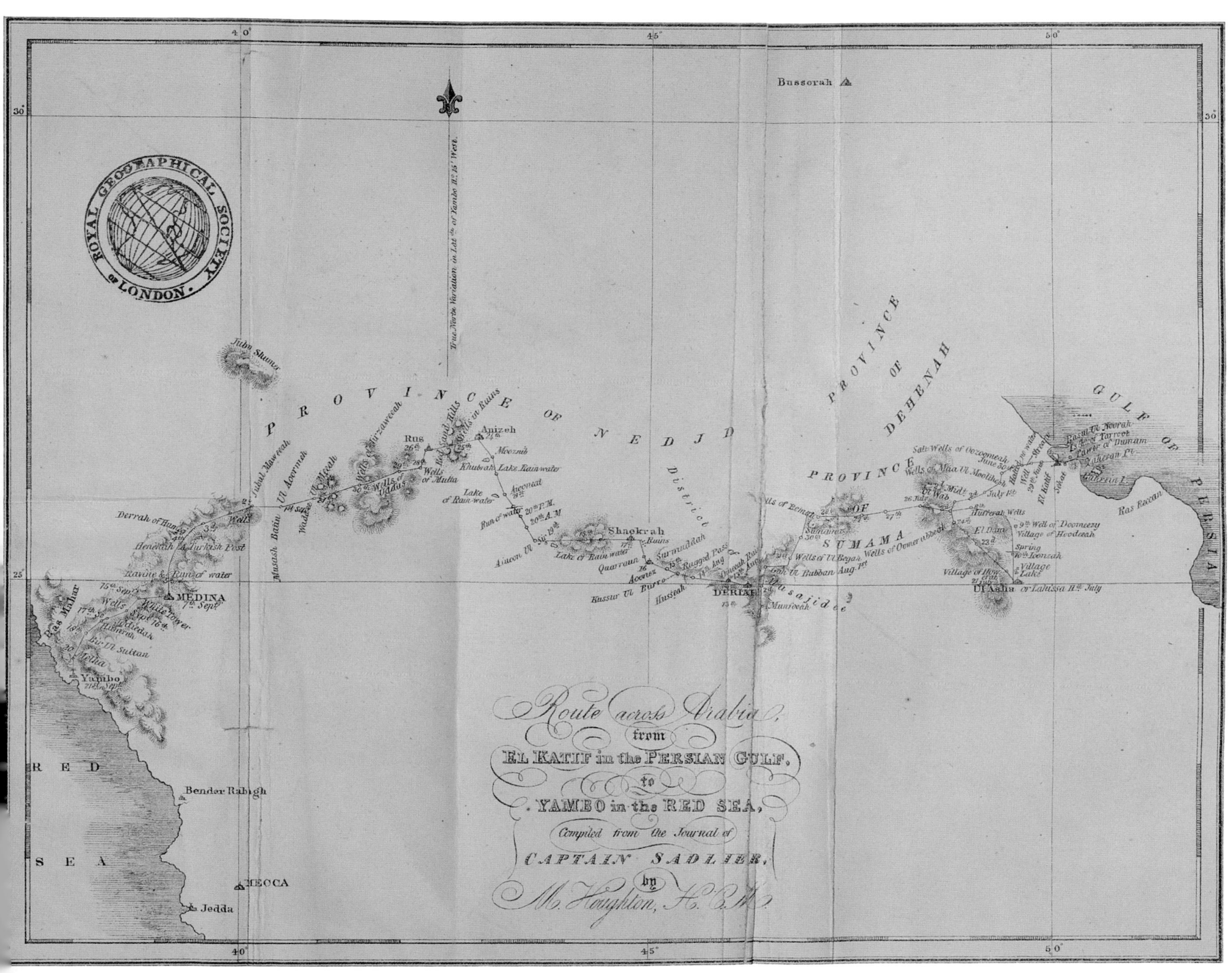
Route across Arabia,
from
EL KATIF in the PERSIAN GULF,
to
YAMBO in the RED SEA,
Compiled from the Journal of
CAPTAIN SADLIER,
by
M. Houghton
ROYAL GEOGRAPHICAL SOCIETY of LONDON
PROVINCE OF NEDJD
PROVINCE OF DEHENAH
PROVINCE OF SUMAMA
GULF OF PERSIA
RED SEA
Bussorah
Anizeh
Rus
Shaqkrah
DERIAH
MEDINA
Yambo
Bender Rabigh
MECCA
Jedda
El Katif
40°
45°
50°
30°
25°

Edward Parry's Remarkable Venture into the Arctic Archipelago

The search for the Northwest Passage.

1819-20

THE NORTHWEST PASSAGE, THAT SPECULATIVE SEA ROUTE around the Arctic shores of North America linking Atlantic and Pacific, languished in the geographical subconscious for two centuries. Abandoned in 1616 as a commercial route to Cathay, shelved by science in favour of more manageable commitments, it lay remote and inaccessible but never quite forgotten. The nineteenth century, however, would see it turn into an irrational obsession whose original motivation – the threat of Russian expansion, the useful employment of the navy's 1200 officers mothballed after the Napoleonic wars, or just natural curiosity – would be lost under a cloud of compulsive endeavour that would draw countless men and ships into the bewildering labyrinth of ice-bound channels and blind alleys that honeycomb the Arctic archipelago.

It all started in 1817 when John Barrow, the Admiralty's secretary and principal planner of all that was to follow, heard from the distinguished explorer William Scoresby that exceptionally mild conditions prevailed in the Arctic. Four comfortably equipped ships, two under the command of David Buchan and John Franklin, the others under John Ross and Edward Parry, were despatched in 1818 for a two-pronged assault, Buchan to the east of Greenland and Ross to the west. Buchan was beset by ice off the northwestern tip of Svalbard, but Ross penetrated to 76°N before conditions turned him towards Ellesmere Island and along the coast of Baffin Island. However, for reasons never properly explained, and to the astonishment of Parry, Ross declared that Lancaster Sound, that one vital gateway into the Northwest Passage which all future expeditions would enter, was a cul-de-sac terminated by mountains only he could see.

In 1819 the Admiralty, swayed by his superior scientific and intellectual abilities, sent Parry back to Lancaster Sound to settle the controversy. In August he successfully navigated the sound, emerging into the even broader Wellington Channel and the vast expanse of Melville Sound. But with the transit of the Passage almost within his grasp, the ice closed in, forcing him and his crews to winter on the coast of Melville Island. Remarkably, through Parry's sympathetic leadership and rigorous attendance to his crew's diet, all but one survived the long Arctic night, but sadly the Beaufort Sea, only a stone's throw away, remained ice-locked when summer returned. In August 1820, denied the fitting climax to his expedition, Parry turned back the way he had come.

Right Parry's men cutting an escape channel through the Arctic ice.

Bellingshausen Navigates a Continent of Ice

Imperial Russia enters the arena.

1819-21

JAMES COOK HAD ADMIRERS THROUGHOUT THE WORLD, but nowhere was there greater reverence than in Russia, where the navy duplicated the British model and voyages in imitation of Cook had been mooted as early as 1786. Wars with Turkey and Sweden diverted its admirals elsewhere, but in 1803 Ivan Fedorovich Krusenstern, a fervent Cook devotee, left Kronstadt naval base for a three-year circumnavigation, during which he successfully established direct maritime contact with the far-flung Alaskan colonies and attempted to open commerce with Japan and China. Then, once again, war intervened, but with the defeat of Napoleon and the weakening of France, Tsar Alexander I began to see Russia as an emergent world power and like his grandmother, Catherine II, sought to extend Russia's influence by peaceful means. A lengthy, prestigious voyage of discovery would not only promise the prospect of collecting a few staging posts in the South Pacific, but would also provide excellent training for his officers and crews. So in May 1819 Captain Faddei Bellingshausen, an Estonian-born Baltic German, was summoned to St Petersburg and given six weeks to prepare for a voyage towards Antarctica. Bellingshausen had envisaged something in the style of his mentor Cook, but impatience precluded the recruitment of specialist scientists and left their work largely in the hands of the officers.

With two ships seriously unmatched in speed, Bellingshausen left Kronstadt in July 1819 and plunged into the South Atlantic, charting the South Sandwich Islands, then crossing the Antarctic circle several times in the longitude of South Africa. In January 1820 he observed the shore of what he would describe as an 'ice-continent' – the first sighting of a continental ice shelf, a formation previously unknown to science. The observation is frequently invoked to honour the Russian with the discovery of Antarctica, but as no 'land', as such, was seen throughout Bellingshausen's frequent close encounters, the accolade might more legitimately fall to the Royal Navy captain Edward Bransfield, who the same month actually spotted from a distance the backbone of the Antarctic Peninsula. Over the next twelve months Bellingshausen went on to accomplish the first circumnavigation of Antarctica in low latitudes, but his remarkable achievement passed almost unnoticed. The mentally unstable tsar had lost interest, and no account of the voyage materialized for ten years. It would be another century, with the Hakluyt Society's English translation, before Bellingshausen could assume his rightful place beside his beloved Cook.

Right Bellingshausen in conference with Pacific islanders. From the Atlas volume of Bellingshausen's *Dvukratnie izyskaniia v Iuzhnom Ledovitom Okeane* (1831).

Clapperton and Lander Resolve the Mystery of the Niger

The riddle of the strong brown god.

1822-30

THE MYSTERY OF THE COURSE OF THE NIGER OBSESSED GEOGRAPHERS for more than thirty years. Mungo Park had died at Bussa during the descent, while reports from Arab traders suggested that the river flowed into Lake Chad and even ultimately into the Nile. In 1822 the Edinburgh doctor Walter Oudney was despatched to open diplomatic relations with the Fulani kingdom, whose legendary trading centre, Kano, was reputed to rival Timbuktu. With him were the naval lieutenant Hugh Clapperton and the army officer Dixon Denham, two men whose characters conflicted to the extent of bitter hatred. To avoid the disease-infested approach through distant Senegal, a route across the Sahara was followed, but when no major rivers were found to enter Lake Chad the party divided, Denham examining the Shari River, the others proceeding to Kano and the Fulani capital Sokoto. Oudney died en route, but Clapperton was courteously received by the ruler, Mohammed Bello, who compliantly drew a map in the sand confirming that the Niger flowed south into the Atlantic. But Bello was soon to realize that in his haste he had laid his kingdom wide open to foreign interlopers. A second map was rapidly fabricated, diverting the Niger northeast to Egypt, while every effort was made to dissuade Clapperton from discovering the river's true course. It left the Scotsman no choice but to rejoin Denham at Lake Chad and trudge wearily back across the Sahara.

Clapperton had not fallen prey to Bello's trickery. Convinced of the veracity of the first map he disembarked on the Nigerian coast in November 1825, determined to strike inland to Sokoto, then descend the Niger to the Atlantic. Within months most of the party had fallen to malaria, and by the time Sokoto was reached only Clapperton and his manservant Richard Lander were left alive. Finally, in February 1827, Bello agreed to allow them to return to the sea by way of the Niger. Success was in the bag, but the next month Clapperton succumbed to malaria and dysentery and died shortly after, leaving Lander to make his way back alone, his plans to negotiate the river frustrated by hostile tribes. However, with official government backing, Lander and his brother John returned to Nigeria in 1830 to successfully descend the last defiant section of the Niger from Bussa to the coast. The task was complete, and by November 1830 the river's course was known from Mali to the Atlantic.

Right Clapperton and Lander's map of the country between Lake Chad and the Atlantic leaves an ominous gap in the course of the Niger.

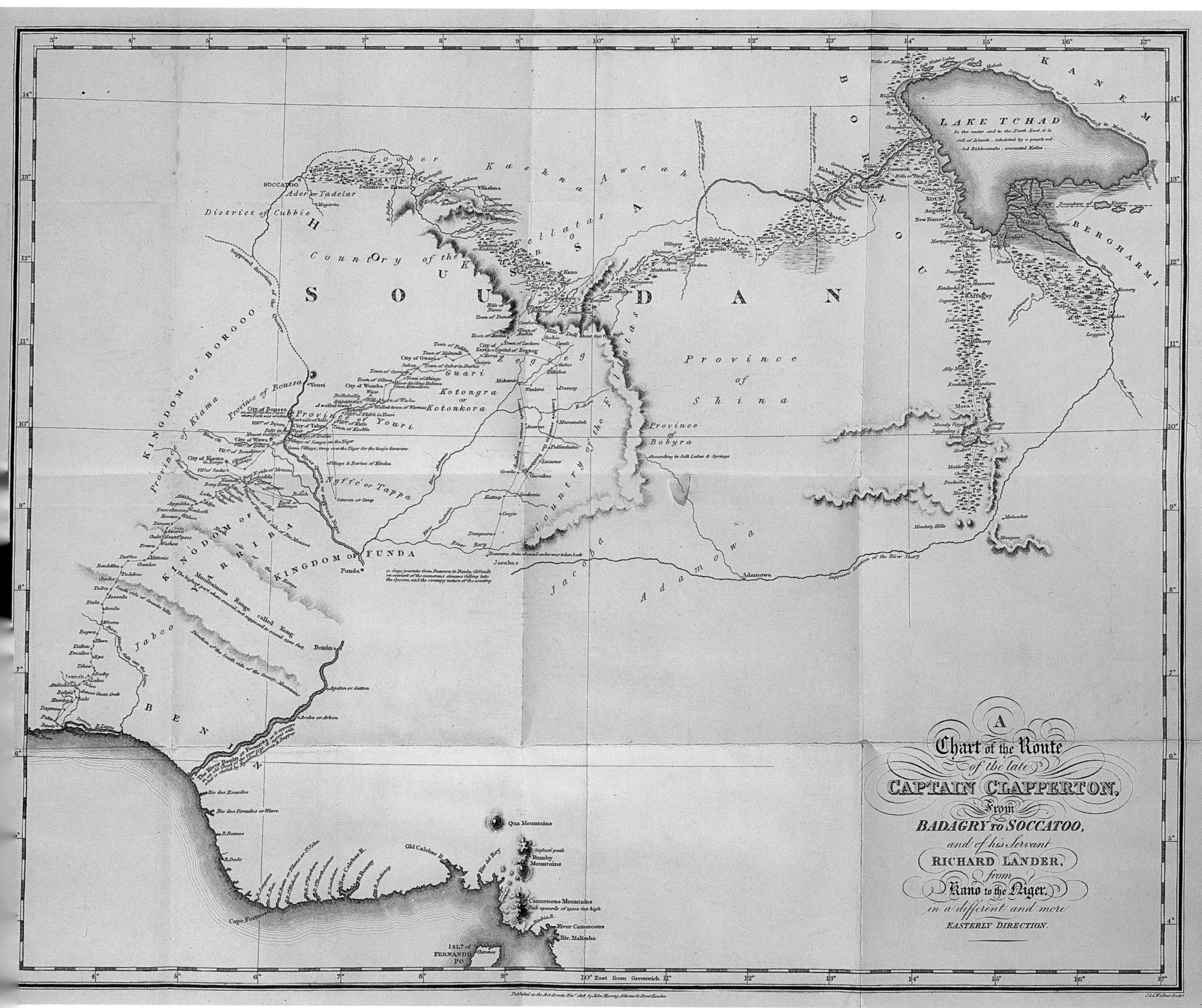
A
Chart of the Route
of the late
CAPTAIN CLAPPERTON,
from
BADAGRY TO SOCCATOO,
and of his Servant
RICHARD LANDER,
from
Kano to the Niger,
in a different and more
EASTERLY DIRECTION.
LAKE TCHAD
SOUDAN
HOUSSA
BORNOU
KANEM
BERGHARMI
Province of Shina
KINGDOM OF BORGOO
KINGDOM OF FUNDA
BENIN
SOCCATOO
Cape Formosa
Cameroons Mountains
Qua Mountains
ISL.D of FERNANDO PO
10° East from Greenwich

1826-40

From Venus to Antarctica

Dumont D'Urville perfects the map of the Pacific.

IN THE ROSTER OF ILLUSTRIOUS FRENCH CAPTAINS who in the eighteenth and nineteenth centuries magisterially plied the world's oceans in the cause of science, the name of Jules Sébastien César Dumont D'Urville stands out above all others. Born to a noble family compelled by the Revolution to seek seclusion in Normandy, and orphaned at six, he entered the navy at seventeen only to spend much of his early career landlocked by a British blockade of French ports. However, the enforced sequestration allowed this timid and studious young man, already well versed in the exploits of his forebears, to indulge a passion for science, botany and languages, of which he spoke eight and would come to master many more. The war over, he joined a hydrographic voyage to the Aegean, during which he was instrumental in procuring for France the statue known as the Venus de Milo. Then in 1822-25 he gained his first experience of distant shores when, on a voyage that was largely his brainchild, he circumnavigated the globe with Louis Isidore Duperrey in the *Coquille*, visiting Australasia and the islands of the Pacific.

Immediately upon his return D'Urville lobbied relentlessly for a voyage under his command – one that would take the *Coquille*, renamed *Astrolabe*, on a three-year cruise to New Zealand and the islands of the southwest Pacific. The expedition returned with a hoard of biological and geological specimens, while its official report ran to thirteen volumes and five sumptuous atlases of plates and maps. Nevertheless, D'Urville, a proud and obstinate man who too easily made enemies, found himself cold-shouldered by his superiors who refused to acknowledge the significance of his work and left him desk-bound for seven years. However, when in 1837 he proposed a second voyage of exploration, he found in King Louis-Philippe a monarch determined to enrol his country in the race for the newly discovered continent of Antarctica. In September D'Urville hurried south with the *Astrolabe* and *Zélée* to spend the austral summer in Antarctic waters, followed by a year's wandering in the Pacific. In January 1840 he turned south again to discover the remote Antarctic mainland, which he christened Terre Adélie after his wife. D'Urville was back in Toulon by the end of the year, but he would never fully enjoy the fruits of his labours, nor see the twenty-three volumes of reports through to their conclusion. He was to die, along with his wife and family, in the fires of an horrific train crash.

Right Dumont D'Urville's crew attempt to open a channel through the Antarctic ice.

René Caillié Beholds the Legendary City of Timbuktu

A journey that failed all expectations.

1827-28

WHILE MOST EXPLORERS OF THE NINETEENTH CENTURY were drawn from the officer class, or could boast at least a medical doctorate or some measure of scientific training, some would emerge from humble obscurity, self-taught and with nothing to commend them beyond an overwhelming passion for exploration. René-Auguste Caillié, son of a baker's assistant, his mother dead and his father in prison, spent his youth poring over geographical texts, excited by the prospect of one day filling the empty spaces that whitewashed the map of Africa. At seventeen he signed as a cabin boy on a ship to Senegal but got little further and spent the next five years working for a Bordeaux wine merchant. But by 1824 he was back in Senegal, determined to become the first European to reach the legendary Timbuktu and claim the 10,000-franc prize on offer for the city's first descriptive account. In 1827, after nine months with a backwoods Moorish tribe, then as manager of an indigo plantation, Caillié converted his savings to gold and set out for the interior disguised as an Egyptian deported to Senegal and now on his way to Mecca.

At Tieme, less than halfway to his destination, Caillié went down with both scurvy and malaria and languished for five months in a primitive grass hut, nursed back to life by an old African woman. Barely able to walk, he started out again in January 1828, and at Djenné boarded a boat for Timbuktu. Weakened by his illness, ranked with slaves and held below deck, he finally disembarked at Kabara and on 19 April 1828 took the short walk into Timbuktu. It was a sight for sore eyes. The grandeur and wealth that the name had evoked for centuries had long since vanished, and Caillié saw nothing but a sleepy huddle of dilapidated buildings swept by desert sands, their residents in perpetual fear of Tuareg attack. To add to his dismay he found that he had been beaten to Timbuktu two years earlier by the Scottish explorer Alexander Gordon Laing, but whose death shortly after leaving the city thankfully disqualified him from receiving the prize. Two weeks in this dreary place was long enough for Caillié, so in April he joined a caravan heading for Morocco. Back in France, although his claim was treated with suspicion and he was cross-examined over the veracity of his travels, the prize was granted.

Right Caillié's unimposing view of Timbuktu – a sleepy, desert town whose grandeur had long since faded.

T. III.
Pl. 6.
Ouest
Sud.
Nord
Est
Vue d'une partie de la ville de Temboctou, prise du sommet d'une colline, à l'Est-nord-est.

FitzRoy, Darwin and the Voyage of the Beagle

An expedition that would create a scientific revolution.

1831-36

If ever an expedition is to be remembered solely by the name of a ship, then the voyage of the *Beagle* is the one most likely to come to mind. Its captain, Robert FitzRoy, who at the tender age of twenty-six was given the task of directing a critical hydrographic circumnavigation, is often forgotten in favour of the expedition's most celebrated affiliate, an adventurous young collector by the name of Charles Darwin. FitzRoy had inherited the *Beagle* on an earlier survey of Patagonian waters when his senior officer shot himself in a fit of depression. Now, in 1831, reappointed to the *Beagle*, he was charged with completing the South American survey, then making precision chronometric measurements at strategic points around the world. Darwin spent most of his time afloat seasick in his cabin, so it came as a relief to find that two thirds of the voyage would be spent at anchor, during which prolonged excursions could be made ashore. While FitzRoy concentrated on the official business of the cruise, Darwin made extensive forays into the hinterland, crossing the Argentine Pampas and experiencing the desolation of the Chilean deserts. But it was not until he reached the Galápagos Islands in September 1835 that he would undertake the observations that would lead him to his theory of natural selection, his precursor to the concept of biological evolution. The voyage continued expeditiously to Tahiti, New Zealand, Australia and Brazil, and returned to England late in 1836.

As acknowledged in the preface to his *Voyage of the Beagle*, Darwin owed an enormous debt of gratitude to FitzRoy, and to the captain's 'undeviating kindness'. Other captains might not have been so amenable to the young collector's demands, and if Darwin had sailed on any other ship the theory of evolution might never have been born. FitzRoy went on to become governor of New Zealand and in later life a pioneer of weather forecasting, establishing weather stations that telegraphed their information to London and hence enabled *The Times* to publish the first daily forecasts of the type that now grace every national newspaper. But his role in assisting Darwin, whose views he never found acceptable, would forever trouble him, and in 1865 FitzRoy took his own life by slitting his throat. An inquest attributed his action to overwork and an unsound mind, but quite probably it was the result of a conflict of conscience with religious conviction.

Right HMS *Beagle* in the Beagle Channel, Tierra del Fuego.

Charles Wilkes Takes on More Than His Men Can Endure

The 'everlasting voyage' of the United States Exploring Expedition.

1838-42

SADLY, THE ENTRY OF THE UNITED STATES INTO THE ARENA of distant maritime exploration would be marked by a voyage of overambitious complexity, disaster and disarray, inept leadership and deficient observation. The expedition's paramount challenge was to explore deep into Antarctic waters where New England whalers and sealers, displaced increasingly southward from their traditional hunting grounds, frequently foundered on uncharted islets and submerged reefs. But the United States Exploring Expedition, with an appropriation of $300,000 from Congress, would blossom into a full-blown scientific expedition intent on rivalling anything accomplished by other nations. Unfortunately, its commander Charles Wilkes, an austere disciplinarian who lacked the wisdom and maturity of his foreign counterparts, would tax his men to such an extent that by the third year they were beginning to see death as a welcome alternative to the privations they were forced to suffer.

The convoy of six vessels that sailed in August 1838 was too unwieldy for satisfactory control in the tumultuous Southern Ocean, requiring constant regrouping of ships that, through damage or unforeseen conditions, had little chance of meeting the proposed rendezvous. After a number of abortive forays south of Cape Horn, where work was frustrated by ferocious storms and blinding fog, Wilkes island-hopped through the Pacific from Tahiti to Hawaii. Then from Sydney in December 1839, after attempts to regroup at an imaginary island, he struck south into impenetrable ice. Sailing west, he sketched what he took to be a range of distant mountains, thereby claiming the first sighting of the Antarctic continent, but later expeditions would follow the same course and see nothing. Confronted by an extensive ice-tongue, Wilkes turned north to spend a year in the Pacific, then in 1841 conduct a wide-ranging survey of the northwest coast of America, during which land parties surveyed inland from Oregon to California. After an absence of forty-six months Wilkes returned to New York in June 1842 by way of the Pacific and the Indian oceans. The voyage received little public acclaim, while Wilkes himself faced a sordid court-martial for the loss of a ship and excessive punishment of his crew. Nevertheless, the scientific achievements of the voyage, which for the first time in American history combined the talents of civilian and military personel, set a milestone in the evolution of United States exploration.

Right Wilkes's expedition, primarily a seaborne undertaking, sent exploring parties overland into country bordering the Pacific coast. However, Wilkes's map of the southwest was considerably less accurate than those of his Spanish predecessors.
Following pages Wilkes's ship, *Vincennes*, at rest in the Antarctic ice.

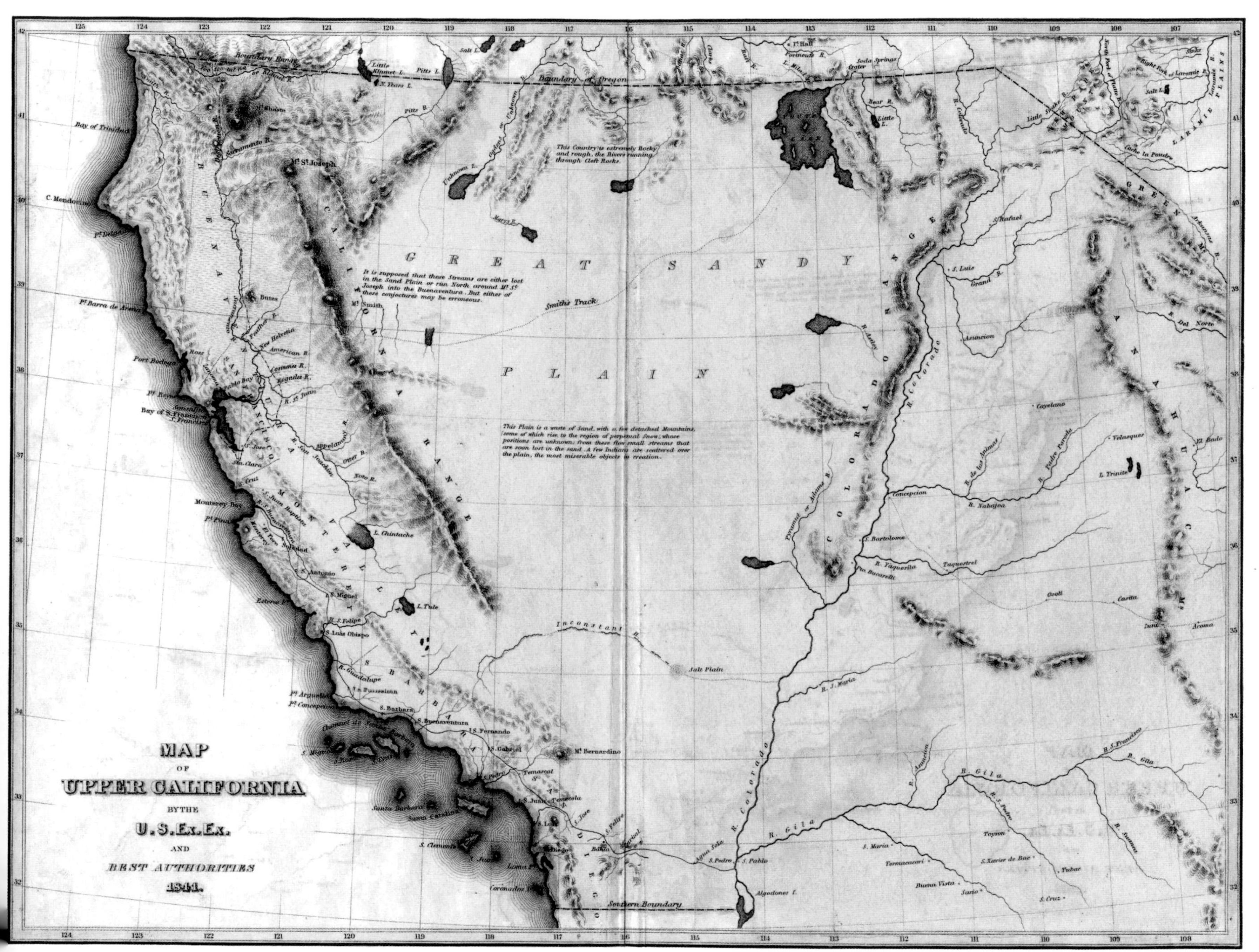
MAP
OF
UPPER CALIFORNIA
BY THE
U. S. Ex. Ex.
AND
BEST AUTHORITIES
1841.
G R E A T S A N D Y
P L A I N
This Country is extremely Rocky and rough, the Rivers running through Cleft Rocks.
It is supposed that these Streams are either lost in the Sand Plain or run North around Mt. St. Joseph into the Buenaventura. But either of these conjectures may be erroneous.
This Plain is a waste of Sand, with a few detached Mountains, some of which rise to the region of perpetual Snow; whose positions are unknown; from these flow small streams that are soon lost in the sand. A few Indians are scattered over the plain, the most miserable objects in creation.
Boundary of Oregon
Southern Boundary
Smith's Track
Salt Plain
Inconstant R.
Monterey Bay
Bay of S. Francisco
C. Mendocino
Mt. St. Joseph
Mt. Bernardino
R. Colorado
R. Gila

The Quest for the Magnetic Poles

James Ross confronts the white cliffs of Antarctica.

1839-43

THE COMPASS AS A NAVIGATIONAL DEVICE had appeared in Europe in the thirteenth century, but, as early oceanic voyagers were soon to discover, its use as a steering device, particularly in the North Atlantic, was extremely limited. Rather than indicating true north it would consistently point at an angle, its 'variation', towards a remote location somewhere in the unknown wilderness of the American Arctic. Around 1600 William Gilbert proposed that the earth's field was generated by a subterranean magnet offset from the earth's axis, and in 1698-1700 the celebrated experimental scientist Edmund Halley took two scientific voyages, the first of their type by an English naval vessel, to chart the variation of the compass throughout the Atlantic. But it was not until the nineteenth century that Arctic exploratory strategies had progressed sufficiently to permit a direct assault on the North Magnetic Pole – the position where a compass would dip vertically downwards towards the earth's centre. In 1831, James Clark Ross, a veteran of five voyages in the Arctic, accurately located the pole on the Boothia Peninsula, a lonely promontory on the shores of Arctic Canada.

With voyages in the southern hemisphere becoming ever more commonplace, thoughts turned towards the even more remote South Magnetic Pole and its position somewhere within the Antarctic circle. In 1839, on a venture funded by Parliament and promoted by the major scientific institutions, James Ross, the ideal man for the job, was sent forth with two specially reinforced and appointed ships, *Erebus* and *Terror*. Rather than haphazardly coasting the continent like his predecessors, Ross took a bearing directly towards the magnetic pole, eagerly hopeful that it would lie beneath a navigable sea. But in January 1841, the pole still some 600 kilometres (370 miles) away, he was abruptly halted by a perpendicular ice cliff, sometimes 60 metres (200 feet) high and as impenetrable as the white cliffs of Dover. He had discovered what became known as the Ross Ice Shelf, which for a generation of future explorers would be the gateway to the South Pole. To his left were the mountains of Victoria Land, and to the south an even more unlikely sight – an active volcano. Ross returned to the Antarctic the following year, but his approach through the Weddell Sea met only with gales and snowstorms. His record south of 78°10 stood for sixty years, and for the next half-century the continent lay undisturbed and almost forgotten.

Right James Clark Ross, from a portrait in the National Maritime Museum, Greenwich.

Edward Eyre Sets Out to Demonstrate the Impossible

Water everywhere, but none to drink.

1841

EDWARD JOHN EYRE, THE ENTREPRENEURIAL SON OF A YORKSHIRE VICAR, migrated to Australia at the age of eighteen and in 1833 took up sheep farming in the Molonglo Plains, near where Canberra now stands. But within a year he had decided that greater profits were to be made by driving livestock overland to the blossoming colonies of Victoria and South Australia. His quest for stock routes led him into waterless deserts, but within five years he had overlanded sheep and cattle from Molonglo to Melbourne, and in 1838-39 driven the first stock directly from Molonglo to Adelaide. As well as satisfying a lust for discovery, he had netted a profit of more than £6000: a small fortune in those days. Eyre's tenacity in locating a stock route from Adelaide to Port Lincoln, on the opposite side of Spencer Gulf, brought the discovery of the immense salt sea named Lake Torrens, but his greatest challenge came in 1840 when confronted by the task of pioneering a stock route from Adelaide to Western Australia. Declaring the coastal route to be 'quite impracticable' he offered to pursue a route through the interior, but three agonizing months were wasted circumventing the soft, shimmering crust of Lake Torrens, which apparently expanded unendingly to the north.

In February 1841, determined to demonstrate the impossibility of a coastal route to Western Australia, and defying instructions to abandon his folly, Eyre departed the furthest outposts of white settlement, taking a single companion, John Baxter, and three Aborigines. The undrinkable ocean washing mockingly forever at their left hand, the party trekked 150 kilometres (90 miles) in temperatures of 45°C (113°F) before locating their first freshwater, and then only by excavating two metres (seven feet) beneath the dunes. To collect sufficient for morning tea, Eyre soaked dew into a sponge from the meagre grass and shrubs. A month out, tragedy struck when two of the Aborigines killed Baxter and made off with vital rations, leaving Eyre alone with only one faithful companion, the Aborigine named Wylie. After four months on the desolate coast, having walked 1100 kilometres (700 miles) and found water only four times, their lives were saved when they chanced upon a French whaling vessel at anchor in a remote bay. Two weeks later, strength restored, Eyre and Wylie resumed the trek, finding just a single oasis but with their thirst assuaged by some welcome rainfall. On 7 July 1841 they stumbled into Albany, the first men ever to arrive in Western Australia overland from the east.

Right The route of Edward Eyre along the desolate and waterless coast of southern Australia.

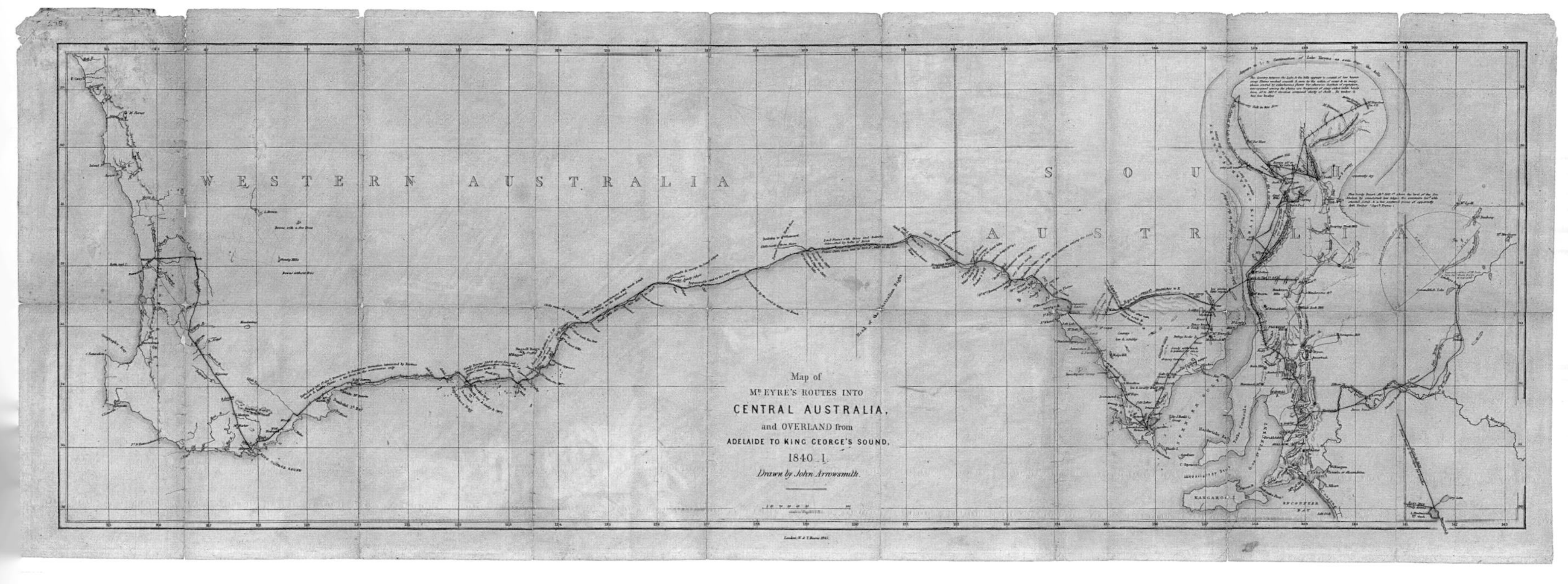
WESTERN AUSTRALIA
SOUTH AUSTRALIA
Map of
M^R. EYRE'S ROUTES INTO
CENTRAL AUSTRALIA,
and OVERLAND from
ADELAIDE TO KING GEORGE'S SOUND,
1840_1.
Drawn by John Arrowsmith.
KANGAROO I.
ENCOUNTER BAY

John Frémont Sets the Paths of Western Expansion

The United States discovers the wealth of its distant provinces.

1842-53

EVEN BEFORE LEWIS AND CLARK RETURNED FROM THEIR LANDMARK JOURNEY across the North American continent, President Thomas Jefferson was already formulating a programme of exploration to unlock the secrets of the trans-Mississippi West. Reconnaissance expeditions were sent out to trace the rivers of the Great Plains, while Zebulon Pike explored the headwaters of the Mississippi, Arkansas and Red rivers. With Jefferson's retirement the zeal for exploration was maintained by Stephen Harriman Long, who laid the bureaucratic and scientific foundation for future explorers and in five expeditions, 1816-23, covered 40,000 kilometres (25,000 miles) of the Mississippi basin. In 1826-27 Jedediah Smith circled the Great Basin of Nevada and in 1832-34 Benjamin Bonneville surveyed a direct passage to Oregon via the Platte River, Wyoming and Idaho. In 1833-34 Joseph Walker examined the Humboldt River route from the Great Salt Lake to southern California. But of the pioneers of the American West none would capture the imagination more than the dashing young Topographical Corps engineer, John Charles Frémont. Backed by the ardent expansionist senator Thomas Hart Benton, whose sixteen-year-old daughter Frémont would secretly marry, in the course of five expeditions between 1842 and 1853 he would see more of the West than any explorer of his day.

While to many Frémont was the archetypal American hero, restless in spirit and impatient in temperament, to others he was a mere adventurer and opportunist who simply revisited routes pioneered by those whose achievements he would overshadow. However, it was Frémont who more than anyone appreciated the vast natural resources of the West, the agricultural potential of what many had dismissed as desert, the geological wealth of the Rockies and the mineral riches that slept beneath the sun-baked landscape of Nevada. In 1842 he followed the Platte route into Wyoming, then in the next two years made a grand sweep of the West, blazing a trail to Oregon, from Oregon to California, then eastward through Nevada, Utah and Colorado. In 1845 he crossed the Colorado Rockies to Utah, then sought the most practical paths across the Sierra Nevada into California. In 1848, and again in 1853, he surveyed new trails across the Rockies, the latter for a projected railroad. A gifted mathematician and topographer, with a solid grounding in all the sciences, Frémont's exhaustive appraisal of the most practical routes west, his siting of forts and staging posts, was critical in establishing the future pattern of migration to Oregon and California.

Right Frémont and his party, en route southward through Oregon and western Nevada, discover Pyramid Lake in January 1844.

The Much Maligned Ludwig Leichhardt

The folk hero of Australian exploration.

1844–45

Of all the great explorers of Australia, none would capture the public imagination, either in his lifetime or in the 160 years since he vanished in the outback, more than Ludwig Leichhardt. Adulated by those for whom he was the archetype of the self-willed, independent adventurer whose achievements outclassed those of his liberally funded, government-backed counterparts, castigated by those jealous of the triumphs of an obscure Prussian upstart or by self-seeking publicists that jumped on the condemnatory bandwagon decades after his death, Leichhardt achieved folk-hero status rivalling Ned Kelly. An erudite 'nonconformist' scholar who pursued knowledge not for degrees and qualifications but for its own sake, Leichhardt arrived in Australia in 1842, his sole ambition being the advancement of science in a little-known part of the world. After a few solitary wanderings between Sydney and Brisbane his attention fixed on an expedition that, under the leadership of veteran explorer Thomas Mitchell, would pioneer an overland route to Port Essington, a colonial outpost at the tip of what is now the Northern Territory. But when the expedition got bogged down in red tape the frustrated Leichhardt decided to attempt the journey under his own steam.

In Brisbane, where businessmen and farmers coveted easier access to the wider world, Leichhardt found no shortage of material support, with the result that in the rivers and ranges encountered en route we find the names of his grocer, ironmonger, his little-known travelling companions, helpful farmers, even squatters and ex-convicts; in fact anybody who had assisted in some small way. Leichhardt's disregard for civil servants and members of the governing élite, whose names customarily dominate explorers' routes, was much enjoyed by the popular press but did him few favours in official circles. With ten men, seventeen horses and abundant provisions, Leichhardt left the Darling Downs in September 1844 and kept a general northwesterly course, reaching the Gulf of Carpentaria the following June. Paralleling the coast across innumerable crocodile-infested streams, then striking directly through unexplored Arnhem Land, the party wandered into Port Essington in December 1845. Substantial monetary rewards awaited Leichhardt in Sydney, and a hero's welcome fitted to one so long given up for dead, but it was an experience never to be repeated. In March 1848 Leichhardt set out from the Condamine River with six companions, his destination the Swan River Colony in Western Australia. He was never heard of again, and to this day his fate remains uncertain.

Right Leichhardt, at the end of his extraordinary journey across northern Australia, arrives at Port Essington, a colonial outpost on the coast of Arnhem Land.

The Torturous Ordeal of Sturt's Central Australian Expedition

'An object worthy to perish one's life for.'

1844–46

NOW IN HIS FIFTIETH YEAR, THE VETERAN EXPLORER CHARLES STURT was (for those days) getting a little too old for the harsh extremes of the Australian outback. Fourteen years earlier he had made the first descent of the Murray River to its mouth, then, in one of the most harrowing journeys on record, had reascended the Murray, rowing against the current, during which one man went mad, others fell asleep at the oars and Sturt suffered partial blindness, which afflicted him for another four years. He subsequently settled into family life as a high-ranking South Australian civil servant, but his yearning to penetrate deeper into Australia's red heart, and his commitment to the notion that at its centre lay a vast inland sea, had never dissipated. Now, in 1844, he suddenly declared his intention to put the finishing strokes to his career 'by unfolding the secrets of the interior and planting the ensign of my country in the centre of the mysterious region'. His expedition left Adelaide in June with fifteen men.

To circumvent the barrier of the great salt lakes reported by Eyre, Sturt's party headed up the Murray and Darling rivers before striking north beyond the site of the Broken Hill silver mines. The season was one of the hottest on record and dead frogs had to be clawed from the waterholes to uncover the last traces of water. Only at Milparinka, 300 kilometres (180 miles) north of the Darling, was the first permanent water found, but the baking heat subjected the party to six months' incarceration in an underground chamber. Ink evaporated from their pens before reaching the paper, metal screws exploded from packing cases, the party's hair stopped growing, and one man turned black from scurvy and died. A little rain fell in July 1845, so in August Sturt hastened towards the continent's dead centre, striking across the northeastern corner of South Australia until in September he came face-to-face with the impenetrable Simpson Desert, the entry of which would have meant certain death. A second attempt further to the east almost condemned the party to a similar fate in the Stony Desert. The return journey was no less of an ordeal. The bulb of the 53°C (127°F) thermometer burst in the shade, and stores and water gave out. Blackened by the sun, prostrated by scurvy and almost totally blind, Sturt was dragged back to Adelaide by cart.

Right A painting by Samuel Thomas Gill depicting the departure of Sturt's expedition from Adelaide in 1844.

The Journey of Huc and Gabet to Tibet

The reconnaissance of the vicariate of Tartary-Mongolia.

1844-46

At the dawn of the nineteenth century the Christian missions in China were in a sorry state of decline. The last of the Jesuits having either fled or suffered martyrdom, their place had been taken by priests of the Congregatio Missionis, commonly called Lazarists or Vincentians. But these too faced widespread persecution, compelling the missionaries to gather their flocks and seek refuge 200 kilometres (125 miles) northwest of Beijing, beyond the Great Wall at a village called Si-Wang (Xiwanzi). Recognizing that this remote territory lay outside any previously defined province of the Catholic Church, the Holy See in 1842 created the vicariate of Tartary-Mongolia, a vast and nebulous swathe of territory that seemed to take in the greater part of Central Asia. The problem was that it remained largely unexplored, little was known of its peoples, and its geographical limits were ill-defined, so when the first vicar apostolic arrived at Si-Wang his immediate priority was to determine the nature and extent of his new dominion. For the task he selected the thirty-year-old French Lazarist priest Évariste Régis Huc and his elder companion Joseph Gabet.

Huc and Gabet left Si-Wang in August 1844, their heads shaven, their identities concealed under the yellow robes of Tibetan lamas. Twice crossing the swollen Yellow River (Huang He) and surviving the blistering heat of the Ordos Desert, they arrived at the massive Kunbum lamasery near Xining. Here they waited eight months, acquainting themselves with Tibetan language and religion, before joining an embassy returning to Lhasa from Beijing. Mingling anonymously with the caravan's 2000 followers, they passed the mystic lake Koko Nor (Qinghai Hu), negotiated the Bayan Har mountains and without hindrance walked sturdily into Lhasa in January 1846. Although welcomed by the Tibetan authorities, their presence was unacceptable to the local Chinese commissioner, who regarded the interlopers as an intolerable security risk. Unaware that a recent treaty, impressed on China by Western nations, had reopened the country to missionaries, he placed Huc and Gabet under armed escort and conducted them through Chengdu to Canton (Guangzhou). Huc remained there for three years before returning to France, writing his bestselling and politically influential *Souvenirs d'un Voyage*, regarded by many at the time as a work of fiction but subsequently seeing countless editions in numerous languages. Gabet returned to France to press the Lazarist cause in Tibet, then departed for Brazil to die in 1853 of yellow fever.

Right A map from Évariste Huc's *Souvenirs d'un Voyage*, 1850.

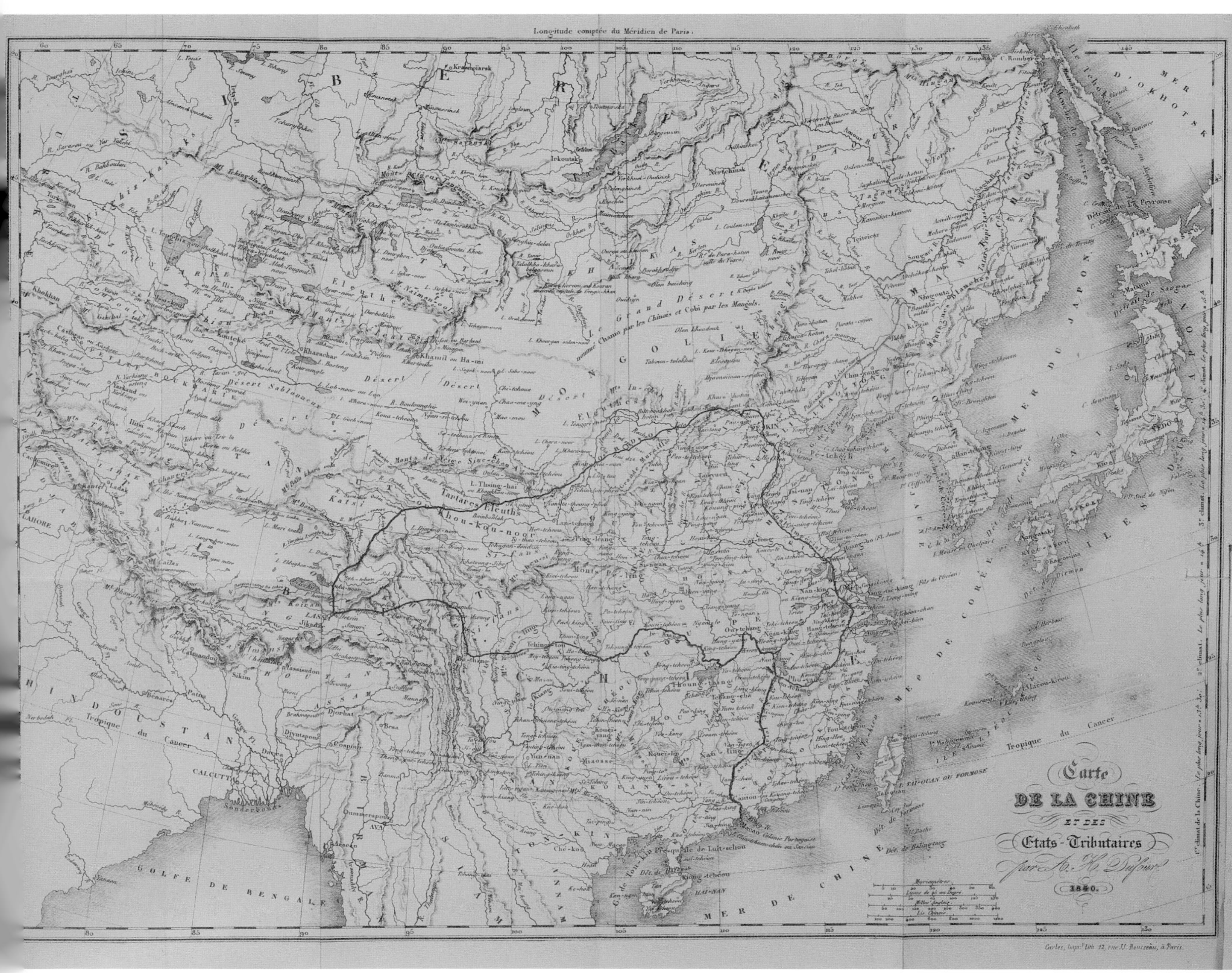
Longitude comptée du Méridien de Paris.
Carte
DE LA CHINE
ET DES
Etats-Tributaires
par A. H. Dufour.
1840.
Carles, Impr. lith. 12, rue J.J. Rousseau, à Paris.
Tropique du Cancer
GOLFE DE BENGALE
MER DE CHINE
MER DU JAPON
MER D'OKHOTSK
HINDOUSTAN
CALCUTTA
TAI-OUAN OU FORMOSE
HAI-NAN
Grand Désert

The Mystery of John Franklin's Last Expedition

The obsessive search for a lost Victorian hero.

1845-47

WHEN SIR JOHN FRANKLIN DISAPPEARED IN 1846 along with the entire company of his two ships, he was already a giant of exploration, a household name and a veteran of many years in the Arctic. He had learnt his seamanship with Matthew Flinders in Australia, and in 1818 he had been with David Buchan's abortive voyage towards the North Pole. In 1819-21 he commanded a major overland expedition to trace the course of North America's northern coastline from the Coppermine River to Bathurst Inlet. Then in 1825-27, as part of a massive onslaught on the Canadian archipelago that comprised three seaborne expeditions, Franklin made a second overland assault on the Arctic coast, descending the Mackenzie River to its mouth and surveying westward beyond the boundary of Alaska. Knighted in 1829, he was for six years an immensely popular governor of Tasmania, eagerly assisting expeditions bound for the Antarctic. Recalled to England in 1843, he found the eighty-year-old John Barrow, the prime mover in the quest for the Northwest Passage, frantically lobbying for an expedition that would finally put the matter to rest. When others declined or were deemed unsuitable, Franklin, despite his fifty-nine years and lack of fitness, happily volunteered to revisit the stomping grounds of his younger days.

With an optimistic and experienced crew, Franklin and his comfortably appointed ships *Erebus* and *Terror* left the Thames in May 1845, and at the end of July were spotted entering Lancaster Sound, gateway into the Northwest Passage. They were never seen again. For a year or two there was little cause for concern, but by 1847 anxiety had grown into consternation over the fate of such a well-loved pillar of the establishment whose devoted family and friends could barely countenance the loss of one so precious. Over the next three years search parties fanned out in every direction, and in the following decades no less than thirty-six ships and overland expeditions answered the call to 'find Franklin', gradually piecing together the last days of the explorer and his men. Ice-bound off the mainland shore, they had abandoned their ships in an heroic attempt to strike overland to the nearest European outpost. Their demise remained a mystery until recent research confirmed that they died not of cold or starvation but of lead poisoning, maybe from the solder in their cans of tinned food, or more likely from the lead plumbing of the unique water system fitted to the expedition's ships.

Right Francis McClintock's expedition discovers a boat and the skeletal remains of two members of Franklin's expedition at Cape Crozier, King William Island, in May 1859.

HARPER'S WEEKLY.

DISCOVERY OF THE FRANKLIN EXPEDITION BOAT ON KING WILLIAM'S LAND BY LIEUTENANT HOBSON.—[SEE PAGE 690.]

Thomas Brunner's Heroic Trek to Rainy Westland

New Zealand's South Island provides an awesome challenge.

1846-48

NEW ZEALAND, SIGHTED BY TASMAN IN 1642, frequented by Cook in the 1770s and haunted by itinerant whalers and flax traders from the 1790s, received no long-term European resident until 1814 when Samuel Marsden came to preach the Gospel in the Bay of Islands. Other dedicated missionaries soon followed in his footsteps and by the 1840s had advanced into the most remote corners of North Island. The first major influx of British settlers arrived in the Wellington area in 1839, tempted by Edward Wakefield and his New Zealand Company's promises of a better life in a virgin land. But too often they found themselves and their belongings dumped on beaches girdled by impenetrable bush and swamp. Almost immediately the company looked across the Cook Strait to the South Island and in 1841 laid out the settlement of Nelson. A grimy, rain-soaked backwater, its hinterland inadequate to support a burgeoning population, it became a second Sydney as its frustrated colonists attempted to break through encircling highlands into pastures new.

Compared with North Island the Tolkienesque landscape of South Island would present an altogether more daunting challenge and would breed a generation of formidable explorers. In 1846 Thomas Brunner set out from Nelson to find an immense plain the Maori had assured him was 'boundless to the eye'. Striking south to Lake Rotoroa, Brunner and his faithful Maori guide Ekuhu descended the densely wooded gorge of the Buller River to the coast. Ceaseless torrential rain spoilt their supplies, compelling them to subsist on the flesh of Buller's favourite dog Rover and on a fern root that thrust the explorer into violent seizures of pain. Following the rainy west coast southward, passing the future coal-rush metropolis of Greymouth, the expedition terminated at Tititira Head, under the shadow of Mount Cook, where Buller, already reduced to walking barefoot, twisted his ankle on a boulder. Returning up the Grey River, his clothes perpetually soaked, almost blind and now paralysed in his left side, the onset of the winter snows obliged him to recuperate in the shelter of a cave. Then to add to his misfortune his notes and sketches, a year's work, were destroyed when they dropped into a fire. However, Brunner, on what would become known as 'The Great Journey', had charted South Island's two major rivers, opened up the fertile Buller Valley and explored for the first time the largely unknown west coast.

Right A map of the Middle Island (now South Island) of New Zealand, printed in 1851 to illustrate Brunner's pioneering journey to the rainy Westland.

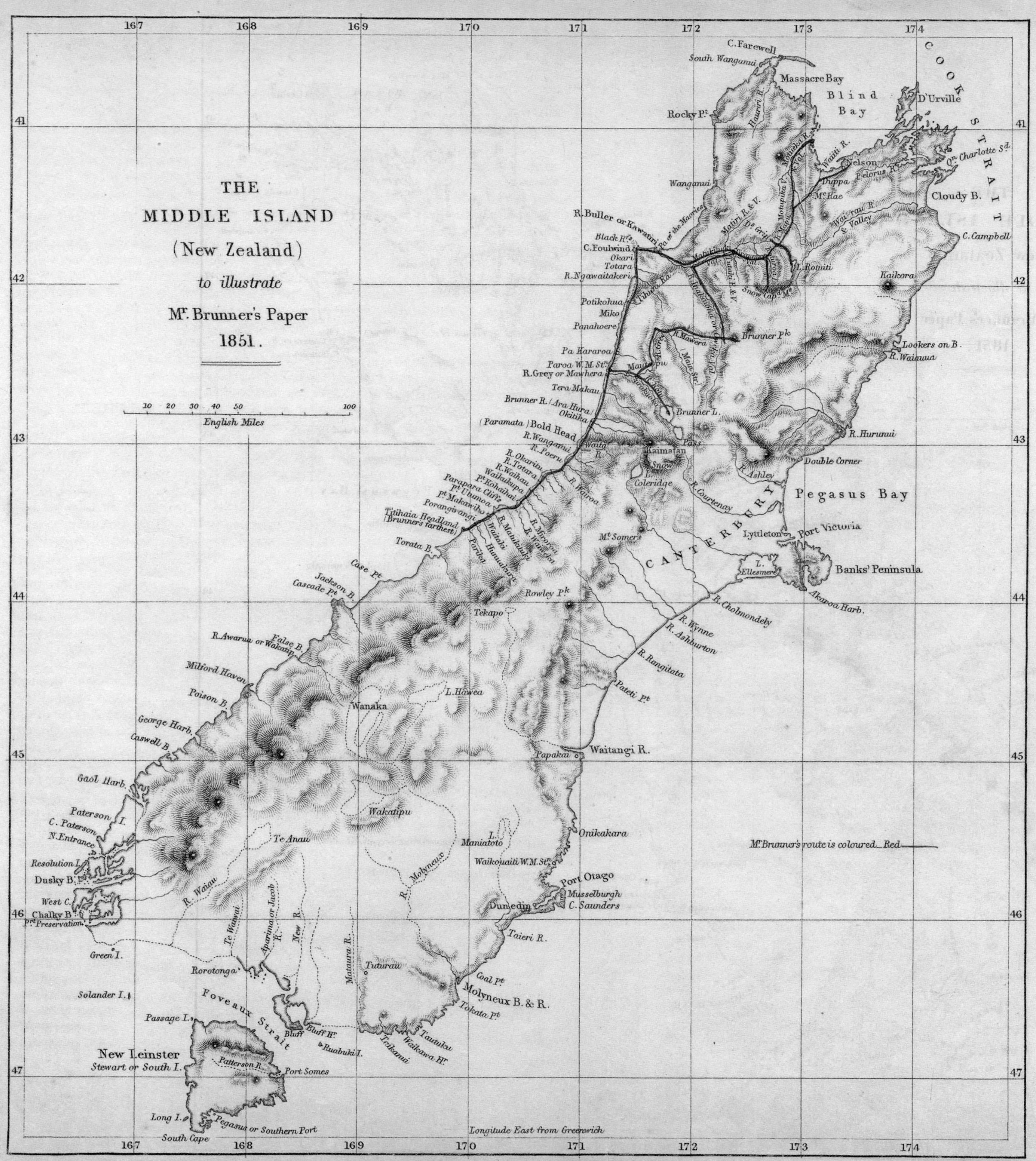

THE
MIDDLE ISLAND
(New Zealand)
to illustrate
Mr. Brunner's Paper
1851.
English Miles
Mr. Brunner's route is coloured Red
Longitude East from Greenwich
COOK STRAIT
C. Farewell
South Wanganui
Massacre Bay
Blind Bay
D'Urville
Rocky Pt.
Nelson
Pelorus R.
Qn. Charlotte Sd.
Cloudy B.
Wanganui
Mt. Rae
C. Campbell
R. Buller or Kawatiri
Black Pt.
C. Foulwind
Okari
Totara
R. Ngawaitakeri
L. Rotuiti
Snow Capd. Mts.
Kaikora
Potikohua
Miko
Panahoere
Brunner Pk.
Lookers on B.
R. Waiauua
Pa Kararoa
Paroa W.M. Stn.
R. Grey or Mawhera
Tera Makau
Brunner R. / Ara Hura
Okitika
Brunner L.
(Paramata) Bold Head
R. Wanganui
R. Poeru
Kaimatau
Pass
Snow
R. Hurunui
Double Corner
R. Ashley
Coleridge
R. Courtenay
Pegasus Bay
Titihaia Headland (Brunners farthest)
Torata B.
Mt. Somers
CANTERBURY
Lyttleton
Port Victoria
L. Ellesmere
Banks' Peninsula
Akaroa Harb.
Case Pt.
Jackson B.
Cascade Pt.
Rowley Pk.
Tekapo
R. Cholmondely
R. Wynne
R. Ashburton
R. Awarua or Wakatip
False B.
R. Rangitata
Milford Haven
L. Hawea
Poison B.
Wanaka
Pateti Pt.
George Harb.
Caswell B.
Waitangi R.
Papakai
Gaol Harb.
Paterson I.
C. Paterson
N. Entrance
Wakatipu
Te Anau
Maniatoto
Onikakara
Resolution I.
Dusky B.
Waikouaiti W.M. Stn.
Port Otago
Musselburgh
C. Saunders
Dunedin
West C.
Chalky B.
Pt. Preservation
R. Waiau
Taieri R.
Green I.
Te Wawai
Aparima or Jacob R.
New R.
Mataura R.
Tuturau
Rorotonga
Coal Pt.
Molyneux B. & R.
Solander I.
Foveaux Strait
Tokata Pt.
Passage I.
Bluff
Bluff Hr.
Ruabuki I.
Tautuku
Waikawa Hr.
Toikanui
New Leinster
Stewart or South I.
Patterson R.
Port Somes
Long I.
South Cape
Pegasus or Southern Port
Pubd. for the Journal of the Royal Geographical Society by John Murray Albemarle St. London 1851.
John Arrowsmith.

72

Andersson and Galton Penetrate the Sands of the Kalahari

The other African desert.

1850–54

WHILE THE SAHARA DREW TRAVELLERS with a particular objective in mind – the course of the Niger, the opening of trade with the flourishing sub-Saharan centres of commerce, or the eradication of the slave trade – another great African desert far to the south attracted men with little more to gain than the glory of discovery in one of the world's most forbidding wildernesses. In 1850 a well-connected young man, Francis Galton, who would later make his name in meteorological circles, landed at Walvis Bay on the Namibian coast. His intention was to boldly cross the Kalahari Desert to Lake Ngami, an immense expanse of water teeming with game, reported by David Livingstone in what is now northern Botswana. For companionship he recruited the likeminded Swedish naturalist Carl Johan Andersson, who just happened to be in London at the time. The expedition made considerable discoveries in central and northern Namibia, largely aided by Galton's persuasiveness in obtaining safe passage from the Hottentots, impressing their chief with his 'fancy dress' of red hunting coat, jackboots and cords. But after fifteen months the explorers halted at what is now the border of Botswana, some 500 kilometres (300 miles) short of their goal. Galton retreated permanently to England to write a narrative of the expedition and the bestselling *The Art of Travel* – a delightful compendium of curious and ingenious contrivances for would-be explorers and a forerunner of the modern survival manual.

While Galton revelled in celebrity status back home, Andersson lingered in Namibia, determined to succeed where he and Galton had failed. In 1853, leaving the safety of the German missions that dotted the more populous regions, he struck east across the desert, passing the previous point of return and arriving safely on the southwestern shores of Lake Ngami. However, an attempt to return by a more northerly route, and hence determine the connection between Ngami and the rivers of southern Angola, was thwarted by local difficulties. Andersson returned to the settled districts to become a prominent trader and mining company manager, his fortunes swinging from rags to riches and back in the space of a few months. In later life, blighted by a leg wound and an addiction to pain-killing opiates, he opened vast swathes of northern Namibia, at the same time collecting for his posthumously published *Birds of Damara Land*. He died prematurely of dysentery, aged forty, on an expedition to the Cunene River.

Right Galton's telescope, used in his exploration of Damaraland in 1850, and his map of Damaraland, showing the results of his expedition with Andersson.

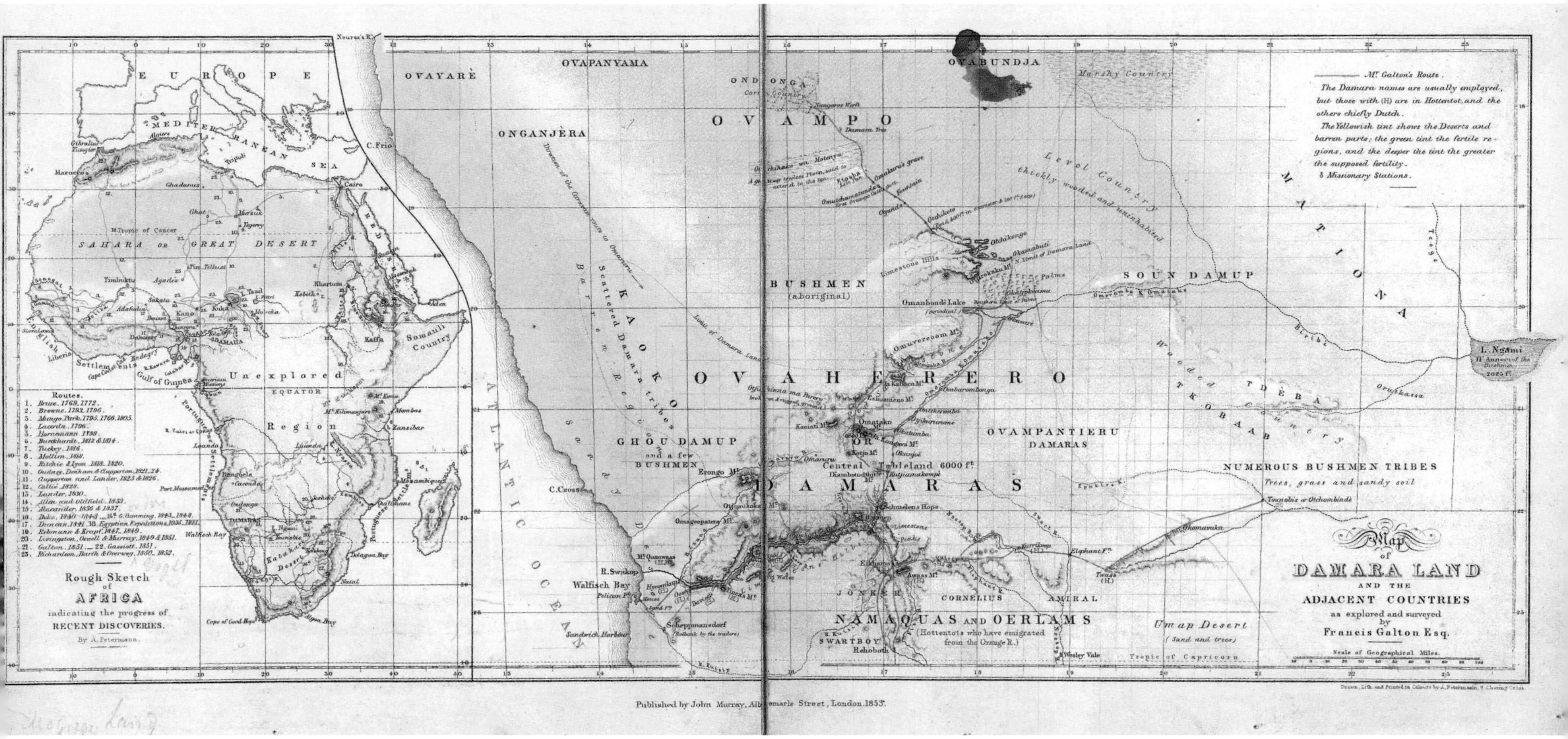

Map of
DAMARA LAND
AND THE
ADJACENT COUNTRIES
as explored and surveyed
by
Francis Galton Esq.

Mr. Galton's Route.
The Damara names are usually employed, but those with (H) are in Hottentot, and the others chiefly Dutch.
The Yellowish tint shows the Deserts and barren parts; the green tint the fertile regions, and the deeper the tint the greater the supposed fertility.
Missionary Stations.

Scale of Geographical Miles.

Rough Sketch of AFRICA indicating the progress of RECENT DISCOVERIES.
By A. Petermann.

Published by John Murray, Albemarle Street, London 1853.

Drawn, Lith. and Printed in Colours by A. Petermann, 9 Charing Cross

Heinrich Barth Wanders Through Sub-Saharan Africa

Patriarch of scientific travellers in the African interior.

1850–55

CROSSING THE SAHARA IN THE NINETEENTH CENTURY was a risky business. Of those foolhardy enough to accept the challenge around eighty per cent died from from disease, were massacred by fanatical Tuareg desperate to protect their monopoly of trade, or were murdered by local despots for showing just a little too much interest in the trans-Saharan slave trade. In fact it was the last of these that brought the English explorer James Richardson to the desert. In 1845, without disguising his Christianity, he had penetrated to the oasis of Ghat, returning with a caravan of slaves and, with his report of the horrors of the trade, stirring strong emotions among abolitionists back home. In 1850 he was sent out again to perform a more thorough examination, taking with him the twenty-nine-year old polymath Heinrich Barth and the geologist Adolf Overweg, both of them recruited from Germany. Harassed every step of the way by hostile tribesmen, the party struck south from Tripoli, and beyond the ancient commercial centre of Agadés, its splendour long since vanished, they separated. Richardson headed for Lake Chad while Barth proceeded to Kano and Overweg circumnavigated Lake Chad in a prefabricated wooden boat they had hauled across the desert. But by the end of September 1852 both Richardson and Overweg had died of fever, leaving Barth alone to decide what to do next.

Barth headed west to Timbuktu, which he found slightly more prosperous than Caillié twenty-five years earlier, then went back to Lake Chad. The round-trip had taken him two years, and on his return to the lake he was amazed to encounter another German explorer, the botanist Eduard Vogel. Vogel had been sent by the British with a small team not only to find Barth but also, somewhat optimistically, to collect specimens and explore in the turbulent tribal regions between the Niger and the upper Nile. The two Germans separated in January 1855, Barth heading back across the desert to Tripoli at the height of summer and eventually returning safely to London after an absence of five years. Vogel, confronted by belligerent tribesmen whichever way he turned, was never heard of again. Several expeditions unsuccessfully sought to asertain his fate and recover his papers, but it was not until 1873 that Gustav Nachtigal reached Ouaddai, some 700 kilometres (435 miles) east of Lake Chad, to find that Vogel had perished in February 1856 at the hands of the local sultan.

Right An engraving by Eberhard Emminger showing the arrival of Barth's caravan at Timbuktu in September 1853.

1853-73

David Livingstone Seeks Highways into the Dark Interior

Missionary or trailblazer for British colonialism in Africa?

VICTORIAN SOCIETY ADULATED ITS MISSIONARIES. While the commonplace geographical explorer might be lucky enough for years of toil to be rewarded with a scant obituary in *The Times*, those who brought the Gospel to the heathen would experience no shortage of biographers eager to secure their subject's rightful place in heaven. William Carey, the pioneer Baptist missionary in India, found around seventy, but nothing approached the idolatory lavished upon the Scottish explorer-missionary David Livingstone whose British Library file boasts an overwhelming 170 biographies, many of them written in his own lifetime. However, while there is no doubting Livingstone's strength of purpose, and in later years his indominitable perseverance in the face of sickness and adversity, his achievements as a proselytizer, geographer and discoverer can too easily be overstated.

Livingstone never remained in one place for long enough to make mass conversions, happily delegating such tedious activities to others whose stations he wandered. And without the formal training of a surveyor his sketch maps often raised more questions than they answered. Nor was he alone in Central Africa, the Portuguese and the Hungarian explorer László Magyar having already covered similar ground. But Livingstone would jealously begrudge the Portuguese their accomplishments, and he would fail to grace Magyar, his unpretentious devotee, with even the courtesy of an audience. However, Livingstone's grand traverse of 1853-56, which took him from the upper Zambezi to the Angolan coast, then back across Africa to Mozambique, did provide the first publicly accessible documentation of the watershed between the Zambezi and the rivers of Angola, even though he remained blissfully unaware of the mighty uncharted Congo.

Livingstone's primary vocation – to delineate a navigable highway that would unlock the African interior to trade, commerce and missionary activity, planting the Gospel and eradicating the loathsome slave trade – was never fulfilled. The Zambezi Expedition, a farcical and costly six-year-long venture that sought to create a missionary arcadia in what is now Malawi, collapsed in 1864 with no converts or new discoveries, only disarray and death, including that of Livingstone's long-suffering wife Mary. Livingstone's secondary objective, the obsessive quest for the source of the Nile which occupied the last ten years of his life in quite the wrong direction, plunged him into the endless reefs and mud of Lake Bangweulu, a slough of despond from which he would never escape alive.

Right The Victoria Falls, discovered by Livingstone in November 1855.

Augustus Gregory's North Australian Expedition

A victim of its own success.

1855–56

WHILE MUCH OF THE STORY OF EXPLORATION IS OF HEROIC ADVENTURERS battling against the odds, and of ripping yarns of survival against the elements, it must be admitted that some of the most geographically enlightening expeditions were relatively bland, prosaic affairs that never quite captured the public imagination. Victims of their own success, nothing went seriously wrong, nobody died in traumatic circumstances and those that participated faded modestly into the obscurity from which they had emerged. Paradoxically, the relative anonymity of such expeditions was often a sign of expert management and meticulous forward planning, or of a leader who shunned the limelight, boasted no triumphs, and in his report bashfully understated the tribulations that must inevitably have been overcome. Of such undertakings, Augustus Charles Gregory's North Australian Expedition is a prime example.

Gregory, the Nottinghamshire-born son of an army officer, had come to Western Australia when his father was granted land in lieu of a pension. A methodical, inventive man, highly skilled in bushcraft, he had worked his way up the Survey Department and had already carried out pioneering explorations in the desert interior. In 1855, at the behest of the Secretary of State for the Colonies, he was commissioned to conduct the first official overland expedition across the north of the Australian continent, to examine such rivers as might provide navigable inland access, and to finish in Brisbane, a daunting 8000 kilometres (5000 miles) from his starting point. The scrupulously organised expedition, which included the eminent scientist Ferdinand von Mueller and the artist Thomas Baines, better known for his African explorations, landed some 300 kilometres (180 miles) south of modern Darwin, at the mouth of the Victoria River. But the Victoria, espoused as the most optimistic stream into the heartland, simply dissolved into the sand, while the creeks further south, watered by recent rains, vanished beyond Lake Gregory into 'one impenetrable desert'. In July 1856 Gregory and six men left the Victoria and struck directly east for the Gulf of Carpentaria. Their most curious discovery, a mystery still unresolved, was the remains of a European encampment 250 kilometres (150 miles) from the nearest coast and occupied some seven years earlier. Paralleling the Gulf coast, then striking southeast via the Burdekin, Fitzroy and Burnett rivers, the party descended to the Pacific at Gladstone in late November. Although honoured by the Royal Geographical Society, Gregory claimed no fame and his characteristically pedestrian and undramatic report failed to stimulate the widespread admiration he deserved.

Right A painting by the expedition artist Thomas Baines, based on sketches made during Gregory's crossing of northern Australia.

Richard Burton, John Speke and the Source of the White Nile

A bitter rivalry that ended in tragedy.

1857-63

In the mid-1850s, the mysteries of the Niger and the Blue Nile solved, scientific curiosity reverted to the next of Africa's great rivers, the White Nile. European missionaries and traders had ascended it as far as the border of Uganda, but beyond here its course was unknown. Did it rise from the snow-capped mountains glimpsed anomalously close to the equator, or was its source in one of the great lakes reported by Arab traders to lie deep in the interior? In June 1857 the celebrated explorer Richard Francis Burton and fellow army officer John Hanning Speke headed inland from Zanzibar to locate the 'Sea of Ujiji' or what is now Lake Tanganyika. An eight-month journey, plagued by a clash of temperaments and every conceivable difficulty, brought them to the shores of the lake, from the northern tip of which flowed a large river, possibly the Nile. But then, on their way back, Speke diverted northward to discover another, even more capacious lake. Named Ukerewe and subsequently rechristened Lake Victoria, it was an equally viable contender for the Nile's source. The revelation strained the relationship almost to breaking point, and by the time Burton returned to London, Speke, the unconfirmed discoverer of the source of the Nile, was already a national hero.

To settle the vicious controversy, and to determine which, if either, of the lakes was the Nile's source, Speke was returned to Africa in 1860, taking with him the quietly methodical Scottish soldier James Augustus Grant. Their route took them beyond the western shore of Lake Victoria and pitched them into the local politics of Buganda, but on 28 July 1862 Speke stood at the place where the Nile flows out of the lake. Tracing the river northward, but unwisely leaving vital sections unseen, the two explorers arrived in February 1863 in southern Sudan, beyond which the river's course was common knowledge. Convinced that they had solved the mystery of the Nile they returned to London, but still Burton refused to give in, questioning whether the lake approached from Buganda was the same as that previously seen by Speke, or whether Speke's river was simply a minor feeder. It was a rivalry that ended in tragedy. On the eve of a scheduled public confrontation with the mighty Burton, Speke, an unwilling public speaker at the best of times, suffered a fatal self-inflicted gun wound while out shooting partridges. Although probably accidental, the Burton camp would forever claim suicide.

Right James Watney Wilson's iconic portrait of Speke at the source of the Nile. Lake Victoria is in the background.

The Ill-Fated Burke and Wills Expedition

A much celebrated catalogue of disasters.

1860–61

THE GRANDILOQUENTLY TITLED VICTORIAN EXPLORING EXPEDITION, which set out to achieve the first traverse of Australia from south to north, was a shambolic affair. Its aims, other than to bolster the prestige of the newly chartered Royal Society of Victoria or to consolidate the emergence of the society's gold-rich home colony on the imperial stage, were nebulous and ill-defined; its organization was chaotic; its contribution to geographical knowledge was minimal; and its legacy would be the death of eight of its members, partly through incompetence, impatience and mismanagement. Yet its principal participants would became icons of the outback, not for their achievements but for their misdirected heroism and untimely demise on the scorched sands of the remote interior. To get the expedition off the ground, £12,000 of public and private money would be allocated – already a record for the period, but it would overspend by 500 per cent. The choice of leader was critical to the expedition's collapse. Rather than soliciting the services of a veteran like Augustus Gregory, whose administrative ability, resourcefulness and experience would have made light work of the enterprise, the Royal Society's naïve and largely sedentary committee was wooed by the charms of an unqualified, impetuous, luxuriantly bearded Irishman named Robert O'Hara Burke.

With camels from Karachi, the loudly trumpeted but overloaded expedition struggled out of Melbourne in August 1860, but by the time it reached the Darling dissension and diffidence had already depleted and divided its higher ranks. With surveyor William Wills, promoted second-in-command after his predecessor had fallen out with the leadership, Burke pressed ahead to Cooper Creek, a rearguard following behind. Burke now calculated that existing provisions were sufficient for himself, Wills, Charles Gray and the cameleer John King, to make a forced dash to the Gulf of Carpentaria and back. They reached the gulf's mangrove swamps in two months, but on returning to Cooper Creek, their condition already desperate, they found it deserted, the rearguard having departed just eight hours earlier. Gray died beside the creek, and Burke decided inexplicably not to chase the rearguard back to the Darling but to strike southwest to a distant police outstation in South Australia. The three men lost their way and fell sick, possibly poisoned by inadequately prepared seeds from the nardoo fern, and by the end of June 1861 Burke and Wills were dead. Only King survived, compassionately tended by Aborigines until rescued by a search party eleven weeks later.

Right An engraving by Nicholas Chevalier showing Burke, Wills and King battling their way southward from the Gulf of Carpentaria.

John Stuart's Traverse of the Australian Continent

The most tenacious of explorers.

1860-62

WITH THE POSSIBLE EXCEPTION OF ANTARCTICA, no continent would present a more formidable challenge than Australia. Unlike Africa or the Americas it had no framework of navigable waterways to help the explorer on his way; it had none of the established trade routes of Asia, Arabia or the Sahara; and it offered no welcoming rendezvous where the traveller could rest, assured of some light relief before continuing on his way. Worse still was the unpredictability of its climate. While one expedition would return with tales of rich grazing lands, gushing springs and babbling creeks, another would reach the same spot a year later only to suffer torment and privation in a barren wasteland.

John McDouall Stuart was all too familiar with the vagaries of the harsh Australian landscape. This slightly built Scottish emigrant who had arrived anonymously in Adelaide when it was little more than a tented encampment would become arguably the most famous, certainly the most persistent of explorers in a land where exploration was the greater part of its history. In 1844-46 he accompanied Sturt to the edge of the Simpson Desert, and in 1858-60 he undertook three pioneering forays into the arid interior of South Australia, riding obliviously through the opal fields of Coober Pedy and stalking the fringes of the Great Victoria Desert. To Stuart speed was the key to success, and unlike his contemporaries, burdened with sluggishly trudging pack trains and overloaded wagons, he took only what could be strapped to the back of a horse. Nevertheless his excursions were maturely orchestrated and throughout his entire career Stuart would lose not a single companion.

On each of his six expeditions Stuart progessed a little further north and in 1860 crossed the MacDonnell Range, passing the continent's dead centre and reaching Tennant Creek before scurvy, shortage of water and unusually hostile Aborigines forced his retreat. Determined to cross the continent on his next attempt, he set out in 1861 with an armed guard, this time finding Newcastle Waters but running short of provisions in a desperate bid to reach the coast via the Victoria River. By April 1862 he was back at Newcastle Waters and after five times failing to find a route to the Victoria he headed directly north. Striking the Mary River, ill with scurvy and nearly blind, he eventually broke through the scrub onto a beach near modern Darwin, the first to cross the Australian continent through its desert heart.

Right A drawing of Stuart by Stephen King, one of the participants in the Central Australian expeditions.

42.
John McDouall Stuart
The great South Australian Explorer
Rough sketch of Stuart
by Stephen King
May be of use to the
Caledonian Society in
designing the proposed
statue
SK

Samuel and Florence Baker Find an Alternative Source of the Nile

A boundless sea of quicksilver, glittering in the noon-day sun.

1862–65

In 1861, while John Speke and James Grant were trudging across East Africa seeking the source of the White Nile under the auspices of the Royal Geographical Society, another man, self-funded and determined to make his name as an explorer, was making his way down the Nile from the opposite direction with the same ambition in mind. Samuel White Baker was a roving adventurer and big-game hunter of independent means who had founded an agricultural settlement in Ceylon and had supervised railway construction in the Balkans. With him was his wife, a voluptuous Transylvanian he had spirited away from a Bulgarian slave market under the nose of the local pasha, saving her from a lifetime in the harem. Taking the name Florence, she would never leave her husband's side, and in England her beauty, charm and elegance would make her acceptable to the highest echelons of Victorian society. In Sudan the couple diverted into the rivers flowing from the Ethiopian highlands. Important discoveries were made, but the delay had cost them the primary objective of their expedition when in February 1862, in southern Sudan, they encountered Speke and Grant on their way back from Lake Victoria and the source of the Nile.

Although naturally disheartened by the unhappy coincidence, and imploring 'does not one leaf of the laurel remain for me', Baker found his enthusiam rekindled when Speke announced that he had omitted an important section of the Nile and produced a map bearing the hypothetical outline of a vast unvisited lake. Striking southward in their quest for the elusive lake, forced to ride oxen, reduced to eating grass, racked with malaria, their boats overturned by hippopotami, the Bakers wandered aimlessly between native villages for nine months. But Florence never flinched from the ordeal, donning men's clothing when her petticoats were saturated with rainwater, and dragged on a stretcher when fever left her too frail to walk. In March 1864 the unnecessarily circuitous route eventually brought the devoted couple to the southern shore of Luta N'zigé, or what Samuel would patriotically christen Lake Albert. Vastly overestimating the size of the lake, the mountains beyond shrouded in mist, he declared: 'Here was the great basin of the Nile that received every drop of water.' The return journey, no less harrowing, took them as far as the Murchison Falls, and it was not until March 1865 that they were back in Sudan, long given up for dead.

Right A painting of giraffes by Florence Baker.

Ladies in a Man's World

Women of discovery and exploration.

WE NEED ONLY CONSIDER the most basic motivations behind distant exploration – the acquisition of empire, the development of overseas trade, the quest for riches, religious proselytization, the advancement of science and the delineation of the earth's islands and continents – to understand why the notion of a woman explorer, in the true sense of the word, was barely imaginable before the nineteenth century and rare before the twentieth. Expeditions did not come cheap, particularly if they needed a fleet of ships, teams of support personnel and vast quantities of food and supplies. The prospective explorer with a large enough personal fortune to finance such an enterprise would be a rare enough phenomenon even amongst the male fraternity, but for an independent woman to have access to such wealth was exceptional. Not only that, but her fortune would have to be her own and not divested in a partner, and she herself would necessarily be free from the impediment of marriage and a doting husband whose worst nightmare was to have his delicate possession swept off to a harem or eaten alive in the Amazonian jungle. She would necessarily be a free-spirited, adventurous spinster with sufficient inherited wealth to indulge a passion for travel in the darker recesses of the globe. Such an essential combination of circumstances and ambition, together with a severe shortage of role models, would make the woman explorer a rare commodity.

The possible alternative would have been to seek financial and material support from governments, religious bodies or scientific institutions, or from wealthy sponsors expecting a return on their investments, but these would also dictate who was to direct the expedition, and would inevitably draw their candidates, invariably male, from disciplines in which ability was already proven. Empires were won by force of arms, by army officers and naval commanders, but there were no women in the military. The expedition that sought golden cities and buried treasure was predominantly a personal affair, a ramshackle quasi-military undertaking suited only to the most battle-hardened mercenary. Trading companies were male-dominated, and their emissaries experienced seamen or seasoned adventurers. Survey expeditions invariably drew their staff from the armed services where there was already an eager reserve of talented surveyors and hydrographers, all of them men. The noble scientific societies and geographical institutions, most of which stubbornly spurned female membership, wanted university-educated doctors and scientists at a time when few universities admitted women. And the missionary societies, the one area in which women would eventually play a key role, rarely sent women to the front line, instead huddling them together in the relative seclusion of convents and mission stations in places already made safe by men. Consequently, job opportunities for women explorers were virtually negligible, and, try as we may, it is almost impossible to find an independent woman who, prior to the late nineteenth century, opened virgin territory unseen by Europeans or was not simply tagging along behind a husband or male family member.

Early colonial literature abounds with harrowing narratives from women like Mary Ingles and Mary Rowlandson, captured from frontier settlements, who suffered frightful ordeals at the hands of savage Indians. And we read of cross-dressers like the pirate Anne Bonny and the Basque trans-sexual adventuress Catalina de Erauso, who forsook the costume and trappings of the gentler sex to flourish in a man's world. Lady Mary Wortley Montagu, wife of the British ambassador to the Ottoman empire, wrote extensively of her travels in the Near East in 1717-18 and became what many regard as the first fully fledged female travel writer. The Ursuline nuns, Marie Tranche-Pain and Marie Hachard, wrote of their missionary wanderings in the Mississippi delta in 1727. And in 1794 Anna Maria Falconbridge described her experiences in Sierra Leone, exposing the destitution of women kidnapped from London's East End to serve as colonial prostitutes. Journals written by ladies who accompanied their husbands to the colonies were fairly commonplace by the beginning of the nineteenth century, although many appeared anonymously, or concealed their femininity under a *nom-de-plume*. Eliza Fay wrote letters from Calcutta; Anne Barnard kept a diary of her travels in South Africa around 1800; Jen Shaw published a narrative of her journey to Carolina and the West Indies in 1774-76; and Maria Randall published in 1792 an account of her travels in the Caribbean. Fanny Parks's remarkable two-volume *Wanderings of a Pilgrim*, describing her twenty-four years in India, bore the authoress's name only in Arabic characters, while further anonimity was assured by denoting the names of friends by initials and by referring to her husband only as 'Monsieur mon mari'.

The narratives of women travellers had always been relatively tame by comparison with the extraordinary tales of heroism and survival emanating from the pens of their male counterparts, but a few enterprising ladies did succeed in accomplishing remarkable journeys at an early date. In 1699-1701, the German naturalist and painter Maria Sibylla Merian, often regarded as the first genuine independent woman explorer, ascended the disease-infested rivers of Dutch Guiana in search of butterflies.

And in 1766-69 the French naturalist Jeanne Barré, disguised as a man, stowed away on Bougainville's voyage to become the first woman to circumnavigate the globe. In 1769 Isabela Godin des Odonais, the Peruvian wife of a participant in La Condamine's expedition, accomplished a nightmarish descent of the Amazon to be reunited with her long-lost husband, stranded in Guiana for the past twenty years. Mary Ann Parker accompanied her husband around the world in 1791 in the warship *Gorgon* to write the first female account of a complete circumnavigation, and in 1824 Maria Graham wrote of her experiences aboard the frigate *Doris*, captained by her husband, on patrol around the South American ports.

Although few women would travel extensively abroad on their own account for several decades to come, the age of the solitary globetrotting woman might be said to have begun in 1846-48 when the Austrian traveller Ida Pfeiffer, her independence guaranteed by a small inheritance, took an adventurous trip around the world, much of it overland across India and the Middle East. Her *Woman's Journey Round the World* caused an immediate sensation and brought offers of free transportation from railway and shipping companies, so in 1851-54 she did the same in the reverse, en route exploring the East Indies, visiting the source of the Amazon and ascending the Mississippi. In her wake came Isabella Bird, who spent the entire second half of the century in almost continuous travel. Increasingly, women were to be seen on the grand tours of the Holy Land, and around the pyramids of Egypt, while some like Amelia Edwards began to extend their journeys far up the Nile and make useful contributions to archaelogical science. In 1863 the Dutch traveller Alexine Tinne, one of the first of her gender to stray far off the beaten track and hence qualify as a true explorer, lost both her mother and maid to disease in southwestern Sudan, then in 1868 set out from Libya to cross the Sahara, only to lose her own life at the hands of fanatical Tuareg tribesmen. About the same time, the beautifully elegant Florence Baker discarded her petticoats to accompany her husband on a gruelling trek to the source of the Nile.

By the 1890s, despite a caustic verse in *Punch* proclaiming the notion of a lady explorer to be 'just a trifle too seraphic', and adjuring that women 'mustn't, can't and shan't be geographic', the woman explorer was beginning to enjoy a reluctant acceptance, almost a reverence only slightly inferior to her male counterparts. This had come about largely as a result of the publicity bestowed on a handful of towering, saint-like women missionaries, whose years of toil in the African jungles or windswept wastes of Central Asia, taming the savage and civilizing the barbarian, were paraded as a call to Christian ladies sufficiently courageous to follow in their footsteps. Mary Kingsley ministered to the gruesomely titled Fang warriors of Equatorial Africa; Kate Marsden went by sledge and horseback through the Siberian wilderness to bring succour and hope to outcast lepers; and the formidable Annie Royle Taylor fought her way across the Tibetan plateau, through blizzards and swollen rivers, only to be turned back just three days from Lhasa. Sadly, when she attempted to make a Christmas pudding from local ingredients she found to her dismay that water boiled at too low a temperature in the high altitude to defrost the pudding at its centre.

By the twentieth century women travellers like Freya Stark and Alexandra David-Neel had begun to acquire sufficient celebrity status to live comfortably on the revenues from their bestselling books. But as genuine explorers their time had come too late. The roads they travelled were deeply rutted by the tracks of their male precursors and their routes could be traced on maps already laid thick with detail. There were a few notable exceptions, like Mina Benson Hubbard's trek across unknown Labrador and Emilia Snethlage's wanderings in the forests of Amazonia, but by now the beckoning white spaces, so prevalent a few years earlier, had all but vanished from the map. As if contriving to ensure that the entire history of geographical discovery could be written without a single reference to a woman, the few genuinely unexplored regions that did remain offered little hope for the woman explorer. Remote and distant, their climate too harsh for the delicate female constitution, they would eventually receive their expeditions, but staffed entirely by men. In 1935 Caroline Mikkelsen, wife of a Norwegian whaling captain, set foot briefly on the Antarctic ice, and in 1947 two women actually overwintered on the continent, but it was not until the late sixties and the age of female emancipation that interested nations began to lift an official embargo on women in Antarctica. Their misplaced caution was demonstrated in 1986 when Anne Bancroft reached the North Pole by dog-sledge, then six years later went on to lead an all-woman skiing expedition to the South Pole, convincingly demolishing the myth of female delicacy and bringing an end to centuries of male domination.

Left Isabella Bird (behind the mast and inset above) at lunch with her boat crew, China 1895.

The Pundits Survey in Secrecy Beyond the Himalayas

Covert operations on the roof of the world.

1863-84

IN A MASSIVE UNDERTAKING THAT PROCEEDED COMPULSIVELY throughout the entire first half of the nineteenth century, British East India Company engineers, officers of the Great Trigonometrical Survey, advanced relentlessly in every direction across India, triangulating the subcontinent to an accuracy that almost defies belief. By 1854 they had reached the fringes of Kashmir and over the next ten years, under the direction of Thomas George Montgomerie, they pressed steadily onwards into the mountainous borderlands, braving unimaginable extremes of altitude and climate to take bearings on even loftier, inaccessible ranges far beyond. The survey was ultimately halted by the borders of empire, but what Montgomerie craved was intelligence of what lay always out of reach, the desolate expanses of the Tibetan plateau, the trade routes into Turkestan, which his officers were forbidden to tread.

When Montgomerie noticed that native Indians passed unhindered across the Himalayan and Karakoram passes it occurred to him that a specially trained Indian surveyor, his instruments concealed or disguised as common objects, could make the journey undetected. Known as pundits, a term commonly applied to local native advisers, the first of these, Mohamed-i-Hameed, set out in 1863 to survey the route to Yarkand (Shache), a focal trading city on the Silk Road. His sextant secreted in a false compartment, the head of his staff flattened to accommodate a compass, and his altitude computed from the temperature at which water boiled in a small copper bowl, Hameed accurately fixed the position and height of Yarkand. In addition he returned with vital political intelligence, and distances estimated by monotonously counting paces, which with the correct training was capable of remarkable precision. Success in the venture now assured, another twelve or more pundits were trained, their identities concealed by code names often taken to the grave. In 1866 Nain Singh, a schoolmaster from Kumaun, calculated the position and altitude of Lhasa to within three kilometres and 30 metres (1.9 miles) of the currently accepted figures, then returned in consecutive years to survey the central Tibetan goldfields and upper Tsangpo Valley. In 1878-82 Kishen Singh, known as 'A K', trekked from Darjeeling to the fringes of the Gobi Desert and returned through the Chinese borderlands. And in 1878-84 Kinthup, a native of Sikkim, solved many of the longstanding mysteries of the Brahmaputra, which by a course only previously conjectured fell a staggering 3000 metres (10,000 feet) on its short journey from Tibet to Assam.

Right Rai Bahadur Kishen Singh Milamwal, one of the native Indian surveyors employed by Montgomerie on clandestine operations beyond the borders of British India.

The Lagrée-Garnier Ascent of the Mekong

The last of the major river-borne expeditions.

1866–68

INDOCHINA, TODAY'S VIETNAM, had for years been a favourite haunt of French missionaries and by the 1830s it boasted a sizeable Christian population. So when the Vietnamese monarchy unleashed a purge on missionary activity it was only natural that the French would react, storming Da Nang in 1858 and Saigon the following year. By 1862 all three provinces of Cochinchina were under French administration, but the benefits, other than a foothold in Southeast Asia and security for the Christians, were debatable. However, optimism was restored when Francis Garnier, a young but perceptive naval officer, suggested that the economic advantages of the newly acquired territory might lay not in the colony itself but in the mighty Mekong that flowed through it. Its course and navigability were uncharted, but it was thought to rise in Yunnan, a Chinese province abounding in minerals and precious stones. An expedition was duly approved in 1865, but Garnier's youth consigned him to take second-in-command under Commander Ernest Doudart de Lagrée, an older man already in fragile health. In the event Garnier would take many of the executive decisions and would find his name most strongly associated with the expedition.

Once described as 'the happiest and most complete of the nineteenth century', no doubt on account of the 700 litres (200 gallons) of wine and 300 litres (80 gallons) of brandy it took with it, the Mekong River Expedition left Saigon in two gunboats in June 1866. Further upstream it transferred to canoes, dragging them around the notorious Sambor rapids and Khone Falls, which together dashed all hope of easy access to China. Sideways excursions were taken to the ruins of Angkor and the Shan states to the west, and despite constant fretting over passports and frequent bouts of fever the party had by September 1867 ascended the Mekong almost to the Chinese border. Striking overland, they examined the upper reaches of the Red River, then at Garnier's insistence proceeded north to Huize. Here Lagrée died, racked by dysentery and malaria. Command passed to Garnier, who had just returned from an abortive trek 250 kilometres (150 miles) to the west. Halted by Muslim rebels at Dali, he failed to reach the upper Mekong but did see the Yangtze further from the coast than any European since Marco Polo. From Yibin the Yangtze was descended by junk to Shanghai, and in June 1868 the party arrived back in Saigon after an absence of a little over two years.

Right A section of the course of the Mekong River through Cambodia, one of the many detailed maps drawn by the Lagrée-Garnier expedition.

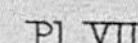

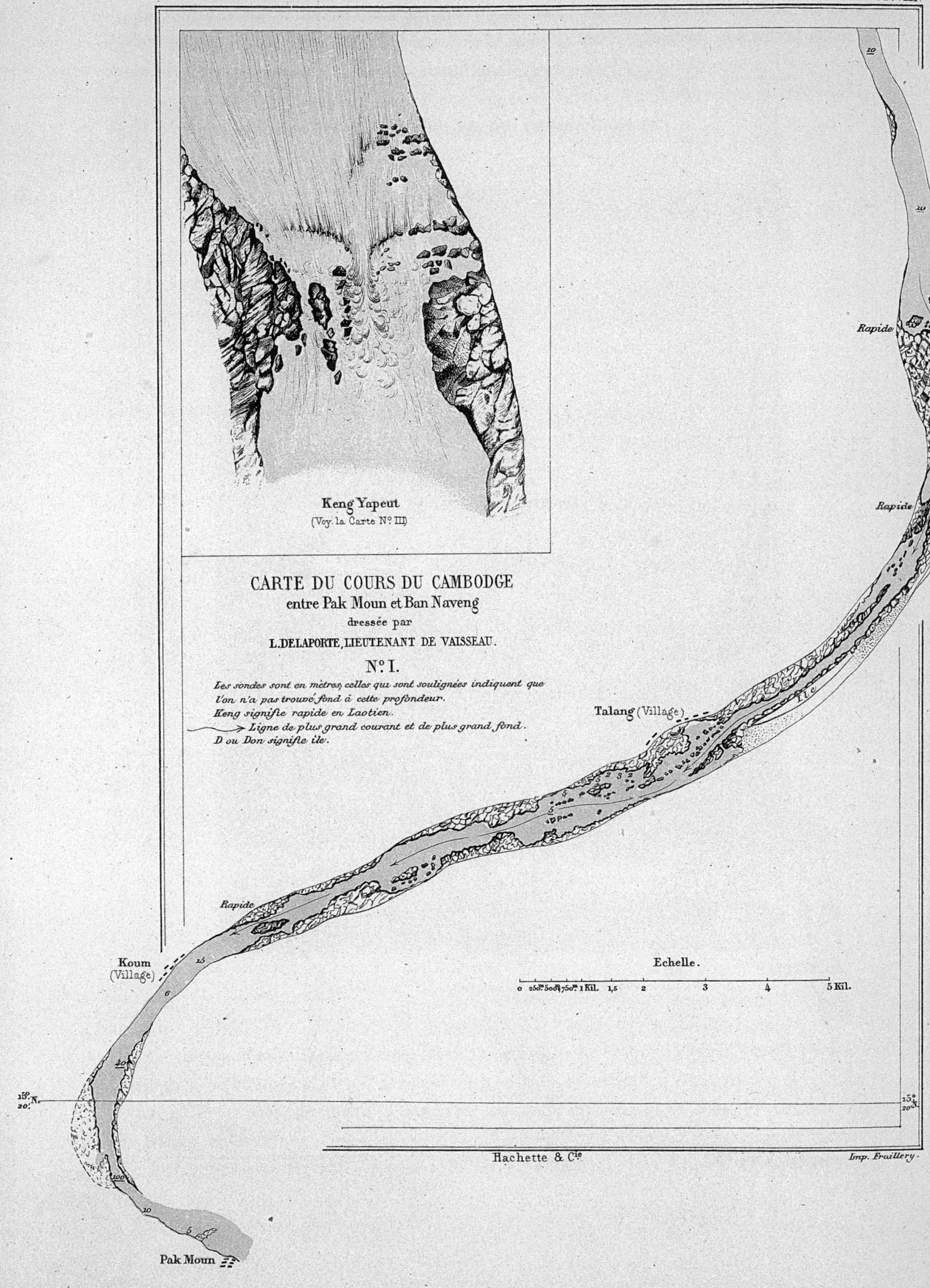

Keng Yapeut

(Voy. la Carte N° III)

CARTE DU COURS DU CAMBODGE

entre Pak Moun et Ban Naveng

dressée par

L. DELAPORTE, LIEUTENANT DE VAISSEAU.

N° I.

Les sondes sont en mètres, celles qui sont soulignées indiquent que l'on n'a pas trouvé fond à cette profondeur.

Keng signifie rapide en Laotien.

→ Ligne de plus grand courant et de plus grand fond.

D ou Don signifie île.

Rapide

Île

Rapide

Île

Talang (Village)

Rapide

Koum (Village)

Echelle.

0 250m 500m 750m 1 Kil. 1,5 2 3 4 5 Kil.

15° 20' N.

15° 20' N.

Pak Moun

Hachette & Cie

Imp. Fraillery.

1867-79

John Wesley Powell Confronts the Terrors of the Colorado

'Three-quarters of a mile in the depths of the earth.'

By the 1850s waves of migrants were pouring across the American West into Oregon, Utah and the goldfields of California. But the journey, by horse or bullock-drawn wagon, was so arduous and danger-fraught that in 1853 Congress despatched three major scientific expeditions to determine feasible routes for a transcontinental railroad. Their results filled seventeen massive volumes but were overshadowed by the outbreak of civil war, which placed a temporary halt on all government-sponsored exploration. Although the general topography of the western territories was understood, the detail, particularly beyond the deeply rutted wagon trails, was sadly lacking. So in 1867 the first of four government survey expeditions, known as the 'Great Surveys', departed for the West with an entourage of topographers, geologists and biologists. Teams under Ferdinand Vandiveer Hayden's direction ranged for twelve years from Nebraska to Idaho and south into Colorado, while Clarence King spent six years on a narrow strip linking Wyoming with the Californian boundary. In the southwest, George Wheeler devoted six years of his life to mapping everywhere from northern California to New Mexico.

Apart from the occasional bitter clash over territorial assignments, these surveyors went quietly about their work, rarely capturing the public imagination. The one exception, which would see its leader a national hero, was the fourth of the Great Surveys, which, under John Wesley Powell, was given the unenviable task of charting the Colorado River. Powell was a gifted academic naturalist who had lost an arm in the Civil War. He had already explored widely in the Rockies when in May 1869 he decided to launch a ragtag band of mountain men into the Green River of Wyoming. Supremely confident of success and often clashing with the independently minded misfits he had hired, Powell drove the expedition down the terrifying whitewater gorges of the Green and Colorado rivers for ninety days, losing one of his boats and most of his provisions in the process. Having successfully negotiated the Grand Canyon, but confronted by rapids that outdid their worst forebodings, three of the party took to the shore only to meet their death at the hands of local tribesmen. The expedition dispersed at the Nevada border, but science had been sacrificed to survival and over the next few years Powell would direct further exploration, descending the river a second time in a more leisurely and organized fashion and steadily unveiling the mysteries of the Colorado and its tributaries.

Right John Wesley Powell (far left) in traditional frontiersman costume, photographed in 1875 with a team of explorers.

Gustav Nachtigal Circumambulates the Eastern Sahara

A wise man bearing gifts for the sultan.

1869–74

LIKE SO MANY GERMAN EXPLORERS IN AFRICA, GUSTAV NACHTIGAL rarely features prominently in Anglophone texts despite accomplishing one of the most remarkable journeys of the nineteenth century. Trained as a military surgeon, he came to Africa seeking relief from tuberculosis, only to spend three years helping Tunis through epidemics of typhoid and cholera. His long-cherished ambition for exploration was finally realized in 1868 when at Tripoli he encountered his mentor, the Saharan explorer Friedrich Rohlfs. Rohlfs had been charged by Emperor Wilhelm I to carry gifts across the desert to the sultan of Bornu, but with other destinations in mind he was only too happy when Nachtigal offered to take the entire affair out of his hands. Leaving Tripoli in January 1869 with only an Italian cook for companionship, Nachtigal struck into the Sahara, his eight camels bending under the weight of an outlandish collection of objects destined for the unsuspecting sultan: life-size portraits of Emperor Wilhelm, Queen Augusta and Crown Prince Frederick, a throne upholstered in crimson velvet, and even a harmonium. Most were abandoned to interested tribesmen along the way, but the throne and harmonium survived intact, albeit in somewhat battered condition.

Although fraught with every conceivable difficulty, the exercise had been well worth the trouble. The sultan loved his gifts and for three years Nachtigal enjoyed hospitality and freedom to travel. In 1871 he penetrated 600 kilometres (370 miles) northeast of Lake Chad, then the next year explored southeast along the Chari River. When in 1873 the time had come to leave Bornu, he decided to head east through the turbulent tribal regions and notoriously dangerous kingdom of Ouaddai that lay between Bornu and the Nile. En route he solved the mystery of Eduard Vogel's disappearance seventeen years earlier, and he took a long diversion south, almost into what is now the Central African Republic. Nachtigal finally reached the Nile a short distance south of Khartoum in August 1874, the first European to have accomplished a west to east crossing of the southern Sahara. An enlightened man, 'discreet, unassuming and honest', who regarded even the most humble African as his equal, Nachtigal was horrified by the Saharan slave trade and, like his British counterparts, saw colonization as the only means to halt it. Ten years later he would become instrumental in Germany's share of the scramble for Africa, annexing Togo and Cameroon and planting the German flag on the coast of Namibia.

Right Nachtigal presents the portrait of Emperor Wilhelm, still intact after being hauled across the Sahara, to the seemingly grateful sultan of Bornu.

Ueberreichung der Geschenke König Wilhelm's an Scheïch 'Omar von Bornû. (S. 594.)

Przhevalskii Unmasks the Complex Geography of Central Asia

The race for Lhasa brings its rewards.

1870–1887

THE HOLY CITY OF LHASA, sheltered by lofty peaks, impenetrable valleys and barren wastelands, had always been a difficult destination, but by the 1860s it had drifted even further from reach. British India was creeping steadily north and Russians were swallowing up the khanates of Turkestan, while China asserted an archaic privilege to everything touching its western borders. Tibet felt threatened from every direction, so any outsiders who ventured towards its capital found themselves politely but firmly turned back well short of their goal. Of those that attempted the journey, none was more persistent than Russia's finest explorer, Nikolai Mikhailovich Przhevalskii. Geographer, historian and naturalist, posted to Irkutsk in 1867, he had already explored vast swathes of eastern Siberia when he enlisted the support of the Russian Geographical Society for an expedition to Tibet.

In November 1870 Przhevalskii struck across the Gobi to Beijing, then west, seeking the mythical lake Koko Nor (Qinghai Hu) where pilgrims rested on their journey to Lhasa. Beset by every conceivable hardship the venture failed, but in 1872 Przhevalskii tried again, this time reaching Koko Nor and ascending the desolate plateau where the rivers of the Orient rise. But 800 kilometres (500 miles) short of Lhasa, supplies and money depleted, he had no option but to turn back and retrace his route to Siberia. In 1876 he tried an alternative approach across the forbidding Dzungaria Basin and Taklamakan Desert, identifying in the system of shifting sands and seasonal ponds the location of Lop Nor, a lake unseen since the time of Marco Polo. Reaching the fringes of Tibet in the dead of winter, he was forced back once again. A third attempt in 1879 from the Altay region brought him again to Tibet, but by now the Tibetans were suspicious that Przhevalskii was spearheading a Russian advance aimed at capturing the Dalai Lama. Halted 270 kilometres (170 miles) from Lhasa, he trekked wearily back to Siberia. A fourth expedition in 1883 followed a route similar to the first but was more professionally organized. The headwaters of the Huang He and Yangtze were examined and much of the geography of the Takla Makan was established, but the wary Tibetans kept the party at arm's length. Sadly, Przhevalskii's fifth attempt, launched from the Tien Shan in 1887, would be his last. He died of typhoid near the lake Issyl Kul and was buried in his travelling clothes, his favourite gun by his side.

Right Przhevalskii's map of Mongolia, China and Tibet, showing the routes taken in 1870–73 on two of his abortive attempts to enter Lhasa.

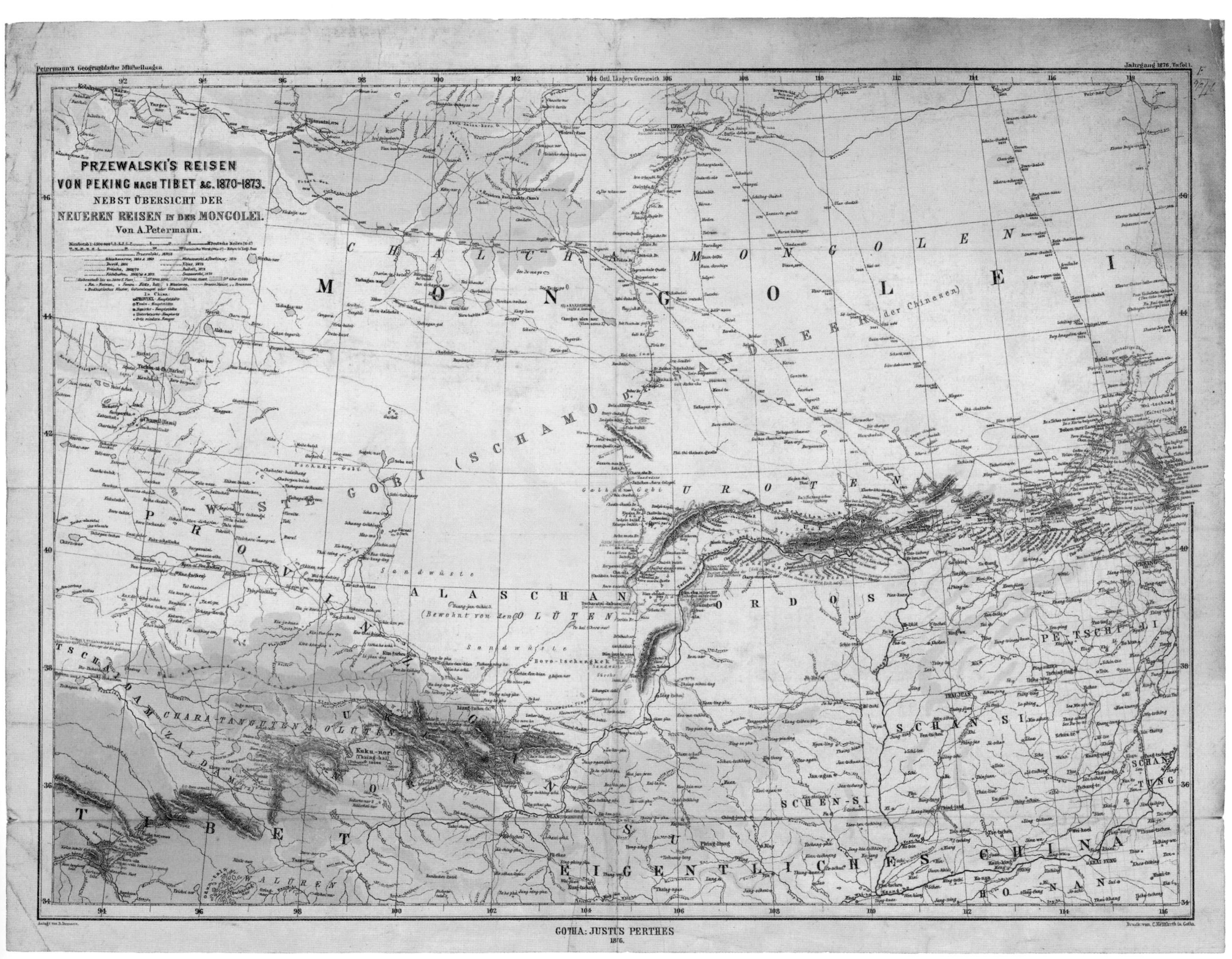
Petermann's Geographische Mittheilungen
Jahrgang 1876, Tafel 1.
PRZEWALSKI'S REISEN
VON PEKING NACH TIBET &C. 1870-1873.
NEBST ÜBERSICHT DER
NEUEREN REISEN IN DER MONGOLEI.
Von A. Petermann.
CHALCHA MONGOLEN
MONGOLEI
GOBI (SCHAMO)
SANDMEER der Chinesen
WÜSTE
PROVINZ
ALASCHAN
ORDOS
TSCHAIDAM
CHARA-TANGUTEN & OLÜTEN
ZAIDAM
Kuku-nor
TIBET
SCHAN-SI
SCHEN-SI
PETSCHI-LI
SCHAN-TUNG
EIGENTLICHES CHINA
HONAN
GOTHA: JUSTUS PERTHES
1876.

Patagonia Gives Up its Secrets

An uninviting wilderness, good for nothing.

1870-1900

DESPITE THE CONSIDERABLE NUMBER OF MARINERS who for centuries had frequented its shores to rest and overhaul their ships, Patagonia, with its relentless winds that could drive settlers insane, remained a virtual no-man's-land. Bleak and inhospitable, allegedly populated by giants and hostile tribesmen and lacking any obvious natural resources, its remote interior had little to offer either the explorer or the colonist. A farming community of ex-patriot Welsh had sprung up around the Río Chubut in 1865, and a wave of brutal campaigns against the Indians had brought northern Patagonia under Argentine control, but it was not until the 1880s that any formal administration in the south came into effect. Eventually this last great wilderness, its serene mountain lakes, its deceptively similar rivers and the richness of its ethnology and anthropology, began to give up its secrets to the explorers. The Englishman George Chaworth Musters undertook a personal odyssey across the interior in the company of Tehuelche Indians in 1869-70, but the real pioneers were two Argentinians, the scientist and ethnologist Francisco Moreno and his close associate, the naval officer Carlos Moyano.

Moreno began his explorations in 1873-76, examining the Río Negro in the north, the Río Santa Cruz in the deep south, and around the Lake Nahuel Huapí where a vast haul of indigenous artefacts brought the tribes of Patagonia to European attention for the first time. In 1878 he joined forces with Moyano to explore the picturesque lake region of southern Patagonia, charting Lago Argentino and discovering Lago Viedma. While Moreno went back to the Negro, Moyano set out to locate a pass through the Andes, coming across Lago San Martin, then ascending the Río Deseado from the Atlantic coast to uncover the last of the region's great lakes, Lago Buenos Aires. Over the next four years Moyano filled whatever blanks remained in the map and in the far south strove unsuccessfully to penetrate the dense forest that had prevented Argentina from establishing a port on the Pacific coast. His marriage to an Englishwoman from the Falklands brought his life of adventure to an end, and in 1887 he finally succumbed to the climate and settled down as a civil servant in Buenos Aires. His old colleague Moreno, however, remained as restless as ever, exploring everything between the Strait of Magellan and the Atacama Desert until his retirement in 1913. Although widely honoured throughout the world for his achievements, he died in poverty six years later.

Right A map of Central Patagonia, 1901, drawn by one of the expeditions sent out to delineate the mountainous boundary between Chile and Argentina.

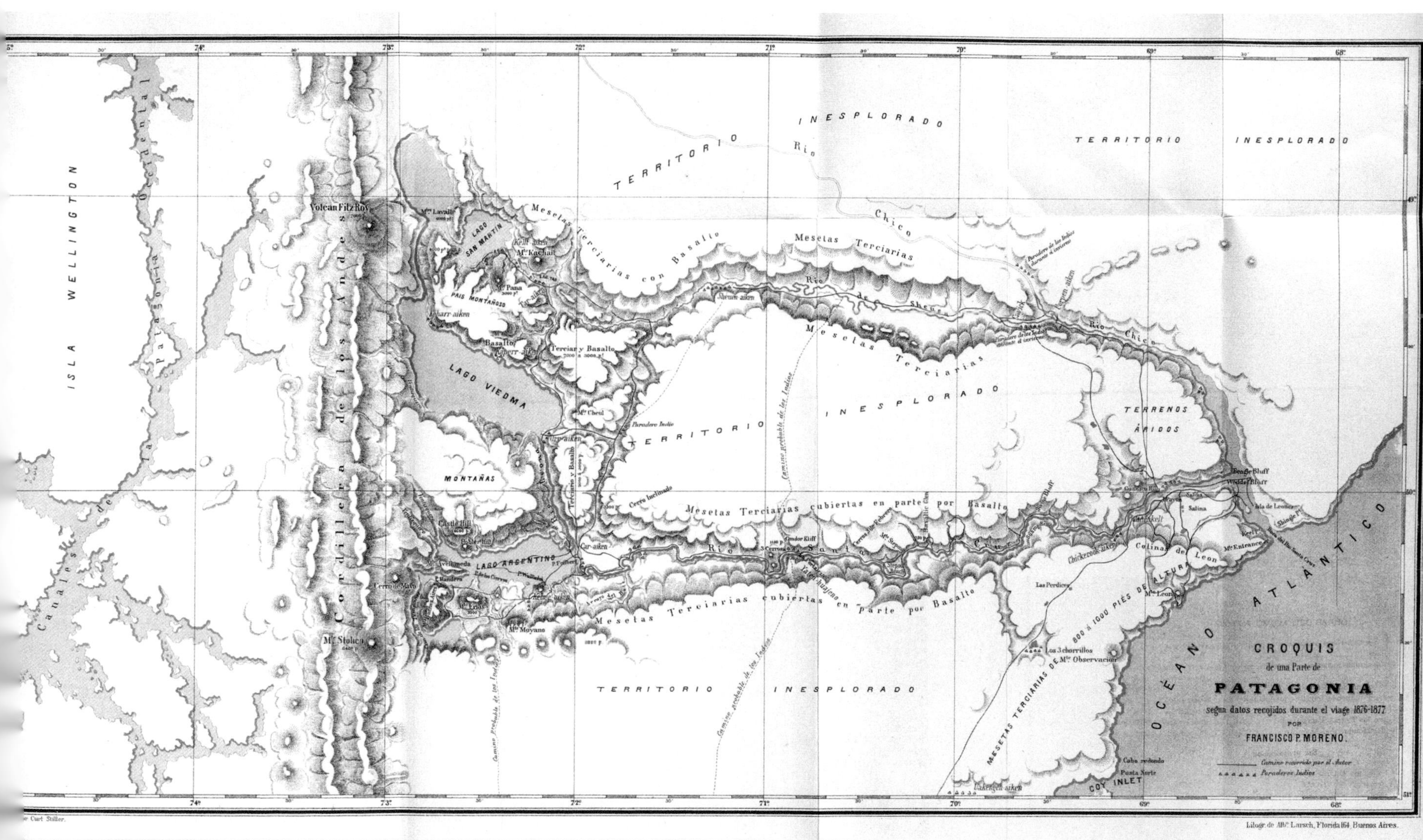
CROQUIS
de una Parte de
PATAGONIA
segun datos recojidos durante el viage 1876-1877
POR
FRANCISCO P. MORENO.
TERRITORIO INESPLORADO
LAGO VIEDMA
LAGO ARGENTINO
LAGO SAN MARTIN
Volcan Fitz Roy
OCÉANO ATLÁNTICO
ISLA WELLINGTON
Cordillera de los Andes
Mesetas Terciarias
Rio Chico
COY INLET
Libogr. de Alb. Larsch, Florida 164, Buenos Aires.

Henry Morton Stanley and the Advent of the Explorer-Journalist

The popular press turns reporters into heroes of discovery.

1871–76

JOURNEYS OF EXPLORATION RARELY GRABBED NEWSPAPER HEADLINES, at best commanding a few column-inches tucked away inconspicuously on an inside page, at worst abandoned to the specialist journals. But all that was to change with the advent of the 'popular press', notably James Gordon Bennett's *New York Herald* and Alfred Harmsworth's *Daily Mail*, aimed at a wider public that had never contemplated purchasing a daily newspaper or simply could not afford it. Real life adventure was ravenously devoured, while a successful outcome to a newspaper-sponsored search for a missing explorer could turn a struggling proprietor into an overnight millionaire. Henry Morton Stanley had already reported on the British Ethiopian campaign for Bennett's paper, bribing telegraph operators to ensure that his copy got through ahead of his rivals, but now in 1868 came the challenge that would give him everlasting fame – to find Livingstone. The missionary-explorer David Livingstone had disappeared in the African interior two years previously and nothing had since been heard. But Bennett chose his timing carefully, and in order to make the most of the story delayed Stanley's expedition for a year or more, hoping that by then speculation over the fate of Livingstone would have reached a fever pitch. In fact it was not until 1871 that Stanley arrived in Zanzibar, by which time reliable intelligence placed Livingstone alive and well on the shore of Lake Tanganyika and the success of Stanley's mission could be guaranteed.

Stanley's meeting with Livingstone at Ujiji in November 1871 catapulted the reporter into stardom, but it would be his next expedition that would earn him renown as a true explorer. By 1874 Stanley had decided his destiny was to continue the work left unfinished by Livingstone and to demarcate the watershed of the Nile from that of the rivers that flow into the Atlantic. However, when Bennett proved reluctant to sponsor an expedition that promised none of the glitter of the Livingstone encounter, Stanley approached Edwin Arnold's *Daily Telegraph*, which promised £6000 on condition that Bennett would match it with a similar amount. Forced into a corner, Bennett reluctantly complied. The outcome was one of the most geographically significant expeditions of the century. Stanley explored lakes Victoria and Tanganyika and arrived on the upper Congo in October 1876. Almost a year later he was on the Atlantic coast having descended the Congo and proved it for the first time to be the major artery into the interior of Africa.

Right Henry Morton Stanley with Kalulu, the boy he adopted as his gun bearer and servant. After the boy's death in 1877, Stanley christened the Kalulu Falls of the Congo in his memory.

The Challenger Lays the Foundation of Modern Oceanography

Plumbing the ocean's depths.

1872-76

In December 1872 the 2306-ton corvette HMS *Challenger* sailed from Portsmouth on what, to this day, would be the longest continuous scientific mission on record. All but two of her eighteen cannon had been removed to make way for scientific equipment; she carried thousands of specimen jars, chemicals for preservation and analysis, thermometers and microscopes; and she was supplied with no less than 290 kilometres (180 miles) of best Italian hemp for sounding, trawling and dredging. At the helm was the popular and seasoned Scottish naval officer George Strong Nares. In charge of the six-man scientific team was Edinburgh professor Charles Wyville Thomson, whose brainchild the expedition was, and who had satisfactorily lobbied the Royal Society and Gladstone's government for a prolonged voyage of exploration. While most of the voyage would be made under sail, the vessel was equipped with an auxiliary steam engine to maintain her stationary while critical measurements were made. Extreme depths would be measured by timing the rate of descent of a lead ball, a remarkably accurate technique devised by Robert Hooke more than two centuries earlier.

In the first year the *Challenger* crossed the Atlantic four times, then in 1874 battled her way through the Southern Ocean, closely approaching Antarctica before heading north to Australia, New Zealand and through the Indies to Hong Kong. Here, to the dismay of the crew, Nares was recalled to take command of a polar expedition, but the *Challenger* pressed onwards into the Pacific under its new captain, Frank Tourle Thomson. By way of Hawaii, Chile and the Atlantic, the *Challenger* returned to Portsmouth in May 1876 after a voyage of 110,000 kilometres (70,000 miles). In the Mariana Trench, southwest of Guam, a record sounding of 8162 metres (26,780 feet) was accomplished, and while no plant life was found below 200 metres (650 feet), dredgings revealed that, contrary to popular opinion, at no depth did living creatures disappear. Small island groups were accurately charted; deep-water temperature measurements were made at 362 stations; and by the end of the voyage 360 million square kilometres (140 million square miles) of ocean floor, often littered with nodules of manganese and iron, had been mapped. Of the curious creatures brought to the surface, some of them with light-emitting organs, 4717 species had never before been seen by man. The reports of the expedition filled fifty volumes totalling 29,500 pages, stimulating a new generation of scientists and launching the era of modern oceanography that continues to the present day.

Right The first page of the journal of Pelham Aldrich, a first lieutenant on the *Challenger* voyage.

1872

Dec. 21st 11.30 a.m. Cast off from the Jetty in Portsmouth Harbor, and with steam commenced our voyage of Scientific exploration and Circumnavigation. For a wonder the sun shone out just as we started and remained out as we discharged our Pilot and a few friends to the Tug which had accompanied us out as far as Spithead – These good people did their best to enliven our departure – and we were greeted with three cheers as they shoved off – and immediately afterwards we proceeded for the Needles. The lively propensities of the ship were soon to be developed, for even before we reached the Needles – signs of motion were observable, and made me anxious to get everything secured as quickly as possible – precautions which were soon to be found necessary – as a falling Barometer and awkward looking sunset gave every indication of a gale from the SW. In the first watch it became thick – and plenty of drizzle – at 2.30 a.m. we got a glimpse

Dec. 22nd of the Start Light abeam – and lost sight of him 2 hours afterwards. The 22nd opened with a fine bright sunshine – the wind having hauled gradually from West round to the Southward a moderate breeze to which we made all Plain sail Except Royals and F. Jib. steering course to W b S. to ~~keep~~ get good Westing in case of falling in with the expected SW. gale – At Midnight the wind and sea began to increase – and necessitated a gradual shortening of sail until 4 a.m. found us under Topsails on the Cap and Courses – There was a nasty confused sea – and the Ship was uncommonly uneasy rolling 22° to Starboard and 14° to Port, with a few hints that she could and would ultimately do more – The Barometer still fell steadily and the ship was kept rap full on the Port Tack to make Westing in

Dec. 23rd case of a shift to the NW. – A lively day promised – under close reefed Topsails and gaff sails with heads hauled in – a fresh Gale from the SSW. the ship rolling 35° to leeward – During the day the Bar. fell and the wind rose. Wore in the hope

Dec. 24th of getting wind from NW – but "Boreas wouldn't" The wind never getting farther round than from SSW. SW. to WSW. a heavy sea running and ship knocking about a great deal – The first night in a gale of wind always produces a few mishaps fortunately ours were confined to those at which one could well afford to laugh – nothing more serious happening than the "gutting" of one or two cabins and the tendency to fly, of a patent ~~wire~~ wire sounding reel – which found its way down into the Cockpit very close to the Paymaster's head.

Peter Warburton Confronts the Great Sandy Desert

An expedition into emptiness and desolation.

1873-74

THE OVERLAND TELEGRAPH THAT CONNECTED DARWIN WITH ADELAIDE in 1871 established a slender swathe of exhaustively surveyed territory across the heart of South Australia and what is now Northern Territory. To the east, beyond the notorious Simpson Desert, the basic topography of the continent had been set by the Burke and Wills expedition, and by Augustus Gregory who in 1857 performed an amazing sweep of the country between Brisbane and Adelaide. However, to the west of the telegraph, from Alice Springs to the pastoral settlements of the west coast, lay only an ominous blank on the map. In 1857-61, Frank Gregory, Augustus's younger brother, had made several abortive forays into the interior of Western Australia, only to be confronted on each occasion by impenetrable wasteland, and in 1869 the government surveyor John Forrest had penetrated some 650 kilometres (400 miles) east of Perth before turning back at the fringe of the Great Victoria Desert.

Peter Egerton Warburton, a retired army captain who had emigrated to South Australia as a commissioner of police, began to indulge his passion for exploration at the relatively advanced age of forty-four. In 1872, now sixty, he was presented with a proposal to deter even the most stalwart adventurer in the prime of life: to command an expedition westward from the telegraph and, if possible, arrive on the Indian Ocean. As it set out from Alice Springs in April 1873 with its neatly aligned caravan of camels, Warburton's expedition looked more like a tranquil, picturesque scene from the Sahara. It would turn into one of the most horrific ordeals in the history of exploration. Unknowingly, the expedition had chosen to cross an already parched landscape in a drought year. Every tentative step involved a desperate reconnaissance for water, sometimes 150 kilometres (90 miles) away and buried deep in the sand. The camels, Warburton's key to success, began to die of a mystery illness, and as the caravan entered the soft, relentless sand-hills of the Great Sandy Desert Warburton despaired of ever seeing water again. To turn back would have meant certain death, so Warburton despatched an advance party to make a dash for the distant Oakover River. The party's heroic trek, and the sufferings it endured to bring relief to the expedition, became a legend in its own time. Strapped to his camel, blind in one eye and close to death after three months in the scorched, shadeless dunes, Warburton descended to the coast in January 1874.

Right In a scene more fitting to the Sahara, Warburton's caravan of camels sets out for the western interior of Australia.

Cameron's Pioneering Traverse of the African Continent

To see 'the Union Jack flying permanently over Central Africa'.

1873-75

LIEUTENANT VERNEY LOVETT CAMERON had joined the navy at the age of thirteen and had seen service in the West Indies, the American Civil War, the Abyssinian campaign and West Africa where he helped suppress the slave trade he so much abhorred. Now aged twenty-six, he was on mundane duties in the Thames estuary. At this point he might forever have passed into obscurity, but Cameron was determined not to fall prey to such an ignominious fate and for two years he pestered the Royal Geographical Society with demands for adventure. Then in 1872 an opportunity arose that would write Cameron into the history books. When news arrived in England that the missionary David Livingstone was alive and well and about to embark on new discoveries in Central Africa, Cameron was selected to seek out the explorer and render whatever assistance would be necessary to his latest venture. Cameron and his three associates set out from Zanzibar in April 1873, but on reaching Tabora one of the party had died, Cameron had suffered weeks of blindness, another was too ill to carry on and the last would shoot himself in a fit of fever. Worse still, Livingstone, whom they had travelled so far to support, had died and his remains were on their way back to the coast.

The objective of the expedition had been satisfied, but Cameron took it upon himself to complete Livingstone's work and to make discoveries that, in his opinion, would pioneer the commercial development of Africa under the British flag. Retrieving the explorer's papers from his base at Ujiji and conducting a wide-ranging survey of Lake Tanganyika, he joined an Arab caravan to Nyangwe, a thriving *entreport* on the upper Congo. Dissuaded from descending the river by Arab traders who by misinformation strove to deflect him from country under their control, Cameron was diverted south with a party of loathsome slave traders into the barren lands of Urua, and hence into the the flooded plains of the Congo-Zambezi watershed. Starving and forced to barter his last possessions for lumps of rotting meat, he entered Angola, finally ridding himself of his obnoxious companions. In torrential rain, smitten with scurvy and barely able to walk, a forced march brought him to the Atlantic coast. Saved by a stranger with a basket of food, Union Jack proudly unfurled, Cameron strode into Benguela in November 1875 – the first European to cross Africa from west to east.

Right Cameron and his native bearers crossing the River Lulindi, between Lake Tanganyika and the Congo.

John Forrest Crosses the Heart of Western Australia

The challenge of 'a great lone land'.

1874

THE 1870S WERE EPIC YEARS IN THE DISCOVERY OF THE AUSTRALIAN WEST, with no less than five major expeditions attempting to cross the vast trackless deserts that lay between the Darwin-Adelaide telegraph line and the settled enclaves of Western Australia. In 1872 Ernest Giles penetrated some 400 kilometres (250 miles) west of the line before he was halted by lack of water. The next year he tried again, taking a more southerly route through the barren ranges around the now popular tourist destination of Uluru, or Ayers Rock. His nightmare journey plunged him headlong into the waterless Gibson Desert, its name celebrating a companion who, sent ahead, was never seen again. En route he crossed the tracks of William Christie Gosse, whose expedition, confronted by an endless expanse of dunes and spinifex, turned back 200 kilometres (125 miles) inside the Western Australian border. Then in 1873 Peter Warburton braved a more northerly route, landing him on the shores of the Indian Ocean but narrowly escaping death in the relentless dunes of the Great Sandy Desert.

In 1872 John Forrest, a courageous native-born Western Australian surveyor of formidable experience and leadership quality, proposed that he should take an expedition east from the coastal settlement of Geraldton and arrive on the telegraph line somewhere in South Australia. His ambitious plan was delayed for two years so as not to appear jealously competitive with the eastern states, but when Giles's and Gosse's attempts proved unsuccessful Forrest delightedly received the go-ahead for the first direct traverse of Western Australia. The party, which included the Aborigine tracker Tommy Windlich, a veteran and crucial component of several successful expeditions, left Geraldton in April 1874 with eighteen pack-horses and provisions for eight months. Following the Murchison River to its source, it struck directly east across the high ground between the Gibson and Great Victoria deserts, its search parties regularly fanning out in search of the next viable source of water. By August, Forrest knew they had reached the point of no return. The waterholes that had so far sustained them, refreshed by recent rains, would soon be dry, and there was no alternative but to take their chances to the east. But Forrest's inspiring self-confidence and popular leadership, his knack of tracing water in obscure locations, would bring success where others had failed. The telegraph line was found near Oodnadatta, and in November the party moved triumphantly through Adelaide's crowd-lined streets.

Right A scene of jubilation. Forrest and his party at the end of their monumental trek across the deserts of Western Australia.

J. Macfarlane

Brazza and the Opening of French Equatorial Africa

The river that led to nowhere.

1875-98

Although the quest for a navigable waterway into the African interior had by the 1860s yielded the Niger, the Nile and the Zambezi, there had been remarkably little success on the equatorial western coast. The Congo, which descends by rapids and falls into the Atlantic, appeared to have little to commend it, while its course above Stanley Pool, some 400 kilometres (250 miles) from its mouth, was virtually unknown. The rivers of Angola rapidly thinned out beyond the coastal plain, and to the south was only desert. Attention therefore focused on the region closest to the equator, where in 1874 the French naturalist Antoine-Alfred Marche had made a pioneering ascent of the Ogooué River. Tribal conflict forced Marche's retreat 200 kilometres (125 miles) upstream, but back in France, one man, Pierre Savorgnan de Brazza, listened with interest to Marche's report. Brazza, a well-connected, Italian-born nobleman who had served with the French navy, had spent his life poring over maps of Africa, imaginatively filling the extensive blanks. Now at last he saw in the Ogooué the long-sought river of the west, optimistically connecting it with Livingstone's Lualaba, the Congo's tail-end more than 2000 kilometres (1250 miles) away.

Brazza's first mission to the Ogooué, partially funded by the colonial treasury, the rest from his own pocket, proved a bitter disappointment. For three years, 1875-78, he and his team, afflicted by dysentery, fever and debilitating leg ulcers, constantly harassed by hostile tribesmen, battled their way through malarial marshlands and up the Ogooué, only to discover that the river petered out just 350 kilometres (220 miles) from the coast. Even more disheartening was the news that Henry Morton Stanley had descended the Congo and confirmed it to be the major artery into the interior. Nevertheless, Brazza came home determined to divert French interests towards his promised land, if only to outrace Stanley who had now joined King Leopold's crusade to carve out a Belgian empire in the African interior. Although suspicious of Brazza, a relatively unknown Italian upstart, the French government complied by returning him to Africa to establish permanent posts and forestall Stanley's brutal march northward. For twenty years Brazza strove to extend French colonialism throughout Equatorial Africa, creating schools, hospitals and training programmes for the native Africans, and establishing the humane government that would contrast so starkly with the bloodthirsty régime of Leopold's empire across the far bank of the Congo.

Right A portrait of Pierre Savorgnan de Brazza.

Au Colonel Bonnier
témoignage de reconnaissance
Comtesse Pierre Savorgnan de Brazza
1905

Charles Doughty and His Travels in Arabia Deserta

A story less important than the manner of its telling.

1876–78

RED-HAIRED AND LUXURIANTLY BEARDED, the reclusive polymath Charles Montagu Doughty came to exploration by an unlikely route. Rejected by the navy on account of his stammer, he read geology and archaeology at Cambridge then devoted five years to an intensive study of early English literature. His devotion to Chaucer and Spenser caused him to lament the sorry state into which, in his opinion, nineteenth-century English had decayed. Determined to instigate a poetic revival of medieval linguistic forms, Doughty started on his travels in quest of a story he could tell in the style of English he was fashioning. After four years wandering throughout Europe he arrived in Egypt, crossed Sinai by camel and scrambled over the ruins of Petra. But there he heard rumours of another rock-hewn city, Mada'in Salih, far to the south and adjudged even more wondrous. Insistent on seeing it for himself, he spent the next year in preparation.

Posing as a Syrian doctor, surveying instruments and notebooks secreted in his effects, Doughty left Damascus in November 1876 with a 6000-strong hajj caravan, his intention being to remain at Mada'in Salih, making notes and copying inscriptions until the caravan returned. But after a few months he was befriended by local Bedouin, even offered a wife on condition that he join the tribe. In their company, alone or with guides that abandoned him to the desert, Doughty meandered through 'fanatical Arabia', visiting Tayma, Ha'il, Buraydah, Unayzah and Taif, many of which had never before seen an infidel European. Uncompromising in his refusal to conceal his Christianity, and openly regarding Islam as 'the most dangerous grown secret conspiracy in the whole world', he suffered humiliation and assault from the ignorant masses, but to others he was something special, a wandering sage, beloved, respected and fondly remembered for generations to come. Doughty returned to England in 1878 and spent ten years labouring over his *Travels in Arabia Deserta*. Turned down by four publishers on account of the demands it made on its readers (who ideally required fluency in Chaucerian English and at least one Semitic language), Doughty refused to alter a single word, adamantly maintaining that the material was less important than the style in which it was told. Eventually accepted by Cambridge University Press, the book became one of the greatest classics of travel literature, even though few would ever profess to having vanquished every word of its intractable prose.

Right Two of the many sketches made by Doughty to illustrate his *Travels in Arabia Deserta*.

JEBEL ʿANÂZ, seen over the lava plain of the Ḥarra (altitude nearly 6000 feet) from the Northward and distant 11 miles: in the foreground part of an antique circle of heaped stones.

MUBRAK EN NÂḲA (EL-MEZḤAM). Looking North.

Adolf Nordenskiöld circumnavigates Asia

The dream of the Northeast Passage becomes reality.

1878-80

THE EIGHTEENTH CENTURY HAD WITNESSED A PERIOD of feverish exploratory activity in the depths of the Siberian wilderness. In a concerted effort that endured for more than five decades, every major river and countless tributaries were charted, and the greater proportion of the Arctic coast was surveyed with such precision that by 1800 it already bore remarkable resemblance to the best modern maps. However, contrary to any impression this might convey, no continuous voyage had successfully followed the entire coast from the Barents Sea to the Bering Strait. Surveys by Russian officers, their names now unfamiliar, were conducted in a coordinated but piecemeal fashion by successive approaches from the west, or by descending the major rivers to their mouth, then sailing or sledging to left or right. In 1742 Semen Chelyuskin dog-sledged across sea ice to reach the northernmost point of Asia, the cape that now bears his name, but it was not until 1823 that Ferdinand von Wrangel charted the notorious Chukchi Sea to finally demolish the myth of a land bridge to America.

In June 1878 Adolf Erik Nordenskiöld left the Swedish port of Karlskrona in the 300-ton barque-rigged steam whaler *Vega* on a voyage that would see him, one year later, emerge from the Bering Strait into the Pacific. Finnish-born, of Swedish descent, and one of Scandinavia's finest explorers, his fourteen years in the Arctic had taken him to Svalbard and Greenland and brought him closer to the pole than any before. Meticulous planning, plus two reconnaissance voyages to the Yenisey to confirm feasibility, had prepared for most eventualities. So, manned by a hardened crew of naval men and walrus hunters, complemented by an enthusiastic team of scientists and hydrographers, the voyage proceeded relatively uneventfully for three months and doubled Cape Chelyuskin without incident. However, optimism for completing the transit in a single season turned to dismay when just 200 kilometres (125 miles) from the Bering Strait a slim but impenetrable ice barrier brought the *Vega* agonizingly to an abrupt halt and imprisoned her for the next 264 days, a mere two days short of her goal. With plentiful supplies and help from the local Chukchi, Nordenskiöld's crew were never in serious danger, but it was not until July the following year that they could resume the final brief lap into the Pacific. Via Japan and the Suez Canal the expedition steamed jubilantly into Stockholm in April 1880, the first to circumnavigate the Eurasian continent.

Right A portrait of Adolf Nordenskiöld by the Swedish painter Georg von Rosen.

1879-84

Joseph Thomson: the Most Amiable of African Pathfinders

'He who goes gently goes safely.'

FOR THE NATIVE AFRICAN WHO HAD NEVER BEFORE SET EYES ON A EUROPEAN, nobody could make that first encounter more happily memorable than Joseph Thomson. At the tender age of twenty-one, this young Scottish geological assistant on a Royal Geographical Society expedition from Dar es Salaam to lakes Nyasa and Tanganyika was suddenly plunged into command when his leader, Alexander Keith Johnston, died on the banks of the Rufiji River. Thomson immediately proved an immense success with local tribesmen, entertaining them with tricks with mirrors and passing round a photograph album stuffed with pictures of nubile young women. While lesser explorers might have challenged unfriendly crowds with guns, Thomson charmed them with parlour games. 'He who goes gently goes safely' was his motto, and throughout his 25,000 kilometres (15,000 miles) of exploration in the dark continent he never knowingly harmed an African nor fired a shot in anger.

In 1879 Thomson discovered 'a perfect Arcadia about which idyllic poets have sung' at the northern tip of Lake Nyasa, then headed north to make important discoveries around Lake Tanganyika and in the remote interior of present-day Tanzania. In 1882 he was commissioned by the RGS to open a direct route from Mombasa to Lake Victoria – a journey that would take him through the domain of the Masai, a people that, as a result of expedient exaggerations by Arab traders, had been imbued with a fearsome and warlike reputation. To make matters worse, Thomson was narrowly preceded by a German explorer, Gustav Adolf Fischer, whose confrontational and aggressive nature, quite the opposite of Thomson's style, had already set the Masai on the warpath. En route, the party paused to string 60,000 beads as gifts for the Masai, and whenever danger approached Thomson would charm his hosts with his magical powers, removing and replacing his two false teeth and dropping effervescent fruit salts into water. Fischer failed in his objective, lacking the diplomacy to deal with the cultured and sophisticated Masai, but Thomson treated the Masai with such profound respect that, although menaced, he was allowed to pass peacefully to Lake Victoria. Although gored by a wounded buffalo, and weakened by malaria and acute dysentery, he returned to England to become the RGS's youngest recipient of its Founder's gold medal. Plagued by acute illnesses throughout his short life, he went on to become one of Britain's most influential African pathfinders and treaty makers, laying the foundations of empire across the continent.

Right 'Reviewing the Expedition.' Joseph Thomson in pensive mood while on his way into Masai country.

Francis Younghusband Ventures into the Heart of Central Asia

Through the Gobi and across the Karakoram.

1887

FRANCIS YOUNGHUSBAND, IMPERIAL ADVENTURER, mystic visionary and legendary Victorian hero, spent most of his first fifty years in the East. Born in India, educated in England and trained at Sandhurst, his passion for exploration was inspired by the memory of his uncle, Robert Barkley Shaw, who in 1868 had been the first European to enter Kashgar, hub of the Central Asian trade routes. Younghusband's first venture into the unknown came in 1886 when as a twenty-three-year old captain he was despatched to Manchuria to ascertain what designs the Russians had on the territory. A difficult trek from Beijing to the Sea of Japan took him through the remote highlands of the Chinese-Korean borderland, which no European had seen since a Jesuit survey of 1709. Finding no evidence of Russian territorial ambition, he returned to Beijing to accept an even more hazardous commission, one which would lead him through the unexplored wastes of the Gobi Desert and return him to India across the mountains of Kashmir.

Leaving Beijing in April 1887 with an interpreter, cook and groom, Younghusband headed beyond the great bend of the Huang He, procured eight camels and struck across the Gobi for 2000 kilometres (1250 miles), following the southern border of Mongolia into the forbidding Dzungaria Basin. Weakened by thirst and exhaustion, he stumbled onto the Silk Road and reached Kashgar in August. At Yarkand (Shache), where merchants remembered his uncle, Younghusband found a letter instructing him to reconnoitre into Kashmir over the 5800-metre (19,000-foot) Mustagh Pass, on the slopes of Mount K2, which no European had succeeded in crossing. The ascent to the pass through steep soft snow was difficult enough, but the near-impossible descent would have defeated all but the bravest. The route blocked by a sheer ice ledge, without ropes or crampons and wearing only worn leather stockings, Younghusband and his handful of mountain men hacked steps out of the ice with a small axe bought in Yarkand. An improvised rope of knotted turbans and pony tethers then allowed them to make the tortuous six-hour descent to the glacier below. Passing the Baltoro Glacier, the highest in the world, Younghusband descended to Skardu and Srinagar, and in December 1887 made his way back to his regimental headquarters at Rawalpindi. Now a national hero, over the next four years he would explore in the Karakoram and Pamirs, and in 1903-04 co-direct the first British mission to Lhasa.

Right Francis Younghusband (centre right) pictured in 1891 with the British consul George Macartney (first left) and other British residents in Kashgar. **Following pages** A hand-drawn map by Francis Younghusband showing his explorations of the remote mountain passes leading from Kashmir to China.

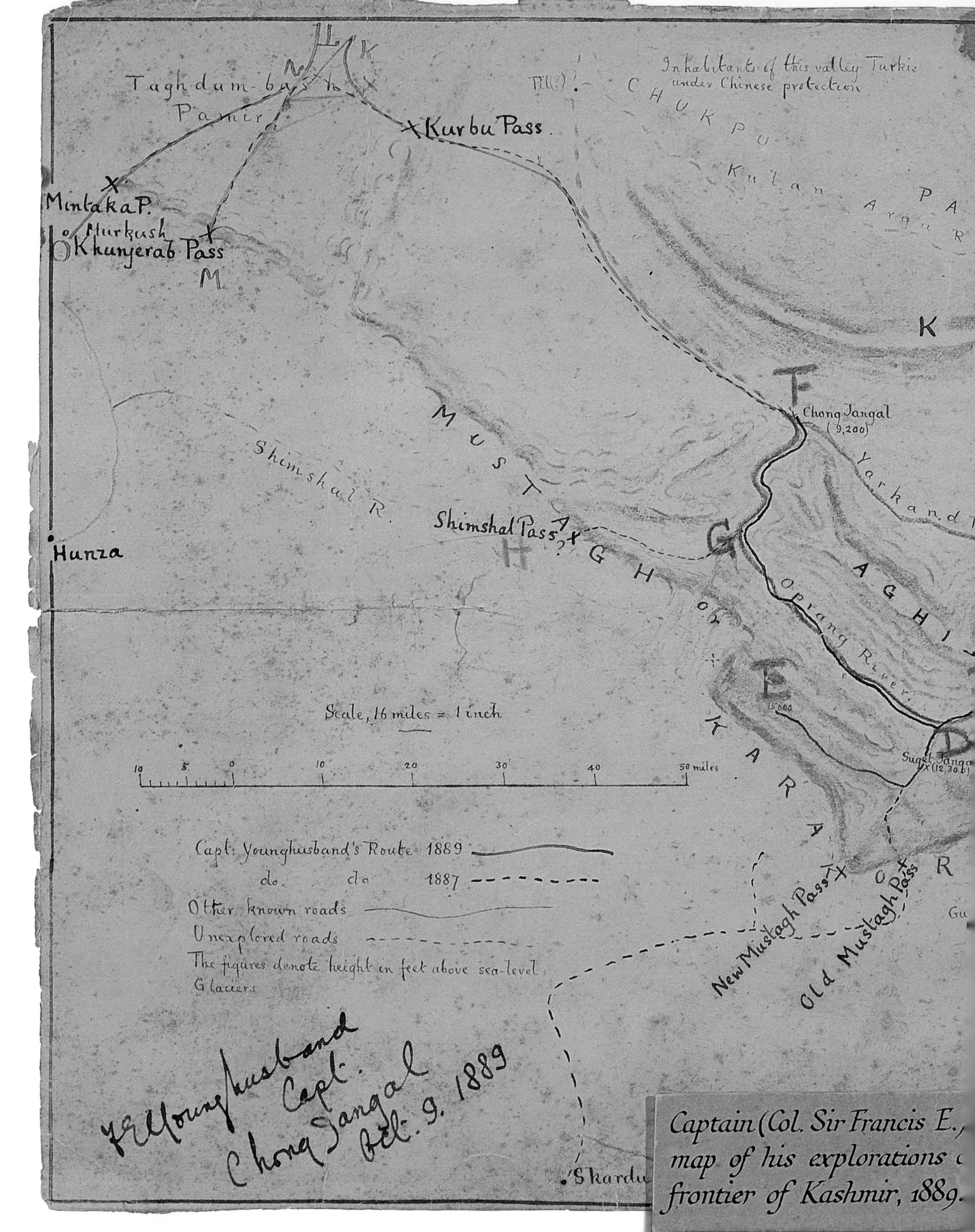

Captain (Col. Sir Francis E., … map of his explorations … frontier of Kashmir, 1889.

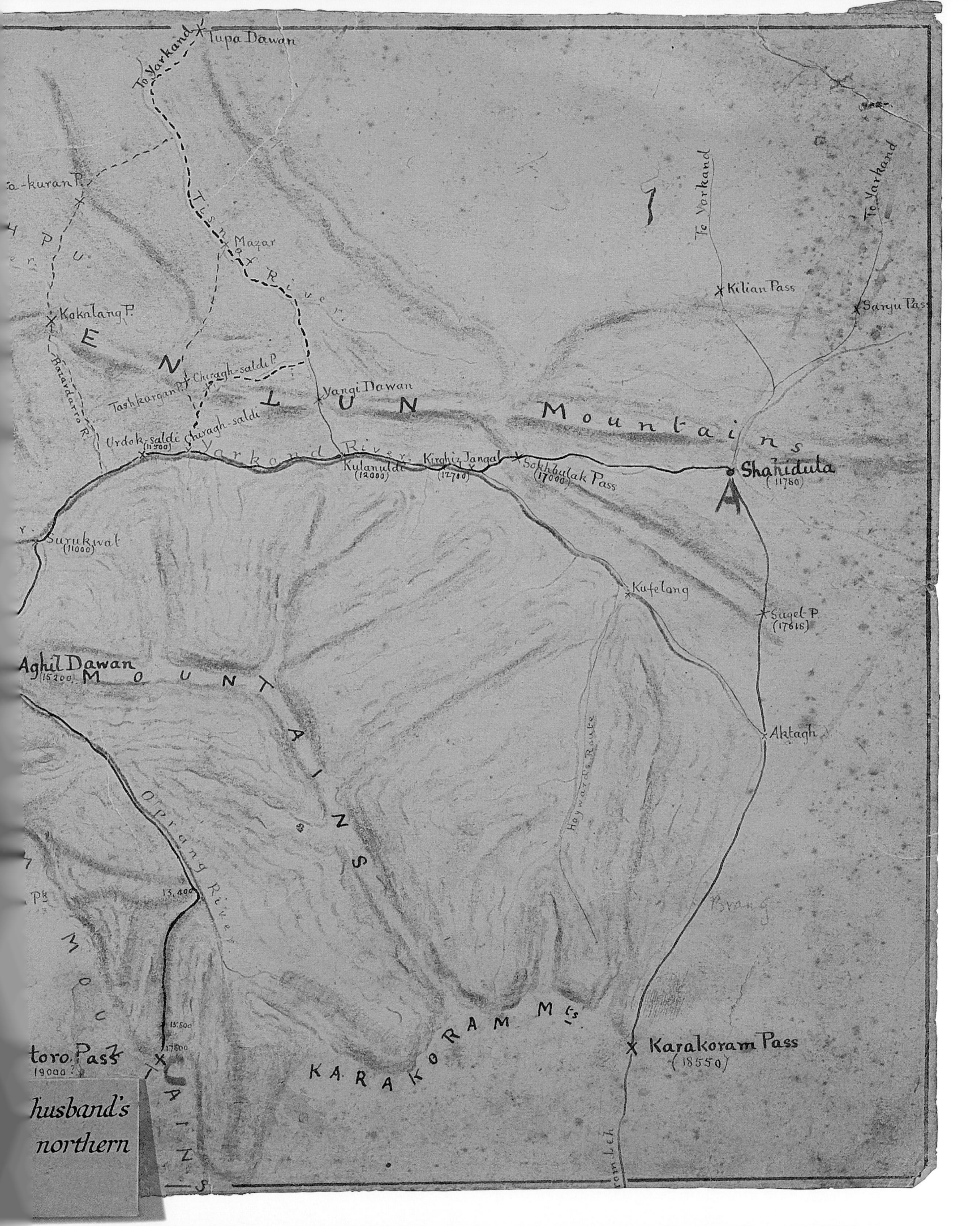

husband's
northern

Vittorio Bottego and the Last of Africa's Great Lakes

Ethiopia opens to a new generation of explorers.

1891–96

FOLLOWING THE EXPULSION OF FOREIGN MISSIONARIES IN 1633, few Europeans entered Ethiopia for more than two centuries. Those that did manage to penetrate its rugged and complex terrain saw little beyond the kingdom of Gonder around Lake Tana, while the remainder of what we now regard as Ethiopia – until the 1850s no more than a collection of remote semi-autonomous tribal fiefdoms constantly at loggerheads with each other – remained virtually unknown. But the efforts of Emperor Tewodros and his successors Yohannes and Menelik to unify the country, and to drag Ethiopia into the modern age, would invite an army of European advisers, traders, ambassadors and arms dealers, all vying to take advantage, commercially and diplomatically, of the country's emergence on the world stage. In their wake came the usual bevy of explorers, British and French, even Russian and Croatian, but the virgin field of endeavour would also arouse a generation of Italian explorers, their country having colonized Eritrea and evasively contrived to reduce Menelik's kingdom to a mere protectorate.

Twenty-seven-year-old Lieutenant Vittorio Bottego already harboured dreams of becoming a national hero when he volunteered for a posting to Eritrea. In 1891, now captain, he explored the forbidding Danakil and paralleled the Red Sea coast from Massawa to Aseb. The next year he ventured southwest into the unexplored Ogaden Desert, then examined the geographically complex Mendebo Mountains, from which the rivers of southern Ethiopia and Somalia flow towards the Indian Ocean. The 3000-kilometre (1800-mile), twelve-month journey eventually landed him on the shores of southern Somalia, but only after his fellow officer had drawn a pistol on the over-adventurous Bottego and defected to make his own way back. In 1895 Bottego returned to Somalia to embark on an even more daring expedition to settle the course of the Omo River, a northern tributary of Lake Turkana. Under the auspices of the Italian Geographical Society, supported by a caravan of 250 colonial troops, he discovered lakes Abaya and Ch'amo, the last of the great Rift Valley lakes to have escaped European detection, then followed the Omo south to Turkana. However, Bottego's decision to return to the coast via the centre of Ethiopia brought him into direct conflict with Menelik, for whom the expedition was nothing less than a backdoor invasion. The Ethiopians launched a full-scale attack, and in the ensuing bloodbath Bottego and many of his followers died.

Right Vittorio Bottego's map of his pioneering exploration of the Ogaden, the remote tribal region of southwestern Ethiopia.

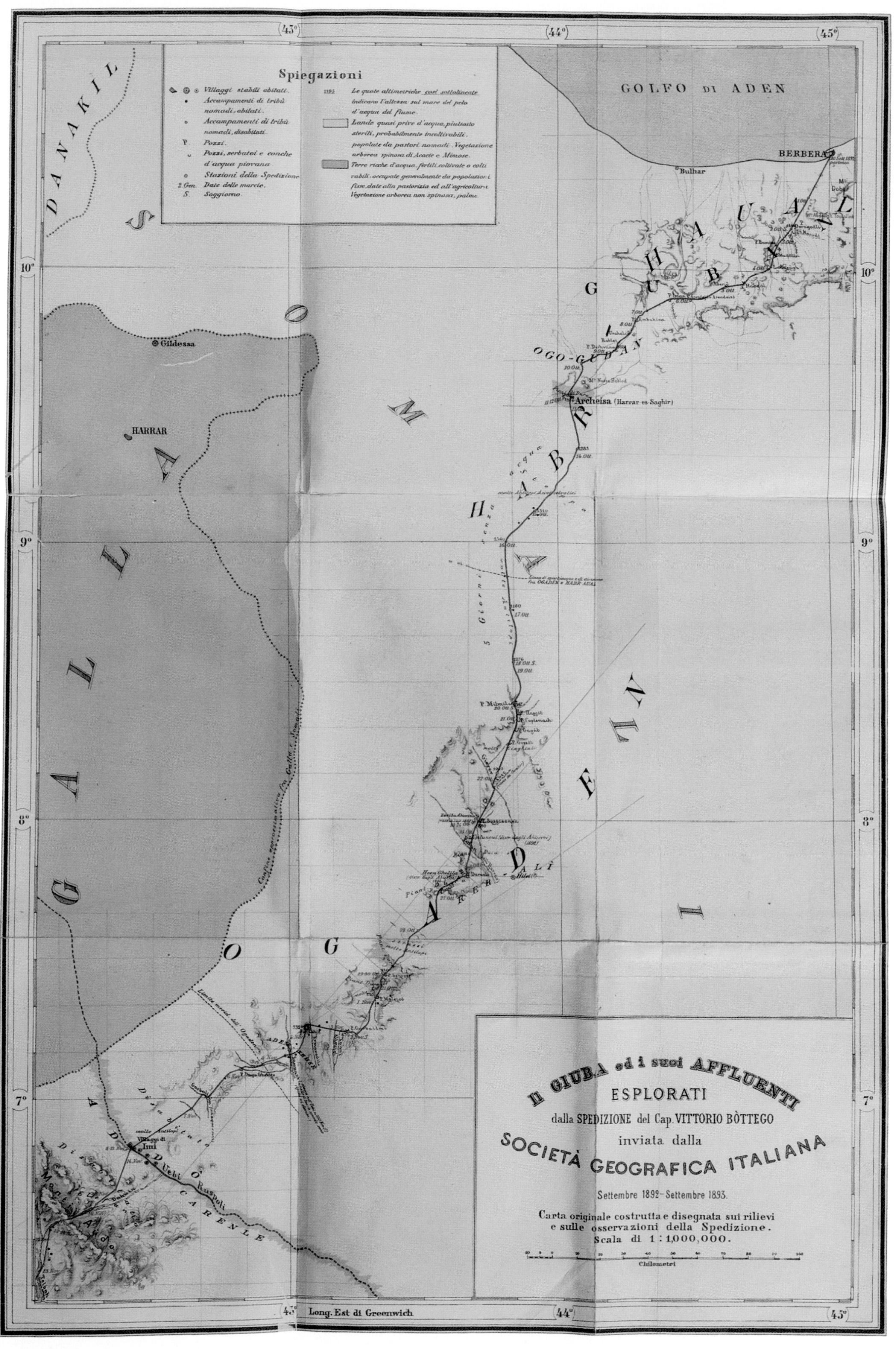
Il GIUBA ed i suoi AFFLUENTI
ESPLORATI
dalla SPEDIZIONE del Cap. VITTORIO BÒTTEGO
inviata dalla
SOCIETÀ GEOGRAFICA ITALIANA
Settembre 1892–Settembre 1893.
Carta originale costrutta e disegnata sui rilievi
e sulle osservazioni della Spedizione.
Scala di 1 : 1,000,000.
Chilometri
Spiegazioni
Villaggi stabili abitati.
Accampamenti di tribù nomadi, abitati.
Accampamenti di tribù nomadi, disabitati.
P. Pozzi.
Pozzi, serbatoi e conche d'acqua piovana.
Stazioni della Spedizione
2 Gen. Date delle marcie.
S. Soggiorno.
1193 Le quote altimetriche così sottolineate indicano l'altezza sul mare del pelo d'acqua del fiume.
Lande quasi prive d'acqua, piuttosto sterili, probabilmente incoltivabili, popolate da pastori nomadi. Vegetazione arborea spinosa di Acacie e Mimose.
Terre ricche d'acqua, fertili, coltivate o coltivabili, occupate generalmente da popolazioni fisse, date alla pastorizia ed all'agricoltura. Vegetazione arborea non spinosa, palme.
GOLFO DI ADEN
DANAKIL
GALLA
SOMALI
OGADEN
HABR AUAL
GUBAN
OGO-GUDAN
BERBERA
Bulhar
Gildessa
HARRAR
Archeisa (Harrar es Saghir)
Imi
Uebi Carenle
Long. Est di Greenwich
43°
44°
45°
10°
9°
8°
7°

Fridtjof Nansen's Voyage Across the Arctic Ice

Polar Sea and Arctic Drift.

1893–96

THE BELIEF IN A POLAR SEA – a wide ice-engirdled pond of open water through which ships could sail unimpeded across the North Pole – lingered in the minds of polar explorers for three centuries. At first it was the effect of the midnight sun that throughout summer bathed the pole in perpetual heat and light. Then it was the presumption that sea ice forms only in proximity to land, or that temperatures minimized around 80°N, beyond which they rose again. But most convincing were the conjectures of the influential geographer August Petermann, who in the 1850s proposed that warm northwesterly currents in the Atlantic and Pacific might dissipate their energy in high latitudes and provide a 'thermometric gateway' to the pole. Quests for Petermann's gateways repeatedly failed, but one would divulge a quirk of polar geography even more profound. In 1879 George Washington De Long's ship *Jeannette* became ice-locked beyond the Bering Strait and throughout the next two years drifted erratically 350 kilometres (220 miles) to the northwest. Eventually it broke up but, quite astonishingly, fragments of the *Jeannette* turned up on the southwest coast of Greenland three years later.

In 1889 the Norwegian explorer Fridtjof Nansen proposed that if a purpose-designed ship could be launched into the ice at the correct position, the Arctic drift would guide it across the pole and eventually disgorge it into open water on the far side of the earth. So in June 1893 the *Fram*, two years in the making, left Oslo to follow the coast of Siberia and in October nestle into the ice north of the Lena delta. For sixteen months the ice took her ever closer to the pole, her listless crew rapidly exhausting her 600-volume library and growing fat on the galley's ample provisions. But by the spring of 1895 it was apparent that the *Fram* would sidestep the pole by some 500 kilometres (300 miles). Nansen and his companion Hjalmar Johansen made a brave assault on the pole, but at 86°N were compelled to submit to a drift that was bearing them southward faster than they could sledge north. Lost and beyond reach of the *Fram*, their flight to safety, which culminated in an extraordinary chance encounter with a British expedition in Franz Josef Land, would become one of the Arctic's finest epics of heroism and survival. The *Fram* was discharged from the ice beyond Svalbard in May 1896, and at Tromsø in September Nansen was finally reunited with his crew.

Right Nansen's ship *Fram*, drifting with the Arctic ice.

1895-1908

Sven Hedin Discovers a Long-Forgotten Civilization

The lost cities of the Taklamakan.

Sweden has always enjoyed a fine reputation for overseas exploration. Its Viking adventurers penetrated as far as Constantinople and the Caspian; its East India Company traded for eighty years with the Orient; the botanist disciples of Carl Linnaeus collected in almost every corner of the earth; and Swedish explorers and navigators spread throughout the world's oceans and islands, making remarkable discoveries in the polar regions. Even in Central Asia, unlikely territory for Sweden's explorers, its countrymen were no strangers. Captured by Russians in 1709 at the Battle of Poltava and transported to Tobol'sk, many subsequently contributed to exploration of Siberia while others, like Johan Renat, found their way deep into the Asian heartlands. It was no wonder therefore that such a tradition should be continued into the twentieth century by Sweden's most celebrated land explorer, Sven Anders Hedin. Inspired by Nordenskiöld's transit of the northern sea route around Asia, trained in the sciences, geography and geology, he began his travels in a gap-year excursion, 1885-86, to the Iranian borderlands, then in 1890 wandered through Russian Turkestan and crossed the Tien Shan to Kashgar.

Over the next twenty years Hedin undertook three major expeditions into Central Asia, covering so much ground that it seemed little of importance remained to be discovered. In 1895 he was the first European to cross the Taklamakan Desert rather than skirting around it, and in so doing became aware of forgotten cities buried beneath the sands, remnants of the long-lost, once-thriving Buddhist civilization reported centuries earlier by Fa Hsien. In 1899 he navigated the mysterious disappearing Tarim River, explored shifting ponds of Lop Nor and stumbled upon the lost city of Loulan. Then in 1901 he attempted unsuccessfully to become the first twentieth-century European to enter Lhasa. When this was achieved by force of arms three years later by Younghusband's mission, Hedin turned his attention to parts of Tibet that were still a blank on the map. In 1906 he examined the northern tributaries that fed the western course of the Tsangpo or upper Brahmaputra, then in 1907 he crossed the mountains of Kashmir to trek diagonally across the Tibetan plateau in the dead of winter. The war years, which lost Hedin many friends through his pro-German sympathies, brought a halt to his explorations, but in 1926 he returned to China at the head of a massive seven-year, multi-disciplinary survey expedition in the country's northwest.

Right Sven Hedin's discoveries in Central Asia pictured on contemporary French trade cards.

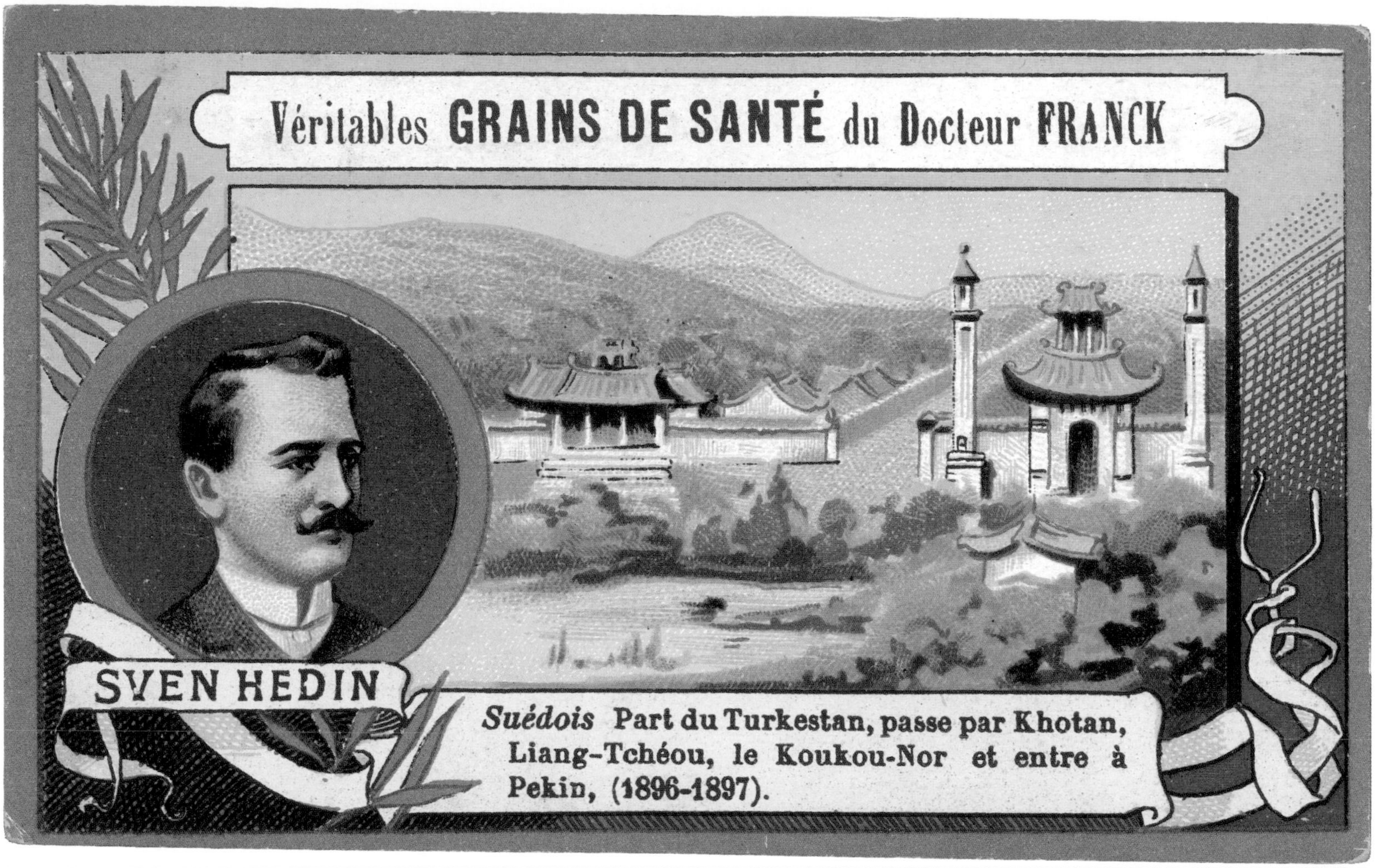
Véritables GRAINS DE SANTÉ du Docteur FRANCK
SVEN HEDIN
Suédois Part du Turkestan, passe par Khotan, Liang-Tchéou, le Koukou-Nor et entre à Pekin, (1896-1897).

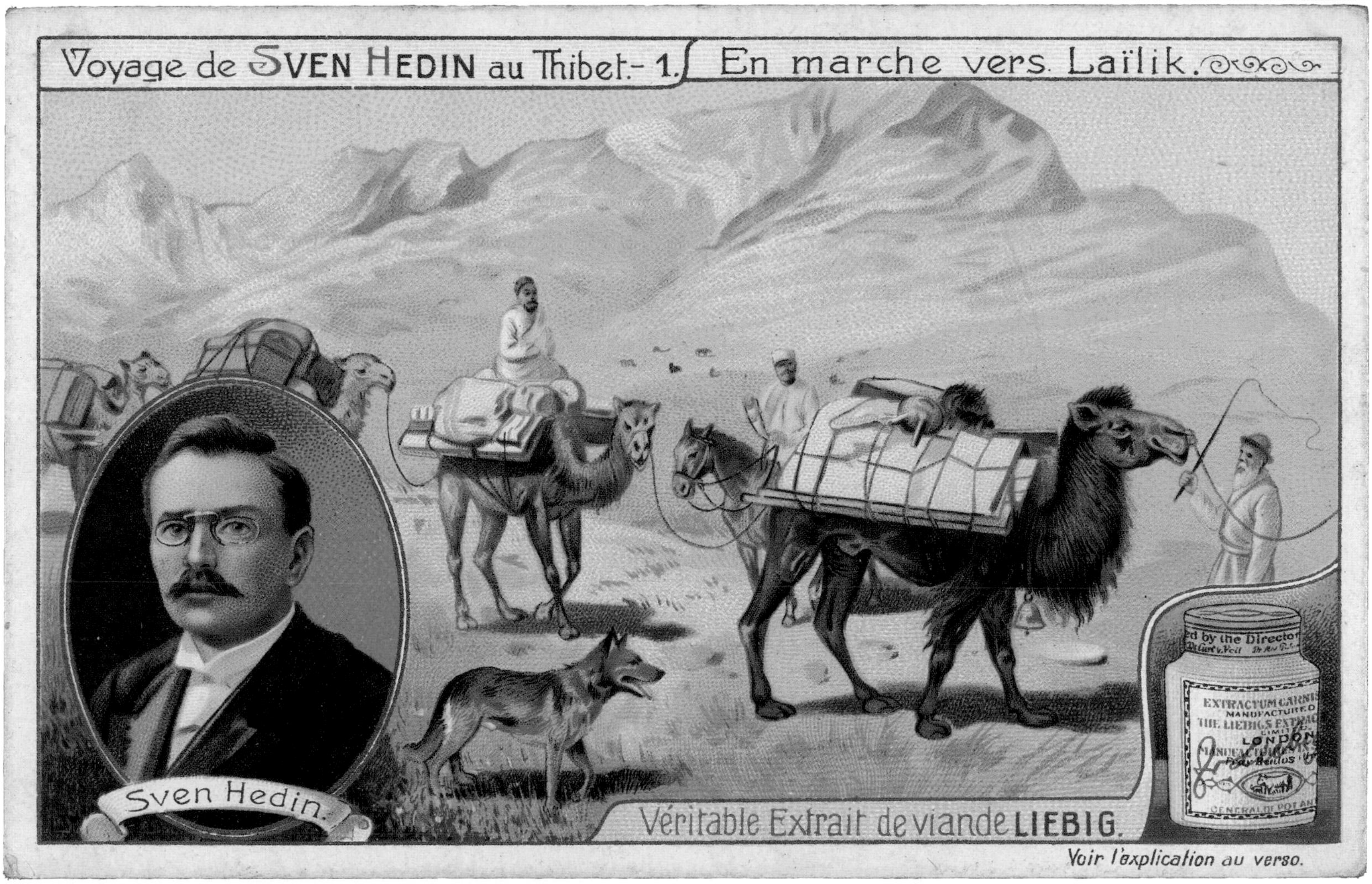
Voyage de SVEN HEDIN au Thibet.- 1. En marche vers Laïlik.
Sven Hedin.
Véritable Extrait de viande LIEBIG.
EXTRACTUM CARNIS
LONDON
Voir l'explication au verso.

Anton Nieuwenhuis Makes the First Crossing of Borneo

Steaming jungles and clouded peaks.

1896-97

THROUGHOUT THE NINETEENTH CENTURY, EVEN INTO THE MID-TWENTIETH, one mention of Borneo would immediately arouse visions of primitive head-hunting tribes, ferocious beasts and explorers adrift in dense, impenetrable jungle. While in reality the beasts tended to keep their distance, and the native peoples were generally cultured, sophisticated and friendly, there is no doubt that Borneo, its mist-shrouded mountains and dark forbidding forests, did present a formidable challenge. The northern part of the island, closely allied to Great Britain since James Brooke's elevation to Rajah of Sarawak in 1840, had become a favourite haunt of missionaries and naturalists. But in Kalimantan, the neglected 'outer province' of the Dutch empire which occupied the southern part, few explorers set foot much beyond the coastal hinterlands until the 1870s. In 1879 the Norwegian, Carl Alfred Bock, examined the southeastern quarter from the Mahakam River to Banjarmasin, and over the next fifteen years a number of Dutch quasi-military expeditions charted the larger river routes into the interior. However, the first to cross the entire island from west to east was the Dutch army surgeon and amateur anthropologist Anton Willem Nieuwenhuis.

In February 1896 Nieuwenhuis hurried alone to Pontianak on the west coast and by steamer ascended the Kapuas River to Putusibau, where the river begins to enter the mountains. Joined there by the rest of his party, a surveyor, a photographer and two Indonesian naturalists, four months were spent gaining the trust and confidence of the local Dayak, on whom the future success of the mission depended. The expedition moved out in July 1896 and in canoes ascended the narrowing tributaries of the Kapuas until navigation became impossible. Following a land route across the highlands, his Dayak scouts always to the fore, establishing supply depots and assessing the friendliness of villagers ahead, Nieuwenhuis crossed the central divide in early August and began his descent to the Penanei River, which would hopefully lead him to the Mahakam and so to the east coast. The descent of the Mahakam lasted a further eight months, much of the time spent mapping, collecting and hunting and addressing problems of food and tribal conflict, but at the end of May 1897 the party successfully entered the estuarine port of Samarinda. Extensive collections were sent back to Holland, then in 1898-99 Nieuwenhuis crossed Borneo a second time before finally coming home to spend his next thirty years as a professor at Leiden.

Right Armed Ma-Suling from the Merasè with their headman Ibau Li. From Nieuwenhuis' *Quer Durch Borneo*, 1904-07.

1896–98

The Inglorious Fate of the Mission Marchand

The last conquistador.

In just fifty years the map of Africa had developed from a hollow shell into a mosaic of colonial enclaves, their landmarks and settlements inscribed with such opacity that, as early as 1885, Joseph Thomson was moved to declare that, with regard to large-scale exploration, 'Africa is played out.' Even so, a few regions, like the Great Sand Sea of the Egyptian borderlands, stayed little known until the 1920s, while others, notably the southeastern sub-Sahara, survived colonially up for grabs well into the late 1890s. In fact it was the latter that would attract what was arguably the largest and most meticulously planned expedition of all time: the so-called 'Mission Marchand'. Named after its director, Jean-Baptiste Marchand, a soldier who had pioneered overland routes from Senegal to the Côte d'Ivoire, it assembled in 1896 near the mouth of the Congo with 12,000 porters, 200 Senegalese troops and a coterie of hand-picked officers and scientists, its purpose being to establish French supremacy across a vast swathe of territory from the Atlantic to Sudan. In addition to the 600 tons of basic provisions, including copious supplies of wines, spirits and foie gras for the officers, it took 70,000 metres (230,000 feet) of textiles and 16 tons of Venetian pearls as gifts to seduce local despots.

Marchand intended to cross the Congo-Nile watershed by the navigable waterways reported by earlier explorers, and a small steamship was carried in sections for this purpose, but beyond the Ubangi the rivers rapidly petered out, requiring the vessel to be disassembled and painfully manhandled 170 kilometres (100 miles) across the Sudanese savannah. The streams feeding the Nile, reduced by drought to mere trickles, proved too shallow even for canoes, and for two weeks the boats had to be dragged through the towering reeds of the mosquito-infested labyrinth known as the Sudd. In July 1898, a year late, Marchand hoisted the French flag on the Upper Nile, only to find that a support expedition from Djibouti had long since dispersed after losing most of its number to fever and desertion. Marchand's fate was finally sealed when a heavily armed Scottish-Sudanese force under Horatio Kitchener arrived from Khartoum to forestall the French invasion. The two commanders introduced themselves in a civilized manner, each congratulating the other on his achievements while their respective ministers back home deliberated on the delicate stalemate. In the end, Kitchener's superior force won the day. Marchand was peacefully despatched to Ethiopia and to a hero's welcome in France.

Right Despite the 'defeat' at Fashoda, the many popular illustrated accounts of the Mission Marchand fired the French with nationalistic pride.

Le Colonel MARCHAND

Fils d'un pauvre menuisier chargé de famille, il naît à Thoissey (Ain), le 22 novembre 1863.

Au collège, où il étonne ses maîtres par sa précocité, il passe tous ses dimanches à lire des histoires de guerre et de voyages et prend la secrète résolution de s'engager.

Sorti brillamment de l'École Militaire de Saint-Maixent, et nommé sous-lieutenant d'infanterie de marine, il vient embrasser son vieux père avant de s'embarquer.

Du fond des colonies, il épargne sur sa solde pour subvenir à l'éducation de ses jeunes frères.

Capitaine à 29 ans, il expose au Ministre des Affaires Étrangères son vaste et hardi projet de traverser toute l'Afrique avant les Anglais et il en reçoit aussitôt la périlleuse mission.

Suivi de son intrépide état-major, et de la petite armée de ses fidèles tirailleurs noirs, il traverse les arides déserts et les marécages de la brousse, où, à toute minute, il court les plus grands dangers.

Après cette expédition qui dure plus de trois ans et que les Anglais avaient déclarée impossible, il plante le premier le drapeau tricolore sur les bords du Nil à Fashoda, s'y établit formidablement et y cultive des légumes et des fleurs.

Il est l'espoir de la France

Vive Marchand!

Il voit arriver les Anglais, et il fait serment, avec ses braves compagnons, de mourir à son poste.

Devant l'énergique attitude de l'héroïque Marchand, le général anglais s'entend avec lui pour qu'un officier de la mission aille en France aviser le gouvernement.

Les tristes nécessités de la politique l'obligeant à se retirer, il quitte Fashoda la mort dans l'âme, et reçoit les honneurs militaires de *toute* l'armée anglaise.

Nommé chef de bataillon et Commandeur de la Légion d'Honneur, il est royalement reçu par Ménélick, Empereur d'Abyssinie, qui le couvre d'honneurs et de présents.

En France, il reçoit, partout sur son passage, l'accueil le plus enthousiaste et il est l'objet à Paris, au Cercle Militaire, d'une ovation triomphale.

Honoré par l'Institut d'un prix de 15,000 francs, il les donne avec un désintéressement admirable à une œuvre de défense nationale : *La Ligue Navale pour la Défense des Côtes.*

Il revoit son village natal qu'il a couvert de gloire.

Au cours d'une visite qu'il fait à l'École de Saint-Cyr, les élèves l'acclament et décident que leur promotion s'appellera *la promotion Marchand.*

A la revue du 14 Juillet, il défile en tête de l'armée de Paris, au milieu de l'amour de tout un peuple.

The First to Overwinter Below the Antarctic Circle

Adrien de Gerlache inaugurates the 'heroic age' of Antarctic exploration.

1897-99

THE FLURRY OF EARLY NINETEENTH-CENTURY ANTARCTIC ACTIVITY, which revealed the existence of an extensive continental landmass and virtually exterminated the seal stocks around the Antarctic Peninsula, ended in 1843, and for the next half-century Antarctica lay almost forgotten. Exploratory whaling expeditions, and sealers anxious to exploit the partial recovery of the species, arrived in the 1890s, but it was not until 1895 that an obscure Belgian naval officer, Adrien de Gerlache, came forward with an ambitious proposal for a scientific expedition, one that would launch the so-called 'heroic age' of Antarctic discovery and would culminate thirty years later in Shackleton's ill-fated bid to cross the continent. Belgium, preoccupied with its newly acquired African empire, had nothing further from its mind, but public subscription, much of it collected at village fairs, raised a considerable sum, which the government felt obliged to match. The expedition sailed from Antwerp in the converted whaleship *Belgica* in August 1897 and reached the coast of Graham Land four months later.

Sadly, De Gerlache's qualities of leadership and planning fell desperately short of his idealistic ambitions. The hurriedly assembled cosmopolitan company of sailors and scientists had little idea of conditions ahead, had no common language, were frequently drunk or at loggerheads and often lacked basic seamanship. Those experienced enough to weather the storm, like Roald Amundsen and the surgeon Frederick Cook, both of whom would achieve fame in their own right, quietly challenged De Gerlache's seemingly irrational decisions. Conditions aboard, into which the Chilean navy had once been called to restore order, deteriorated unimaginably when the *Belgica* became locked in pack ice, committing an already miserable and dispirited crew to an unforeseen winter in the Antarctic. Scurvy became rampant, and Dr Cook, who would receive a knighthood for his services, assumed moral command of the crew, many of whom suffered mental instability in the long Antarctic night, while one set forth on the ice to walk back to Belgium. Not until March 1899, after blasting an open channel through the ice, did the expedition clear the pack and begin its return to the heroes' welcome awaiting in Belgium. Scientifically the enterprise had been a remarkable success, establishing geological connections between Antarctica and South America and, as the first to overwinter in the southern continent, returning with an entire year's meteorological data. In fact, so overwhelming were the findings that publication of official reports was still in progress fifty years later.

Right The track of De Gerlache's expedition along the western coast of the Antarctic Peninsula, now Graham Land.

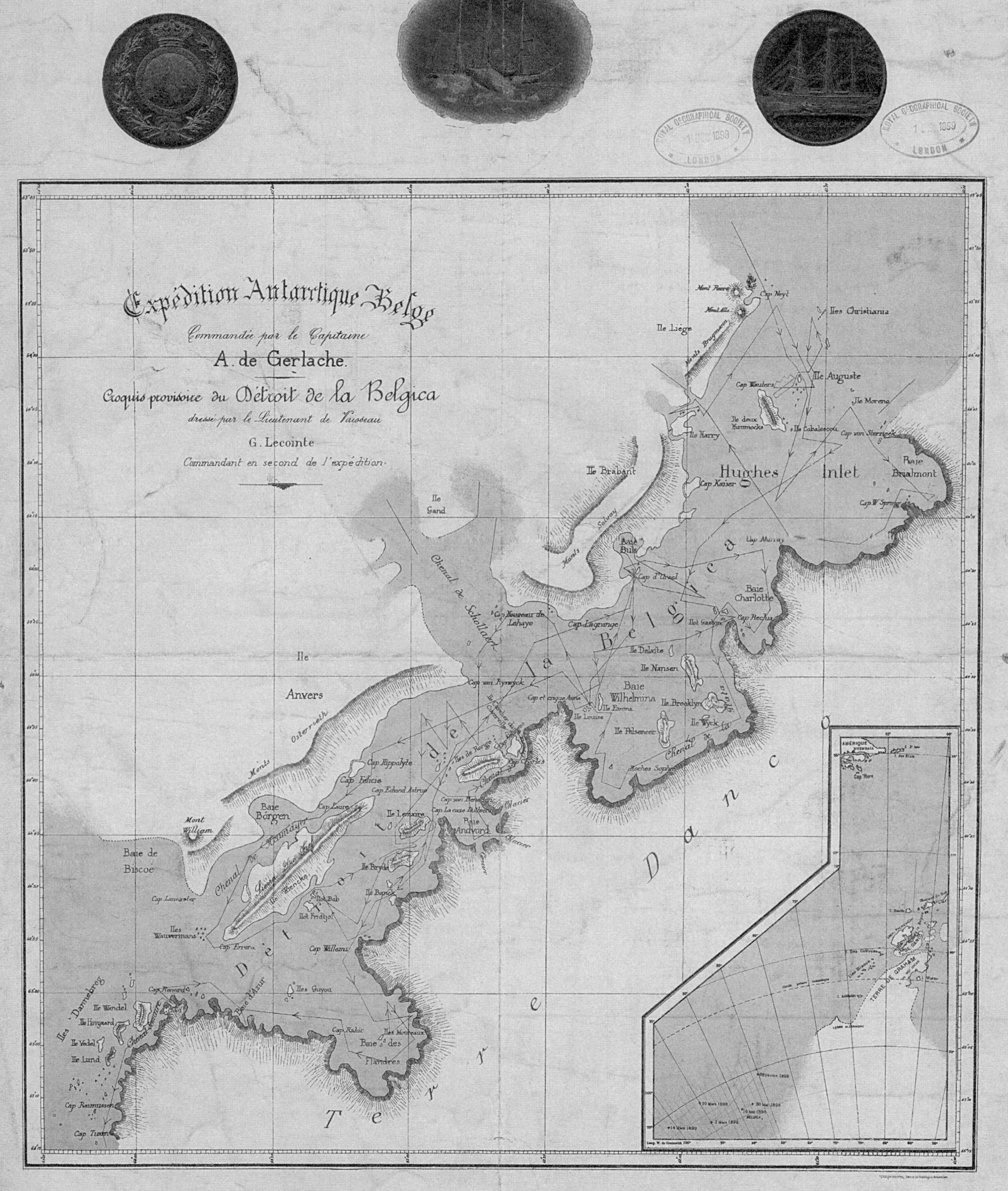

SOCIÉTÉ ROYALE BELGE DE GÉOGRAPHIE

SEANCE DU 18 NOVEMBRE 1899

1898-1902

Otto Sverdrup Completes the Map of the Canadian Arctic

Charting the world's most remote island.

THE NAME OF OTTO NEUMANN SVERDRUP is seldom heard outside his native Norway. A quiet and modest man, in the words of Hjalmar Johansen: 'He walked aboard, silently and calmly, noticed everything, spoke so little, but accomplished all the more.' Perhaps this is why this 'prince of polar explorers' remains to this day overshadowed by giants like Nansen and Amundsen. In fact Sverdrup had been instrumental in the success of Nansen's Arctic drift expedition and had captained the *Fram*, but his contribution to the official report, which he should have co-authored, was relegated by Nansen to a mere appendix. However, Sverdrup's moment of glory would arrive when he was selected to direct an expedition that was to chart one of the last white spaces on the map, a region so remote and uninviting that none had ventured there before.

The refitted *Fram* was borrowed back from the Norwegian government, and with a hand-picked crew Sverdrup left Oslo in June 1898, his intention being to map the unknown wilderness of northern Greenland. However, extensive ice off Greenland's northwest coast halted progress, causing Sverdrup to rethink his plans and instead investigate what might lay west of Ellesmere Island, the fringe of the known world. Sverdrup and his team spent three winters in the Arctic, the last forced upon them when ice around the *Fram* failed to melt. Sledge parties fanned out in every direction, mapping the fjords of Ellesmere Island's remote western coast, trekking to the edge of the frozen Beaufort Sea and naming the islands of Axel Heiberg, Amund Ringnes and Elef Ringnes after the expedition's sponsors. Sverdrup returned to a heroes' welcome in September 1902 with such a wealth of information that publication continued for more than fifteen years.

Sverdrup had taken possession of the newly discovered islands for Norway, but only in the 1920s did it suddenly dawn on the Canadian government that an extensive part of its northern archipelago legitimately belonged to another nation. Although Norway had taken little interest in its remote Arctic bequest, an amicable settlement was essential, so in 1930 Canada decided to buy off the Norwegians by purchasing Sverdrup's maps and appeasing the explorer himself with an annual pension. However, when it was suggested that Sverdrup might live to a ripe old age, this was commuted to a lump sum of $67,000. The decision cost the Candians dearly. Sverdrup died two weeks later.

Right Sverdrup's ship *Fram* locked in the ice off Ellesmere Island.

'Mischievous Rivalry'

The devolution of Scottish scientific exploration: William Bruce and the Scottish National Antarctic Expedition.

1902-04

SCOTLAND PRODUCED SO MANY FINE EXPLORERS that one is tempted to remark that the history of post-1750 British exploration is more Scottish than it is English. Mackenzie, Livingstone, James Bruce, Stuart, Mitchell, Thomson, Clapperton, Nares, Park and Grant already have pages in this book. All were Scots, although they were often travelling under the auspices of institutions south of the border. However, by the late nineteenth century Scottish exploration had begun to assume an identity of its own. The celebrated *Challenger* voyage, the first to be entirely devoted to oceanographical science, was almost exclusively Scottish in its composition of scientists and crew, and its collections were administered from Edinburgh. Then in 1892-93 the city of Dundee, which required whale oil for its jute industry and built ships specifically for polar waters, sent an early survey expedition to Antarctica and made important discoveries there. Scottish universities became pre-eminent in the sciences, leaving many of their southern counterparts stranded in the Dark Ages, while an upsurge in Scottish nationalism, under the guidance of scientists like Patrick Geddes and William Speirs Bruce, viewed scientific advancement as a component of a romantic Scottish-Celtic cultural revival. Others, however, like James Wordie, the future *éminence grise* of polar exploration, jumped the border to share in an English polar renaissance that would subsequently strand their Scottish colleagues in isolation.

William Bruce, son of an Edinburgh surgeon but English born and educated, was so impressed by the intellectual vibrancy of Edinburgh that he decided to stay. He participated in the Dundee expedition and in excursions to Franz Josef Land and Svalbard, but he declined a senior post on Robert Scott's first Antarctic venture, partly because its uncertain objectives seemed largely to hinge on the sensationalistic attainment of the pole, but mainly because he already envisaged a uniquely Scottish enterprise under his own leadership. When the British government refused to sponsor a project that a grandee of the Royal Geographical Society condemned as 'mischievous rivalry', Bruce rapidly acquired local funding, and his own team of scientists, and sailed in November 1902 in the *Scotia*, bound for the Weddell Sea and South Orkneys. While Scott and his party, from their Dundee-built ship *Discovery*, spent two years vagrantly sledging the polar ice and achieving comparatively little, Bruce's Scottish National Antarctic Expedition filled large blanks in the map, established a meteorological station still manned to this day, and brought back more oceanographic, geographical and scientific information than any that had gone before.

Right The *Scotia* and her crew in the ice off Coats Land, 1904, where important discoveries were made.

Roald Amundsen Conquers the Northwest Passage

Wisdom succeeds where heroism had failed.

1903–06

BY THE END OF THE NINETEENTH CENTURY the obsessive quest for the Northwest Passage had unveiled a host of feasible routes through the maze of ice-bound channels that disect the American Arctic archipelago. Remarkably, a few British crewmen had traversed the passage as early as 1853, sledging between expeditions that approached from opposite directions, but still no single ship had left the Atlantic to emerge into the Pacific. However, the challenge that had defeated the might of the Royal Navy was soon to be vanquished by a relatively obscure Norwegian adventurer, his crew of six and a diminutive, thirty-year-old herring fishery sloop named *Gjøa*. Roald Engelbregt Gravning Amundsen was well prepared for the realization of his boyhood dream. A meticulous and thoughtful planner for whom 'heroism' was synonymous with wanton self-sacrifice and bungling, he had no desire to repeat the mistakes of others. A skilled seaman and proficient skier, he had witnessed the psychology of survival as an unpaid mate with Adrien de Gerlache's Antarctic expedition. He had consulted with Arctic veterans, taken a crash course in magnetism and sailed the *Gjøa* on a trial run in the most deplorable conditions. Even so, much of his success would depend on his willingness to absorb the wisdom of the native Inuit, the art of warm dressing in loose furs, and how to drive dogs.

The De Gerlache expedition had posed many questions about the conjectural drift of the earth's magnetic poles, and it was the precise siting of the North Magnetic Pole that would become a key feature of Amundsen's enterprise. Leaving Oslo in June 1903, collecting dogs, sledges and kayaks in Greenland, he took the *Gjøa* through Lancaster Sound, then south to the Boothia Peninsula where James Ross had fixed the pole's position in 1831. While the *Gjøa* stayed locked in its ice-bound harbour for two years, precisely as Amundsen had planned, sledging parties made extensive forays, encircling the pole and confirming a drift of 60 kilometres (37 miles) to the northeast. The anchor was weighed in August 1905 and in less than a month the *Gjøa* had completed the passage into the Beaufort Sea. Another ice-bound winter postponed the final leap into the Pacific, but Amundsen, impatient for recognition, sledged 800 kilometres (500 miles) across Alaska to the nearest telegraph office and made a $700 reverse-charge call to Fridtjof Nansen announcing his monumental achievement to the waiting world.

Right Amundsen's party, ice-bound at King Point in the spring of 1906 after their successful transit of the Northwest Passage.

The Strange Case of Colonel Fawcett

A mystery to grip the imagination of the millions.

1906–25

LOVE HIM OR LOATHE HIM, there is no doubt that the enigmatic Colonel Percy Harrison Fawcett would inspire a generation of explorers, armchair and otherwise, with a passion for adventure in the darkest recesses of the Amazonian jungle. His narrative, *Exploration Fawcett*, selectively edited by his son Brian, appeared thirty years after the explorer's disappearance, pre-dating the mindless deforestation of recent years and not too late for the aspiring disciple to experience the landscape much as Fawcett had portrayed it. The book, with its unfulfilled promise of hidden cities and latter-day El Dorados, sold by the million and was acclaimed by many as the finest of its genre, but in its pages lurked an undercurrent of mystery and secret ambition never quite disclosed. Fawcett, a soldier who had hunted buried treasure in Ceylon and knew something of surveying, first came to South America in 1906. Sent by the Royal Geographical Society at the request of the Bolivian government, his commission was to delineate national boundaries in the disputed rubber-rich forests of the country's northernmost provinces. The task, which subsequently encompassed the eastern and western borderlands, occupied him until 1912, beyond which he would travel largely on his own account.

It was in Bolivia that Fawcett heard tales of advanced cultures that had once flourished in the interior, confirming his belief that a lost city lay buried somewhere deep in the jungle. The war years interrupted further travels, but his obsession with vanished civilizations never faded. By 1920 he was back in South America, his focus having shifted to the unexplored darkness beyond the Mato Grosso, the dense trackless forests that lay between the southernmost tributaries of the Amazon. His first expedition met with every conceivable disaster, while a second in 1921, this time from the Atlantic coast and destined for a location designated 'Z', somewhere beyond the Rio Xingu, appears to have come to little. A third attempt in 1925, with son Percy and a friend named Rimell, approached 'Z' from the Mato Grosso and reached an earlier camp from which Fawcett wrote to his wife: 'You need have no fear of failure.' The party was never seen again. Whether, as some maintain, it was lured into a subterranean Atlantis, was abducted by a she-god, took a drug-induced time-trip or survived to establish a secret theosophical community, we shall never know with certainty, but most likely it simply perished at the hands of hostile Indians.

Right Colonel Fawcett, photographed during his travels in South America.

The North Pole and the Cook-Peary Controversy

Problems of priority, credibility and validation.

1908–09

QUESTIONS OF PRIORITY ARE ALL TOO COMMON in the history of exploration. Little more than tiresome intellectual distractions if the discoveries were accidental, but quite a different matter where they relate to long-sought goals for which substantial rewards, prestigious and often financial, were on offer. And of the latter, none would kindle a more heated debate, a controversy that would persist to the present day, than the race to the North Pole. In September 1909 the American explorer Frederick Cook, returning from months of shadowy wanderings in the Arctic, telegraphed the outside world to claim his attainment of the pole in April the previous year. He had certainly set out to accomplish this mission, and he would author a 600-page book about the journey, but his map failed to show islands over which he must have passed, and his photographs of the pole were adjudged by critics to be cropped versions of those taken years earlier in Alaska. It was argued that Cook had perpetrated an almighty fraud; one that would sadly blight the life of an otherwise benevolent and kind-hearted man.

But what of Cook's principal rival, the self-aggrandizing Robert Peary, an altogether less savoury character who often humiliated his co-workers and had once rejected Doctor Cook's compassionate concerns for his health? Pennsylvania-born Peary had since his early twenties sought to write himself into history, an ambition that began in 1886 with an unsuccessful bid to be the first across the Greenland ice cap. For the next twenty years he would commute with the Arctic, but not until 1909 was he sufficiently organized for an assault on the pole. From a location on Ellesmere Island support teams and advance parties invaded the polar ice, but only 213 kilometres (132 miles) from the pole Peary decided inexplicably to make the final four-day dash with only his faithful black servant Matthew Henson and four Inuit, none of whom could corroborate the accuracy of his latitude calculations. When in 1969 Wally Herbert and his team fought their way across daunting ridges of polar ice, they found that precise attainment of the pole was almost unachievable due to the relentlessly disorientating drift of the ice, while the tiniest of observational errors could project them into an endless spiral. Under such conditions, Peary's sixth sense for navigation must have finally failed him and presented a dilemma, maybe one he had foreseen, that not even he could escape.

Right 'The plum job'. The bear-like figures of Cook and Peary wrestle their claim to the top of the world. A painting by the Portuguese caricaturist Tomás Leal da Câmara.

Nº 446
16 Octobre 1909
50 Centimes

L'Assiette au Beurre

RÉDACTION
ET ADMINISTRATION
62, Rue de Provence,
PARIS
Téléphone : 283-74

Le Pôle Nord

par

Leal da Camara

The Arctic Expedition that Conquered the South Pole

Roald Amundsen's hidden agenda.

1910-12

THERE WERE MANY EXPEDITIONS, particularly in the early days of European reconnaissance, that for sound commercial or political reasons were planned and executed in an atmosphere of secrecy. But nothing quite compares with the extraordinary sequence of events, the subterfuge and blatant deception that preceeded Roald Amundsen's conquest of the South Pole. Returning from a successful transit of the Northwest Passage, Amundsen straightaway prepared for an assault on the unconquered North Pole, his idea being to equip Nansen's old ship *Fram* for a five-year drift in the Arctic ice that would hopefully deposit him within walking distance of his destination. However, just as preparations were underway, reports arrived that Cook or Peary, or both, had beaten him to it. The news was shattering, but the infinitely adaptable Amundsen decided on an immediate and preposterous volte-face. Rather than forfeit the considerable backing already received for the projected Arctic enterprise, he would direct the *Fram* into the Atlantic as though heading for the Bering Strait, then once in open waters suddenly declare to his officers and crew that they were going not to the Arctic, but to the South Pole!

It is a tribute to Amundsen's organizational expertise that he could with meticulous detail simultaneously plan two expeditions, one real, the other imaginary, and that the deception would stay hidden even when his carpenter was asked to design a prefabricated hut of somewhat questionable use in the Arctic. Suspicions lurked unvoiced, but it was only on leaving Bergen in August 1910 that the senior officers were brought in on the secret, and only at Madeira that the rest of the crew and the world at large were informed. By January 1911, Amundsen and his eighteen men, hand-picked for initiative and adaptability, had settled into the contentious hut to see out the winter. To the west, 600 kilometres (370 miles) along the Ross Ice Shelf, lay a rival British expedition under Robert Scott, its sights also set on the pole. In October, Amundsen and four companions made their departure, their four sledges each hauled by thirteen dogs. The ascent to the plateau in driving snow was by no means pleasant, but compared with the harrowing ordeal suffered by Scott it was relatively easy-going. In less than two months the pole was reached and by the end of January, three months before Scott and his men lay dying in their tent, Amundsen and his team were safely returned to base.

Right Amundsen proudly unfurls the Norwegian flag at the South Pole, 12 December 1911.

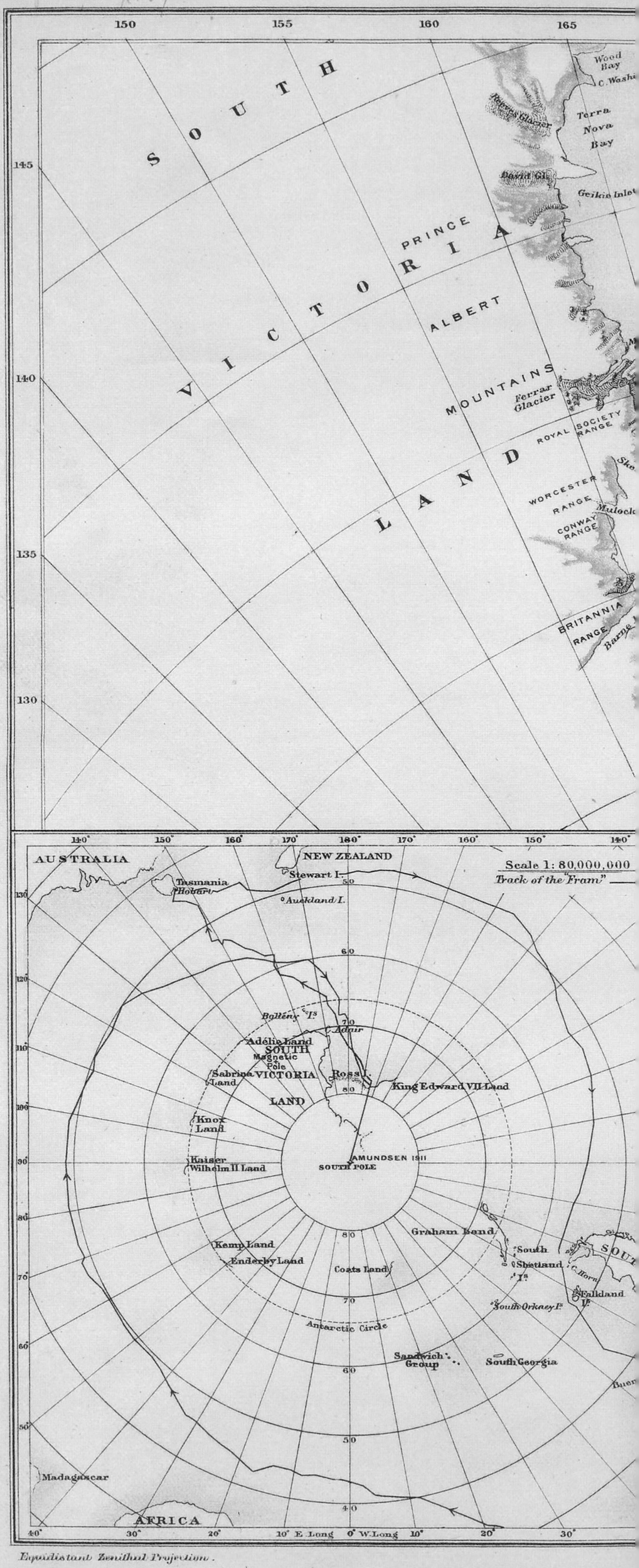

Above Amundsen in the Antarctic during his bid for the south pole.
Right A map of Antarctica showing his route to the pole and back.

SOUTH VICTORIA LAND
PRINCE ALBERT MOUNTAINS
Wood Bay
Terra Nova Bay
David Gl.
Geikie Inlet
Ferrar Glacier
ROYAL SOCIETY RANGE
WORCESTER RANGE
CONWAY RANGE
BRITANNIA RANGE

Scale 1: 80,000,000
Track of the "Fram"
AUSTRALIA
NEW ZEALAND
Tasmania
Hobart
Stewart I.
Auckland I.
Balleny Is
Adare
Adélie Land
SOUTH Magnetic Pole
Sabrina Land
VICTORIA LAND
Ross I.
King Edward VII Land
Knox Land
Kaiser Wilhelm II Land
AMUNDSEN 1911
SOUTH POLE
Graham Land
South Shetland Is
Falkland Is
South Orkney Is
Kemp Land
Enderby Land
Coats Land
Antarctic Circle
Sandwich Group
South Georgia
Madagascar
AFRICA
10° E.Long 0° W.Long
Equidistant Zenithal Projection.

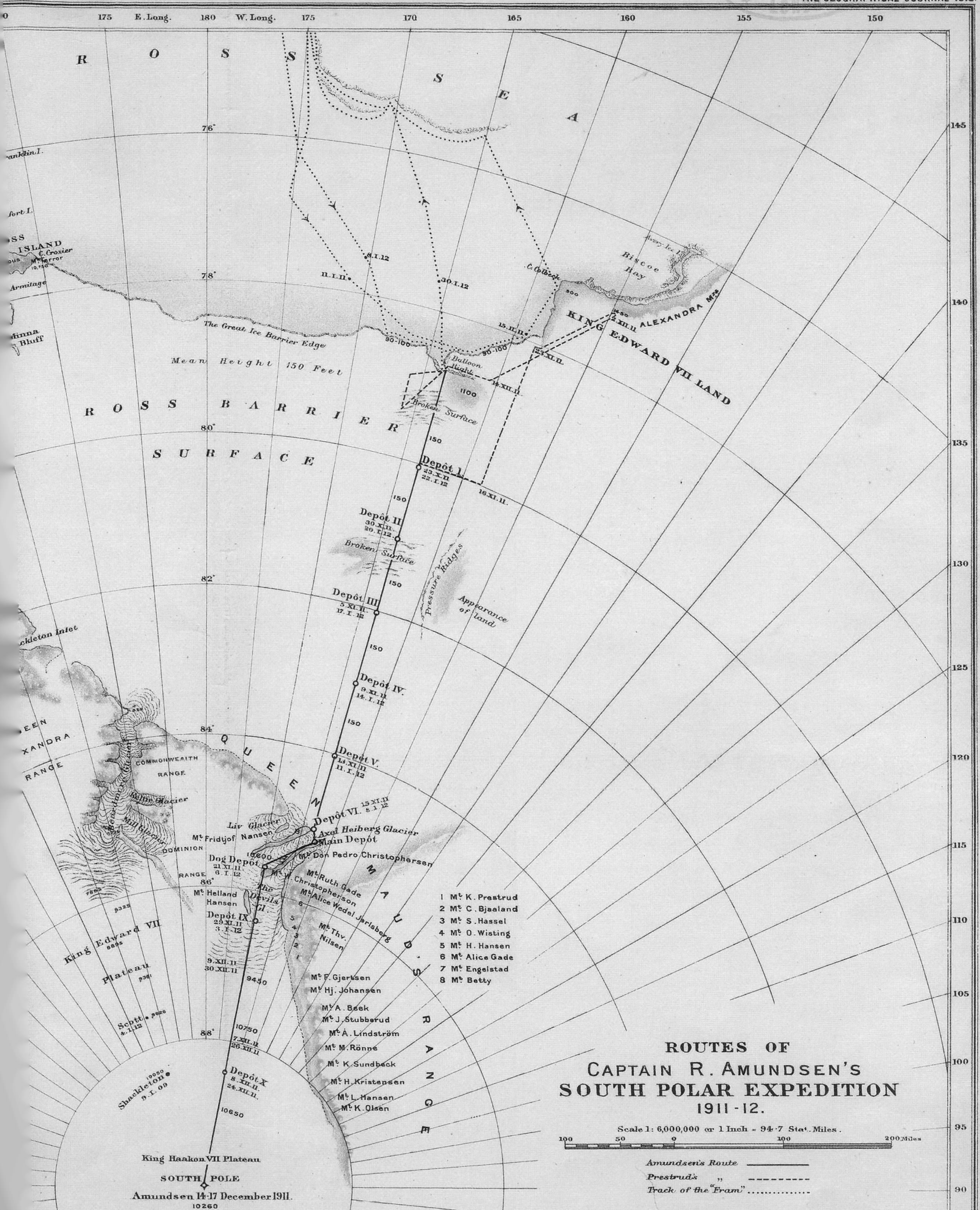

175 E. Long. 180 W. Long. 175 170 165 160 155 150

ROSS SEA

ROSS BARRIER SURFACE

Mean Height 150 Feet

The Great Ice Barrier Edge

KING EDWARD VII LAND

ALEXANDRA Mts

Biscoe Bay

C. Colbeck

Balloon Bight

Broken Surface

Pressure Ridges

Appearance of land

ROSS ISLAND

C. Crozier

Mt Terror

Depôt I. 23.X.11 22.I.12

Depôt II 30.X.11 20.I.12

Depôt III 5.XI.11 17.I.12

Depôt IV. 9.XI.11 14.I.12

Depôt V. 13.XI.11 11.I.12

Depôt VI. 15.XI.11 8.I.12

Axel Heiberg Glacier

Main Depôt

Liv Glacier

Mt Fridtjof Nansen

Mt Don Pedro Christophersen

Dog Depôt. 21.XI.11 6.I.12

Mt Ruth Gade

Mt H. Christophersen

Mt Alice Wedel Jarlsberg

Mt Helland Hansen

The Devils Gl.

Depôt IX 29.XI.11 3.I.12

Mt Thv. Nilsen

Mt F. Gjertsen

Mt Hj. Johansen

Mt A. Beck

Mt J. Stubberud

Mt A. Lindström

Mt M. Rönne

Mt K. Sundbeck

Mt H. Kristensen

Mt L. Hansen

Mt K. Olsen

Depôt X 8.XII.11 24.XII.11

QUEEN MAUD'S RANGE

COMMONWEALTH RANGE

DOMINION RANGE

King Edward VII Plateau

Shackleton 9.I.09

Scott 4.I.12

King Haakon VII Plateau

SOUTH POLE

Amundsen 14-17 December 1911.

10260

1 Mt K. Prestrud
2 Mt C. Bjaaland
3 Mt S. Hassel
4 Mt O. Wisting
5 Mt H. Hansen
6 Mt Alice Gade
7 Mt Engelstad
8 Mt Betty

ROUTES OF CAPTAIN R. AMUNDSEN'S SOUTH POLAR EXPEDITION 1911-12.

Scale 1: 6,000,000 or 1 Inch = 94·7 Stat. Miles.

100 50 0 100 200 Miles

Amundsen's Route ————

Prestrud's „ - - - - - -

Track of the "Fram" ....

88 88 86 84 82

Published by the Royal Geographical Society

Exploration for National Pride and Duty

Robert Scott's assault on the South Pole.

1910–12

IT SEEMS ONLY NATURAL that the epics of exploration we are most likely to recall will be those of explorers battling against the odds, emerging or even dying as heroes in a valiant attempt to achieve the impossible. But the simple truth is that the circumstances that made them so memorable were more often the consequence of inadequate preparation, a mindless denial of conditions that lay ahead or of a leader consummately unsuited to the task. Robert Falcon Scott, for ten years a rather dull naval lieutenant facing the nightmare of promotional neglect, had no ambitions as an explorer, no qualifications or experience in that direction, and absolutely no predeliction for the icy wastes of Antarctica. Yet with remarkable ease he had reinvented himself as an unlikely protégé of Clements Markham, the Royal Geographical Society's formidable president, who was scavanging around for somebody to take charge of a forthcoming Antarctic enterprise. Other far more suitable contenders had appeared on the scene, but it was Markham's will, and the Royal Navy, that prevailed, and in July 1901 Scott had set forth at the head of an expedition whose aims were from the outset muddled and ill-defined.

The expedition was a disappointment, the only notable achievement arising in December 1902 when Scott accomplished the first major Antarctic sledge journey, marching out into the unknown, ill-prepared and with no specific strategy, just some hazy notion of reaching the pole. Frustrated by the apparent vagaries of the dogs that drew his sledges, confronted by scurvy, snow-blindness, depleted food stocks and dissension among his men, he managed to get little beyond 82°S. However, when Scott was returned to Antarctica in 1910 for a concerted assault on the pole, it was not simply his dislike of dogs that would prove his undoing, nor his decision to use horses that fell inextricably into crevasses, nor the motorized vehicles that promptly broke down. It was his unrealistic notion that true exploration could be realized only 'when a party of men go forth to face hardships, dangers and difficulties with their own unaided efforts' – the product of a Victorian upbringing that believed that men bonded as a team could overcome any adversity. So while his unheroic rival Amundsen sped quietly towards the pole with dog sledges, everything planned in meticulous detail, Scott's party, afflicted by every conceivable difficulty, wearily man-hauled their necessities to the pole, only to arrive late, then suffer death in a blizzard-torn tent just 16 kilometres (10 miles) from salvation.

Right 'Leaving for the west, September 1911': the departure of one of Scott's depot-laying expeditions.

Eric Bailey Unveils the Mystery of the Tsangpo Gorges

The last of the world's major rivers divulges its secrets.

1911–13

Frederick Marshman Bailey, known since childhood as Eric, rarely features in the catalogue of great explorers. An invincibly modest man who 'concealed his unusual talents beneath the gentlest of exteriors', his most exceptional feats slumbered unremarkably in the pages of the *Scottish Geographical Magazine*, while the full story of his subsequent undercover operations in post-revolutionary Russian Central Asia had to wait forty years. The son of an Indian Army major, Bailey's career as an explorer began in 1904 when, as a young officer on Younghusband's mission to Lhasa, he was detached to explore the upper course of the Tsangpo (Zangbo) River, known in Assam as the Brahmaputra or Dihang, westward from Lhasa to the sacred lake Mansarowar (Mapan Yumco). But what fascinated Bailey was the mysterious eastern course of the Tsangpo, which somehow left the Tibetan plateau at an elevation of 2700 metres (8850 feet) and arrived in Assam, less than 200 kilometres (125 miles) distant, at a height of only 500 (1650). Were the Tsangpo and the Brahmaputra the same, or was there, deep in the labyrinthine topography of southeastern Tibet, a mighty waterfall to rival anything on earth?

Approaches from the south were obstructed by unfriendly hill people and discouraged by the Indian government, while an advance from the northeast required crossing the entire width of China, then negotiating the precipitous valleys of the Tibetan borderlands. Bailey opted for the latter, ascending the Yangtze and its gorges in March 1911, then working overland to the upper reaches of the Mekong, Salween and Irrawaddy. Moving into tribal lands that had never before seen a European, Bailey, now only 150 kilometres (90 miles) from the Tsangpo, was suddenly halted by a fearsome tribe whose territory nobody dared to enter. Unable to obtain local assistance, he had no alternative but to take the shortest route into Assam. In 1913 he tried again, this time from Assam in the company of a small survey party under the direction of Captain Henry Treise Morshead. By June they had reached the Tsangpo-Brahmaputra at a point 80 kilometres (50 miles) south of the river's great bend, and over the following month approached the river from sufficient vantage points to confirm that the two rivers were the same, connected by swift-flowing rapids and minor waterfalls in deep impenetrable gorges. Bailey and Morshead returned by a complex route through the mountains of Bhutan, accomplishing possibly the longest land survey completed on foot in the twentieth century.

Right Bailey (extreme left) as a member of Captain G A Nevill's survey party overlooking the valley of the Simong River, northern Assam, in February 1913.

Science and Survival in the Windiest Place on Earth

Douglas Mawson in the 'Home of the Blizzard'.

1911–14

DOUGLAS MAWSON, a man so respected in his native Australia that for twelve years his face shone through every $100 banknote, seemed too much of an academic scientist to capture the limelight in an age when even the most extreme advances in geographical discovery took second place to epic tales of heroism that contributed little to the understanding of our planet. Although Mawson's sense of adventure was greater than most, and his suffering and endurance equal to many, heroism would be the accidental consequence of a quest for enlightenment and truth. Trained in the Sydney school of geology, which under its celebrated mentor Edgeworth David did so much to advance science in the western Pacific, Mawson came to Antarctica with Shackleton in 1908 and was one of those that made the first gruelling trek to the South Magnetic Pole. But for Mawson the greater concern was how little was really known about the continent. Was it a single continuous landmass or simply a collection of large islands shrouded in ice? And what of the immense shoreline that lay neglected between the Ross Sea and the longitude of South Africa?

Mawson found no shortage of friends when he visited England in 1911 to raise funds for an enterprise that would delineate a third of the entire Antarctic coast and by the end of the year the painstakingly organized expedition, staffed predominantly by Australians, had departed Hobart in the Dundee sealer *Aurora*. Radio communication was maintained via Macquarie Island and bases were placed 2000 kilometres (1250 miles) apart on the Adélie Coast and the Shackleton Ice Shelf. At the former, throughout March and April 1912, a relentless wind, sometimes averaging 150 kilometres (90 miles) per hour, battered Mawson's camp, while miniature whirlwinds threw equipment high into the air. At the latter, eight men wintered in a six-metre-square (20-feet-square) hut. Sledging operations began the following summer, one of which would thrust Mawson into a struggle for survival equal to the best of his illustrious contemporaries. When one of his companions disappeared into a crevasse, together with a dog team and fully laden sledge, and the other died from eating toxic dog's liver, Mawson, alone and seriously debilitated, his shoes disintegrating and fingers frostbitten, cut his sledge in half with a pocket saw and dragged it 160 kilometres (100 miles) back to base. When the expedition returned in 1914 it was hailed as the greatest Antarctic scientific expedition to date, and Mawson had become a hero.

Right Snow drifted so thickly into the verandahs of the Main Base hut that tunnels had to be dug to reach the outside world.
Following pages To read the instruments outside the hut, Mawson's team had to battle against blizzards, crawling on hands and knees.

The Mystic Quest of Alexandra David-Neel

A Parisian lady in Lhasa.

1911-24

BORN IN PARIS BUT RAISED IN BELGIUM, the offspring of an unhappy union, from an early age Alexandra David-Neel longed 'to go beyond the garden gate, to follow the road that passed it by, and to set out for the unknown'. At seventeen, with only a raincoat and a copy of Epictetus's *Manual*, she crossed the Saint Gotthard Pass on foot, and later in Paris studied oriental languages, joined secret spiritual societies and even became *première chanteuse* with an operatic company. She toured India in 1890-91, then in Tunis married a wealthy railway engineer. But married life was incompatible with Alexandra's feminist leanings – she had written that housewives should be paid for their work – and in 1911 she bade farewell to her husband and set out for Sikkim to study Buddhism. By 1914, in the company of a young monk named Aphur Yongden, she was residing hermit-like near the Tibetan border, which she crossed several times to converse with the Panchen Lama in Xigaze. When the British prohibited further cross-border travel she migrated to Japan, where an encounter with the celebrated traveller-monk Ekai Kawaguchi fired her with a passion to enter the holy city of Lhasa.

Alexandra spent three years with the monks of the Kumbum monastery in northwestern China, then in 1921, dressed as a beggar and accompanied by Yongden, she finally set out for Lhasa. For three years they tramped through the rugged Chinese borderlands, across the deep gorges of the upper Mekong and Salween, then into Tibet by the track that parallels the Zangbo or upper Brahmaputra. Entering Lhasa in January 1924, they stayed for two months, visiting the major sites and blending with pilgrims arriving for the New Year festival. Via Sikkim they returned to a heroes' welcome in Paris where Alexandra camped in a tent outside the Guimet Museum. She settled at Digne in Provence, built her Samten-Dzong or 'fortress of meditation', then in 1937 returned to China to see out the war years in the mountains of Sichuan. Back in Europe, at the age of eighty-two she camped in the high Alps in the depth of winter, then in 1969, aged one hundred, she renewed her passport in anticipation of future travels. Sadly she died at Digne the following year while in the process of writing biographies of Mao Zedong and Jesus Christ. Her ashes were scattered into the Ganges at Benares.

Right Alexandra David-Neel and her faithful companion Aphur Yongden en route to Lhasa.

The Expedition to the 'River of Doubt'

A Brazilian explorer and a United States president.

1913-14

THE NAME OF CÂNDIDO DA SILVA RONDON, champion of the Indians and arguably Brazil's finest explorer, is little known beyond his native country. But fifteen major rivers were discovered by him, and the state of Rondônia now bears his name. By 1913, his forty-eighth year, he had travelled an estimated 22,000 kilometres (13,700 miles) in the interior, and that was only the start. Born in Mato Grosso of mixed blood, he underwent his apprenticeship as a military engineer in the most apalling conditions, working on the strategic telegraph line that linked Brazil's western outposts with the populous east. In 1907 he accepted the unenviable task of pushing the line northwest from Cuiabá towards the Rio Madeira, carving out a line-of-sight route through forests inhabited by uncontacted Indians. His advance party, in a desperate condition after four months living on what they could scavenge from the forest, eventually reached the Madeira around Christmas 1909. The next year Rondon, an enlightened and compassionate man, received command of Brazil's newly created Indian Protection Service. Shamed by his country's hitherto inhumane treatment of the Indians, he rocked the nation by announcing that under no circumstances should his subordinates kill an Indian, not even in self-defence. His saintly proclamation marked a turning point in Brazilian attitudes and would gain him worldwide admiration.

The telegraph expedition had come across a large and hitherto unmapped Amazon tributary, so in 1913 Rondon was sent back to chart the river from its source. His co-leader was a most unlikely figure, the American ex-president Theodore Roosevelt, a man of prodigious intellect and learning whose passion for scientific exploration had only been hampered by his involvement in politics. Rondon with his hardened Brazilian officers, and Roosevelt with his unsuspecting entourage of family and friends, plunged into the Mato Grosso and in February 1914 reached the source of the so-called 'River of Doubt'. What followed tested the party to its limits. Rapids and whirlpools, fever and dysentery almost brought the ex-president to a premature demise, while canoes were lowered laboriously over waterfalls and termites devoured the party's clothing. Only after two months did the expedition reach the safety of the Madeira. Roosevelt's career as an explorer was over, but Rondon's continued for another twenty-five years, taking him to the Mato Grosso, the tributaries of the Madeira, the Venezuelan and Colombian border regions and to the remote tribes of the Xingu.

Right Roosevelt (left) and Rondon at the Navaite rapids on the 'River of Doubt'. A photograph by the expedition's naturalist George Cherrie.

The Climactic Conclusion to an Age of Heroism

Ernest Shackleton's triumphant failures.

1914–17

OF THE MANY THAT ASPIRED TO DISTINCTION AS EXPLORERS, few would realize the opportunity or make that chance encounter that would turn their dreams to reality. But Ernest Henry Shackleton, a previously obscure but ambitious merchant sea captain, would make just such an encounter when, ferrying troops to the Boer War, he happened to befriend a young lieutenant whose father turned out to be a principal backer of Scott's first Antarctic expedition. Introductions successfully discharged, Shackleton joined Scott's ship *Discovery* and in December 1902 quite fortuitously found himself among those that made the closest approach, 770 kilometres (480 miles), to the pole so far. The dent to Shackleton's pride caused by his physical collapse and premature removal from the expedition only heightened his ambition to be the first to the pole, but it was not until 1906 that a suitable sponsor came forth – a wealthy industrialist whose wife Shackleton had seduced with his charm and brooding good looks. The next year, with the *Nimrod* and a hand-picked team, Shackleton was back in the Antarctic, and in January 1908, while one detachment desperately sought magnetic south, he and his companions fought their way through a blizzard that brought them frustratingly to a halt just 180 kilometres (110 miles) from the pole.

The British public, which gloried in heroic failure as much as success, cheered Shackleton's homecoming and lavished honours upon him, but his moment of glory was soon to be eclipsed by polar defeats and successes even more triumphant. For a while he busied himself with abortive money-making projects, but an announcement in 1913 by Wilhelm Filchner, that a huge ice shelf in the Weddell Sea provided a realistic entry point for a trans-Antarctic expedition, spurred Shackleton into a renewed lease of life. In July 1914, narrowly avoiding mobilization for the coming war, he and his teams set out on a massive, multi-pronged assault on the Antarctic continent. But the Weddell Sea proved Shackleton's undoing. His ship *Endurance* broke up in the pressure of the ice, forcing his men into refuge for months on a barren, rocky islet. In a small boat, Shackleton plunged into mountainous seas to sound the alarm in South Georgia, 1300 kilometres (800 miles) away, and so bring the party to safety. Antarctica would forever present a formidable challenge, but the 'age of heroism' had fittingly ended with one of its most spectacular tales of endurance.

Right The *Endurance* breaks up in pack ice in the Weddell Sea, its crew stranded 3000 kilometres (1800 miles) from civilization.

Philby Maps the Unknown Heart of Arabia

A lifetime in the desert wilderness.

1918–32

THE BRITISH GOVERNMENT HAD ALWAYS FELT RELUCTANT to get entangled in the complex domestic affairs of the Arabian Peninsula, but the years preceding the First World War saw a number of British emissaries working their way inland, openly and without disguise, fostering relationships with King Ibn Sa'ud and coincidentally filling the white spaces on the map. In 1912 Gerard Leachman visited Riyadh and brought back photographs of the Saudi royal family, and in 1914 William Henry Shakespear reached Riyadh from Kuwait, then continued overland to Suez by a route untrodden by Europeans. But it was only at the outbreak of war that the British came to fully appreciate the advantages of cultivating Ibn Sa'ud's friendship in their campaign against the Turks. In 1917 Harry St John Philby, a Cambridge-educated civilian administrator in Iraq, visited Riyadh to negotiate support for Ibn Sa'ud's attack on the Rashids of Ha'il, allies of the Turks. His official business done, unheeding all concerns for his safety, Philby took the opportunity to ride across the desert to Jiddah by the most southerly crossing yet. So began a lifelong acquaintanceship with Ibn Sa'ud, and an association with Arabia that would last forty years.

In 1918 Philby returned to Riyadh and with a small escort, in the baking height of summer, pushed south for nearly 500 kilometres (300 miles) along the wholly unknown Jabal Tuwayq as far as As Sulayyil. His constant detours for triangulation purposes brought his men, always resentful of having to cooperate with an infidel, to the brink of mutiny, but the journey for the first time mapped the most inaccessible heart of Arabia and defined the northern boundary of the infamous Rub' al Khali, the vast sand desert known as the Empty Quarter. Posted to Jordan in 1921, Philby became increasingly uncomfortable with British government policy. He resigned, settled in Jiddah at the head of a trading company and in 1930 formally converted to Islam. In 1932 he set out from Hufuf with fourteen men and thirty-two camels to complete his survey of the Rub' al Khali, heading southwest across the desert to the point where the borders of Yemen, Oman and Saudi Arabia all meet, then from this most desolate of places struck due west to connect at Sulayyil with his former survey. Philby's explorations continued well into the 1930s, by which time he had travelled every track and had seen virtually every settlement of the Arabian Peninsula.

Right Philby was one of the first Europeans to introduce motor vehicles into the deserts of Arabia. Most of his later explorations used this mode of transport.

Karius and Champion: From the Fly to the Sepik

Unsung heroes of the New Guinea Patrol.

1927-28

NEW GUINEA WAS DISCOVERED BY PORTUGUESE NAVIGATORS IN 1526 and named 'the island of the Papuans' – a name that survives until the present day. But remarkably, for more than three centuries, no European set foot in its densely forested interior, ascended its jungle-clad streams or glimpsed the shimmering, snow-capped peaks that rise incongruously from the sweltering canopy below. A naturalist's delight, an ethnologist's dream, an explorer's nightmare, every aspect of the island's wildly varying topography presented an extreme challenge. By the twentieth century vast tracts of its inter-riverine landscape still remained unseen from the ground, and its native tribes, some manifestly cannibalistic, dwelt in blissful ignorance of the wider world. Despite abortive attempts at settlement in the far northwest, the island remained a territorial no-man's-land until the 1870s when missionaries founded Port Moresby and the Italian adventurer Luigi d'Albertis undertook the first significant excursion into the interior, ascending the Fly River for 930 kilometres (575 miles). The partitioning between Great Britain, Germany and the Netherlands brought a surge of exploratory activity, which in the British sector was closely controlled and largely undertaken by little-known officers of the local police force, the New Guinea Patrol.

Charles Henry Karius, a Queenslander who had volunteered for the Western Front but arrived a week after the war had ended, returned home in 1920 to join the New Guinea Patrol as an officer cadet. By this time explorers and mineral prospectors had crossed New Guinea in the narrow peninsular east, but none had accomplished the more daunting traverse of the island's dead centre, where an impenetrable, mountainous barrier of precipitous valleys and razor-sharp limestone formations separates the tributaries of the southward-flowing Fly from those of the Sepik, the great river of the north. In 1926 Karius was appointed to the task, choosing as his second-in-command Ivan Francis Champion, later to become one of New Guinea's most celebrated explorers. Their first attempt failed, but in 1927, with a support party of thirty-six, they ascended the Fly and entered the Victor Emmanuel Range, climbing on hands and knees up almost vertical walls of rock and across broken limestone with knife-like edges. Crevices of unfathomable depth were spanned by fallen trees or by clinging to slimy, moss-covered roots, where a single mistake would mean instant death. After overcoming 'obstacles too numerous to describe', the Trans-Guinea Patrol descended to the Sepik and followed it to the coast.

Right Charles Karius outside his tent in the village of Kapatia, New Guinea, in 1927.

At KAPATIA. 27.

1930-31

Bertram Thomas Crosses the Empty Quarter

'The last unwritten plot of earth.'

ONE MIGHT REASONABLY CONJECTURE THAT BY THE 1930S, deep into the age of the motor car and aeroplane, little of great significance could possibly have escaped the attention of European explorers. But while the remotest recesses of the Amazon jungles, the heartlands of Australia, Africa and Antarctica had steadily yielded their secrets to man's curiosity, there remained one vast *terra incognita* – the waterless, sun-baked wastes of the Rub' al Khali, the immense sand desert known as the 'Empty Quarter' that fills much of the southern Arabian Peninsula. James Wellsted had skirted its fringes in the 1830s; Leo Hirsch spied it from the Wadi Hadramawt in 1893; and since the 1880s explorers had ventured hesitantly beyond the ruins of Marib. For some, like Richard Burton and Gerard Leachman, the desert became a lifelong ambition denied, but for Bertram Sidney Thomas the secret dream of being the first across the Empty Quarter would become a reality.

Bertram Thomas arrived as a soldier in the Middle East in 1917 and after the war stayed on in a number of civil and diplomatic posts. While most of his colleagues took their leave in summer, retreating to the more temperate Indian hill stations, Thomas took his in winter, the season most suited to exploration. In 1927-28 he took an extraordinary 1000-kilometre (600-mile) camel ride along the entire southeastern coast of Oman, and in 1929-30 he made his first approach into the Rub' al Khali, striking inland from Salalah for 250 kilometres (150 miles) to the edge of the sand desert. To gain the friendship and confidence of those on whom his future success would depend he grew a beard, adopted local dress and gave up drinking and smoking. Then, the next October, 1930, his mission shrouded in secrecy but sanctioned by both Britain and Muscat, Thomas dropped furtively from a British oil tanker, regrouped his Bedouin associates and headed inland from Salalah. In January he plunged into the interminable dunes of the Empty Quarter where mysterious tracks led to the ancient city of Ubar, long swallowed by the shifting sands. Despite merciless heat and severe sandstorms, his party emerged from the 430 kilometres (270 miles) of dunes after eighteen days, and in early February entered the tranquility of Doha. For his achievement Thomas was widely honoured, the last of that generation of Arabian greats that, in the words of T E Lawrence, 'walked the inviolate earth for newness' sake'.

Right The explorer stares into the unknown. Bertram Thomas contemplates the Empty Quarter's next horizon.
Following pages Bertram Thomas and his caravan on route to the Rub' al Khali, the last of earth's undiscovered wildernesses.

Wilfred Thesiger Fills the Last Blanks on the Map

The heroic age of exploration finally closes.

1933–48

RAISED IN ETHIOPIA WHERE HIS FATHER WAS BRITISH MINISTER, Wilfred Thesiger's career began in 1930 when, as a guest at Haile Selassie's coronation, he asked whether some hidden recess of Ethiopia still awaited its explorer. Time allowed only a brief excursion down the Awash, a river which lost itself inland from the Red Sea, but in 1933 Thesiger went back to carry out a more detailed examination, following the river into the sun-baked landscape of the Danakil where human habitation is forced to its limit. Two years later a posting with the Sudan Political Service brought him to the deserts of northern Darfur, and in 1938 to the Tibesti Mountains in the remote northern borderlands of Chad. The war years were spent largely in the Middle East, then in 1945 Thesiger eagerly accepted a commission to explore into the Rub' al Khali, the 'Empty Quarter' whose interminable featureless dunes monotonously cloak much of southeastern Arabia.

Thesiger's official assignment was to collect information on locust movement, but to him the Empty Quarter represented the final challenge – the only extensive blank on the map where a man could still make his mark as a real explorer. Although penetrated twice before, by Bertram Thomas and Harry Philby, vast tracts remained unseen from the ground. In 1946, from Salalah on the Arabian Sea, Thesiger reconnoitred the outer fringes of the desert, then, returning to the coast, followed an inland route to the Wadi Hadramawt. By the end of 1947 he was back in the Empty Quarter, this time to cross it well to the east of Thomas's traverse through what, beyond Antarctica, was probably the most obscure and least visited corner of the earth. After forty-eight days, ragged, hungry and desert-scoured, he emerged at Abu Dhabi, a sleepy little place that, with its small fort and handful of reed huts, 'did not exist to any sort of extent'. Thesiger returned by an inland route through Muscat and Oman, then in 1948 made his second crossing of the Empty Quarter, plunging into the desert from Hadramawt and making a wide sweep to the west of Philby's tracks. Thesiger would spend most of his remaining years in remote tribal areas, the marshlands of Iraq, the highlands of Pakistan and Afghanistan, the deserts of Iran and the plains of northern Kenya.

Right Thesiger's map of his explorations in the Hijaz Mountains, south-western Saudi Arabia, in 1946.

ARABIA

A journey through THE TIHAMA, THE 'ASIR & THE HIJAZ MOUNTAINS in 1946 by W. Thesiger

Scale 1:1 000 000

Miles

10 0 10 20 30 40

Heights in feet from aneroid readings
Tribe names in red and sub sections listed and indexed
Wells and springs • Route ——

Zahran Tribe
1 Quraish
2 Bani Adhwan
3 Bani 'Amr
4 Bani Kanana
5 Bal Khazmar
6 Bani Hassan
7 Baidhan
8 Bani 'Umr

Ghamid Tribe
1 Bani 'Abdillah
2 Bani Kabir
3 Bani Dhabyan
4 Al Bisham

Tribes of Rijal al Hajar
1 Bani 'Amr
2 Bani Shahr
3 Bal Asmar
4 Bal Ahmar

W. Yaba Tribes
Nuwashira
Mahamid
Bani Yala
Bal 'Air
Hasana
Shugaifa
Shardi

Badu Tribes
1 Rabi'a
2 Tahahin
3 Musaifara
4 Bani Hilal
5 Minjaha

Shahran Tribe
1 Tamniya
2 Sirhan
3 Bani Majar
Masqi
Wadi ibn Hashban
Nahis
Kaut Tintaha
Hwad
Qaru
Al Jahra
Al Musairiq

Qahtan Tribe
1 Rufaida
2 Bani Bishr
3 Abida
4 Shuraif
5 Sanhan
6 Wada'a
7 Āl al Siri

'Asir Tribes
1 Rabi'a wa Rufaida
2 Bani Malik
3 Al Qam
4 'Asam
5 Rijal al Ma
6 Bani Mughaith

Khaulan Tribes
1 Āl Thalid
2 Bani Malik
3 Bal Ghazi
4 Harub

'Abs Qahtan Tribe
1 Āl Raith
2 Āl 'Aziyin
3 Āl al Haqu

WADI HALI DELTA

SA'UDI ARABIA · RED SEA · TIHAMA · 'ASIR · HIJAZ · YAMAN

Drawn by G. W. Whibley & K. C. Jordan

Published by the Royal Geographical Society

SA'UDI ARABIA
Thesiger

Antarctica Ring-Fenced with Swastikas

Alfred Ritscher: colonization or conspiracy?

1938–39

ALTHOUGH THE BIZARRE AND ECCENTRIC are hardly uncommon in the history of exploration, little compares with some of the enterprises launched under the patronage of the Third Reich, the totalitarian dictatorship that dominated Germany between 1933 and 1945. In 1938, on the eve of war, SS chief Heinrich Himmler, a man obsessed by weird science and perverted anthropological convictions, sent a prolifically documented expedition to Tibet to trace the origins of the Aryan race. Its directors, the naturalist Ernst Schäffer and the anthropologist Bruno Beger whose racial theories were taken to their obscene conclusion at Auschwitz, took head-casts from unsuspecting locals and freely distributed pennants bearing the swastika – a symbol equally revered in Tibet. A similar expedition planned for the Caucasus in 1942 never quite got underway, and the war would be over before Schäffer had managed to locate the haunt of a red horse with a white mane that Himmler had read about in Nordic fairy tales.

Undercover Nazi expeditions have continued to furnish inexhaustible fodder for conspiracy theorists, but none more so than Alfred Ritscher's operations in Antarctica. If his purpose was really to search for lost sub-glacial civilizations, or provide a research facility for anti-gravity devices, or reconnoitre a post-war subterranean sanctuary for high-ranking Germans, Hitler included, we will never know with certainty. His major publicized objective, somewhat less sensational, was to establish stations that would ensure an uninterrupted supply of whale oil, but why Ritscher felt it necessary to take innumerable colour photographs of monotonous wasteland, or stake out a vast outpost of empire in an icy wilderness, posed intriguing questions that, for some, demanded unconventional explanations. Ritscher's expedition departed in December 1938 with an expensively refitted Lufthansa 'aeroplane mothership', and within a month was off Dronning Maud Land, an Antarctic sector vociferously claimed by Norway. Two hydroplanes, launched from a steam-driven catapult, flew sorties across 600,000 square kilometres (230,000 square miles) of the continent, penetrating some 600 kilometres (370 miles) inland. Aerial photographs were recorded on six 390-metre-long (1300-foot-long) films; the 11,000 frames, few of which carried geographical coordinates, providing a challenge for analysts well into recent years. The territory, christened Neu-Schwabenland, was 'colonized' by encircling it with swastika-tailed aluminium darts, dropped every 20 kilometres (12.5 miles) and capable of penetrating 30 centimetres (12 inches) into solid ice. Congratulatory telegrams from Hitler and Göring greeted Ritscher's return in April 1939, but projected follow-ups were prevented by the outbreak of war.

Right top Alfred Ritscher optimistically plants the swastika on the Antarctic ice.
Right below The ephemeral German colony of Neu-Schwabenland, showing the results of Ritscher's surveys.

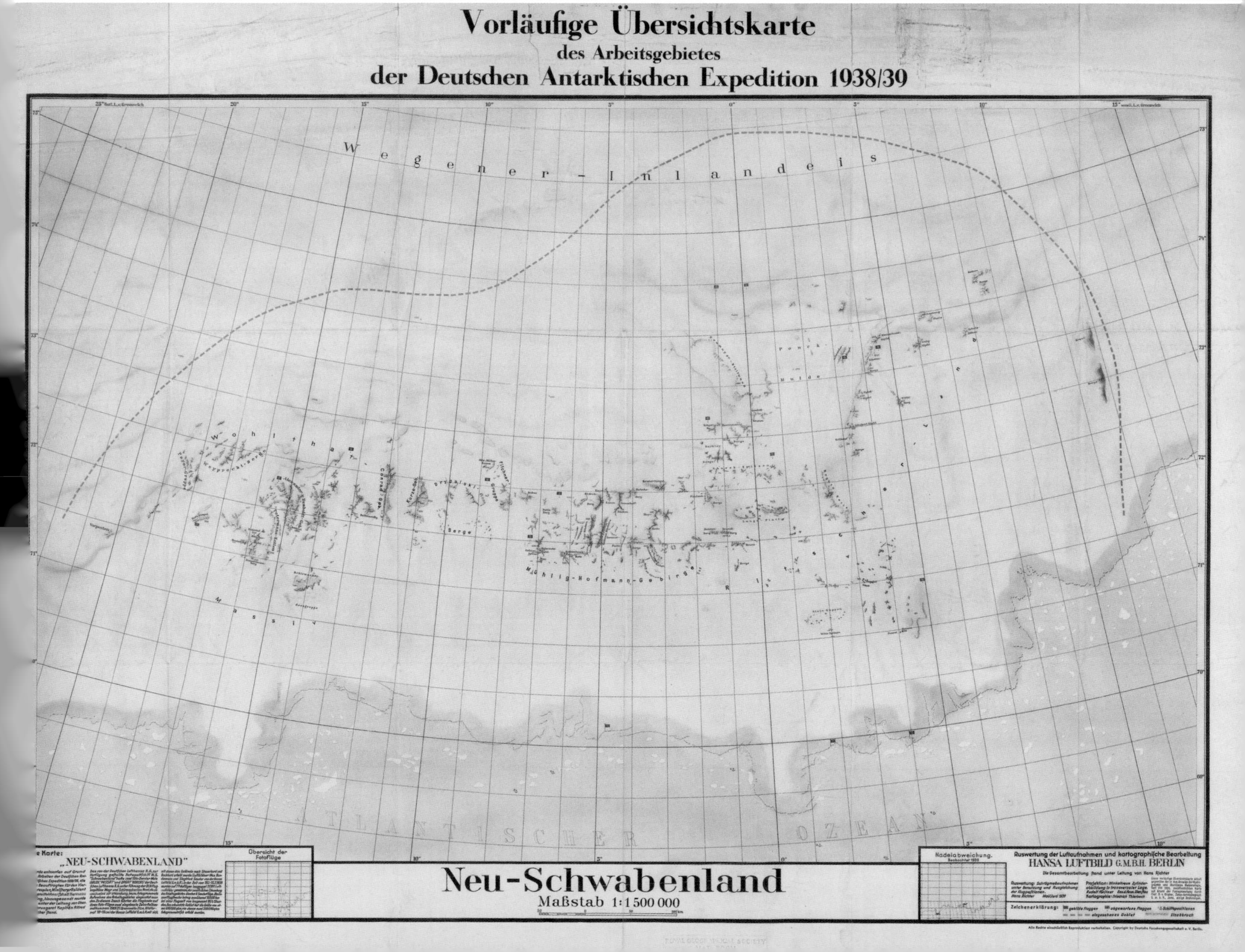

Vorläufige Übersichtskarte
des Arbeitsgebietes
der Deutschen Antarktischen Expedition 1938/39

Wegener-Inlandeis

Wohlthat-Massiv

Mühlig-Hofmann-Gebirge

Ritscher-Hochland

ATLANTISCHER OZEAN

…e Karte:

„NEU-SCHWABENLAND"

Übersicht der Fotoflüge

Neu-Schwabenland

Maßstab 1:1 500 000

Nadelabweichung.
Beobachtet 1939

Auswertung der Luftaufnahmen und kartographische Bearbeitung
HANSA LUFTBILD G.M.B.H. BERLIN

Die Gesamtbearbeitung stand unter Leitung von Hans Richter

Auswertung: Schrägmeßaufnahmen unter Benutzung und Ausgleichung der Flugpositionen.
Hans Richter Mai/Juni 1939

Projektion: Winkeltreue Zylinderabbildung in transversaler Lage.
Rudolf Förstner Ass. d. Verm. Dienstes
Kartographie: Friedrich Thierbach

Zeichenerklärung: gehißte Flaggen · abgeworfene Flaggen · Schiffspositionen · eingesehenes Gebiet · Eisabbruch

Eight Men Winter in a Wooden Box

Vivian Fuchs's Trans-Antarctic Expedition.

1955-58

ONE MIGHT IMAGINE that with all the technological advances of the twentieth century an overland crossing of the Antarctic continent should have become a relatively simple matter. But in the forty years since Wilhelm Filchner and Ernest Shackleton failed, Antarctica remained defiant as ever, reminding all who dared set foot on its icy wastes that the age of heroism was by no means dead. When in 1955 Vivian Fuchs set out for Antarctica at the head of the Commonwealth Trans-Antarctic Expedition his strategy was similar to Shackleton's. He would approach the continent from a forward base on the Weddell Sea while a support party under Edmund Hillary, better known for his conquest of Everest, would await Fuchs's arrival on the far side of the continent. Near disaster, worryingly reminiscent of previous attempts, struck early when Fuchs's mother ship *Theron* was trapped by ice in the Weddell Sea until a floatplane scouted a way out. However, it was Ken Blaiklock and his seven men of the advance party that would see heroism thrust upon them with all the vengeance the continent could muster.

Cast ashore beside the Weddell Sea, the components of their prefabricated hut in crates and most of their provisions strewn out across adjacent sea ice, Blaiklock's team began building a permanent shelter for the oncoming winter. But, hardly had the wooden framework been completed, a blizzard blew up, confining the team to their tiny windswept tents and forcing them to improvise communal quarters in the 6x3x3-metre (20x10x10-foot) packing case that had once contained their tractor. Their skeleton hut filled with snow, and on extricating themselves from their icy tomb they found to their dismay that not only had the sea ice broken up and carried most of their supplies out to sea, but the crates housing building materials had vanished deep into the drift. Nevertheless, the party survived the winter in good health and, after frantic tunnelling beneath the snow to retrieve the missing crates, they completed the hut in time for the return of Fuchs in December 1956. By comparison, the crossing of the continent during the summer of 1957-58, with motorized vehicles and air support, was something of an anticlimax. Hillary's party was encountered at the pole in early January, and by following his marked route to the base on the Ross Sea the first crossing of the continent, 3473 kilometres in ninety-nine days, was completed by early March.

Right One of the 'Sno-Cats' used by Fuchs in his pioneering crossing of the Antarctic continent.

TRANS ANTARCTIC
EXPEDITION
TUCKER SNO-CAT
TUCKER SNO-CAT

Wally Herbert and his British Trans-Arctic Expedition

First across the top of the world.

1968–69

IN 1909 A LITTLE-KNOWN ENGLISH-BORN EXPLORER, ALFRED HARRISON, approached the Royal Geographical Society with an elaborately conceived and mathematically calculated proposal for an expedition that would take him across the polar ice from Alaska to Svalbard via the North Pole. With 100 dogs working in 1.32-kilometre (0.8-mile) relays, hauling sixty sledges, ten at a time, bearing 5.4 tons of provisions, Harrison computed that he could complete the journey in precisely 912 days. The RGS refused to countenance a scheme that would commit its originator to almost certain death, but Harrison's intelligently contrived plan highlighted the one seemingly insurmountable problem of long journeys across the polar ice – that of transporting sufficient provisions to sustain the traveller for a period that could extend to two or three years. The development of aviation, and the prospect of food being dropped from the air, did much to alleviate this difficulty, but it was not until the 1960s that any explorer felt confident enough to put Harrison's dream into action. In fact when Wally Herbert submitted his plan to the RGS in 1965 he met with a similar reaction to that afforded to Harrison, but within a year, with the support of eminent men and advances on book and film rights, preparations were under way.

In February 1968, Wally Herbert, Allan Gill, Fritz Koerner and Kenneth Hedges set out with dogs and sledges from Point Barrow, Alaska, on a journey that would become the longest in Arctic history, and as heroic as anything that had gone before. In front of them lay 3200 kilometres (2000 miles) of shifting, fractured ice, the drift of which consistently undermined their projected schedule and perpetually directed them off course, expanding their trek to an extraordinary 5800 kilometres (3600 miles). After a full year, when they established winter camp on an ice flow, they were still 480 kilometres (300 miles) from the pole, and it was not until April 1969, after battling across towering ridges of ice, that the pole itself was attained. Beyond was unknown territory where no surface expedition had ever passed before and conditions were uncertain, but resolutely they forced their way south across broken and ever-thinning ice until in mid-May they caught their first sight of land, a rocky outcrop northeast of Svalbard. From a flow that adverse currents threatened to sweep out to sea, Gill and Hedges scrambled across perilous ice to make landfall and complete the first surface-based crossing of the top of the world.

Right A hand-drawn map by Wally Herbert showing the route of the party across the polar ice.

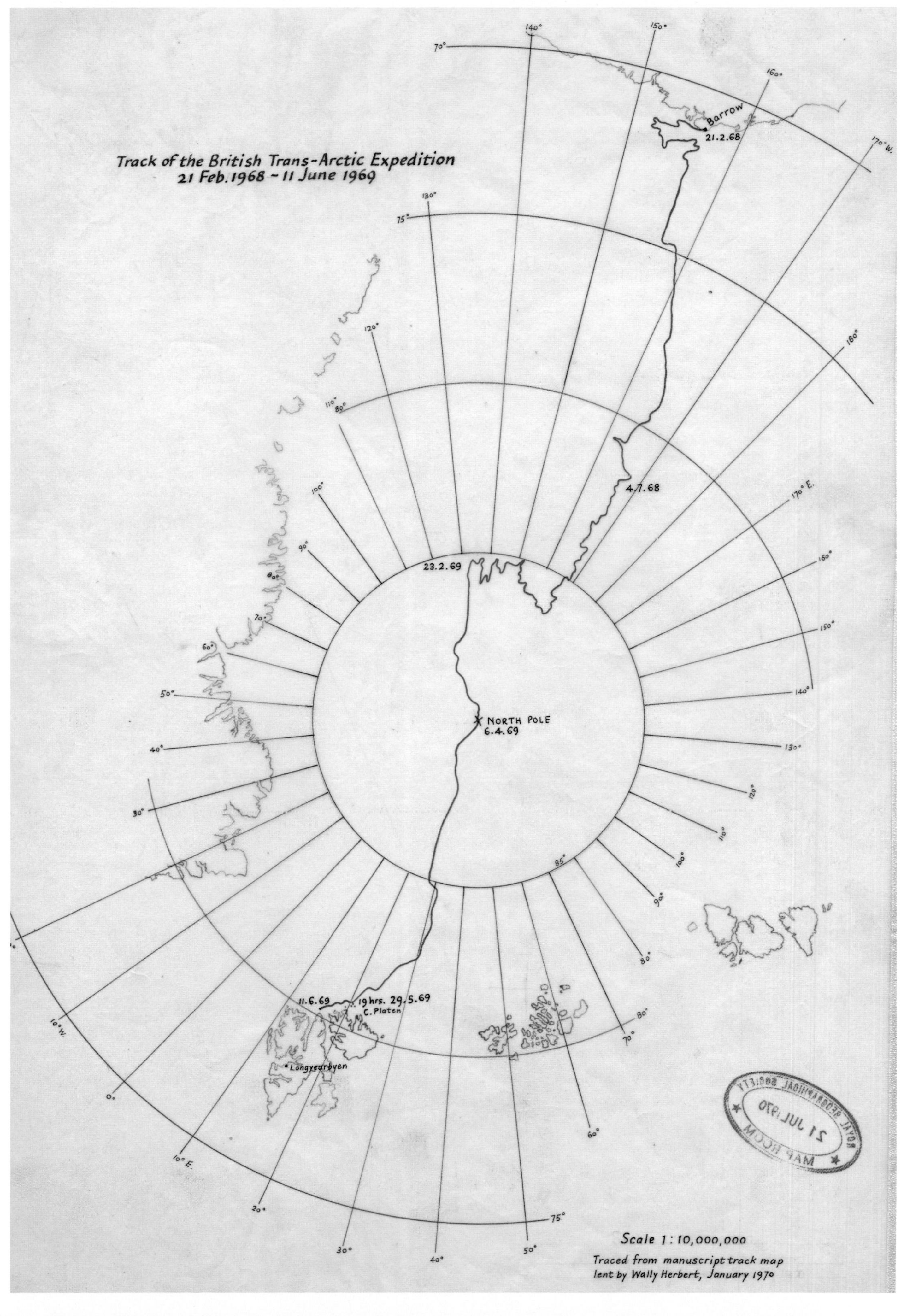
Track of the British Trans-Arctic Expedition
21 Feb. 1968 – 11 June 1969
Barrow
21.2.68
4.7.68
23.2.69
NORTH POLE
6.4.69
11.6.69
19 hrs. 29.5.69
C. Platen
Longyearbyen
Scale 1 : 10,000,000
Traced from manuscript track map
lent by Wally Herbert, January 1970

Picture Credits

The publishers would like to thank the following sources for the permission to publish the illustrations in this book. Additional thanks to Jamie Owen and the staff of the Reading Room at the RGS in London for their help in sourcing images.

Endpapers Private Collection/The Bridgeman Art Library; page 1 Royal Geographical Society, London; 2-3 Scott Polar Research Institute, Cambridge, UK/The Bridgeman Art Library (Sledge Hauling on the Great Ice Barrier, 1903 by Wilson, Edward Adrian); 11 UN/Ancient Art & Architecture Collection Ltd; 13 Paul Almasy/Corbis; 15 The Art Archive/Gianni Dagli Orti; 17 akg-images/Eric Lessing; 19 Mark Boulton/Alamy; 21 The collection of the Author; 23 The Art Archive/Museo Prenestino Palestrina/ Alfredo Dagli Orti; 25 British Library, London (Add. 19391, ff.17v-18); 27 UN/ Ancient Art & Architecture Collection Ltd; 29 The Bodleian Library, University of Oxford (MS. Pococke 375, fols. 3c-4r); 31 Arnamagnaen Collection, Denmark/The Bridgeman Art Library; 33 Beinecke Rare Book and Manuscript Library; 35 UN/ Ancient Art & Architecture Collection Ltd; 37 Copyright © Archivio Segreto Vaticano (ASV, A.A., Arm. I XVIII, 1802 (2)); 39 Bibliothèque nationale de France (MSS Espagnol 30); 41 bpk Berlin, Photo: Iris Papadopoulos/Museum für Asiatische Kunst, Kunstsammlung Süd-, Südost- und Zentralasien, (SMB / MIK III 6911); 43 The Bodleian Library, University of Oxford (MS. Laud. Or. 317, fols. 10v-11r); 45 www.mapsorama.com; 47 Biblioteca Marciana, Venice © 1990 Photo Scala, Florence; 49 Biblioteca Estense, Modena © 1990 Photo Scala, Florence – courtesy of the Ministero Beni e Att. Culturali; 51 British Library, London (Add. 15760, ff.68v-69); 53 British Library, London (W 7726, title page); 55 Museo Naval, Madrid (P-257); 57 © 2003 Photo Scala Florence/HIP; 59 Biblioteca Estense, Modena © 1990 Photo Scala, Florence – courtesy of the Ministero Beni e Att. Culturali; 61 Library of Congress, Washington; 63 Academia das Ciencias de Lisboa, Lisbon, Portugal/ Giraudon/The Bridgeman Art Library; 65 Royal Geographical Society, London; 67 Bibliotheque Nationale, Paris, France/Giraudon/The Bridgeman Art Library; 69 Newberry Library, Chicago, Illinois, USA/The Bridgeman Art Library; 71 Princeton University Library ((Ex)1804.379.11q); 73 Bibliothèque nationale de France (CPL GE FF 14410 RES Plate 12); 74-75 Courtesy of the Hispanic Society of America, New York; 77 British Library, London (G 6409); 79 National Maritime Museum, Greenwich, London; 81 Bibliotheque Nationale, Paris, France/Lauros/Giraudon/The Bridgeman Art Library; 83 Bibliotheque Nationale, Paris, France/The Bridgeman Art Library; 85 Wittliff Collections/Texas State University-San Marcos (1555 edition of La relación y comentarios by Álvar Núñez Cabeza de Vaca); 87 British Library, London (Add.15217 f. 35 v); 89 Bibliotheque Nationale, Paris, France/Lauros/Giraudon/The Bridgeman Art Library; 91 Library and Archives Canada; 93 Bibliothèque nationale de France (CPL GE DD 683 RES folios 3v (left) - 4v (right)); 95 British Museum, London, UK/The Bridgeman Art Library; 97 British Library, London ; 99 British Library, London, UK/The Bridgeman Art Library; 101 The Art Archive/Kobe Municipal Museum/Laurie Platt Winfrey; 103 The Bridgeman Art Library; 105 Private Collection/The Bridgeman Art Library; 107 Private Collection/The Bridgeman Art Library; 109 Library and Archives Canada; 111 Art Museum of Tomsk, Russia/The Bridgeman Art Library; 113 British Library, London © 2003 . Photo Scala, Florence/HIP; 115 The collection of the Author; 117 British Library, London (Add. 17940 A,); 119 British Library, London (C.133.e.34, Ri); 121British Library, London (2354.h.8.(3), plate LVIII); 123 Library of Congress, Washington; 125 Courtesy The Newberry Library, Chicago. Call Number: Novacco 2F 247; 127 National Library of Australia, Canberra (map-ra265-s125); 129 National Library of Australia, Canberra (map-rm750); 131 National Library of Australia, Canberra (map-rm3704); 133 Mitchell Library, State Library of New South Wales (Ref: ML 863); 135 Private Collection/The Bridgeman Art Library; 137 Archives of the Society of Jesus in Canada Q-0001,687; 139 From the Collection of the James Ford Bell Library, University of Minnesota; 141 Royal Geographical Society, London; 142-143 National Library of Australia, Canberra (nla.pic-an9406669); 148-149 British Library, London (4051.a.13); 151 British Library, London (Maps. 83040,(4)); 153 The Bodleian Library, University of Oxford (203 f.154); 155 From the Collection of the James Ford Bell Library, University of Minnesota; 156-157 From the Collection of the James Ford Bell Library, University of Minnesota; 159 Library and Archives Canada; 161 Royal Geographical Society, London; 163 ©NTPL/John Hammond; 165 British Library, London (Add.15499 f.25); 167 Royal Geographical Society, London; 168-169 Royal Geographical Society, London; 171Royal Geographical Society, London; 173 British Library, London (Add. 15513, No.16); 175 Princeton University Library ((Ex) 1270.441q); 177 Library of Congress, Washington; 179 Map of the North-West Territory of the Province of Canada [1814] - Archives of Ontario (F 443, R-C(U), AO 1541); 181 Chateau de Versailles, France/The Bridgeman Art Library; 182-183 National Library of Australia, Canberra (1797. MAP T 835); 185 National Library of Australia, Canberra (nlc001139-v6); 187 Dixson Galleries, State Library of New South Wales; 189 Library of Congress, Washington; 191 Private Collection/The Bridgeman Art Library; 192-193 Royal Geographical Society, London; 195 Royal Geographical Society, London; 197 Nationalgalerie, SMPK, Berlin, Germany/The Bridgeman Art Library; 199 top right Mitchell Library, State Library of New South Wales/The Bridgeman Art Library 199 top left and bottom Royal Geographical Society, London; 200-201 Mitchell Library, State Library of New South Wales (ML 443); 203 Library of Congress, Washington; 205 British Library, London; 207 National Library of Australia, Canberra (nla.pic-an5263464); 209 Royal Geographical Society, London; 211 Private Collection/The Stapleton Collection/The Bridgeman Art Library; 213 Royal Geographical Society; 215 Royal Geographical Society, London; 217 Private Collection/Archives Charmet/The Bridgeman Art Library; 219 Bibliotheque Nationale, Paris, France/The Bridgeman Art Library; 221 Down House, Kent, UK/The Bridgeman Art Library 223 University of Arizona Library; 224-225 Peabody Essex Museum, Salem, Massachusetts, USA/The Bridgeman Art Library; 227 National Maritime Museum, Greenwich, London; 229 Image courtesy of the State Library of South Australia (SA Memory website). Mr Eyre's routes into Central Australia, and overland from Adelaide to King Georges Sound, 1940-41, (cartographic) John Arrowsmith, London, 1845; 231 Private Collection/The Bridgeman Art Library; 233 Royal Geographical Society, London; 235 National Library of Australia, Canberra (nla.pic-an7350668); 237 Royal Geographical Society, London; 239 from the collection of Russell A. Potter; 241 Royal Geographical Society, London; 243 top and bottom Royal Geographical Society, London; 245 Bibliotheque Nationale, Paris, France/Archives Charmet/The Bridgeman Art Library; 247 Princeton University Library ((Ex)DT731.L739); 249 National Library of Australia, Canberra (nla.pic-an2273869-v); 251 Royal Geographical Society, London, UK/The Bridgeman Art Library; 253 National Library of Australia, Canberra (nla.pic-an7372844); 255 Image courtesy of the State Library of South Australia.(SLSA: B 486/42); 257 Royal Geographical Society, London; 262-263 Royal Geographical Society, London; 263 inset Private Collection/The Bridgeman Art Library; 265 Royal Geographical Society, London; 267 Royal Geographical Society, London; 269 © Bettmann/CORBIS; 271 Royal Geographical Society, London; 273 Royal Geographical Society, London; 275 Royal Geographical Society, London; 277 Royal Geographical Society, London; 279 Royal Geographical Society, London, UK/The Bridgeman Art Library; 281 National Library of Australia, Canberra (nla.pic-an8960261-v); 283 Private Collection/The Stapleton Collection/The Bridgeman Art Library; 285 National Library of Australia, Canberra (nla.pic-an9025855-6-v); 287 Musee des Arts d'Afrique et d'Oceanie, Paris, France/Archives Charmet/The Bridgeman Art Library; 289 top and bottom Royal Geographical Society, London; 291 © The Nationalmuseum, Stockholm; 293 Royal Geographical Society, London; 295 British Library, London (C13636-34); 296-297 Royal Geographical Society, London; 299 Royal Geographical Society, London; 301 National Library of Norway, Picture Collection; 303 top and bottom Mary Evans Picture Library; 305 Royal Geographical Society, London; 307 Bibliotheque Nationale, Paris, France/Archives Charmet/The Bridgeman Art Library; 309 Royal Geographical Society, London; 311 National Library of Norway, Picture Collection; 313 Royal Scottish Geographical Society, Perth; 315 Royal Geographical Society, London; 317 Royal Geographical Society, London; 319 Mary Evans Picture Library; 321 Private Collection/Ken Welsh/The Bridgeman Art Library; 322 left Mary Evans Picture Library; 322-323 Royal Geographical Society; 325 Royal Geographical Society, London; 327 Royal Geographical Society, London; 329 National Library of Australia, Canberra/Frank Hurley (nla.pic-vn3122262), 330-331 National Library of Australia/Frank Hurley (nla.pic-an24615776); 333 Royal Geographical Society, London; 335 Private Collection/The Bridgeman Art Library; 337 © Underwood & Underwood/CORBIS; 339 Royal Geographical Society, London; 341 National Library of Australia, Canberra (nla.pic-an10571028-24); 343 Royal Geographical Society, London; 344-345 Royal Geographical Society, London; 347 Royal Geographical Society, London; 349 top akg-images/ullstein bild; 349 bottom Royal Geographical Society, London; 351 Value RM | © Morton Beebe/CORBIS; 353 Royal Geographical Society, London.

Index

Published by Bloomsbury USA, New York

All papers used by Bloomsbury USA are natural, recyclable products made from wood grown in well-managed forests. The manufacturing processes conform to the environmental regulations of the country of origin.

LIBRARY OF CONGRESS CATALOGING-IN-PUBLICATION DATA HAS BEEN APPLIED FOR.

ISBN: 978-1-60819-059-1

First published in Great Britain in 2009 by Weidenfeld & Nicolson
First U.S. edition 2009

1 3 5 7 9 10 8 6 4 2

Edited by Debbie Woska and Jo Murray; Design by Clive Hayball and Tony Chung; Picture research by Emily Hedges; Index by David Atkinson

Colour reproduction by Altaimage Ltd; Printed and bound in Italy by Printer Trento Srl and L.E.G.O. SpA